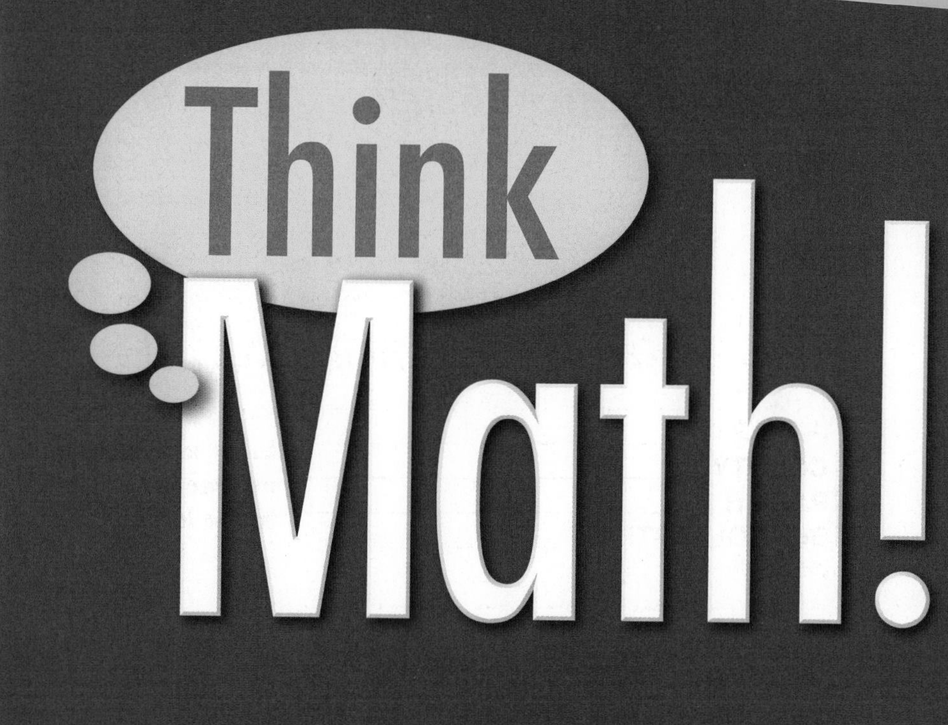

Student Work Text

Lesson Activity Book

Developed by Education Development Center, Inc.
through National Science Foundation

Grant No. ESI-0099093

Published and distributed by:

www.Math.SchoolSpecialty.com

Think Math! Lesson Activity Book

Printing 6 – 6/2010

Worldcolor, Dubuque, IA

1358080

978-0-15-341847-1

This program was funded in part through the National Science Foundation under Grant No. ESI-0099093. Any opinions, findings, and conclusions or recommendations expressed in this program are those of the authors and do not necessarily reflect the views of the National Science Foundation.

Principal Investigator

E. Paul Goldenberg

Curriculum Design and Pedagogy Oversight

E. Paul Goldenberg
Lynn Goldsmith
Nina Shteingold

Research

Director: Lynn Goldsmith
Nina Arshavsky
Cynthia Char
Sabita Chopra
Sophia Cohen
Andrea Humez
Suenita Lawrence
Katherine Schwinden
Eugenia Steingold

Editorial

Director: Frances Fanning
Nicholas Bozard
Eric Karnowski

Writing

Director: Eric Karnowski
Jean Benson
Abigail Branch
Sara Cremer
E. Paul Goldenberg
Stacy Grossman
Andrea Humez
Suenita Lawrence
Debora Rosenfeld
Paisley Rossetti
Nina Shteingold
Kate Snow
Julie Zeringue

Graphics and Design

Directors: Laura Koval and **Korynn Kirchwey**
Jessica Cummings
Jennifer Putnam
E. Charles Snow
Jenny Wong

Project Management

Directors: Eric Karnowski and **Glenn Natali**
Amy Borowko
Nannette Feurzeig
Kim Foster
Alexander Kirchwey
Helen Lebowitz
June Mark
Kimberly Newson
David O'Neil
Cynthia Plouff

Mathematics Reviewers

Richard Askey, Professor of Mathematics, Emeritus
University of Wisconsin, Madison, Wisconsin

Roger Howe, Professor of Mathematics
Yale University, New Haven, Connecticut

Harvey Keynes, Professor of Mathematics
University of Minnesota, Minneapolis, Minnesota

David Singer, Professor of Mathematics
Case Western Reserve University, Cleveland, Ohio

Sherman Stein, Professor of Mathematics, Emeritus
University of California at Davis, Davis, California

Additional Mathematics Resource

Al Cuoco, Center Director, Center for Mathematics Education,
Education Development Center, Newton, Massachusetts

Advisors

Peter Braunfeld
David Carraher
Carole Greenes
Claire Groden
June Mark
Ricardo Nemirovsky
James Newton
Judith Roitman
Deborah Schifter

Evaluators

Douglas H. Clements
Cynthia Halderson
Mark Jenness
Julie Sarama

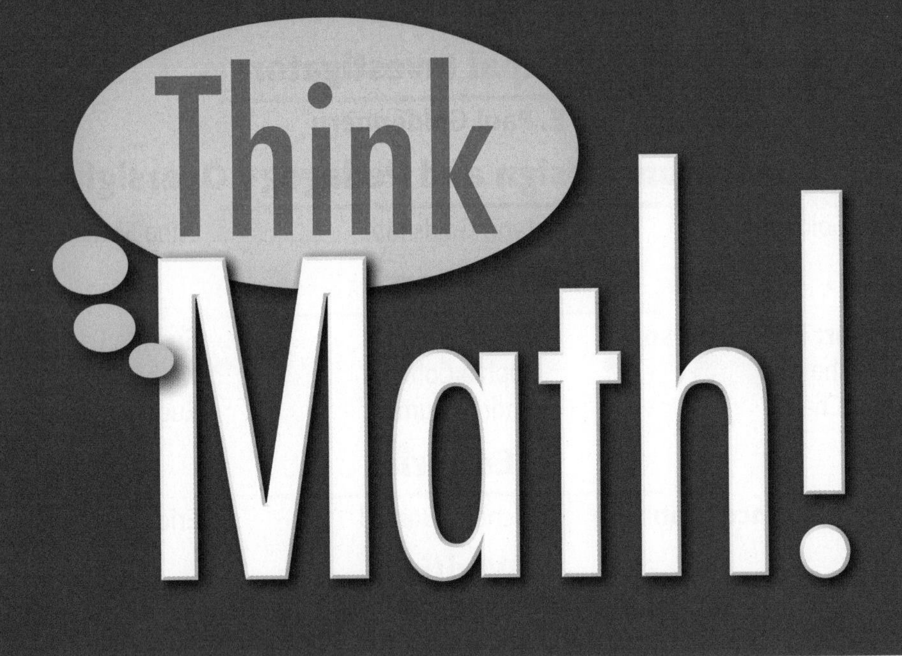

Chapter 1 Magic Squares

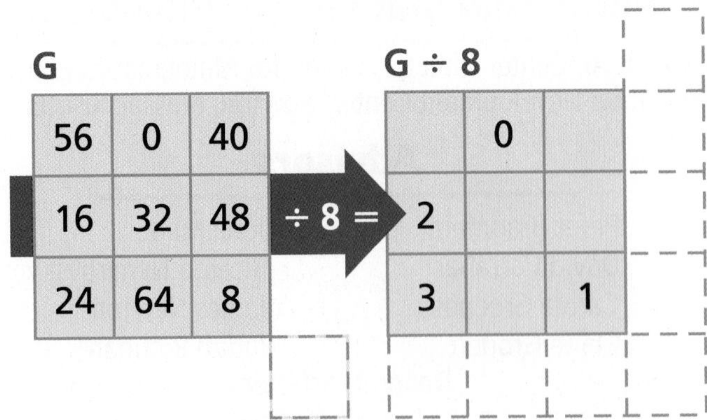

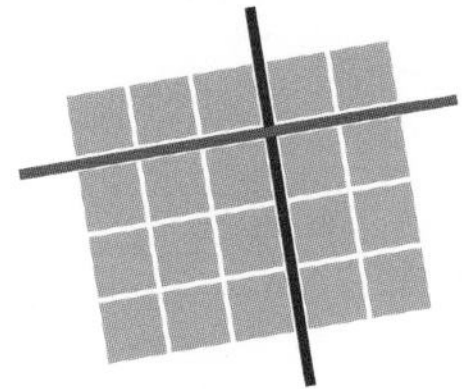

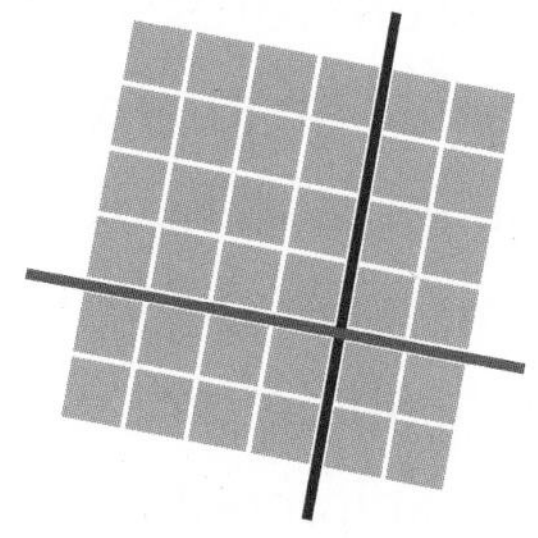

Chapter 2 Multiplication

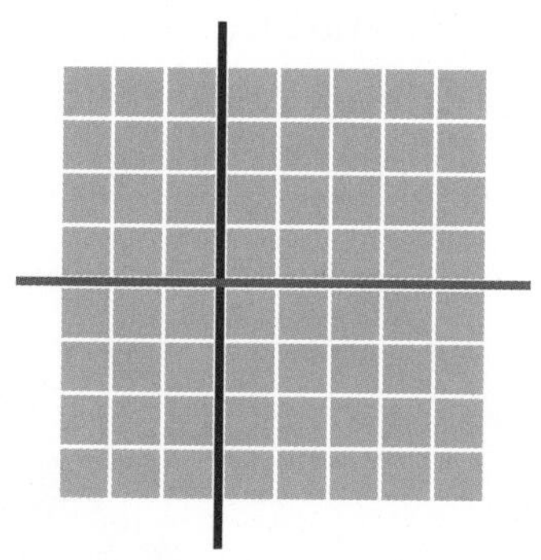

Think Math! Contents

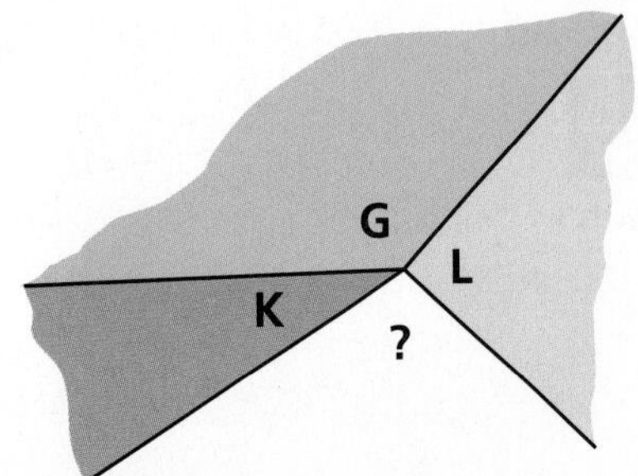

Chapter 5 Area and Perimeter

Chapter 6 Multi-Digit Multiplication

Contents

Chapter 7 Fractions

Chapter 8 Decimals

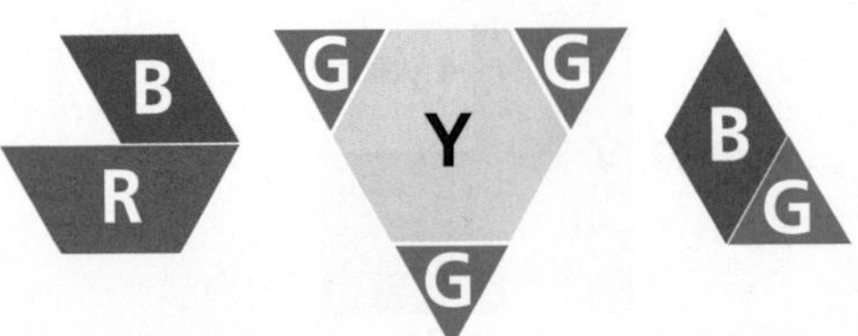

Chapter 9 Measurement

Chapter 10 Data and Probability

Think Math! Contents

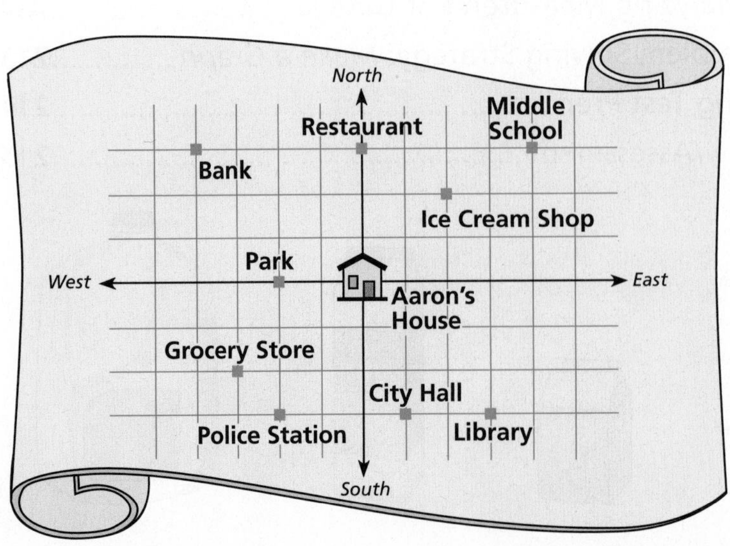

Chapter 13 Division

Chapter 14 Algebraic Thinking

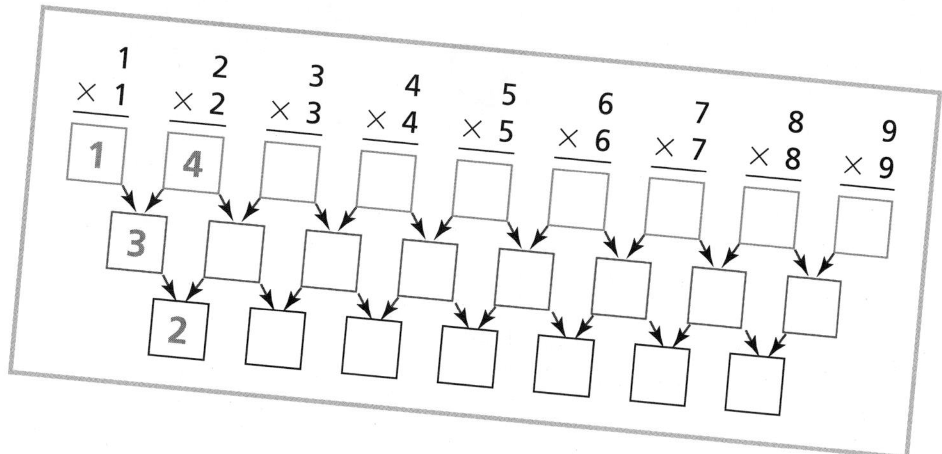

Think Math! **Contents**

Chapter 15 Estimation

Chapter 1

Lesson 1

Name ______________________ Date ____________

Introducing Magic Squares

NCTM Standards 1, 6, 7, 8, 10

In a magic square, each row, column, and diagonal sums to the same number. Complete each magic square and complete the number sentence for one of the rows, columns, or diagonals.

1.

		1	
2	1		
1		2	3
		3	

1 + ☐ + 2 = 3

2.

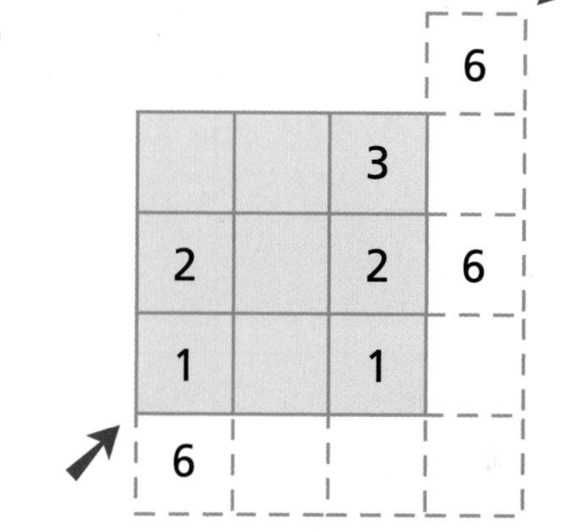

1 + ☐ + 3 = 6

3.

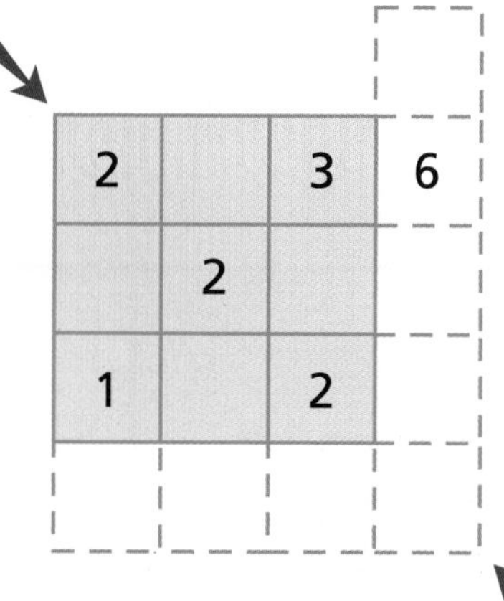

2 + 2 + 2 = ☐

4.

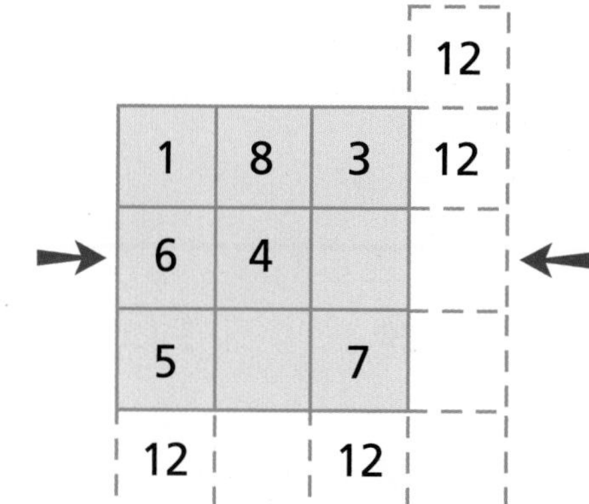

6 + 4 + ☐ = ☐

Complete each magic square.

5

	5	2	
1	4		12
6	3		
		12	

6

			30
	10		
18		9	
	30		30

7

3	19		
	10	5	
	1		
			30

8

	25		
		21	42
23		16	

9 Katy and Sasha each have the same number of coins. Katy has 3 quarters, 2 dimes and 8 nickels. Sasha has 5 quarters and 1 dime. If the rest of her coins are nickels, how many nickels does Sasha have?

______ nickels

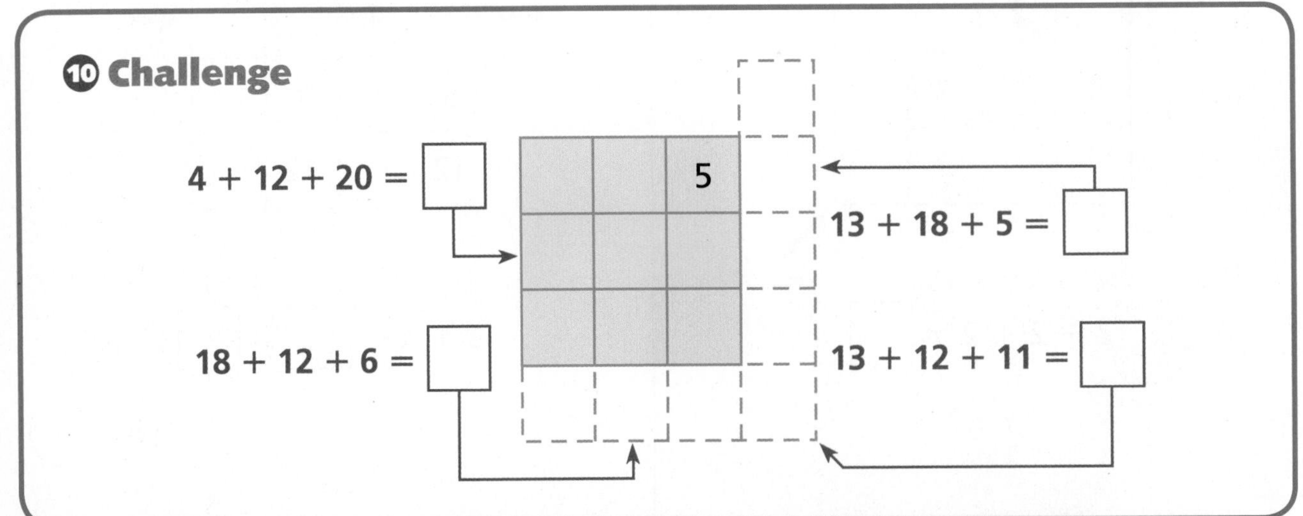

Chapter 1
Lesson 2

Name ______________________ Date ____________

Adding Magic Squares

NCTM Standards 1, 2, 6, 7, 8, 10

Is the sum of two magic squares always a magic square? Complete the magic squares and then add them together.

1

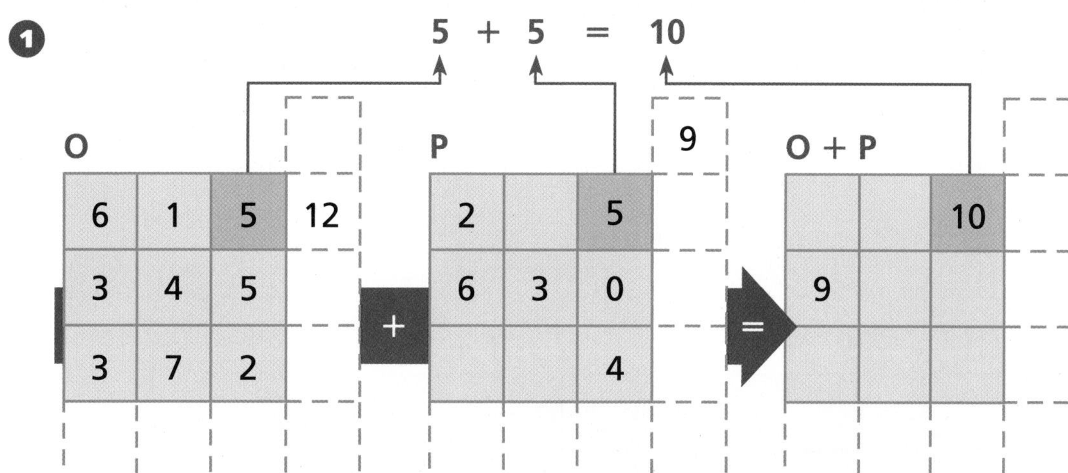

O + P is a magic square.

True ◯

False ◯

2

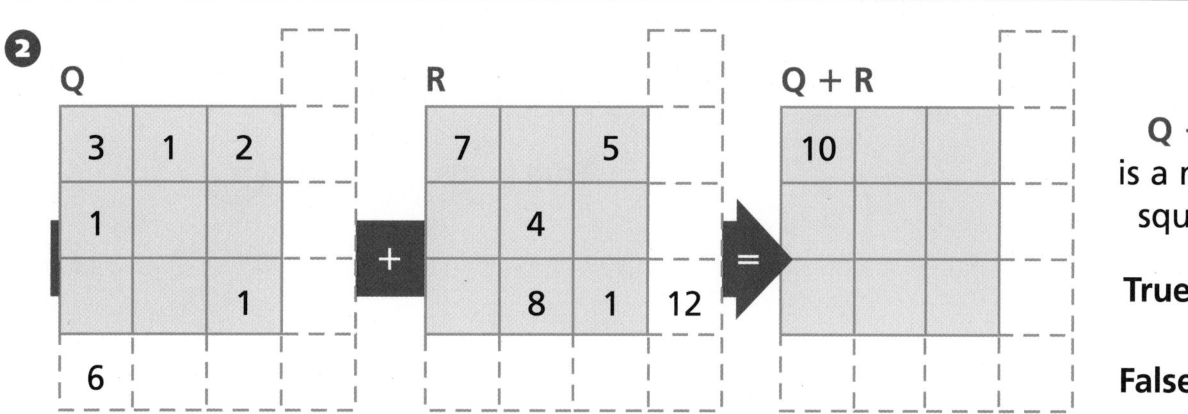

Q + R is a magic square.

True ◯

False ◯

3

X

7		5	
	4		
	8	1	12

\+

Z

	0	0
0		

=

X + Z

7		5	
	4		
	8	1	12

X + Z is a magic square.

True ◯

False ◯

4

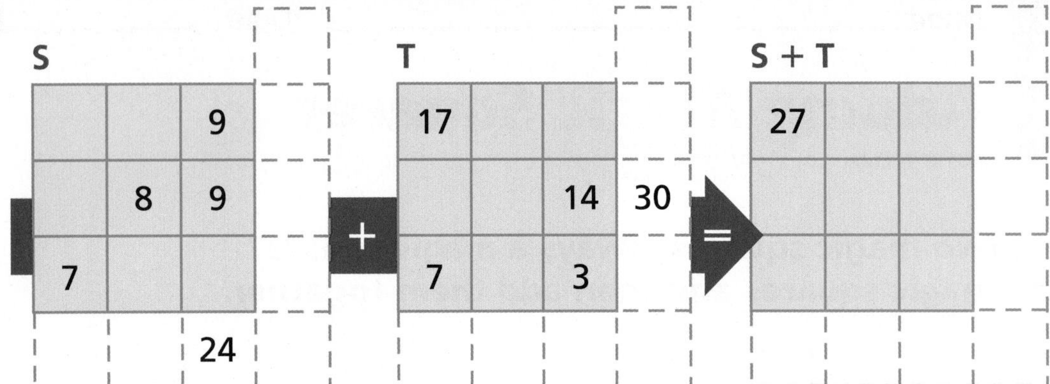

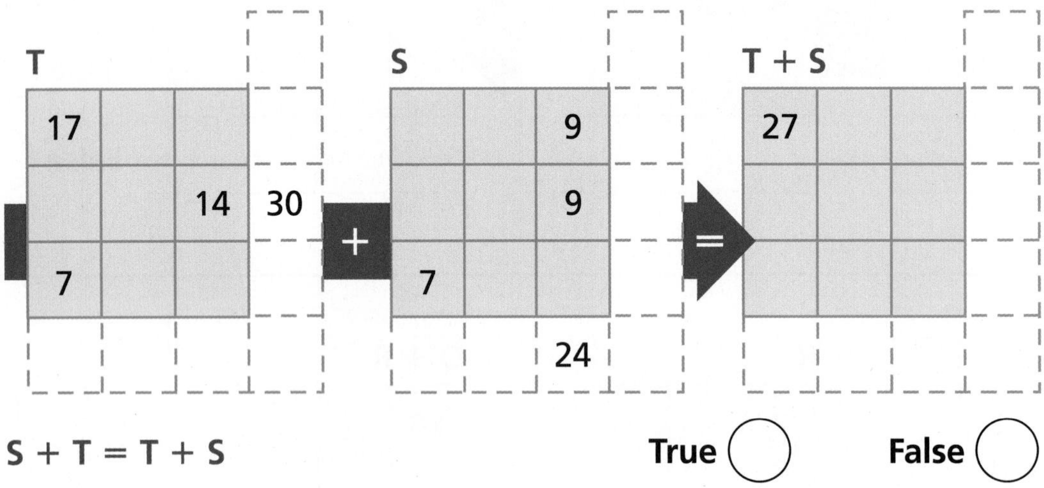

S + T = T + S

True ◯ False ◯

5 Challenge Complete these magic squares.

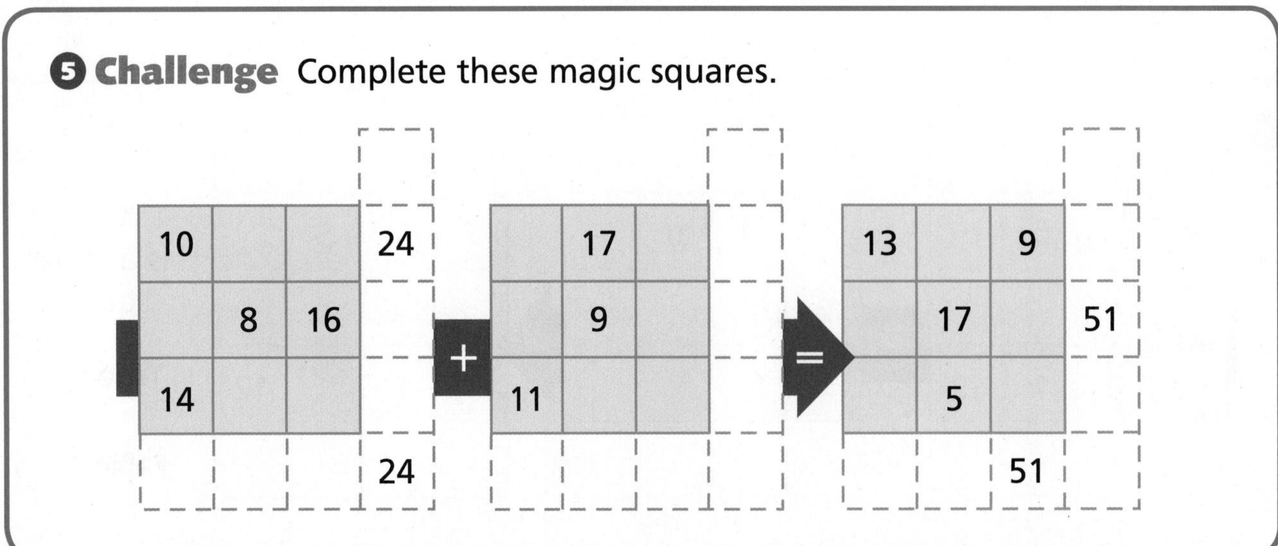

Chapter 1
Lesson 3

Name ______________________ Date ____________

Subtracting Magic Squares

NCTM Standards 1, 2, 6, 7, 8, 10

Complete the magic squares. Find their difference.

1

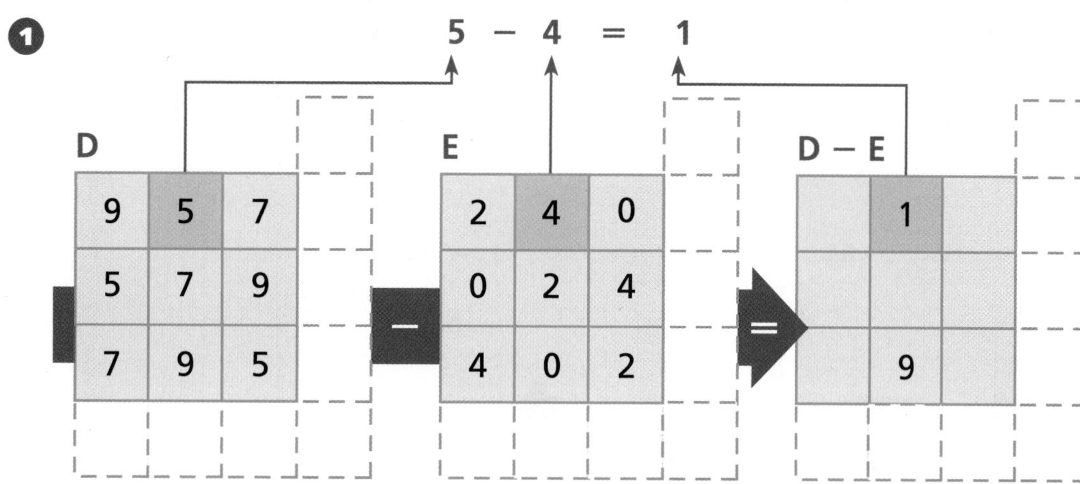

D − E is a magic square.

True ◯

False ◯

2

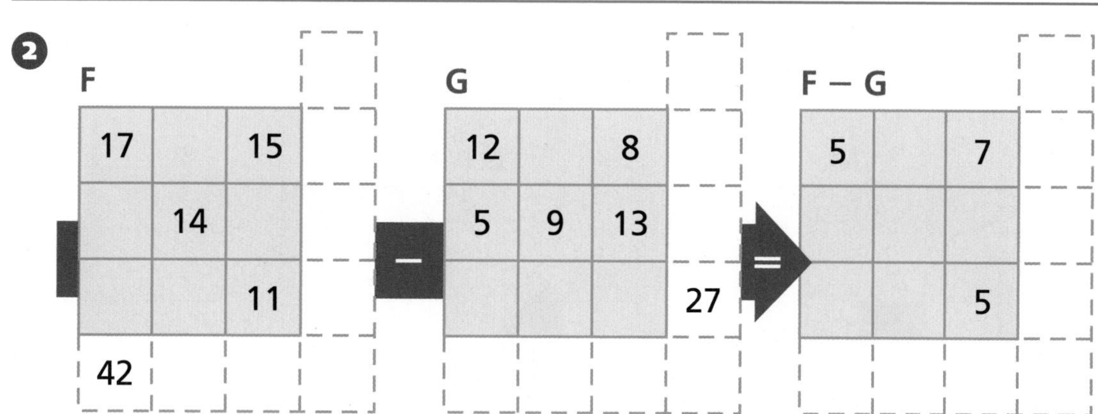

F − G is a magic square.

True ◯

False ◯

3

H

		20
30	5	40

75

I

10		
	15	
20		20

45

H − I

0		
10		20

H − I is a magic square.

True ◯

False ◯

4

J

14			
11	10		
5		6	
			30

−

K

6		9	
		2	

=

J − K

		6	
3	5		
		2	
			15

5

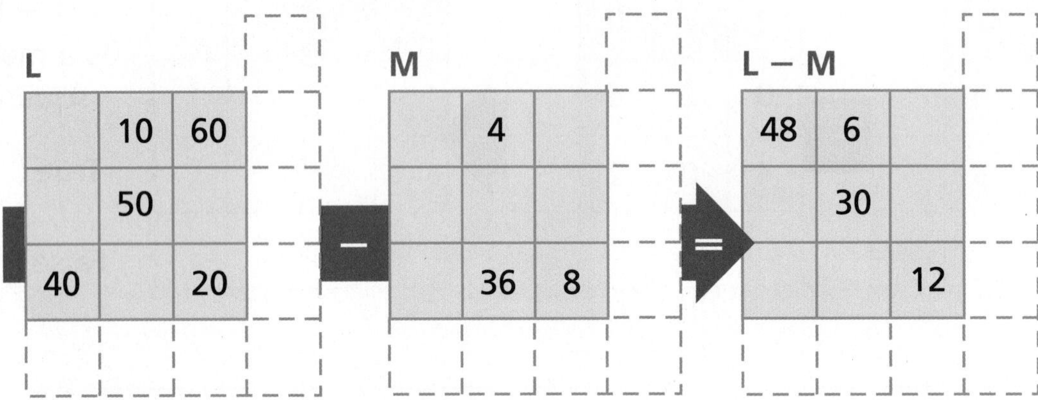

6

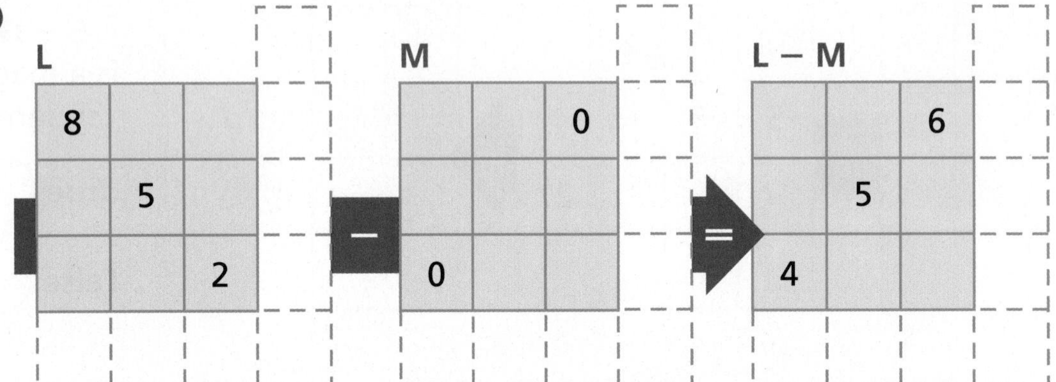

7 Challenge Jennifer paid for a stamp with a $1 bill. The stamp cost 53¢. How much change did she receive?

______

If the cashier gave her the fewest possible coins in change, how many coins did she receive? What were they?

____

Chapter 1
Lesson 4

Name ______________________ Date ____________

Multiplying Magic Squares

NCTM Standards 1, 2, 6, 7, 8, 10

Multiply each magic square by the given number.

1

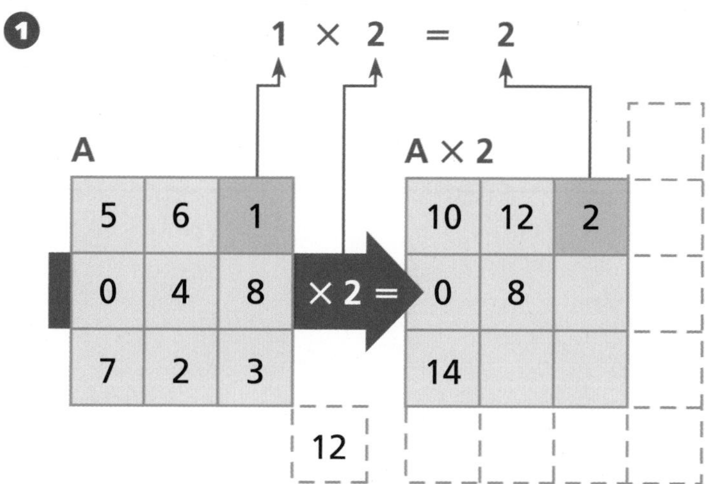

Row, column, or diagonal sum before multiplication	12
Numbers in A are multiplied by	2
Row, column, or diagonal sum after multiplication	24

2

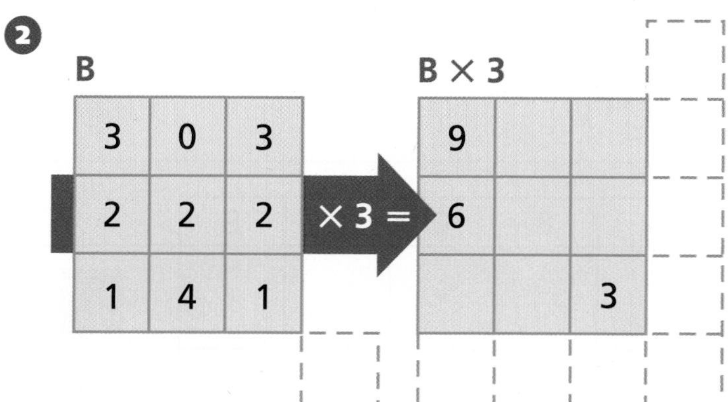

Row, column, or diagonal sum before multiplication	
Numbers in B are multiplied by	
Row, column, or diagonal sum after multiplication	

3

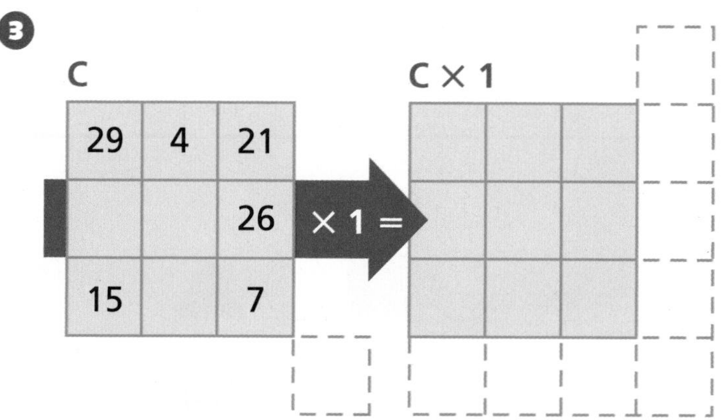

Row, column, or diagonal sum before multiplication	
Numbers in C are multiplied by	
Row, column, or diagonal sum after multiplication	

4

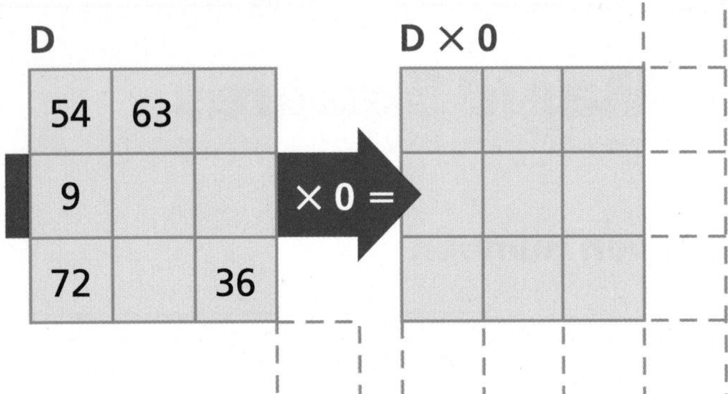

5

E

		1
	4	
7		5

× 10 =

E × 10

6

	A	B	C	D	E	
Row, column or diagonal sum before multiplication						■
Numbers are multiplied by						▲
Row, column, or diagonal sum after multiplication						★

7 Challenge Fill in the blanks with + , − , × , ÷ , or = .

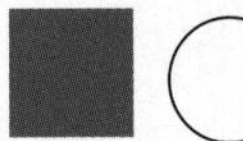  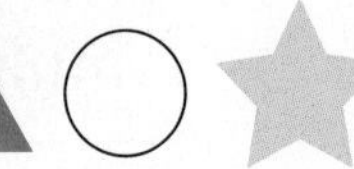   

  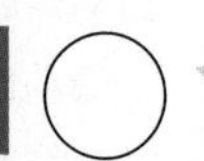 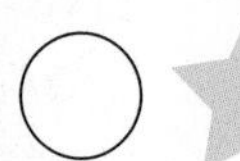  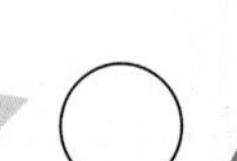  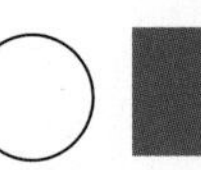

Chapter 1
Lesson 5

Name ______________________ Date ____________

Dividing Magic Squares by Numbers

NCTM Standards 1, 6, 8, 9, 10

Divide each magic square by the given number.

1

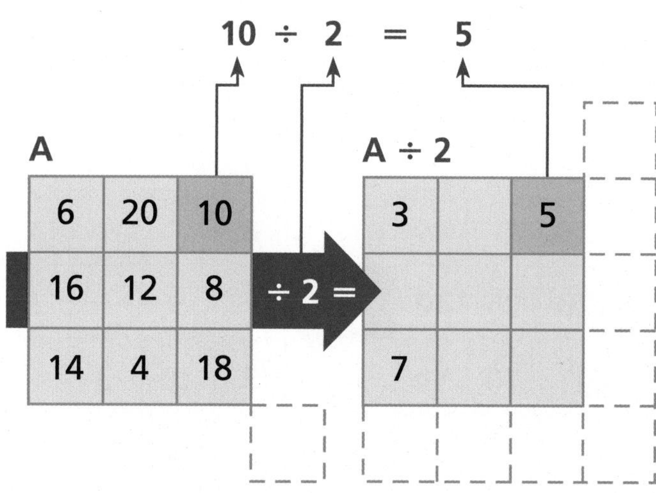

2

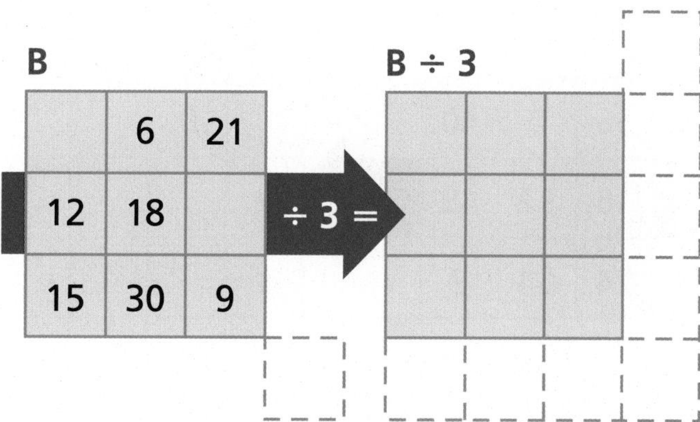

3

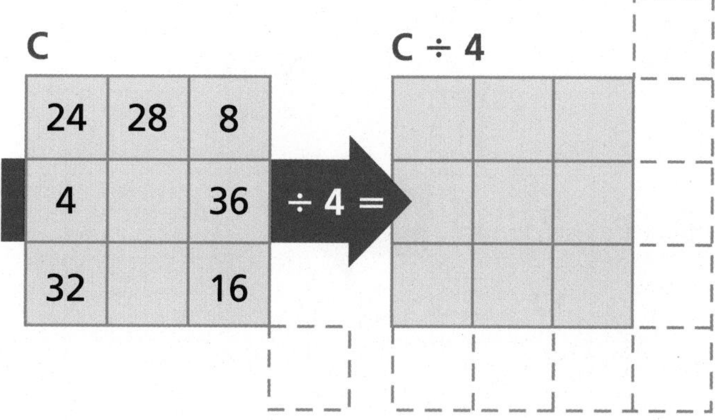

4

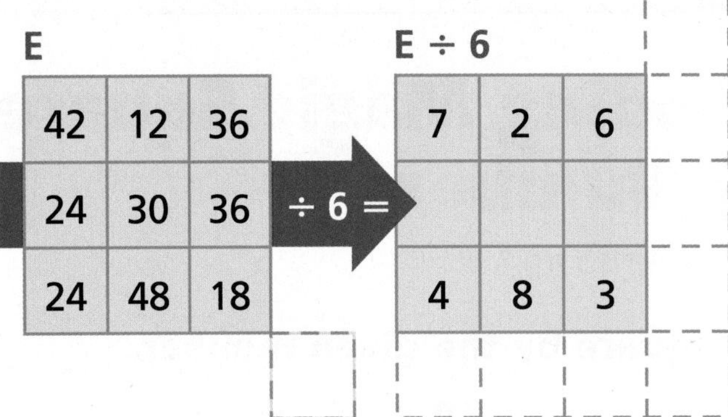

5

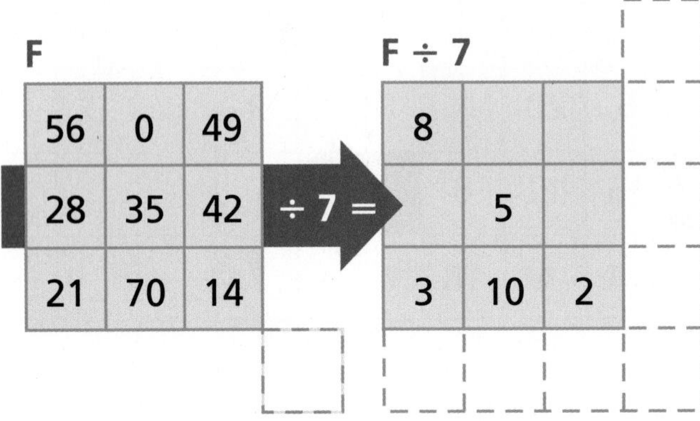

F
F ÷ 7
56 0 49
28 35 42
21 70 14
÷ 7 =
8
5
3 10 2

6

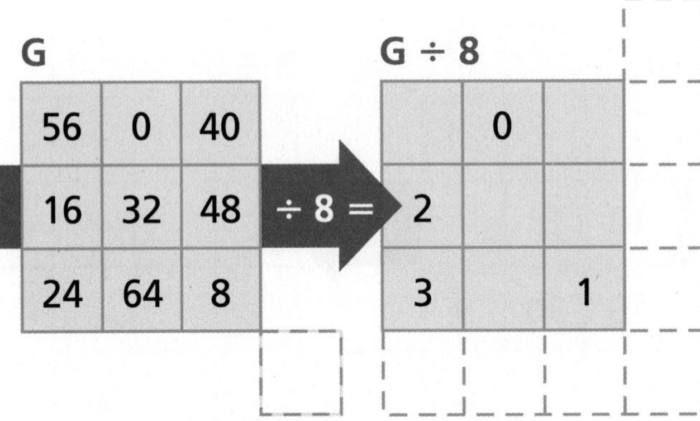

G
G ÷ 8
56 0 40
16 32 48
24 64 8
÷ 8 =
0
2
3 1

7 Challenge

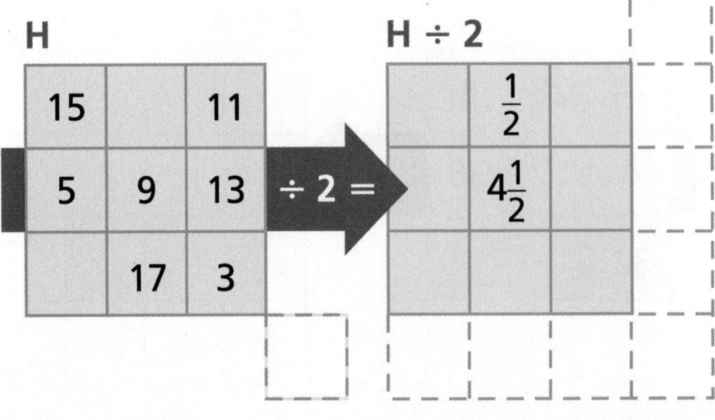

Chapter 1
Lesson 6

Name ______________________ Date ____________

Working Backward and Forward

NCTM Standards 1, 6, 8, 9, 10

Complete the magic squares.

1

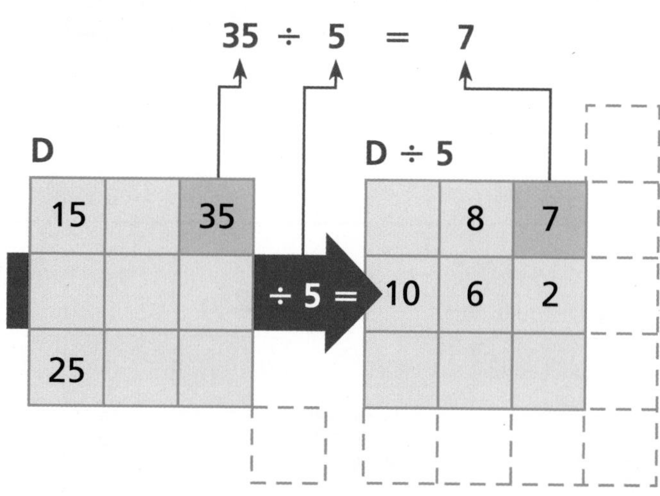

2

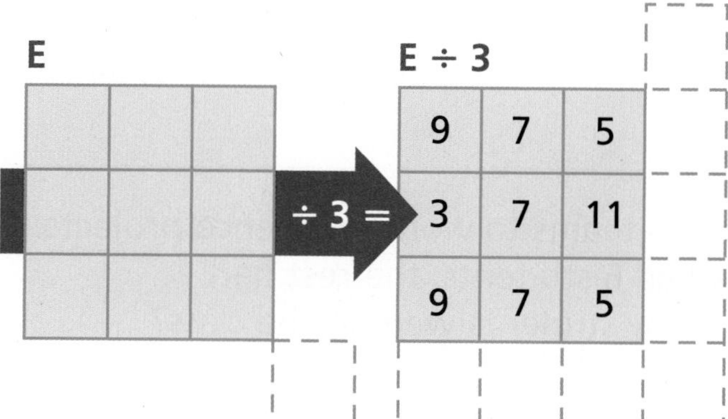

3

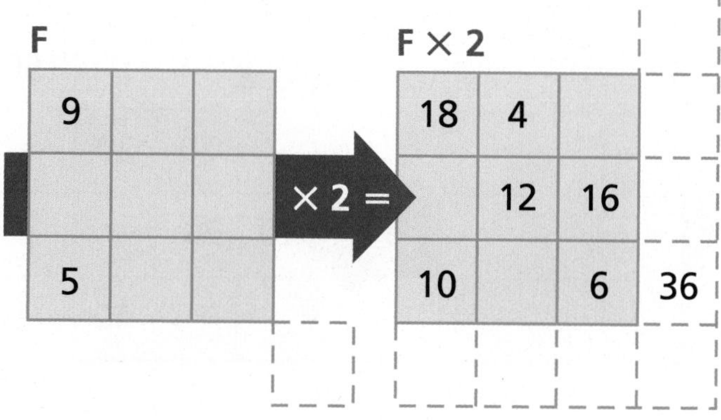

4

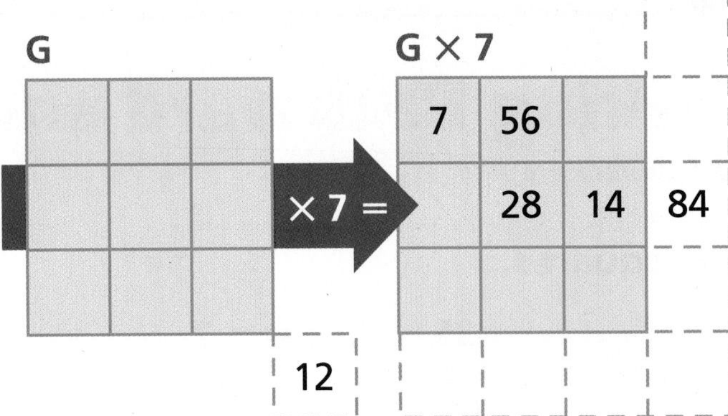

5

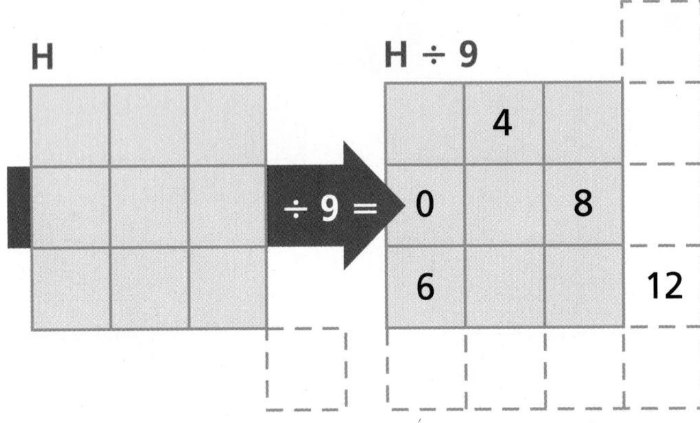

6 A class split up into 6 teams to work on science projects. Two of the teams had 6 students, the rest had 5 students. How many students were in the class?

_____ students

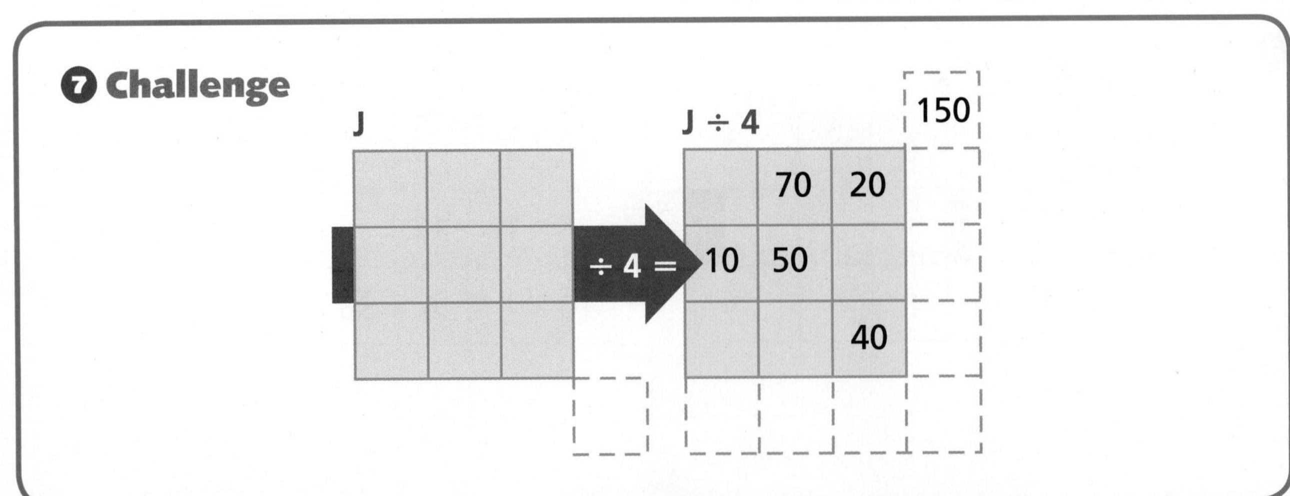

Name ______________________ Date ____________

Chapter 1
Lesson 7

Problem Solving Strategy
Work Backward

NCTM Standards 1, 2, 6, 7, 8, 10

Understand
Plan
Solve
Check

Solve each problem.

1 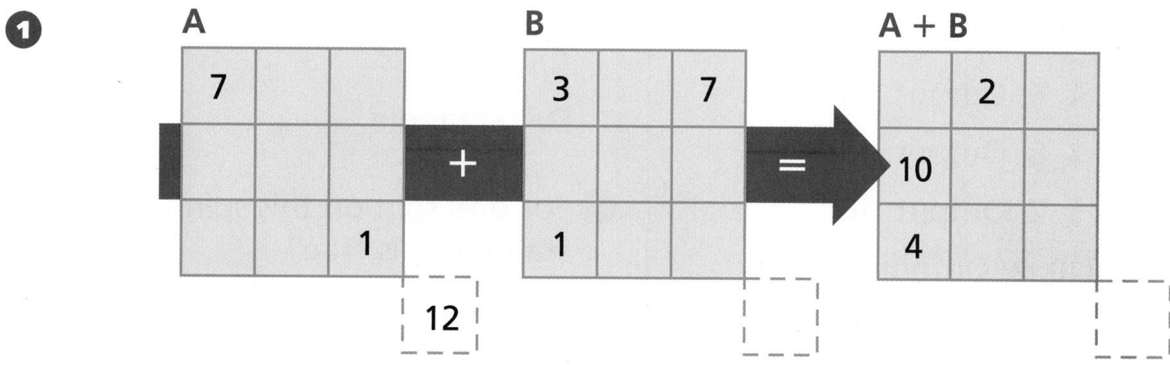

2 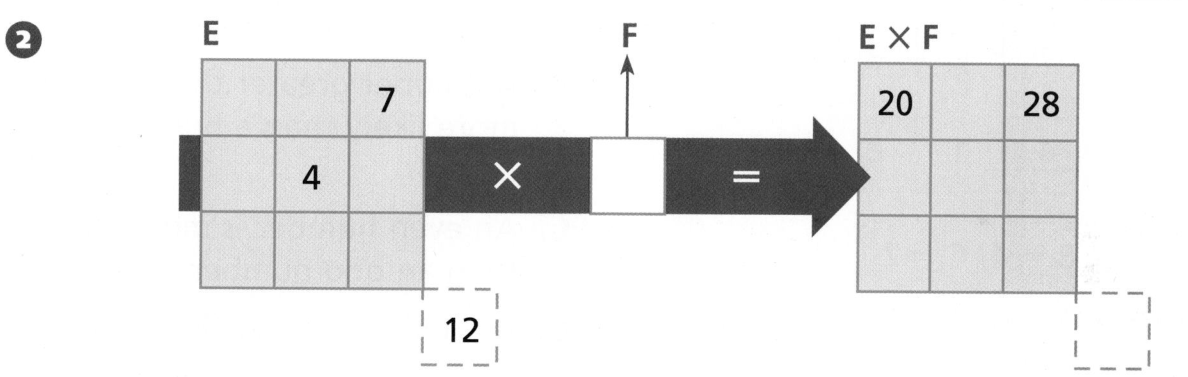

3 Todd sold ornaments at a craft fair. The first customer bought 5 ornaments. The second customer bought half of what Todd had left. The third customer bought 8 ornaments. After that Todd had 2 ornaments left. How many ornaments did Todd start with?

______ ornaments

Problem Solving Test Prep

Choose the correct answer.

1. Which set of input-output values follows the rule in the table?

INPUT	2, 7	3, 9	1, 0	5, 1
OUTPUT	14	27	0	5

A. Input: 4, 6; Output: 10

B. Input: 2, 8; Output: 10

C. Input: 5, 2; Output: 10

D. Input: 10, 2; Output: 10

2. The sum of the magic square is 15. What are the values of A, B, and C?

A	9	B
7	C	3
6	1	8

A. A = 5, B = 4, C = 2

B. A = 5, B = 2, C = 4

C. A = 4, B = 5, C = 2

D. A = 2, B = 4, C = 5

3. Which is the only figure that is **not** a parallelogram?

A. trapezoid

B. square

C. rhombus

D. rectangle

4. For one spin on this spinner, which statement is true?

A. An odd number is more likely than an even number.

B. A number greater than 5 is more likely than a number less than 4.

C. An even number is more likely than an odd number.

D. A number greater than 4 is more likely than a number less than 4.

Show What You Know

Solve each problem. Explain your answer.

5. Jason wants to buy a book for $19. He has a $10 bill and two $1 bills. His father lends him money to pay the rest. What is the least number of bills his father can give him to buy the book? Explain.

____

____

Name ______________________ Date ____________

Chapter 1

Review/Assessment

NCTM Standards 1, 2, 6, 8, 9, 10

Complete the magic squares. Lesson 1

1

24		18	
		6	
			45

2

3		7	
1			
12			

Complete the magic squares. Then add them. Lessons 2 and 3

3

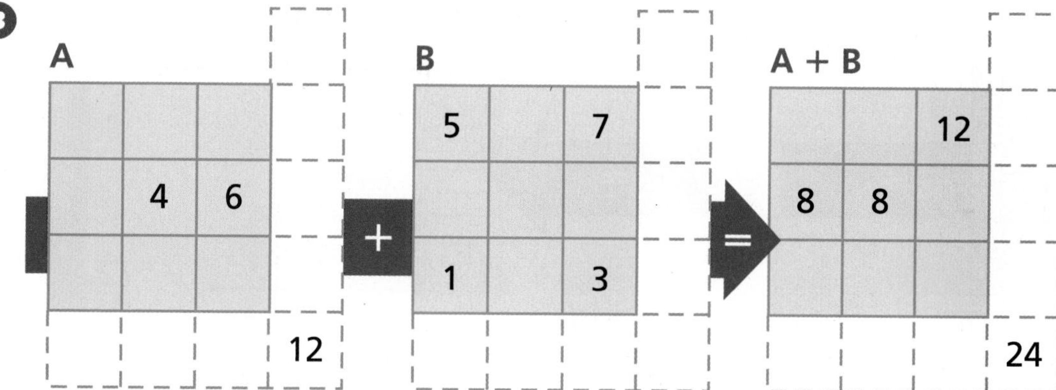

4 There are 27 students in Mrs. Albia's class. Fifteen of the students are girls. Write a number sentence to show how many boys are in Mrs. Albia's class. Lessons 2 and 3

____

5 Solve. Lessons 4 and 5

$(14 \div 2) \times 2 =$ ______

$(36 \div 2) \times 2 =$ ______

Multiply and divide. Lessons 4 and 5

6

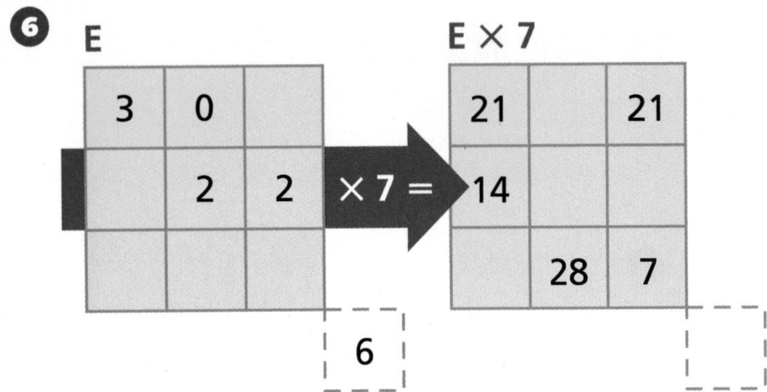

7

H

13	6	8
4	9	14
10	12	5

× 3 =

H × 3

÷ 3 =

(H × 3) ÷ 3

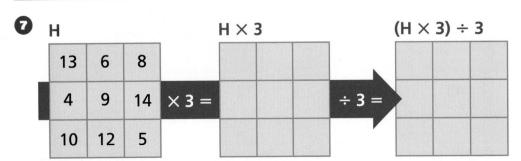

Complete the magic square. Lessons 5 and 6

8

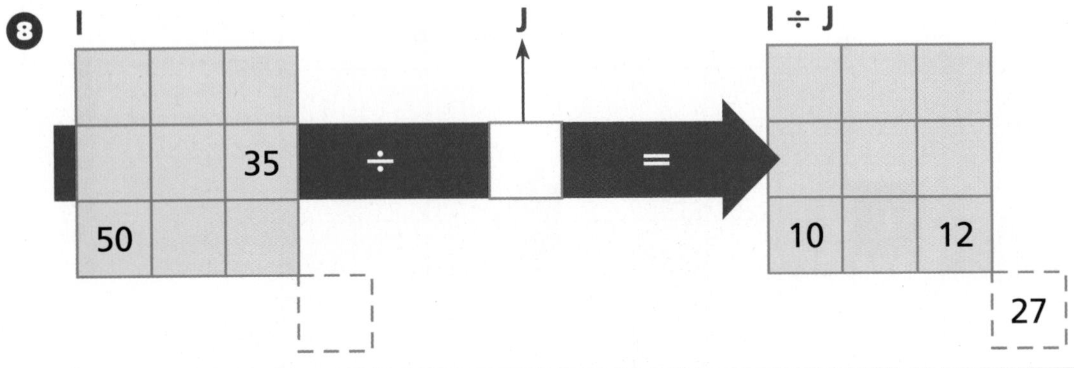

9 Phillip went to the music store and bought a CD for $14 and a DVD for $9. He had $6 in his wallet when he got home. How much money did he have before he went to the music store? Lesson 7

10 Maria had 36 stamps in her collection. Each week she added 6 more stamps. How many weeks passed until Maria had 72 stamps? Explain. Lesson 7

Chapter 2

Lesson 1

Name ______________________ Date __________

Introducing Arrays

NCTM Standards 1, 2, 6, 7, 8, 9, 10

Use counting shortcuts to find the number of squares in each array.

1. 

   4

2. 

   6

3. 

4. 

   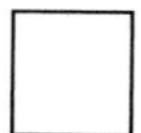

5. 

6. 

7. 

8. 

9. 

10. 

11. 

    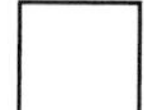

12. 

13. Mrs. Wu arranged the desks of her classroom into 4 rows of 7 desks. How many desks are there in her classroom? Show how you solved the problem with words, pictures, or numbers.

    _____ desks

14. Use counting shortcuts to find the number of squares in each array.

A

B

C

D

E

F

G

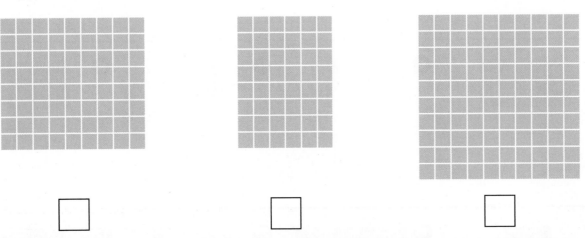

15. **Challenge** Write the letter of each of the above arrays A through G in the appropriate white box in the table. You will write some letters twice.

×	1	2	3	4	5	6	7	8	9	10
1										
2										
3									A	
4										
5										
6										
7										
8										
9										
10										

Name ______________________ Date ____________

Chapter 2

Lesson 2 Separating Arrays

NCTM Standards 1, 2, 6, 7, 8, 9, 10

Complete the diagrams and number sentences.

1 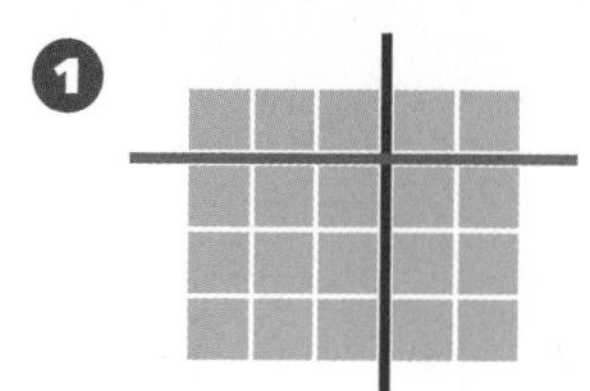

1 × 3	
	3 × 2

	2
9	

$(1 \times 3) + (3 \times 3) + (1 \times 2) + (3 \times 2) = \boxed{20}$

---

2 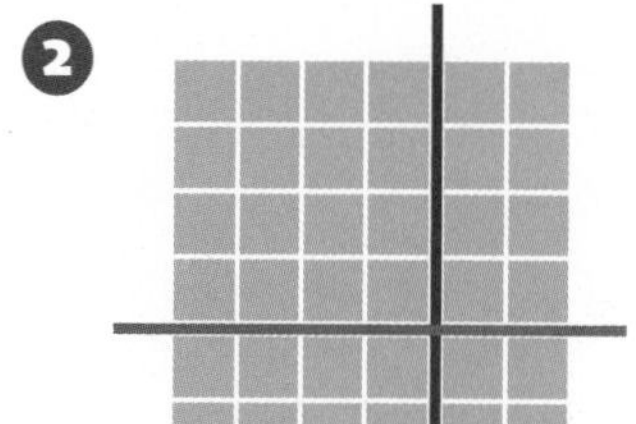

4 × 4	

8	

$(4 \times 4) + (2 \times 4) + (\square \times \square) + (2 \times 2) = \square$

---

3 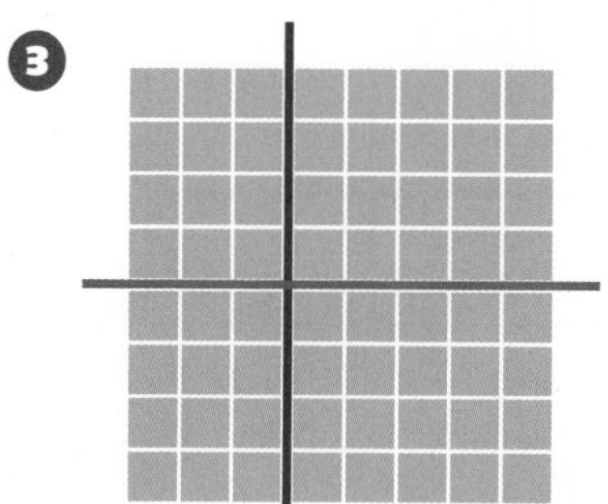

4 × 3	

	20

$(4 \times 3) + (4 \times 3) + (4 \times 5) + (\square \times \square) = \square$

4

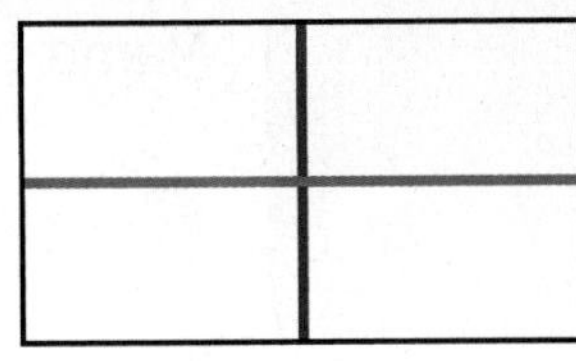

(□ × □) + (□ × □) + (□ × □) + (□ × □) = □

5

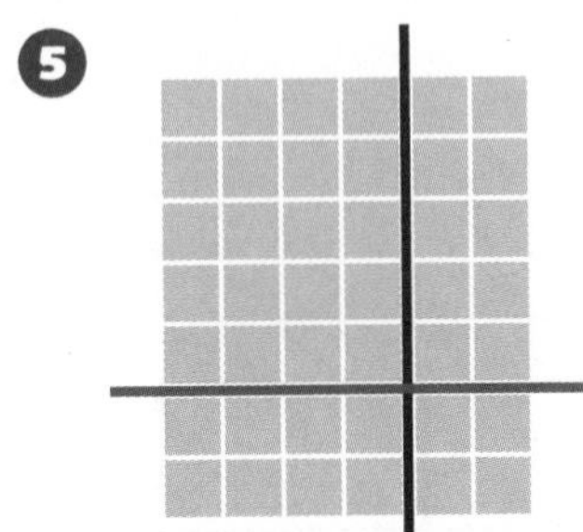

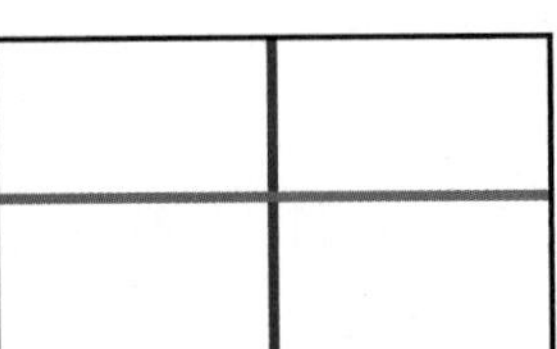

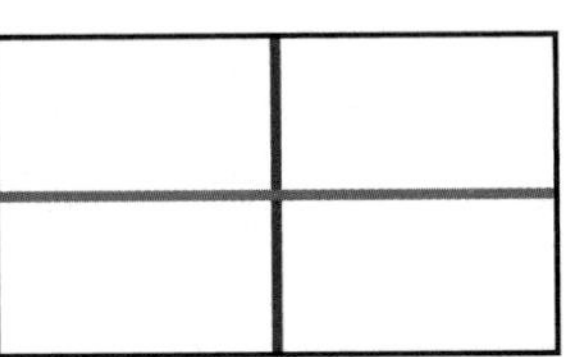

(□ × □) + (□ × □) + (□ × □) + (□ × □) = □

6 Challenge Separate the array into four sections and complete the diagrams.

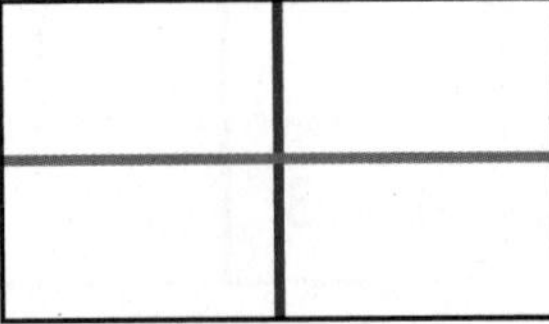

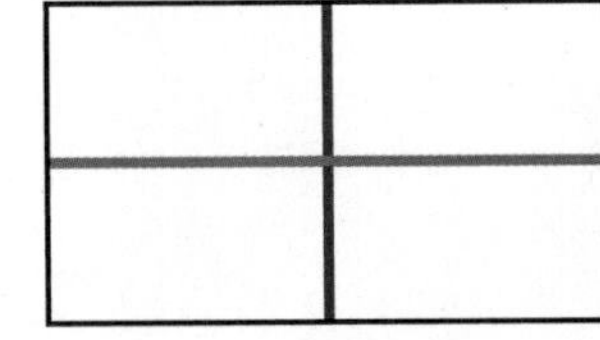

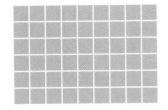

Write a number sentence to help find the total number of squares in the array.

Name ______________________ Date ____________

Chapter 2

Lesson 3 Adding Array Sections

NCTM Standards 1, 2, 6, 7, 8, 9, 10

Complete the diagrams. Then find the number of squares in each array.

1

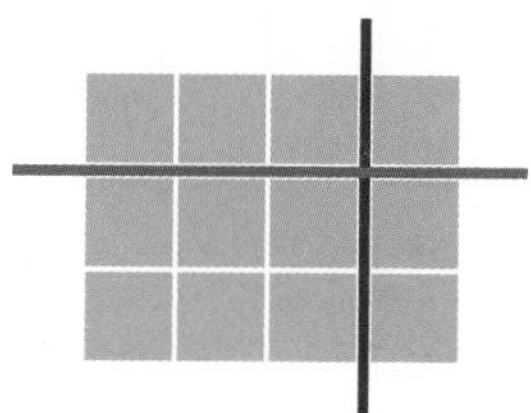

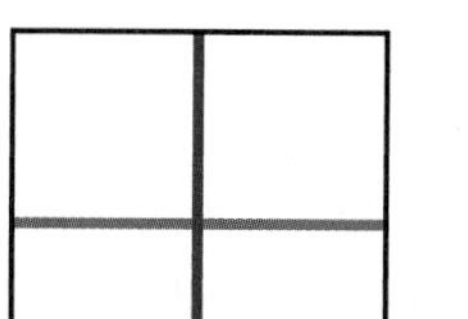

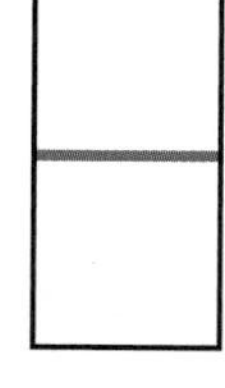

$3 \times 4 =$ ☐

2

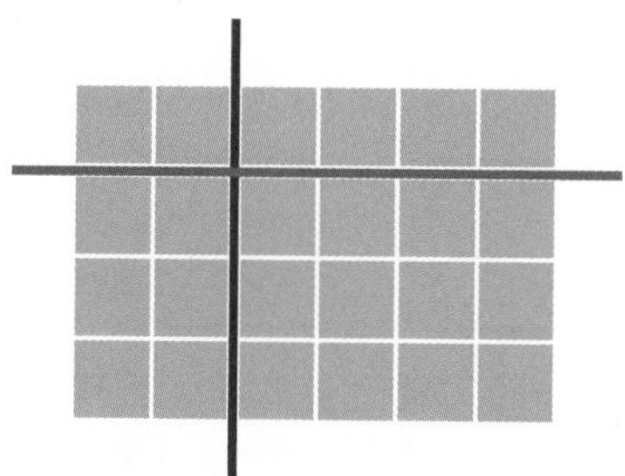

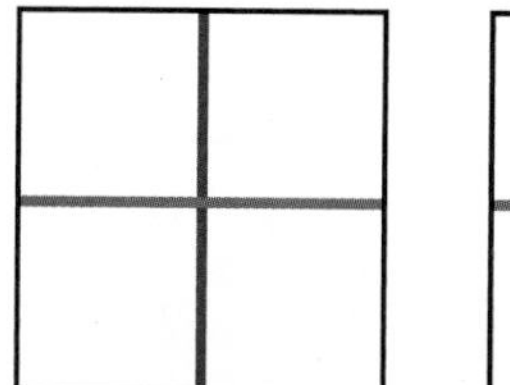

$4 \times 6 =$ ☐

3

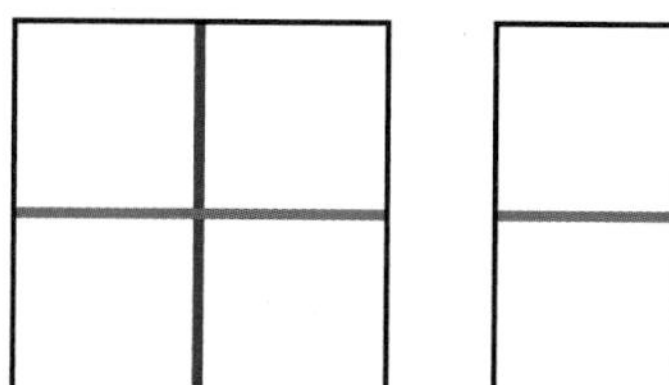

$5 \times 6 =$ ☐

4

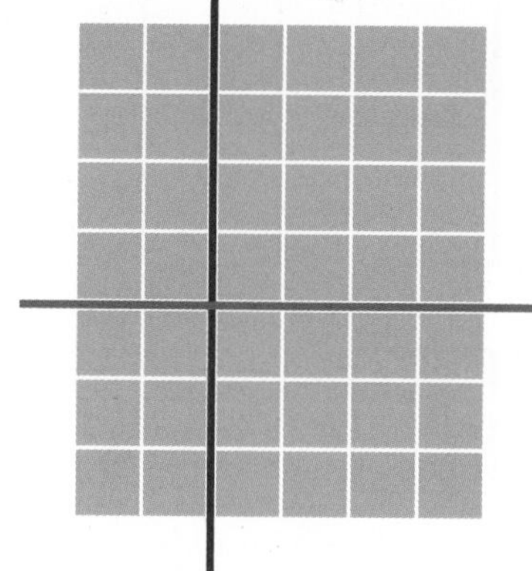

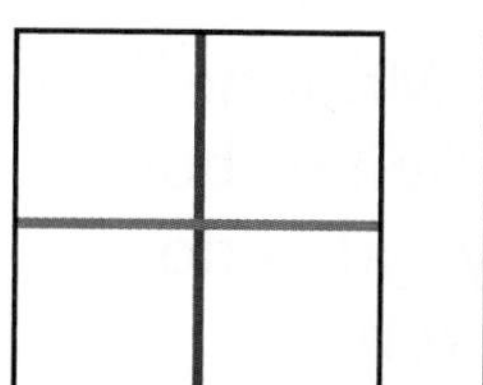

$7 \times 6 =$ ☐

5

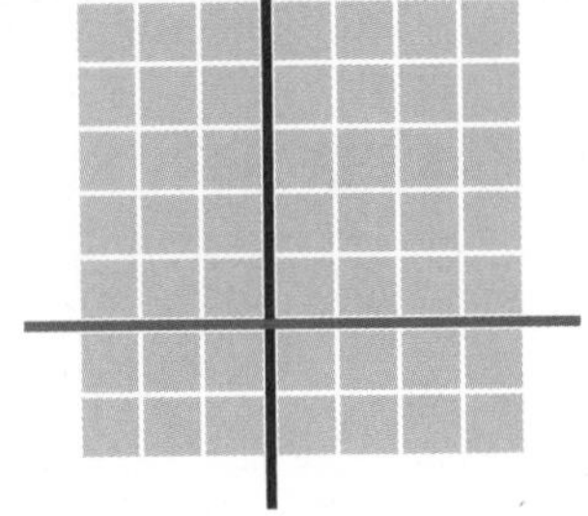

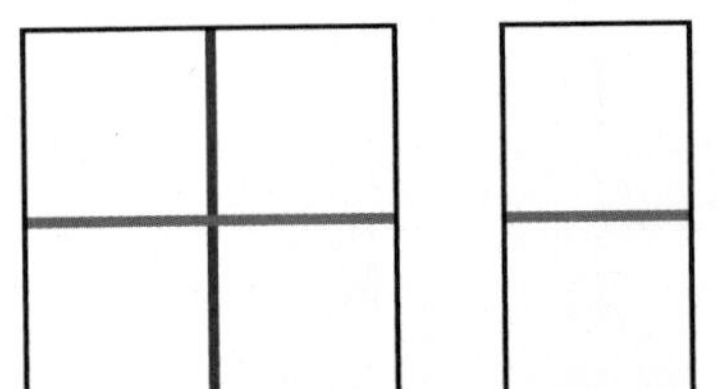

$\square \times \square = \square$

6

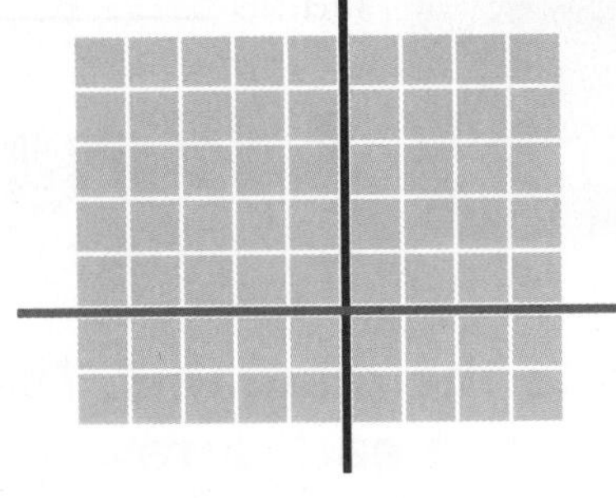

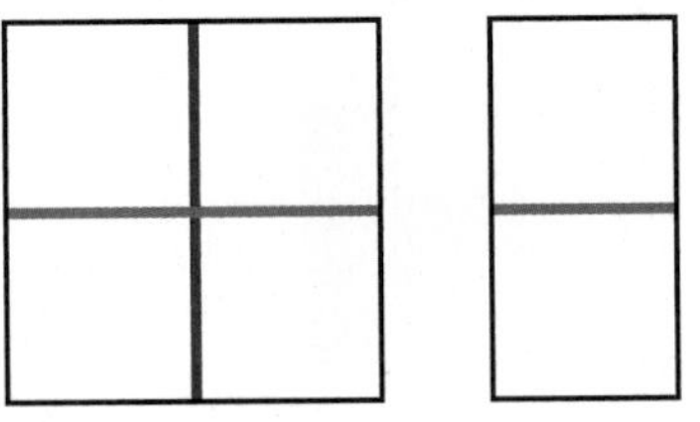

$\square \times \square = \square$

7

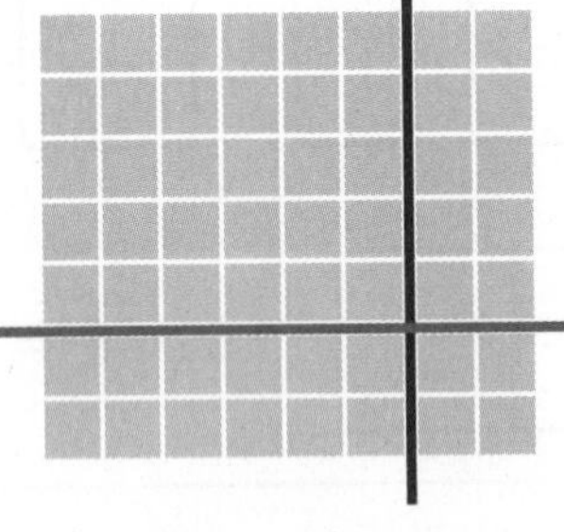

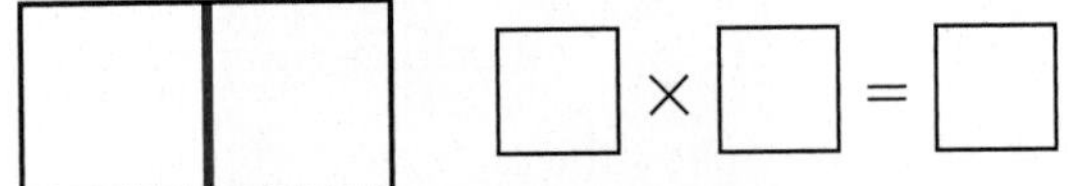

8

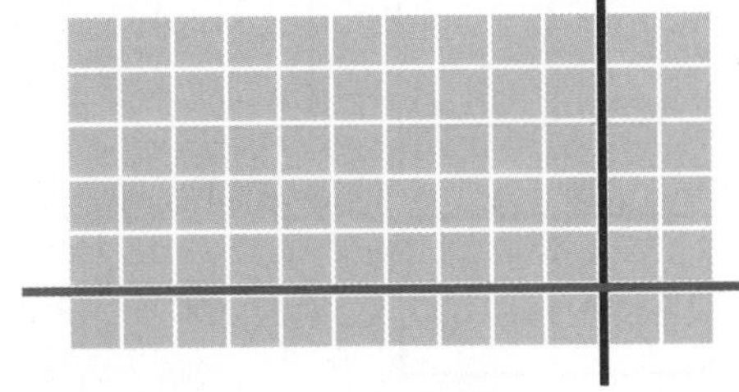

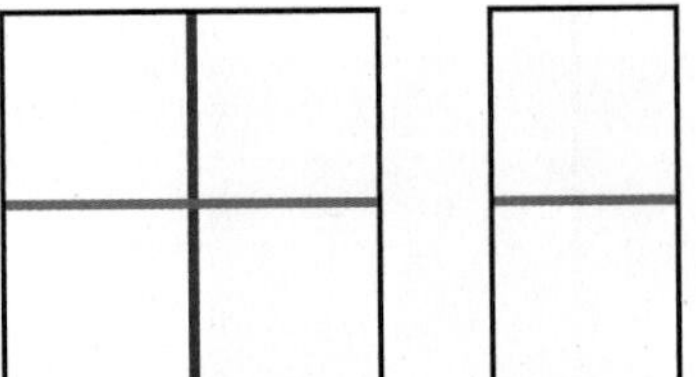

$\square \times \square = \square$

9 **Challenge** Mr. Jones bought 7 six-packs of yogurt. Mr. Gomez bought 4 six-packs of yogurt. How many yogurts do they have? Show how you solved the problem.

_____ yogurts

Chapter 2

Lesson 4

Name ____________________ Date ____________

Exploring a Multiplication Shortcut

NCTM Standards 1, 2, 6, 7, 8, 9, 10

Look for shortcuts in completing the tables and finding the number of squares in the arrays.

1.

	6	2	8	10	11
× 2	12				

2.

	2	5	9	0	10
× 3	6				

3.

	1	3	5	6	8
× 2					
× 4					
× 6					

4.

	2	0	10	6	9
× 3					
× 6					
× 9					

5.

	1	4	5	9	10
× 5					

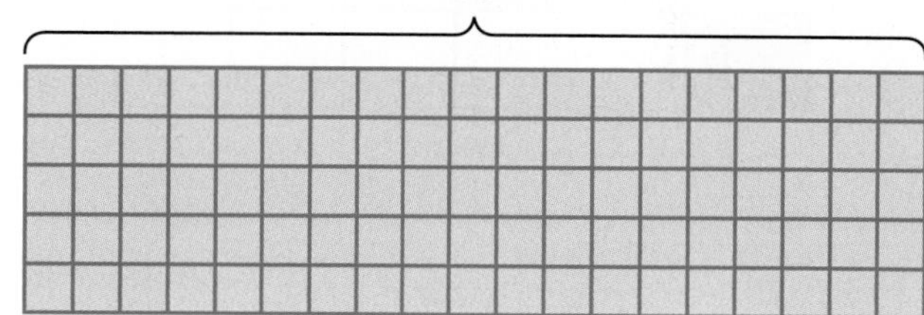

_____ squares

6.

	3	4	7	8	11
× 4					

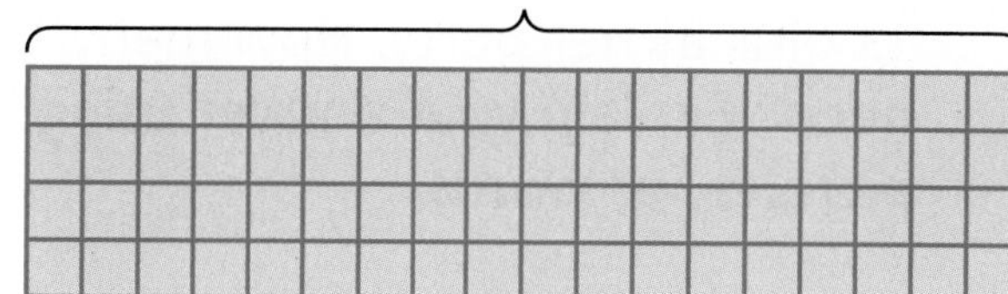

_____ squares

7

	3	4	5	7	12
× 7					

15

_____ squares

8

	2	3	5	8	11
× 9					

16

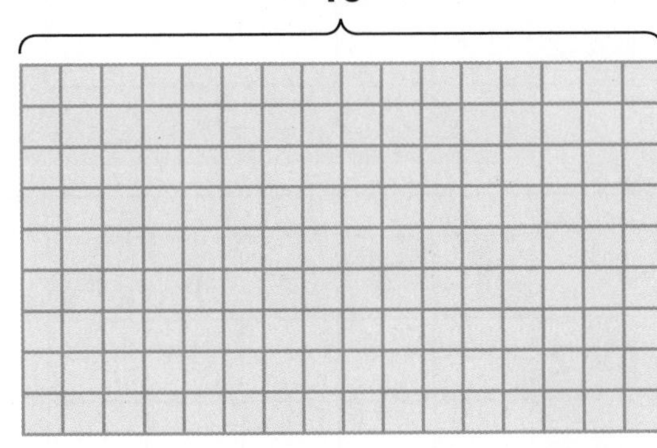

_____ squares

9

	2	4	5	9	14
× 8					

17

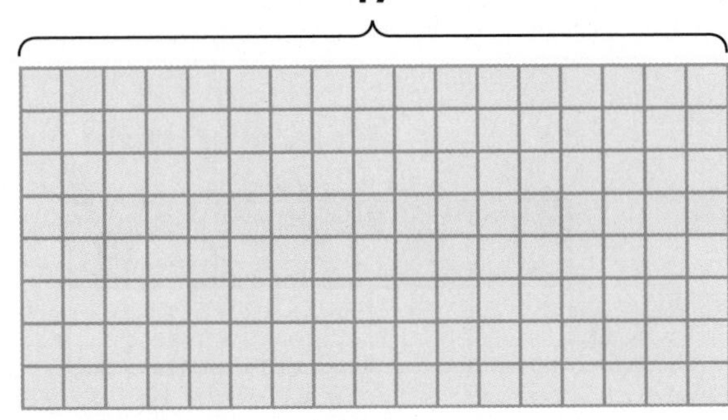

_____ squares

10 Challenge Sue wants to give 7 party favors to everyone at her party. There are 14 boys and 13 girls at her party. How many favors does she need? Explain your answer using numbers, pictures, or words.

_____ favors

Name ______________________ Date ____________

Chapter 2

Lesson 5

Using a Multiplication Shortcut

NCTM Standards 1, 2, 6, 7, 9, 10

Fill in the addition and multiplication tables.
Look for shortcuts to help you.

1

+	1	5	2	6	4	10
3				9		
1						
4			6			
5						
7						

2

×	1	5	2	6	4	10
3						
1		5				
4			8			
5						
7						

3

×	3	6	9	10	5	15
6						
2			18			
8						
9						

How many more squares are needed in an array when a factor is increased by 1 or 2? How many squares in all?

4

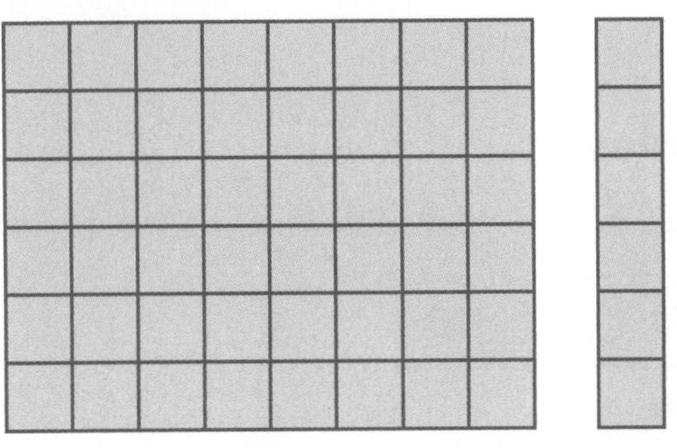

(6 × 8) + 6 = ☐

5

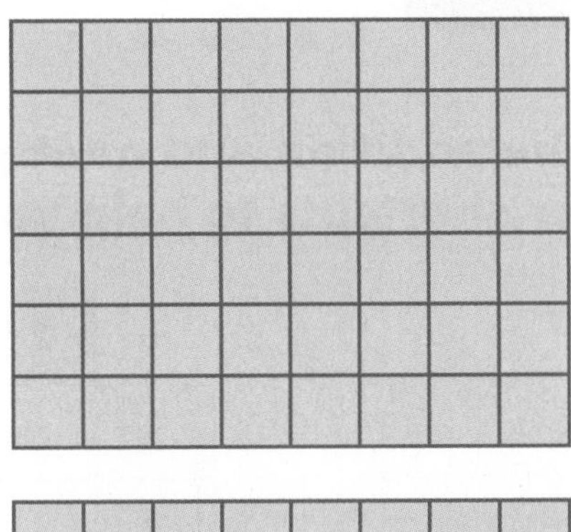

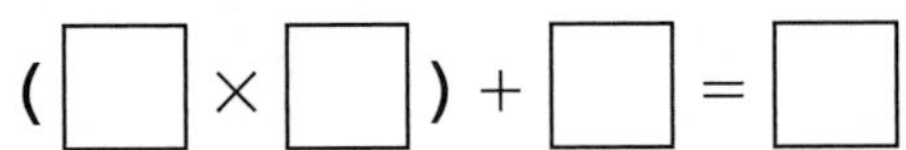

(☐ × ☐) + ☐ = ☐

6

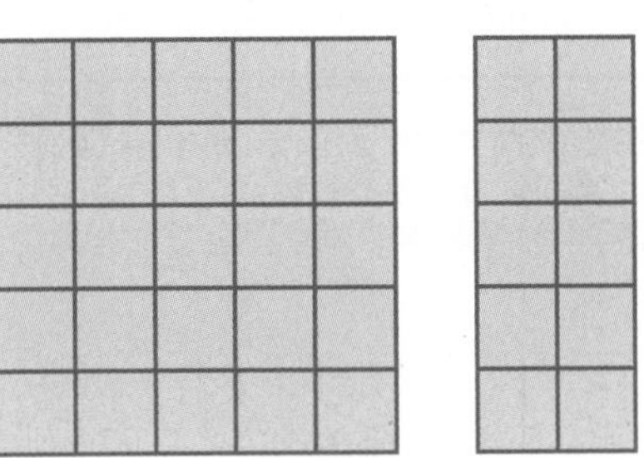

(5 × 5) + (☐ × ☐) = ☐

7

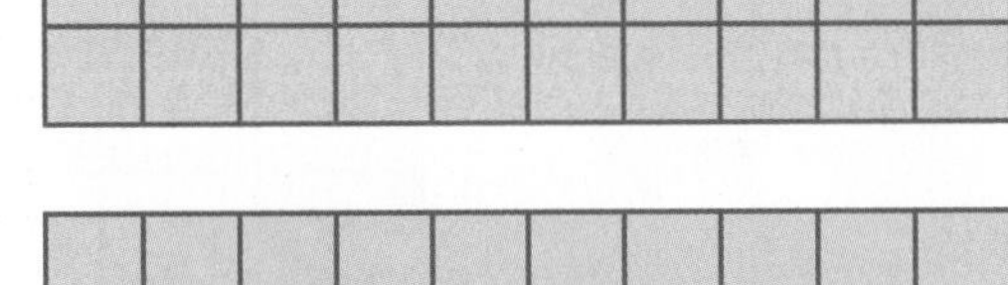

(☐ × ☐) + (☐ × ☐) = ☐

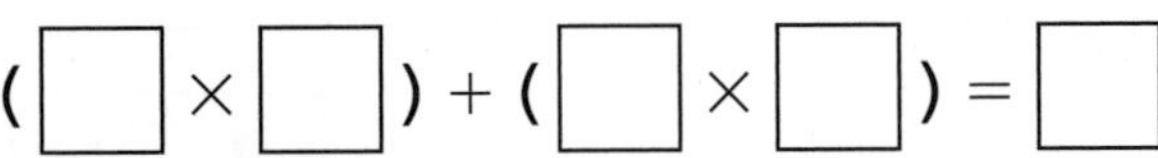

8 Challenge Reese has 14 birds and 25 dogs. How many legs do her pets have? Show your work by writing a number sentence.

______ legs

Chapter 2
Lesson 6

Name ______________________ Date ____________

Connecting Multiplication and Division

NCTM Standards 1, 2, 6, 7, 8, 9, 10

Find the missing numbers to complete the fact family.

1

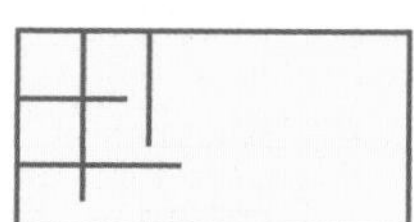

3 × ☐ = 18

☐ × 3 = 18

18 ÷ 3 = ☐

18 ÷ ☐ = 3

2

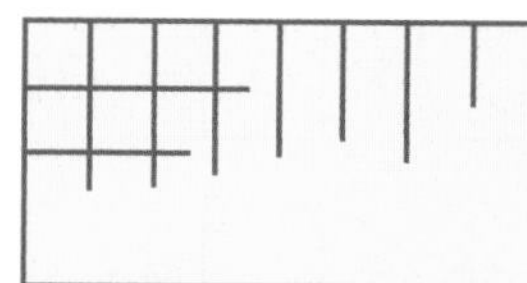

☐ × 8 = 32

8 × ☐ = 32

32 ÷ ☐ = 8

32 ÷ 8 = ☐

3

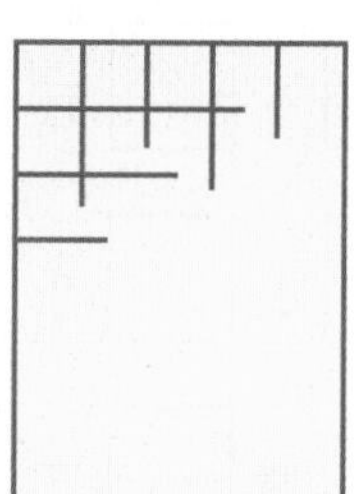

☐ × 5 = 35

5 × ☐ = 35

35 ÷ ☐ = 5

35 ÷ 5 = ☐

4

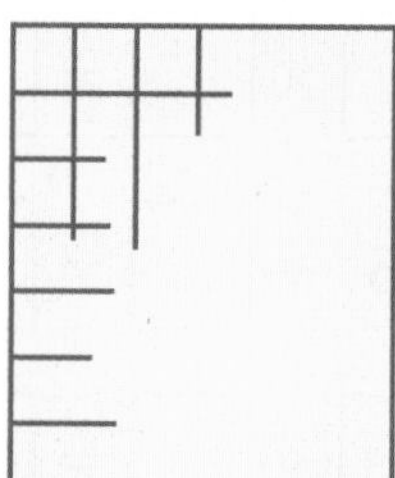

7 × ☐ = 42

☐ × 7 = 42

42 ÷ 7 = ☐

42 ÷ ☐ = 7

5

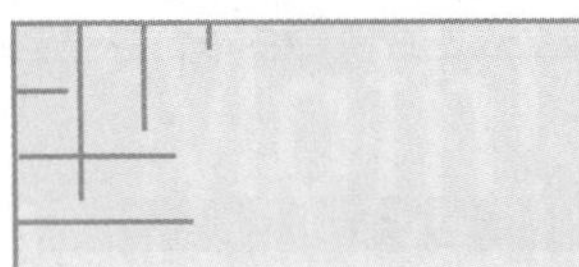

□ × □ = 36

□ × □ = 36

36 ÷ □ = □

36 ÷ □ = □

6

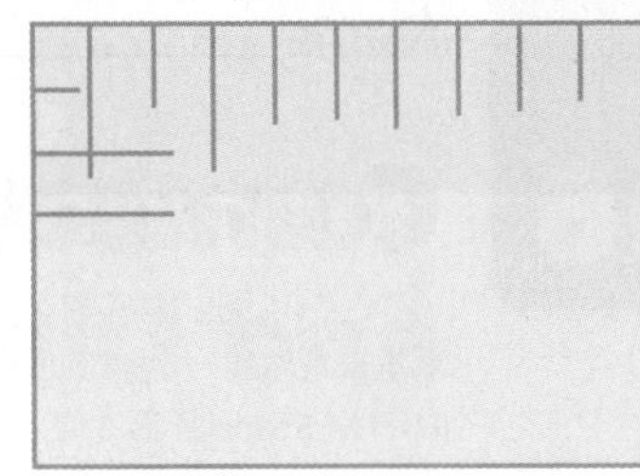

□ × □ = 70

□ × □ = 70

70 ÷ □ = □

70 ÷ □ = □

7

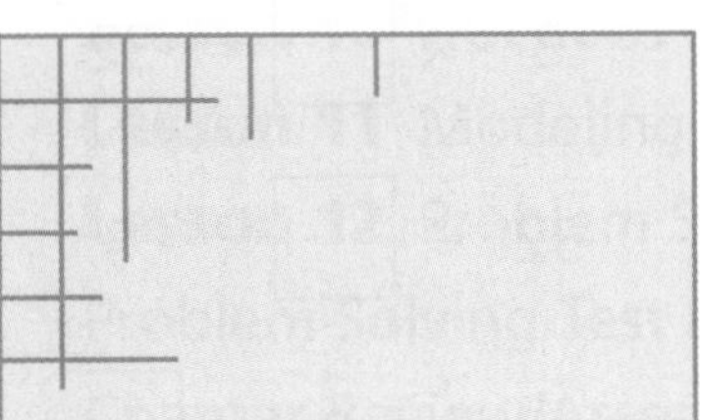

□ × □ = □

□ × □ = □

66 ÷ □ = □

□ ÷ □ = □

8

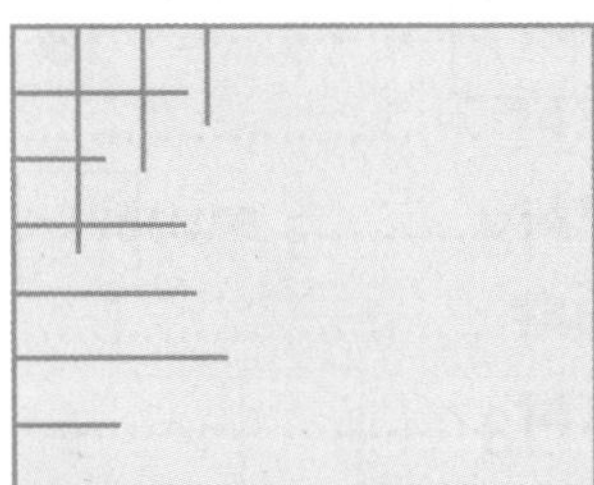

□ × □ = □

□ × □ = □

□ ÷ □ = □

63 ÷ □ = □

9 Challenge Gregory wants to arrange his 60 books on 5 shelves. He puts the same number of books on each shelf. How many did he put on each shelf? Explain your answer using numbers, pictures, or words.

______ books on each shelf

Chapter 2
Lesson 7

Name ______________________ Date ____________

Arrays with Leftovers

NCTM Standards 1, 2, 6, 7, 8, 9, 10

Fill in the missing numbers for the full columns and the tiles left over.

1. $2\overline{)8}$

Number of full columns	4
Number of tiles left over	0

2 {

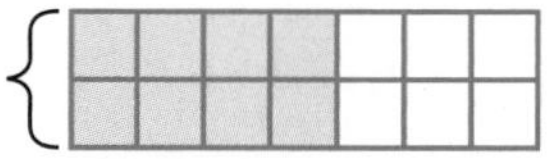

2. $2\overline{)7}$

Number of full columns	
Number of tiles left over	1

2 {

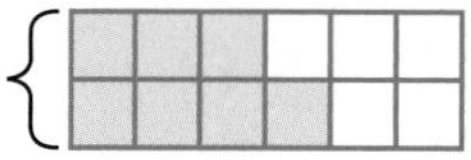

3. $3\overline{)9}$

Number of full columns	
Number of tiles left over	

3 {

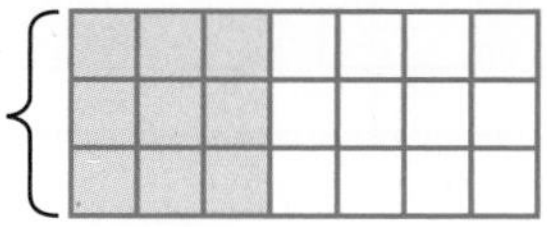

4. $3\overline{)10}$

Number of full columns	
Number of tiles left over	

3 {

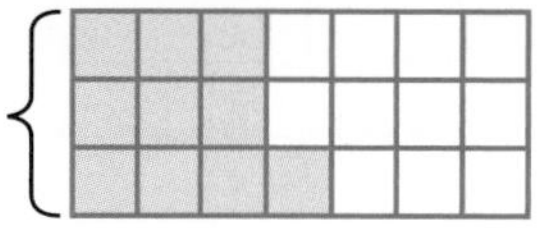

5. $2\overline{)12}$

Number of full columns	
Number of tiles left over	

2 {

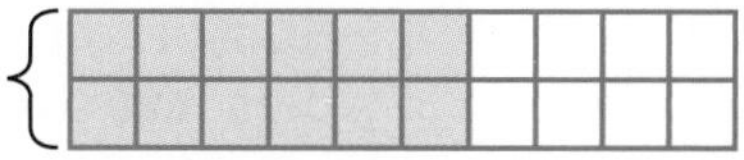

6. $2\overline{)15}$

Number of full columns	
Number of tiles left over	

2 {

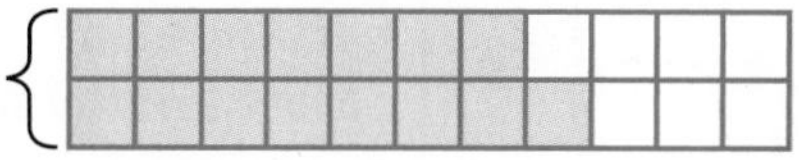

For each of the problems, find the arrangement of tiles with the greatest number of complete columns.

7 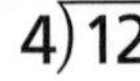 $4\overline{)12}$

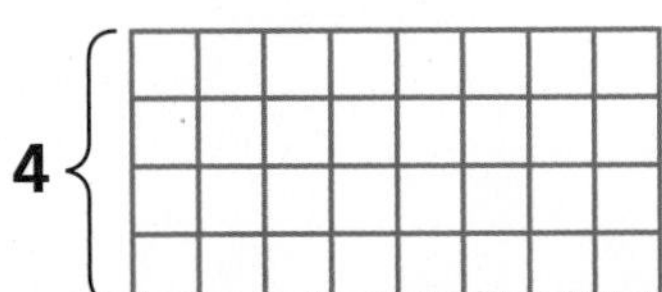

Number of total tiles	12	Number of full columns	
Number of tiles in a full column	4	Number of tiles left over	0

8 $4\overline{)18}$

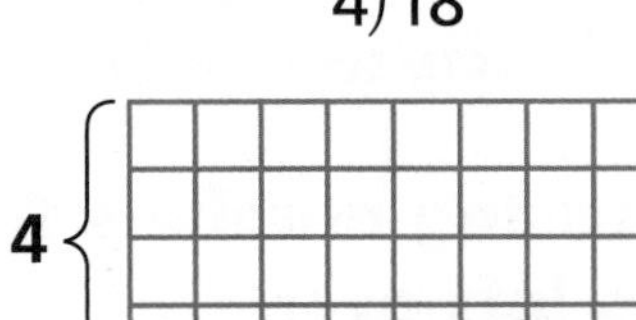

Number of total tiles	18	Number of full columns	4
Number of tiles in a full column	4	Number of tiles left over	

9 $5\overline{)17}$

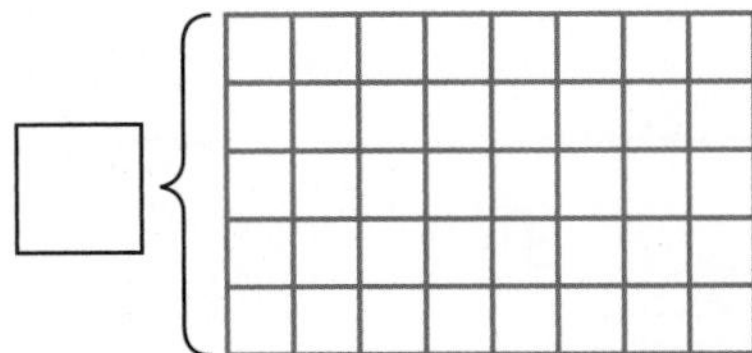

Number of total tiles	17	Number of full columns	
Number of tiles in a full column	5	Number of tiles left over	

10 $5\overline{)24}$

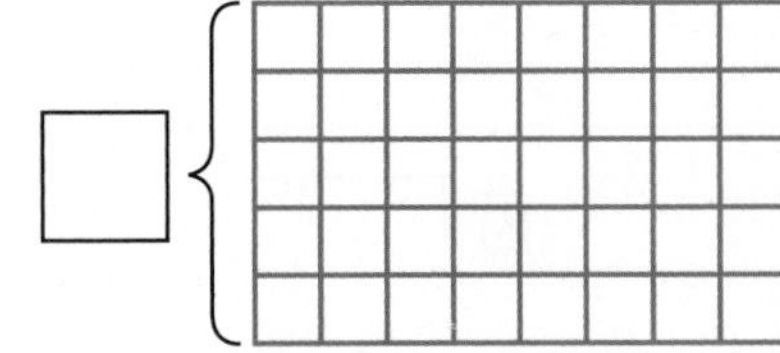

Number of total tiles	24	Number of full columns	
Number of tiles in a full column	5	Number of tiles left over	

11 Challenge $3\overline{)16}$

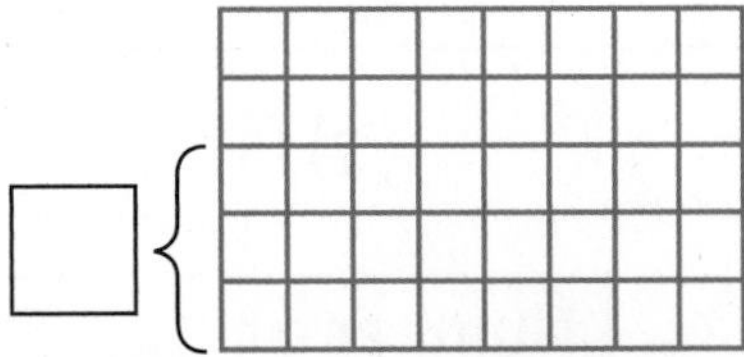

Number of total tiles	16	Number of full columns	
Number of tiles in a full column	3	Number of tiles left over	

12 Challenge $4\overline{)14}$

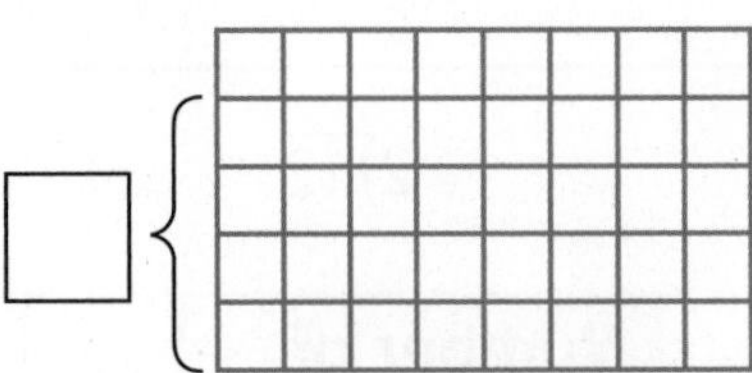

Number of total tiles	14	Number of full columns	
Number of tiles in a full column		Number of tiles left over	

Name ______________________ Date ____________

Chapter 2

Lesson 8 Working with Remainders

NCTM Standards 1, 2, 6, 7, 8, 9, 10

Make a diagram of each arrangement and then complete the shorthand based on the diagram.

1

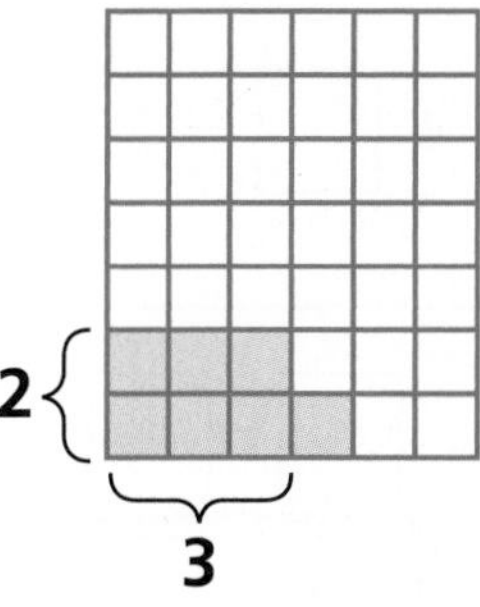

3 r ☐

2 ⟌ 7

2

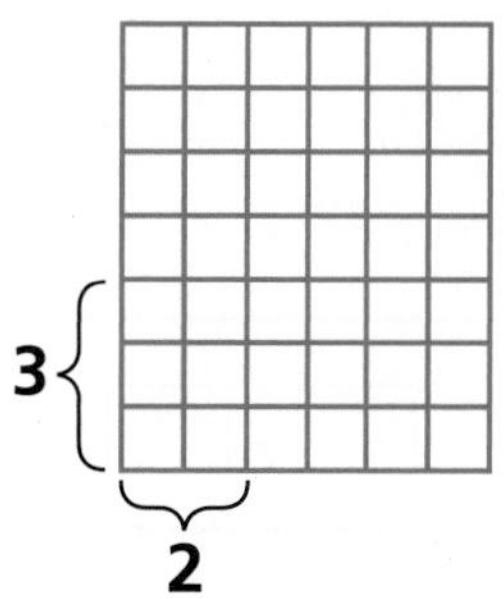

☐ r 1

3 ⟌ 7

3

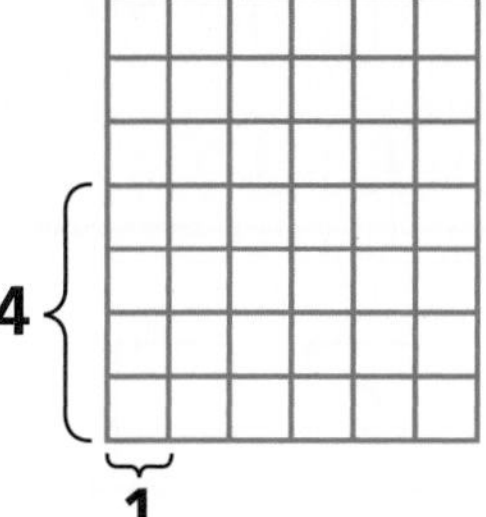

1 r ☐

4 ⟌ 7

4

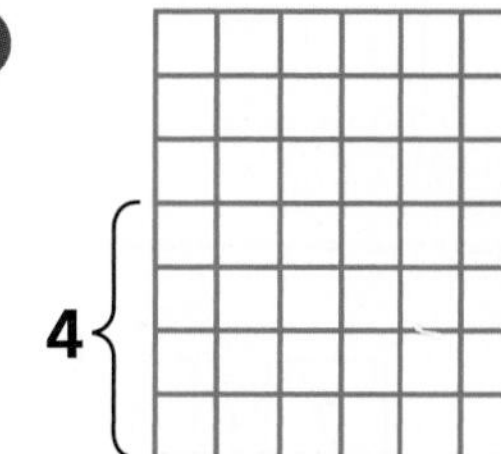

☐ r ☐

4 ⟌ 10

5

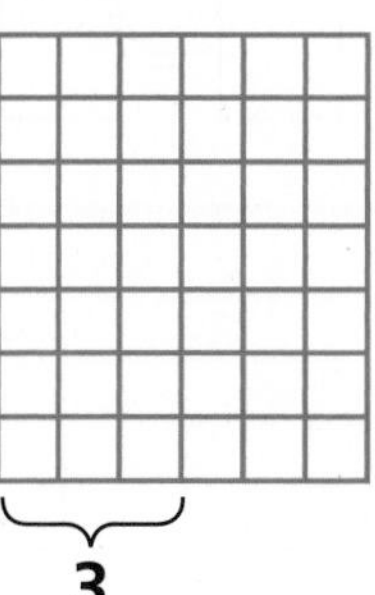

3 r 0

☐ ⟌ 9

6

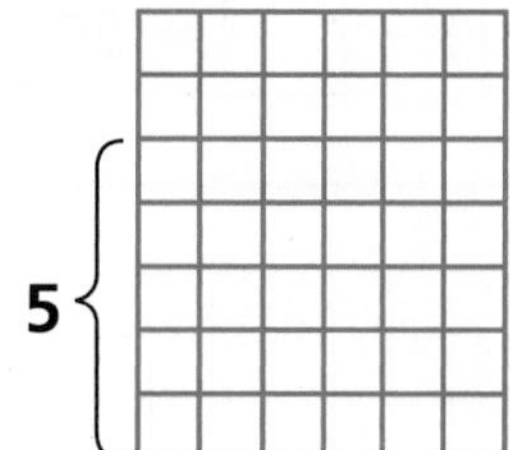

☐ r ☐

5 ⟌ 14

7

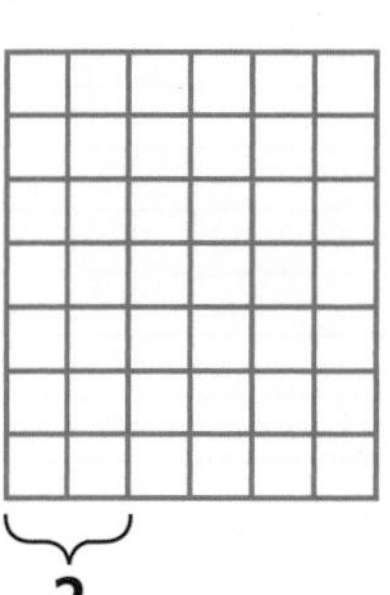

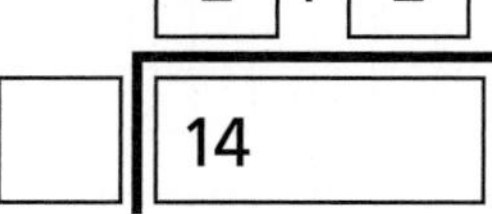

8

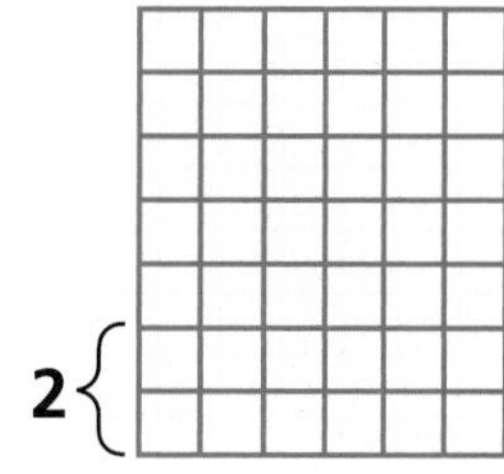

☐ r ☐

2 ⟌ 12

Complete the shorthand below. Complete the number sentences to check your answers. Draw diagrams if you wish.

9

8 r ☐

3) 25

(☐ × ☐) + ☐ = 25

10

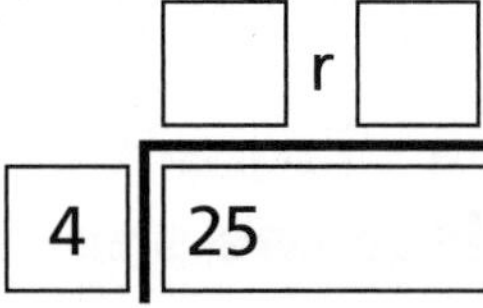

☐ r ☐

4) 25

(☐ × ☐) + ☐ = 25

11

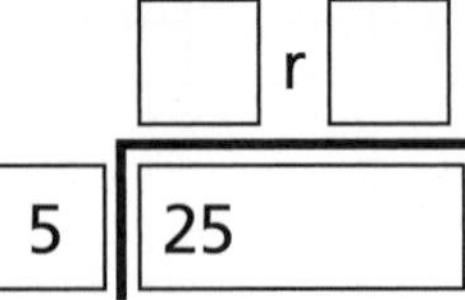

☐ r ☐

5) 25

(☐ × ☐) + ☐ = 25

12

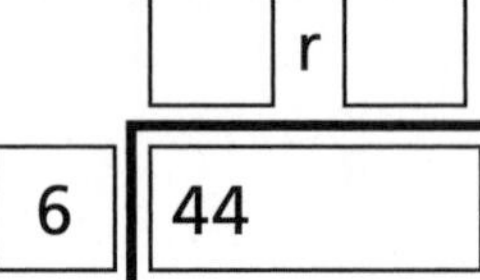

☐ r ☐

6) 44

(☐ × ☐) + ☐ = 44

13 Challenge

7 r 1

☐) 50

(☐ × ☐) + ☐ = 50

14 Challenge

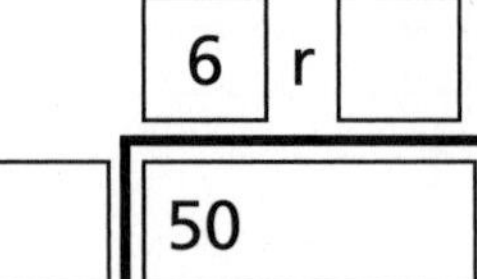

6 r ☐

☐) 50

(☐ × ☐) + ☐ = ☐

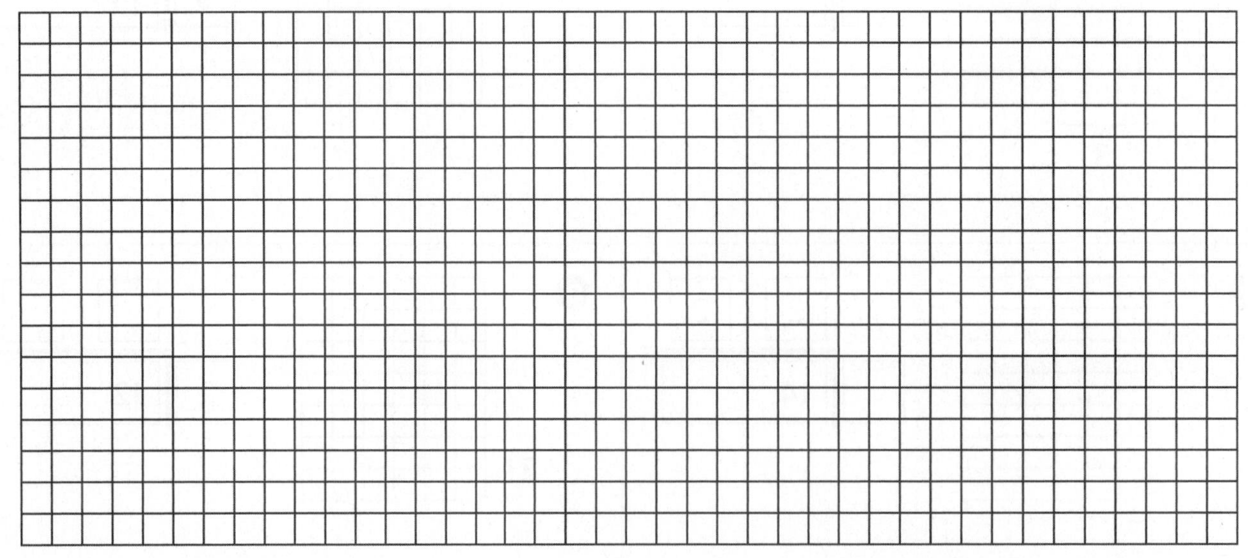

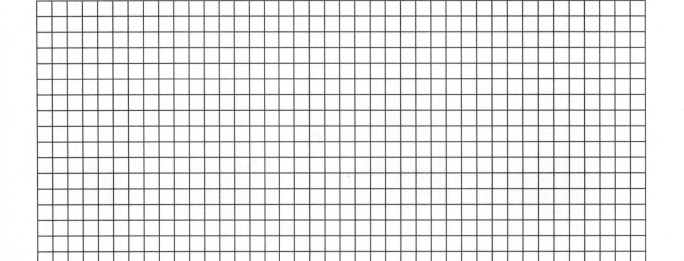

Chapter 2
Lesson 9

Name ______________________ Date ____________

Problem Solving Strategy
Solve a Simpler Problem

NCTM Standards 1, 2, 6, 7, 8, 9, 10

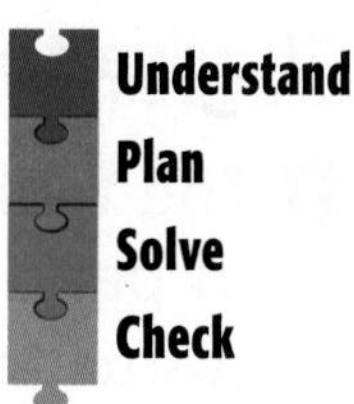

Solve each problem. Show your work.

1. Each of the 19 members of the swim team swam 8 laps. How many laps did the team swim?

_____ laps

2. Joey ate 13 pumpkin seeds on each of the 31 days in October. How many pumpkin seeds did he eat in October?

_____ seeds

3. Mrs. Mann gave each of her 21 students a box of crayons. Each box had 16 crayons. How many individual crayons did Mrs. Mann give her students?

_____ crayons

4. Mr. Zee bought some supplies for his class. The books cost \$19.95, the markers cost \$8.95, the paper cost \$11.07, and the rulers cost \$7.89. Mr. Zee quickly tried to figure out the cost so he knew which dollar bills to pay with. About how much will everything cost?

\$_____

Problem Solving Test Prep

Choose the correct answer.

1. The table below represents the cost of pencils at a school store. Todd wants to buy 6 pencils. How much money will he need?

PENCIL COSTS	
Number of Pencils	Cost
1	6¢
2	12¢
3	18¢

A. 24¢ **C.** 36¢

B. 30¢ **D.** 42¢

2. Tomas is learning about multiplying by multiples and wants to solve this riddle.

I am a multiple of 10 and when you multiply me by 4, you get 400.

Which multiple solves this riddle?

A. 100

B. 40

C. 10

D. 4

Show What You Know

Solve each problem. Explain your answer.

3. Nic has a secret number, *k*. He wrote a clue on the chalkboard for his classmates.

$k + (6 \times 2) = 17$

What is Nic's secret number? Explain.

4. About how much farther is it from Baltimore to Bethesda if you travel through Cumberland than if you travel through Annapolis? Explain.

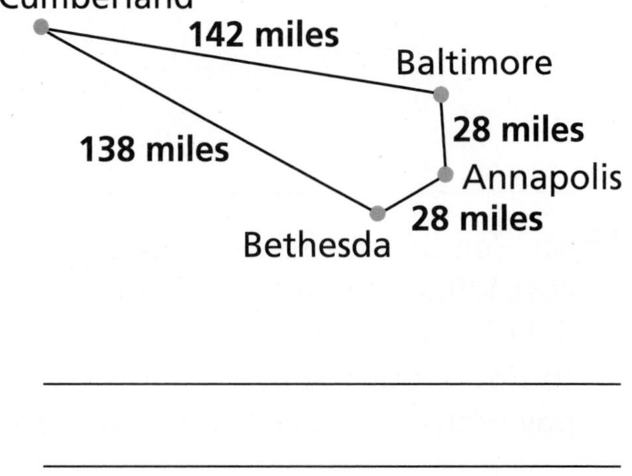

Name ______________________ Date ____________

Chapter 2 Review/Assessment

NCTM Standards 1, 2, 6, 7, 8, 9, 10

Find the number of squares in each array. Lesson 1

1

☐

2

☐

3 Complete the table. Find the total number of squares in the array. Then explain how you got your answer. Lesson 4

	2	3	4	5	8	10
× 7						

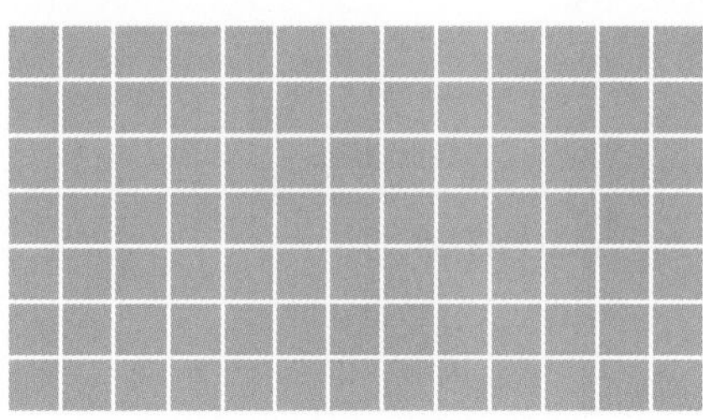

$7 \times 13 =$ ☐

____

____

____

4 Use the array to complete the diagrams. Find the total number of squares in the array. Lessons 2 and 3

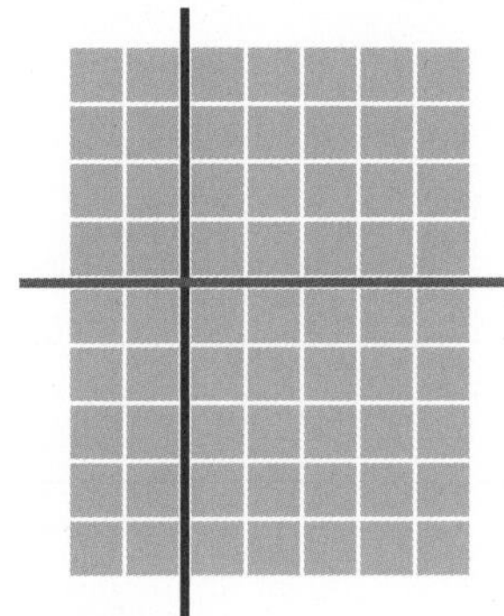

4 × 2	

8	

$9 \times 7 =$ ☐

5 Find the missing numbers to complete the fact family. Lesson 6

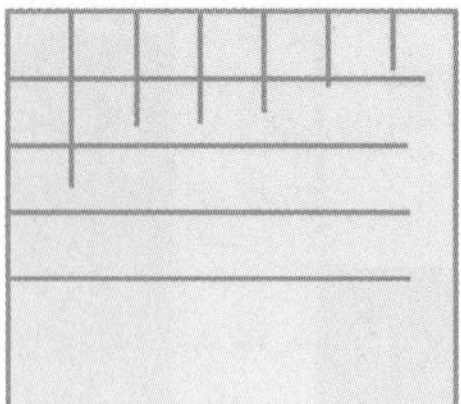

$\square \times \square = 42$

$\square \times \square = 42$

$42 \div \square = \square$

$42 \div \square = \square$

Shade the tiles to show the arrangement with the largest number of full columns. Then complete the tables. Lesson 7

6 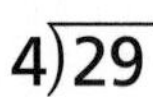

4)29

4 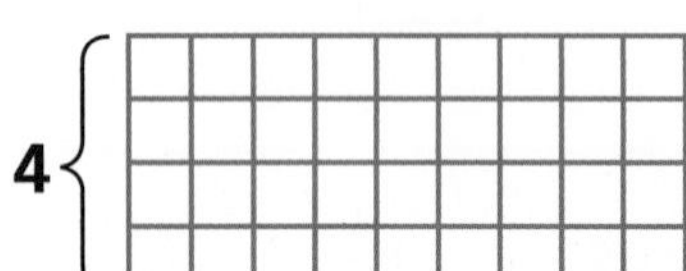

Number of full columns	
Number of tiles left over	

7 5)13

5 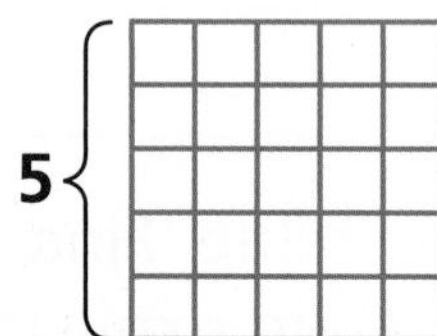

Number of full columns	
Number of tiles left over	

---

8 Use the array to complete the shorthand below. Then complete the division and multiplication number sentences to check your answer. Lesson 8

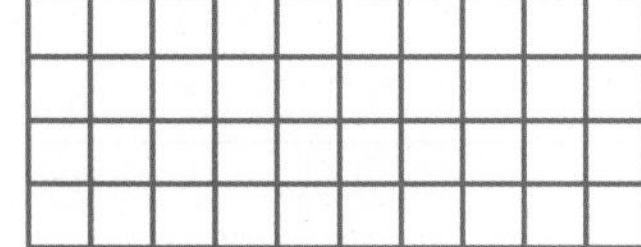

□ r □

4 | 37

$(\square \times \square) + \square = 37$

Solve the problem. Explain your answer. Lesson 9

9 Each member of the club has 23 cards. If the 8 members each bring all their cards to a meeting, how many cards are there all together? Explain.

____

____

____

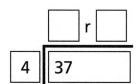

Name ______________________ Date __________

Chapter 3

Lesson 1

Introducing the Eraser Store

NCTM Standards 1, 2, 6, 7, 8, 9, 10

1. Fill in this chart to help with the rest of the page.

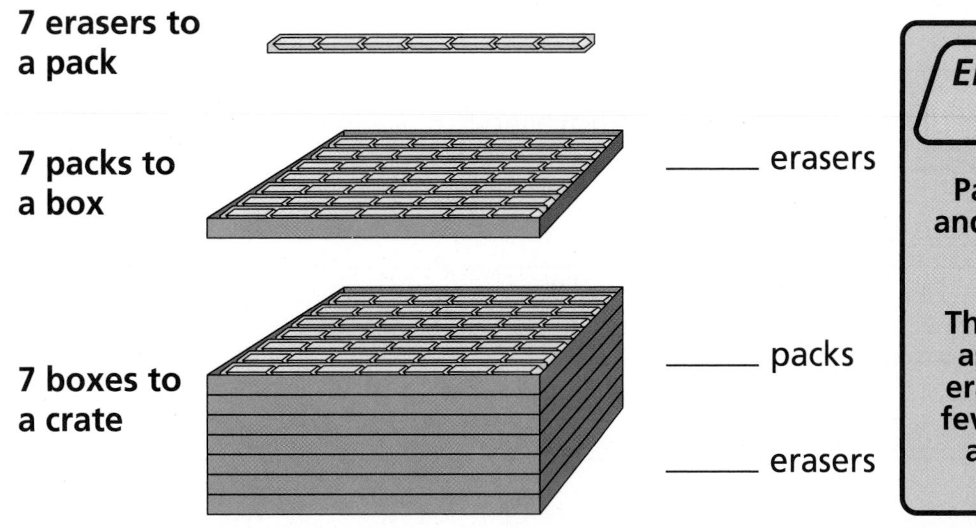

Eraser Store Rules

Packs, boxes, and crates must be FULL!

There must be as few loose erasers and as few containers as possible.

Find the missing number of packages or the number of erasers that are in each shipment.

Shipment	Packages	Total Number of Erasers
2	0 crates, ___ boxes, ___ packs, ___ erasers	4
3	___ crates, ___ boxes, ___ packs, ___ erasers	9
4	0 crates, 1 box, 2 packs, 5 erasers	
5	0 crates, 1 box, 3 packs, 5 erasers	
6	0 crates, 2 boxes, 3 packs, 5 erasers	
7	0 crates, 0 boxes, 6 packs, 6 erasers	
8	___ crates, ___ boxes, ___ packs, ___ erasers	72
9	___ crates, 3 boxes, 0 packs, ___ erasers	150
10	1 crate, 0 boxes, 0 packs, 2 erasers	
11	1 crate, ___ boxes, ___ packs, ___ erasers	346

Shorthand for Recording Shipments

• an eraser —— a pack of 7 erasers ▢ a box of 7 packs (_____ erasers)

▢ a crate of 7 boxes (_____ packs or _____ erasers)

Find the missing number of packages or the total number of erasers that are in each shipment.

Shipment	Shorthand	Total Number of Erasers
12	—— • • • •	
13		42
14		53
15	crate ——	
16		100
17		70
18	crate crate —— ——	
19	box box box box	
20		200
21	crate box —— •	
22 Challenge	crate box box —— •	
23 Challenge	crate	392
24 Challenge	crate crate	695
25 Challenge		294

Chapter 3
Lesson 2

Name ______________________ Date ____________

Shipment Records at the Eraser Store

NCTM Standards 1, 2, 6, 7, 8, 9, 10

Record Keeping in the Eraser Store

Shorthand for recording shipments

• an eraser —— a pack of 7 erasers ☐ a box of 7 packs (_____ erasers)

a crate of 7 boxes (_____ packs or _____ erasers)

Complete the records.

Shipment	Total Number of Erasers	Shorthand	crate, box, pack, eraser
1	8		0, 0, 1, 1
2	35		0, 0, 5, 0
3	353	crate — • • •	___, ___, ___, ___
4		crate =	___, ___, ___, ___
5		☐ — • •	0, 1, 1, 2
6	48		0, 0, 6, ___
7		☐ ☐ = • • • •	0, 2, 2, 4
8	67		0, 1, 2, 4

Oops! Someone packed this shipment incorrectly. Find the total number of erasers and fill in the blanks to show the correct way to package the shipment.

Remember:

- Packs, boxes, and crates must be full.
- There must be as few loose erasers and as few containers as possible.

Shipment	Total Number of Erasers	Shorthand	crate, box, pack, eraser
9		☐ ☐ • • • • • • • • • •	___, ___, ___, ___

These shipments have the correct number of erasers, but some are packed incorrectly. Circle each incorrect shipment and write the correct numbers of packages below it.

Shipment	Total Number of Erasers	cube, square, line, dot
10	1,285	3, 5, 1, 4 ___, ___, ___, ___
11	250	0, 4, 7, 5 ___, ___, ___, ___
12	591	1, 4, 7, 3 ___, ___, ___, ___
13	1,515	4, 2, 5, 10 ___, ___, ___, ___
14	601	1, 5, 1, 6 ___, ___, ___, ___
15 **Challenge**	2,105	6, 0, 6, 5 ___, ___, ___, ___
16 **Challenge**	1,080	2, 7, 6, 9 ___, ___, ___, ___
17 **Challenge**	344	0, 6, 6, 8 ___, ___, ___, ___

Chapter 3

Lesson 3

Name ______________________ Date ____________

Organizing Shipment Data

NCTM Standards 1, 2, 6, 7, 8, 9, 10

Shade the bar graph using the Organizing Shipment Data: AM13.

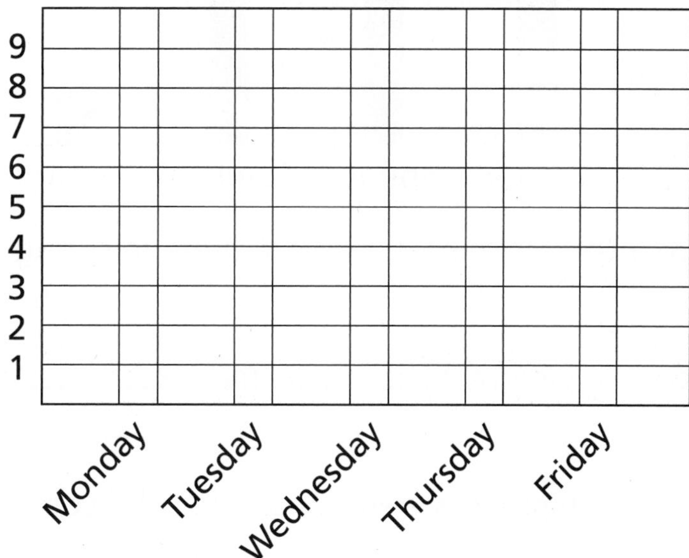

1. Which day had the most small shipments? ______________________

2. Which day had the fewest small shipments? ______________________

3. Between which two consecutive days did the number of small shipments increase?

____

4. Between which two consecutive days did the number of small shipments decrease?

____

Answer the questions using the graph.

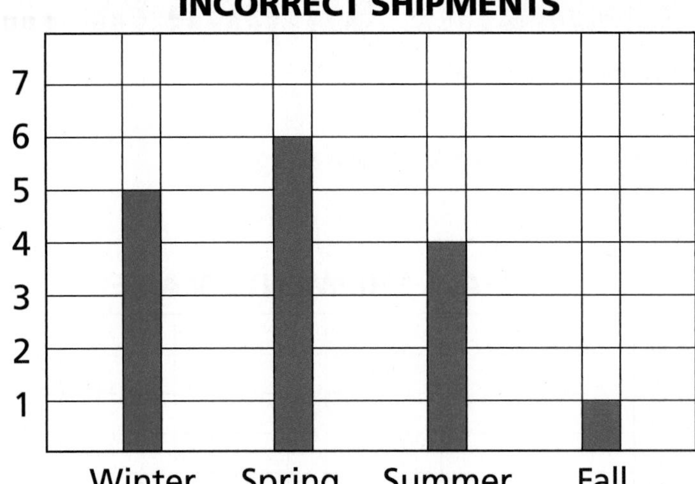

5. How many more incorrect shipments were there in spring than fall? ______

6. When were the most incorrect shipments made? ________

7. How many incorrect shipments were made over the year? ______

8. **Challenge** Here are two shipments:

T	

U	•

Without finding the number of erasers in each shipment, tell how many more erasers there are in shipment **U** than there are in shipment **T**. Explain your reasoning.

____

____

____

____

Name ______________________ Date ____________

Chapter 3

Lesson 4

Combining and Reducing Shipments

NCTM Standards 1, 2, 6, 7, 8, 9, 10

Watch the add and subtract symbols!

• an eraser

— a pack of 7 erasers

a box of 7 packs

a crate of 7 boxes

Find the results of the shipments after orders are increased or decreased.

1

	0,	0,	2,	3
add	0,	0,	1,	2

___, ___, ___, ___

2

	0,	3,	1,	4
add	0,	1,	2,	4

___, ___, ___, ___

3

	0,	0,	2,	1
remove	0,	0,	0,	3

___, ___, ___, ___

4

	0,	0,	2,	2
+	0,	0,	1,	6

___, ___, ___, ___

5

	0,	0,	3,	2
−	0,	0,	1,	4

___, ___, ___, ___

6

	0,	0,	4,	0
−	0,	0,	2,	6

___, ___, ___, ___

7

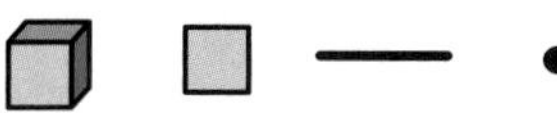

	1,	0,	2,	4
−	0,	0,	1,	5

___, ___, ___, ___

8

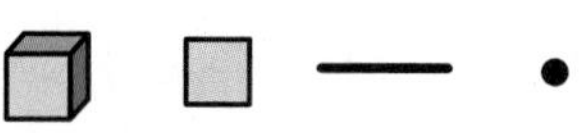

	1,	6,	6,	6
+	0,	0,	0,	1

___, ___, ___, ___

9

	2,	0,	0,	0
−	0,	0,	0,	1

___, ___, ___, ___

10

		—	•
1,	2,	3,	1
− 0,	1,	1,	4

____, ____, ____, ____

Use pictures, words, or numbers to explain how you solved the problem.

11 Challenge A school ordered **165 erasers.** Use pictures to show your work. The shipment would be:

But the school changed the order to 3 times as many. Use pictures to show your work. This shipment would be:

Circle the parts of your picture that need repackaging and then write the new shipment.

Chapter 3
Lesson 5

Name ______________________ Date ____________

Packaging Erasers in Tens

NCTM Standards 1, 2, 6, 7, 8, 9, 10

Bigger containers have arrived!

Watch the add and subtract symbols!

• an eraser — a box of 10 packs

— a pack of 10 erasers — a crate of 10 boxes

Add or subtract the shipments.

1

	1,	0,	0,	6
+	3,	0,	0,	7

___, ___, ___, ___

2

	1,	8,	6,	9
+	0,	6,	0,	1

___, ___, ___, ___

3

	5,	2,	6,	4
−	1,	1,	0,	8

___, ___, ___, ___

4
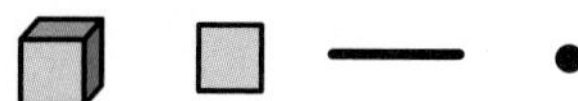

	4,	0,	2,	3
−	0,	7,	1,	7

___, ___, ___, ___

5

	4,	0,	9,	7
+	3,	0,	0,	5

___, ___, ___, ___

6

	0,	4,	2,	3
−	0,	2,	0,	7

___, ___, ___, ___

7 Donna ordered **3 boxes** and **2 packs** of erasers. Then she realized she didn't have enough money for this order, so she removed **1 box** and **5 packs** from her order. What is her new order?

☐ crates, ☐ boxes,

☐ packs, ☐ loose erasers

	0,	3,	2,	0
−	0,	1,	5,	0

___, ___, ___, ___

8 Joel ordered some erasers. His brother ordered **5 packs** and **3 loose erasers**. The total shipment contains **1 box**, **3 packs**, and **7 loose erasers**. What did Joel order?

☐ crates, ☐ boxes,

☐ packs, ☐ loose erasers

	crates	boxes	packs	loose
	0,	1,	3,	7
−	0,	0,	5,	3
	___,	___,	___,	___

9

	3,	7,	4,	6
+	6,	1,	5,	___
	___,	___,	___,	1

10

	2,	0,	5,	3
+	5,	2,	9,	___
	___,	___,	___,	6

11

	6,	3,	0,	0
−	3,	1,	5,	___
	___,	___,	___,	7

12

	2,	3,	5,	___
−	0,	3,	7,	3
	___,	___,	___,	6

13

	0,	0,	0,	1
+	0,	9,	9,	9
	___,	___,	___,	___

14

	1,	0,	0,	0
−	0,	0,	0,	1
	___,	___,	___,	___

15 Challenge

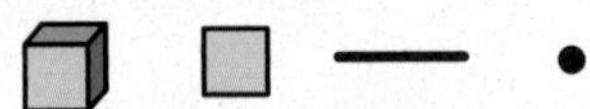

	4,	3,	7,	5
−	0,	___,	0,	___
	___,	2,	___,	4

16 Challenge

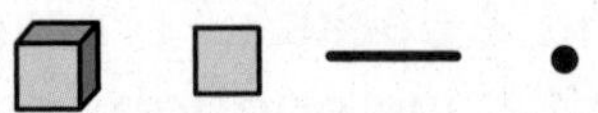

	4,	5,	5,	8
+	___,	7,	5,	___
	9,	___,	___,	6

17 Challenge

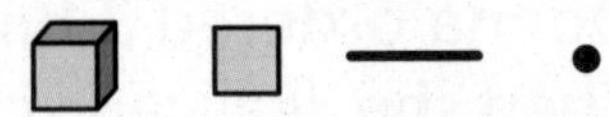

	___,	___,	0,	0
−	4,	1,	___,	___
	2,	8,	7,	5

Chapter 3
Lesson 6

Name ______________________ Date ____________

Multiple Shipments

NCTM Standards 1, 2, 6, 7, 8, 9, 10

- • an eraser
- — a pack of 10 erasers
- ☐ a box of 10 packs
- a crate of 10 boxes

Find the total shipments.

1
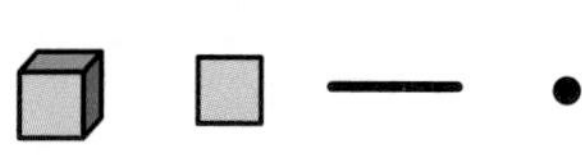
0, 3, 2, 1
× 3
____, ____, ____, ____

2

0, 4, 0, 7
× 2
____, ____, ____, ____

3

0, 4, 2, 5
× 3
____, ____, ____, ____

4

2, 3, 0, 1
× 3
____, ____, ____, ____

5
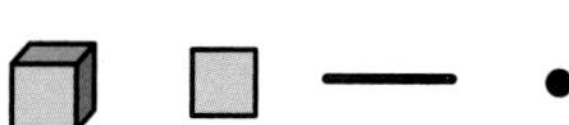
1, 0, 0, 9
× 9
____, ____, ____, ____

6

0, 8, 4, 3
× 7
____, ____, ____, ____

7 Debbie's father ordered erasers for Debbie, Charlie, Abby, and Nick. Each child got **1 box, 3 packs,** and **5 loose erasers.** What was the total shipment?

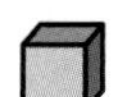
0, 1, 3, 5
× 4
____, ____, ____, ____

8

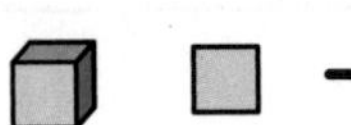

0, 2, 3, 1

× 7

___, ___, ___, ___

9

1, 7, 1, 3

× 4

___, ___, ___, ___

10

1, 0, 9, 6

× 8

___, ___, ___, ___

11

___, 0, 5, 8

× 3

9, ___, ___, ___

12

2, ___, 2, 4

× 4

___, 6, ___, ___

13

1, 5, 2, ___

× 3

___, ___, ___, 5

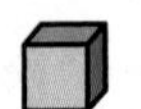

14

2, 1, 3, 2

× 4

___, ___, ___, ___

15

1, 3, 8, 6

× ___

9, ___, 0, 2

16

1, 7, 0, 4

× ___

5, 1, 1, 2

17 Challenge

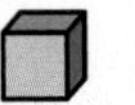

1, 7, 0, 0

× ___

5, ___, ___, ___

18 Challenge

___, 4, 6, 3

× 6

8, ___, ___, ___

19 Challenge

___, 5, 5, 5

× 4

2, ___, ___, ___

Chapter 3
Lesson 7

Name ____________________ Date ____________

Sharing Shipments

NCTM Standards 1, 2, 6, 7, 8, 9, 10

• an eraser — a box of 10 packs

— a pack of 10 erasers — a crate of 10 boxes

1 If **3** students share **6** boxes, **7** packs, and **2** loose erasers, how many boxes, packs, and loose erasers will each student get?

0, 2, ___, ___

3) 0, 6, 7, [1]2

2 Tim and his two sisters share **2** boxes, **4** packs, and **9** loose erasers. How many boxes, packs, and loose erasers will each of them get?

___, ___, ___, ___

3) 0, 2, [2]4, 9

3 Four classes share a shipment of **5** boxes and **4** packs of erasers. How many boxes and packs will each class get?

___, ___, ___, ___

4) 0, 5, [1]4, [ ]0

4 Five friends share **4** packs and **5** loose erasers. How many packs and loose erasers will each friend get?

___, ___, ___, ___

5) 0, 0, 4, [ ]5

Watch the operation symbols.

5

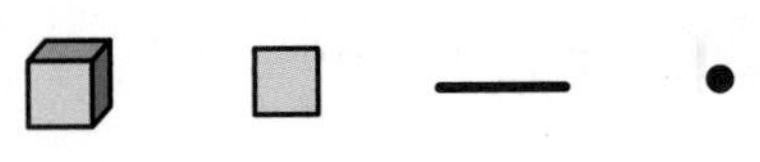

___, ___, ___, ___

2 | 0, 9, □ 3, □ 8

6

___, ___, ___, ___

9 | 0, 2, □ 8, □ 8

7

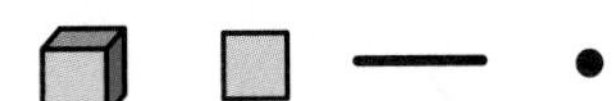

	2,	1,	8,	0
+	4,	7,	3,	9
	___,	___,	___,	___

8

	1,	8,	9,	0
−	0,	3,	___,	8
	___,	___,	1,	___

9

	3,	6,	1,	___
+	4,	7,	9,	8
	___,	___,	___,	2

10

	0,	3,	7,	8
×				5
	___,	___,	___,	___

11

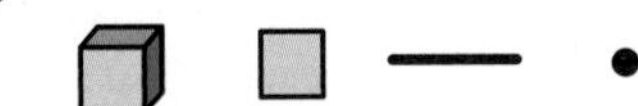

	1,	7,	3,	6
×				___
	___,	___,	0,	8

12

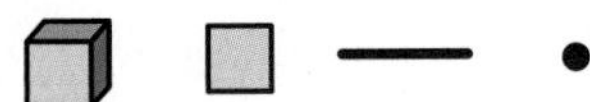

	6,	9,	1,	9
−	2,	1,	8,	0
	___,	___,	___,	___

13 **Challenge**

	9,	6,	3,	0
−	5,	4,	___,	7
	___,	___,	4,	___

14 **Challenge**

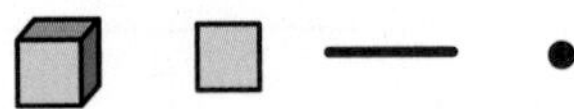

	1,	___,	7,	2
+	0,	7,	3,	9
	___,	6,	___,	___

15 **Challenge**

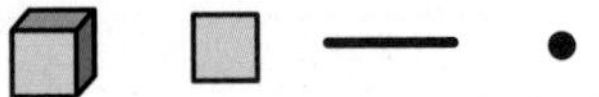

	1,	3,	6,	___
×				4
	___,	___,	7,	6

Chapter 3
Lesson 8

Name ______________________ Date ______________

Multiplying and Dividing Shipments

NCTM Standards 1, 2, 6, 7, 8, 9, 10

• an eraser
— a pack of 10 erasers
a box of 10 packs
a crate of 10 boxes

1

____, ____, ____, ____

3) 0, 2, □ 0, □ 4

2

____, ____, ____, ____

5) 0, 7, □ 1, □ 5

3

2, ____, 3, 7

× ____

____, 5, ____, 8

4

____, 1, 5, 6

× 3

9, 4, ____, ____

5

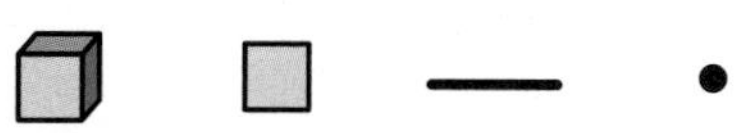

____, ____, ____, ____

5) 2, □ 3, □ 4, □ 0

6

____, ____, ____, ____

8) 3, □ 2, 2, □ 4

7

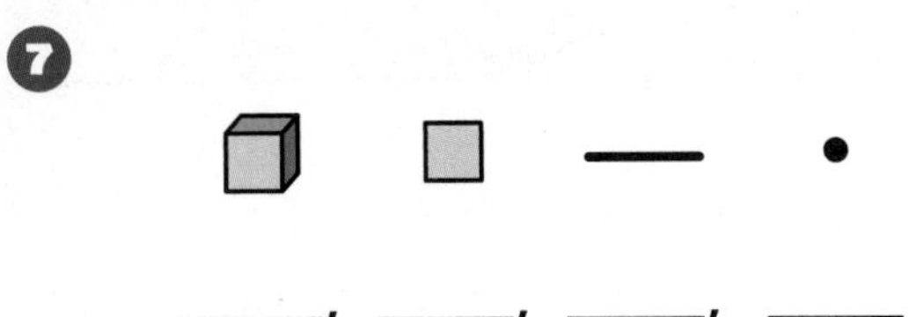

___, ___, ___, ___

9 | 9, 3, 7, 8

8

___, ___, ___, ___

7 | 9, 4, 3, 6

9

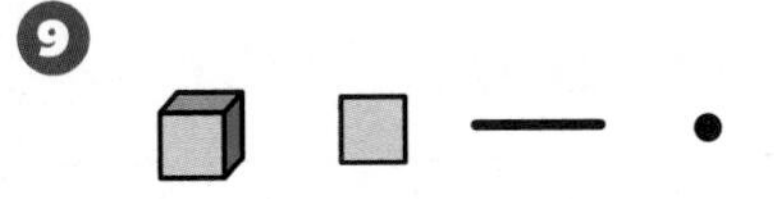

0,	___,	8,	5
×			4
1,	9,	___,	___

10

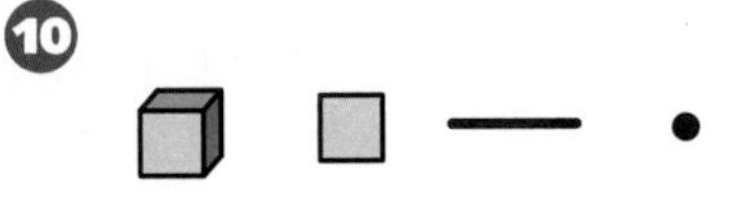

1,	0,	3,	7
×			___
___,	2,	2,	2

11

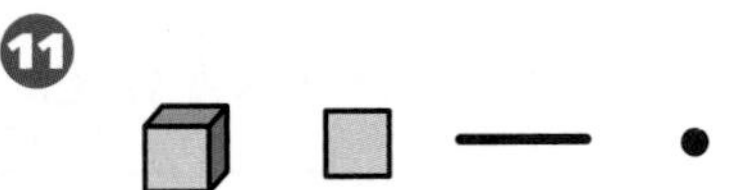

2,	0,	5,	9
×			___
8,	___,	___,	___

12

1, 7, ___, ___

5 | ___, 8, 7, 5

13

1, 2, ___, ___

___ | 9, 6, 3, 2

14 Challenge When the Eraser Store has a very big shipment to prepare, the employees put **10 crates** on a pallet. A customer ordered **3 pallets, 4 crates, 2 boxes, 5 packs,** and **4 erasers.** Then the customer decided to divide the shipment into 2 equal halves.

How large should each half be?

Original Order	Half Order
___, ___, ___, ___, ___	___, ___, ___, ___, ___

Chapter 3

Lesson 9

Name ______________________ Date ____________

Connecting Shipment Records to Place Value

NCTM Standards 1, 2, 6, 7, 8, 9, 10

Solve these Eraser Store problems.

1

	3,	1	4	8
+	5,	6	9	3

___, ___ ___ ___

2

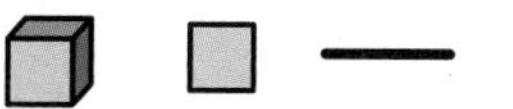

	6,	4	1	9
−	2,	2	3	7

___, ___ ___ ___

3

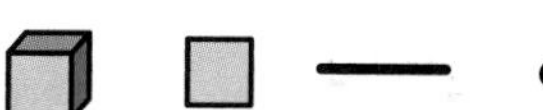

	1,	4	2	6
×				3

___, ___ ___ ___

4

___, ___ ___ ___

3) 3, 7 □1 □4

5

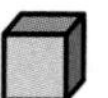

___, ___ ___ ___

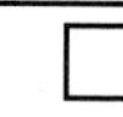

2) 2, 3 □1 □4

6

___, ___ ___ ___

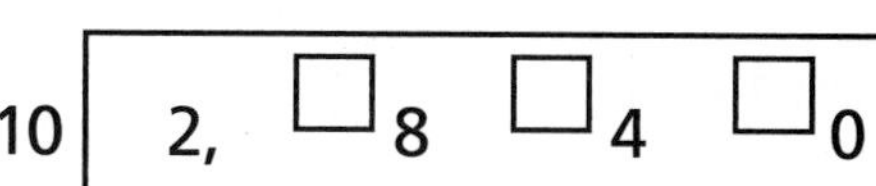

10) 2, □8 □4 □0

7

1,650 ÷ 10 = ______

8

8,790 ÷ 10 = ______

9

4,	0	7	8
+ 3,	8	6	1
___,	___	___	___

10

6,	0	3	4
−	8	5	7
___,	___	___	___

11

1,	8	___	4
×			4
___,	5	3	___

12

	8	6	6
×			___
___,	___	3	2

13

2,	2	5	8
×			3
___,	___	___	___

14

2,	___	2	6
×			4
9,	7	___	___

15

___, ___ ___ ___
4) 5, 5 3 2

16

___ ___ ___
3) 1, 4 4 6

17

___, ___ ___ ___
2) 3, 5 7 8

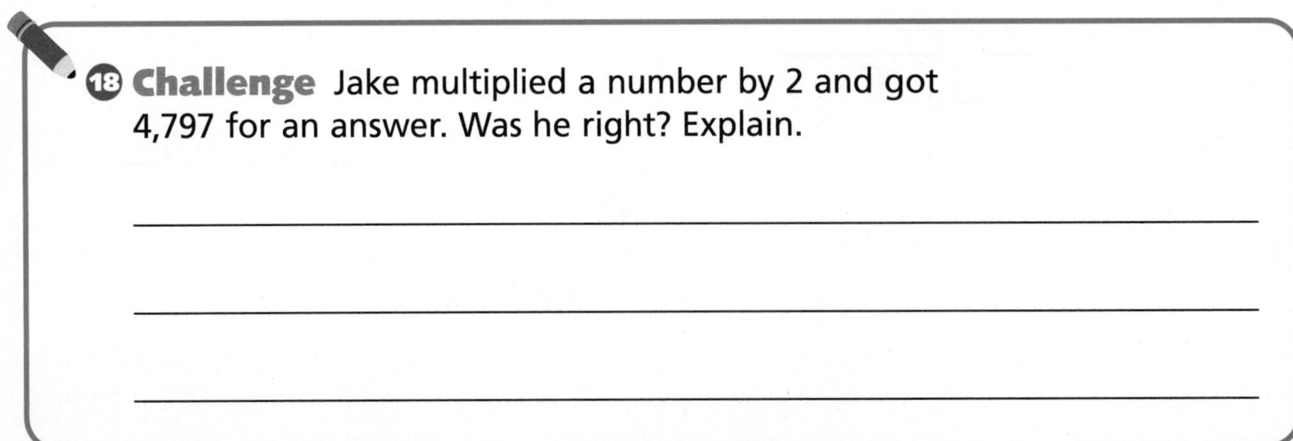

18 Challenge Jake multiplied a number by 2 and got 4,797 for an answer. Was he right? Explain.

___

___

___

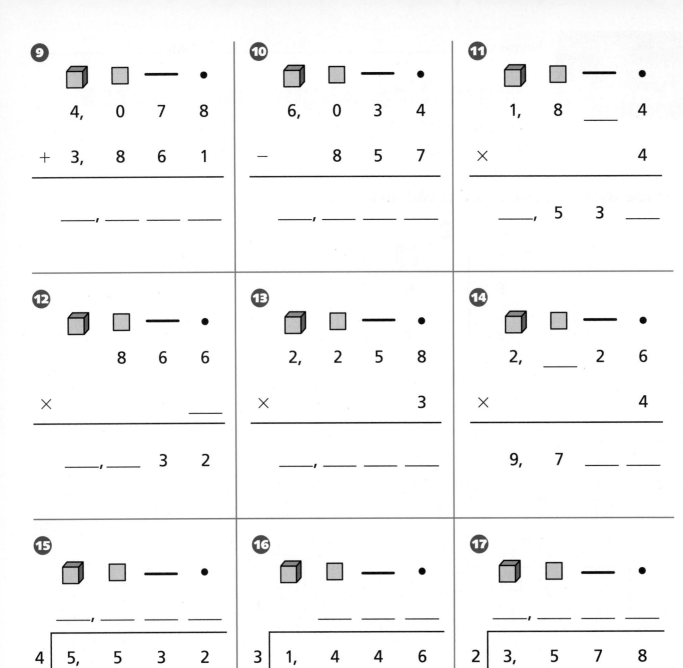

Name ______________________ Date ______________

Chapter 3
Lesson 10

Estimating Shipment Orders

NCTM Standards 1, 2, 6, 7, 8, 9, 10

Match each expression with its best estimate.

	Expression		Estimate
1	605 + 403	●	► 100
2	1,742 − 261	●	► 200
3	247 × 8	●	► 500
4	890 ÷ 10	●	► 1,000
5	2,023 × 2	●	► 1,500
6	1,407 ÷ 7	●	► 2,000
7	1,917 + 3,064	●	► 3,000
8	5,692 − 2,518	●	► 4,000
9	49 × 9	●	► 5,000
10	4,987 + 5,062	●	► 10,000

Estimate the answers.

11

$$\begin{array}{r} 6,001 \\ -\ 2,798 \\ \hline \_\_,XXX \end{array}$$

12

$$\begin{array}{r} 4,008 \\ \times\ \ \ \ \ 8 \\ \hline \_\_\ \_\_,XXX \end{array}$$

13

$$\begin{array}{r} \_\_,XXX \\ 8\overline{)\,9,464} \end{array}$$

14

$$\begin{array}{r} 84,898 \\ +\ 12,158 \\ \hline \_\_\ \_\_,XXX \end{array}$$

15

$$\begin{array}{r} 25,696 \\ -\ \ 3,753 \\ \hline \_\_\ \_\_,XXX \end{array}$$

16

$$\begin{array}{r} 56,381 \\ +\ 49,555 \\ \hline \_\_\ \_\_\ \_\_,XXX \end{array}$$

17

$$\begin{array}{r} \_\_,XXX \\ 5\overline{)\,5,635} \end{array}$$

18

$$\begin{array}{r} \_\_\ XX \\ 7\overline{)\,4,074} \end{array}$$

19

$$\begin{array}{r} \_\_\ XX \\ 9\overline{)\,6,579} \end{array}$$

20 Challenge

$$\begin{array}{r} \_\_,XXX \\ \times\ \ \ \ \ \ 6 \\ \hline 37,926 \end{array}$$

21 Challenge

$$\begin{array}{r} 13X \\ \_\_\overline{)\,1,179} \end{array}$$

22 Challenge

$$\begin{array}{r} 27,106 \\ -\ \_\_\ \_\_,XXX \\ \hline 15,627 \end{array}$$

Chapter 3
Lesson 11

Name ______________________ Date ____________

Problem Solving Strategy

Make a Table

NCTM Standards 1, 2, 6, 7, 8, 9, 10

Understand
Plan
Solve
Check

1. Sedrick ordered erasers from the Eraser Store before the store bought new containers. So, each pack contained 7 erasers, each box contained 7 packs, and each crate contained 7 boxes. He can't remember how many erasers he ordered, but when his order arrived, there were 3 containers and no loose erasers. What are all the possible orders he might have made?

---

2. The Eraser Store now has pencils too! Pencils cost 3¢ each, or 4 for 10¢. Erasers cost 4¢, or 4 for 15¢. There is a limit of 5 pencils and 5 erasers per customer.

Alison spent 25¢. What purchases might she have made?

____ pencils, ____ erasers,

or ____ pencils and ____ erasers,

or ____ pencils and ____ erasers.

Problem Solving Test Prep

Choose the correct answer.

1. Lisa started watching a movie at 7:40 P.M. The movie lasted 2 hours 13 minutes. At what time did she finish watching?

   A. 8:55 P.M.
   B. 9:53 P.M.
   C. 10:03 P.M.
   D. 10:13 P.M.

2. Derrick is making a design using squares and circles. He has 3 different-size squares and 5 different-size circles. If he chooses 1 square and 1 circle, how many pairs can he make?

   A. 6 **C.** 12
   B. 8 **D.** 15

3. Which subtraction sentence is equivalent to the one shown?

$$\begin{array}{r} (400 + 20 + 3) \\ -\ (200 + 80 + 7) \\ \hline \end{array}$$

   A. $423 - 280 = 143$
   B. $420 - 280 = 140$
   C. $423 - 287 = 136$
   D. $420 - 287 = 133$

4. Which number sentence represents this story?

   You have 17 stickers and share them evenly among yourself and 4 friends.

   A. $17 \div 5 = 3$ r2
   B. $17 \div 4 = 4$ r3
   C. $17 \div 5 = 2$ r3
   D. $17 \div 4 = 4$ r1

Show What You Know

Solve each problem. Explain your answer.

5. At the Snack Shop, large drinks cost \$2 and small drinks cost \$1.50. If you want to spend exactly \$14.00 on drinks, what can you order? Explain.

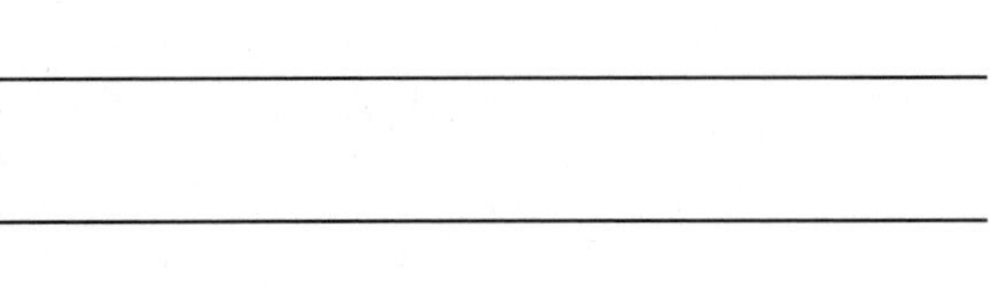

6. Jessie has 1-gallon and 3-gallon containers. She wants to measure exactly 2 gallons of water. Explain how she can do it using the least number of pours between containers.

Name ______________________ Date ____________

Chapter 3 Review/Assessment

NCTM Standards 1, 2, 6, 7, 8, 9, 10

- • an eraser
- — a pack of 7 erasers
- ☐ a box of 7 packs
- a crate of 7 boxes

Find the new number of each type of package. Lessons 1, 2, 4, and 5

1

	0,	5,	6,	1
+	1,	4,	3,	5
	___,	___,	___,	___

2

	2,	0,	3,	5
+	0,	1,	5,	2
	___,	___,	___,	___

3

	6,	6,	5,	2
−	1,	0,	4,	5
	___,	___,	___,	___

4 Complete the bar graph using the data. Then answer the question. Lesson 3

ORDERS SHIPPED	
Monday	2
Tuesday	4
Wednesday	3
Thursday	1
Friday	5

ERASER STORE ORDERS SHIPPED

5
4
3
2
1

M Tu W Th F

If 1,000 erasers were shipped in each order, how many more erasers shipped on Friday than on Monday?

_______ more erasers

There are 10 erasers in a pack, 10 packs in a box, and 10 boxes in a crate. Lessons 6 and 7

5. The Eraser Store has run out of crates. Orders must now be shipped in smaller boxes of 500. The Bell School ordered 2 crates, 6 boxes, 1 pack, and 5 loose erasers. Mr. Z's class ordered 1 crate, 4 boxes, 9 packs, and 4 loose erasers. How many boxes of 500 will you need to ship the order?

_______ smaller boxes of 500

Find the missing numbers. Lessons 8 and 9

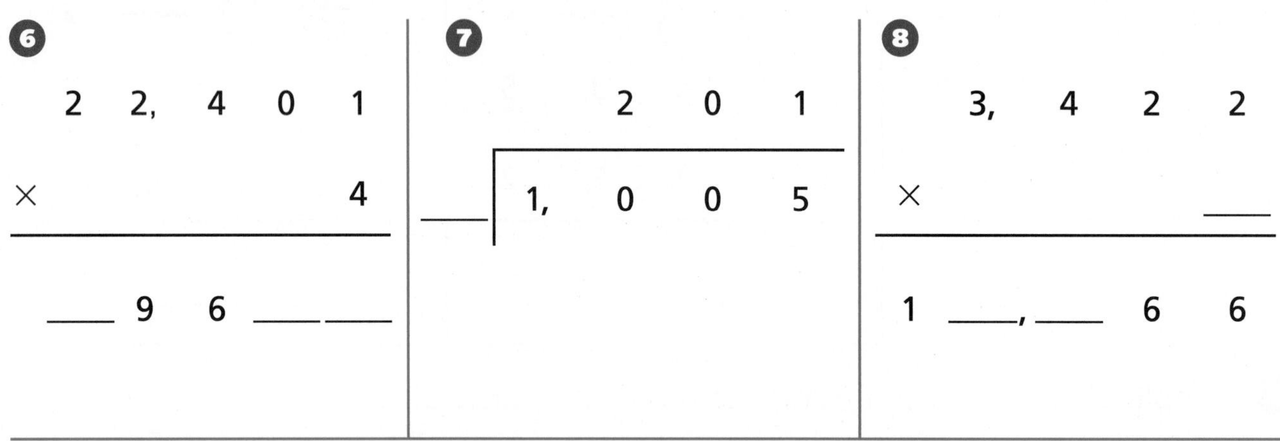

6.
```
  2 2, 4 0 1
×          4
------------
  __ 9 6 __ __
```

7.
```
      2 0 1
    -------
__ | 1, 0 0 5
```

8.
```
  3, 4 2 2
×       __
----------
1 __, __ 6 6
```

9. Devon is ordering prizes for the school carnival. She needs about 4 prizes per student. If there are 1,089 students in her school, about how many prizes does Devon need? Explain how you found your answer. Lesson 10

____

____

10. Doug works at the Eraser Store. The table at the right shows the orders he has received from three different grade levels at Highland Elementary School. He wants to package the orders into one shipment. What is the fewest number of packages he can ship? Lesson 11

Grade	Erasers
3	689
4	752
5	587

____

Chapter 4
Lesson 1

Name ______________________ Date ____________

Introducing Angles

NCTM Standards 1, 2, 3, 6, 7, 8, 9, 10

A group made a graph of their 4-person spinner game.

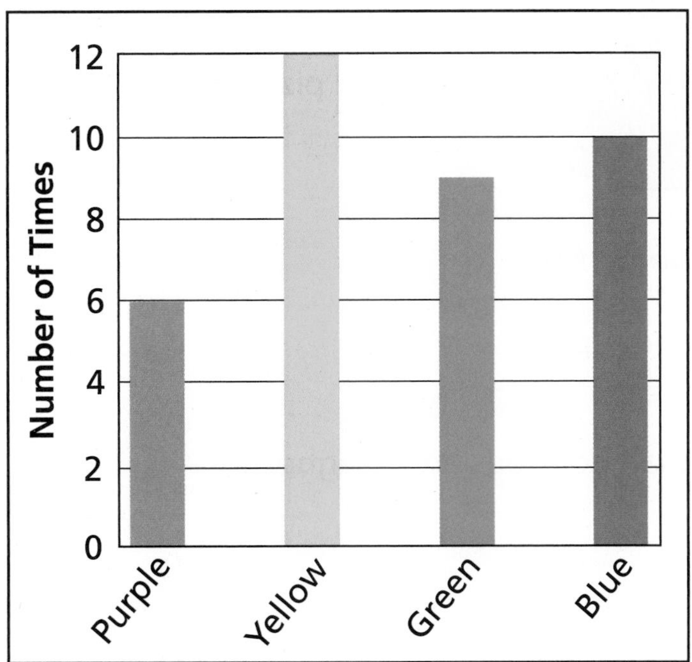

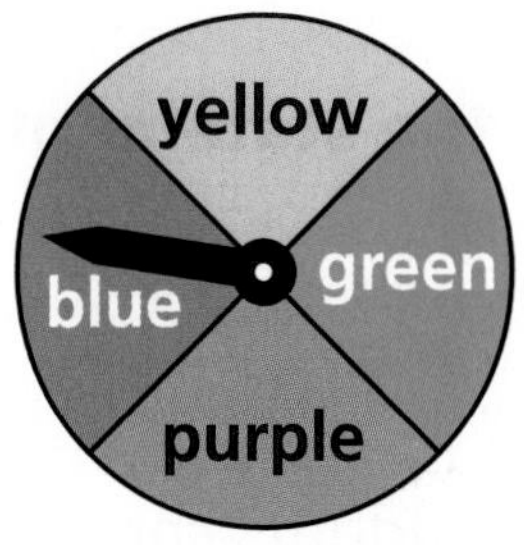

1. Which color won the game? ______________

2. How many times did the spinner stop on green? ______

3. If purple and yellow were a team, and blue and green were a team, which team won?

____

4. The spinner stopped on yellow ______ more times than on green.

5. How many times did this group spin the spinner? ______

The students at Jefferson School were asked about their favorite school lunches.

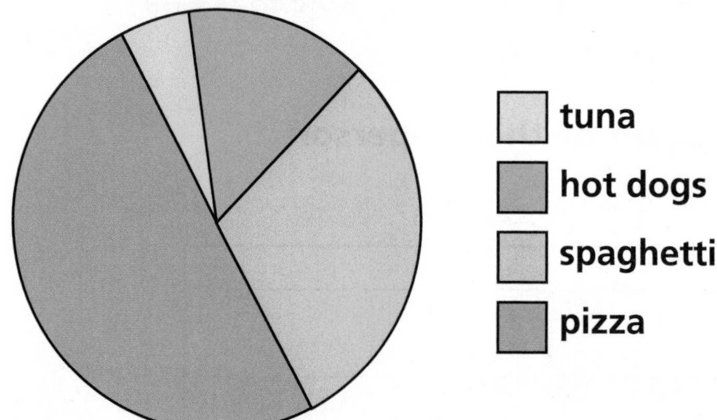

Write if the statement is *true* or *false*.

6. About half of the students chose pizza. __________

7. More students chose pizza than hot dogs and spaghetti put together. __________

8. No one liked tuna. __________

9. Hot dogs were less popular than spaghetti. __________

10. About half as many students chose tuna as chose pizza. __________

11. **Challenge** If you created a spinner that looked like the pie chart above, would it be a fair spinner? Why or why not? Use pictures, numbers, or words to explain your answer.

____

____

____

Chapter 4
Lesson 2

Name ______________________ Date ____________

Classifying Angles

NCTM Standards 3, 4, 6, 7, 8, 9, 10

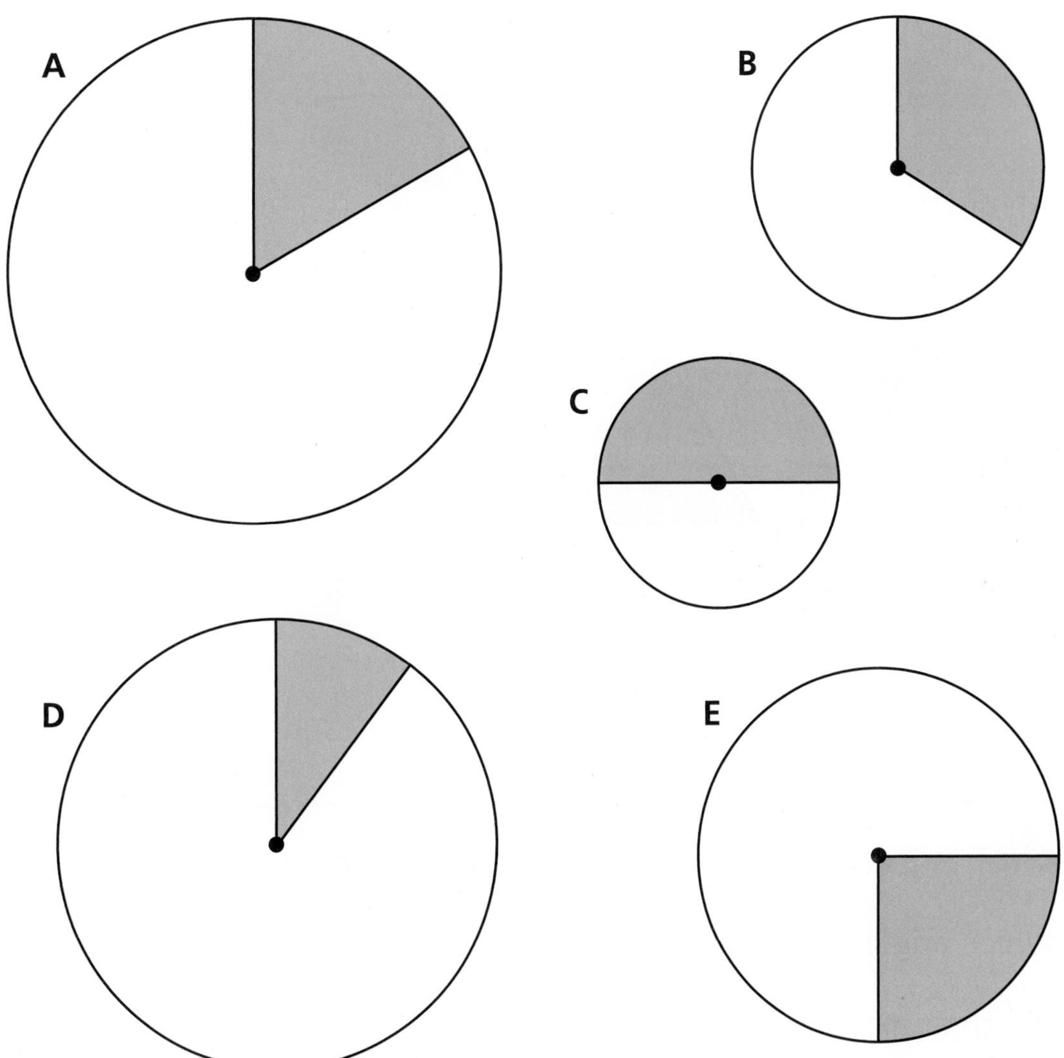

You can choose which spinner base to play with. If the spinner lands on the shaded part of a base, you win.

1. Which spinner base gives you the best chance of winning? spinner base ______

2. Which spinner base gives you the worst chance of winning? spinner base ______

3. Order the spinner bases from best to worst chance of winning. ______, ______, ______, ______, ______

4 Order the angles from the smallest to the largest.

________, ________, ________, ________, ________, ________, ________

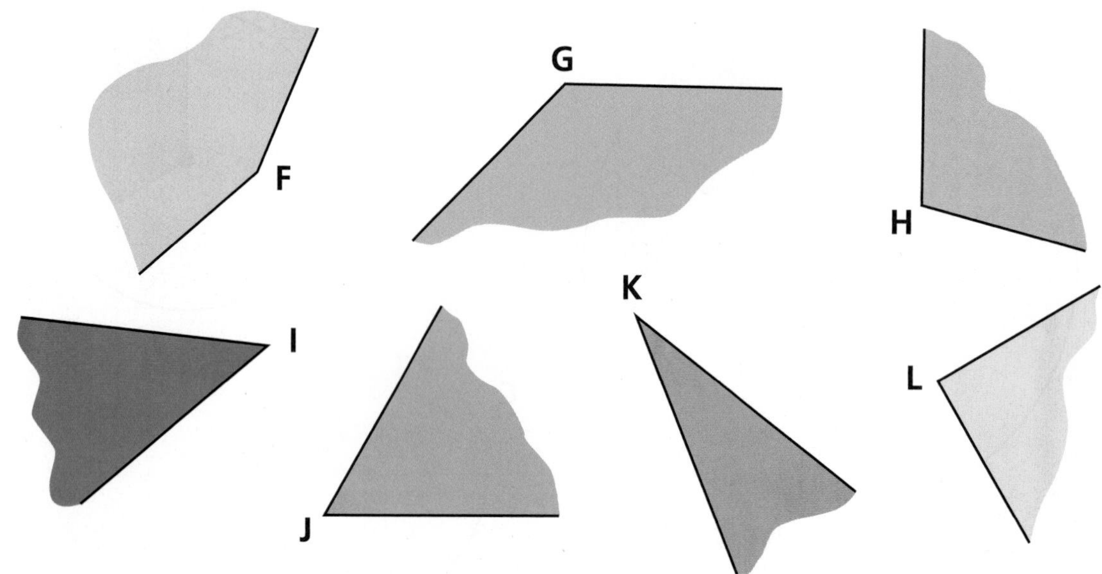

5 **Challenge** Compare each angle to a right angle.

Which angles are less than a right angle? ________, ________, ________

Which angle is equal to a right angle? ________

Which angles are greater than a right angle? ________, ________, ________

6 **Challenge** Angle ________ would fit in the empty space.

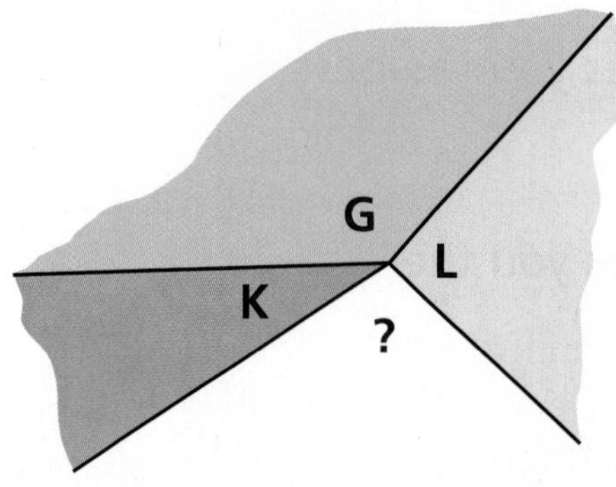

Chapter 4
Lesson 3

Name ______________________ Date ____________

Classifying Triangles by Angles

NCTM Standards 3, 4, 6, 7, 8, 9, 10

These are triangles.

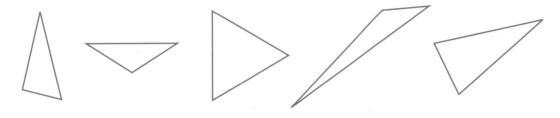

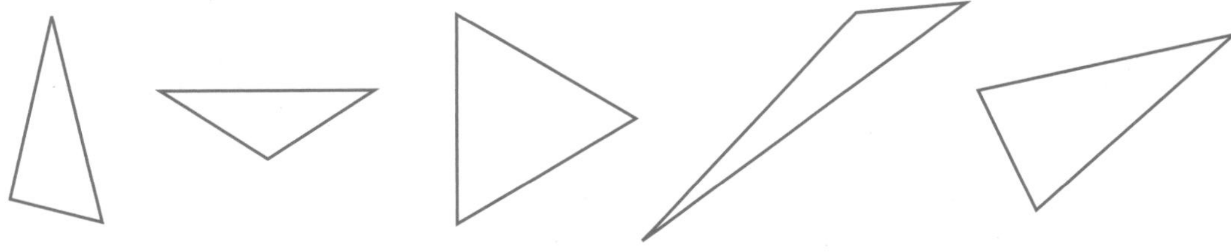

These are not triangles.

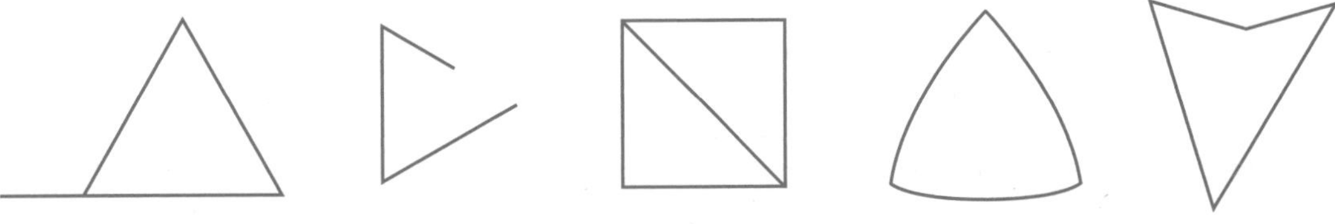

1. Which of these are triangles? Circle the triangles.

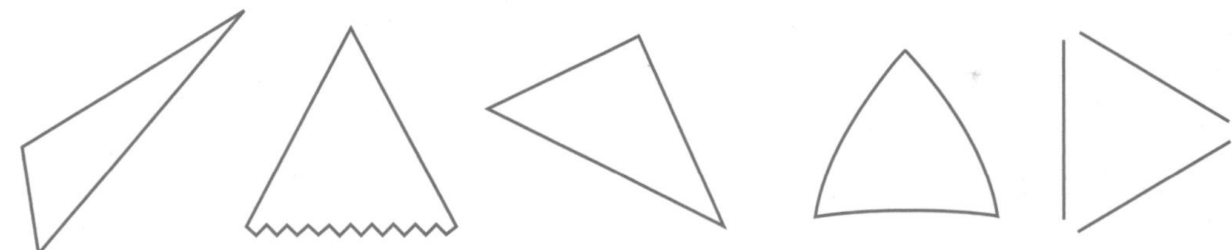

2. Draw a triangle that is different from the others on the page.

3. Describe a triangle in your own words.

____

____

____

____

____

____

4 Circle the triangles and label them *acute*, *right*, or *obtuse*.

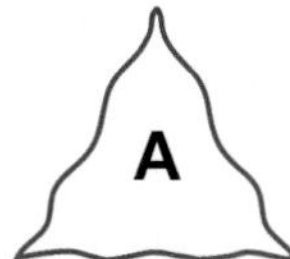

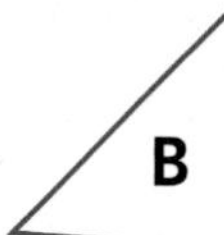

_______________ _______________ _______________

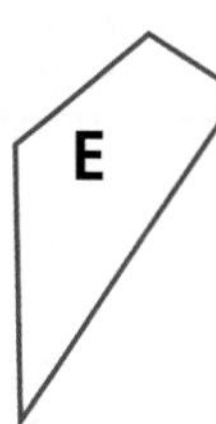

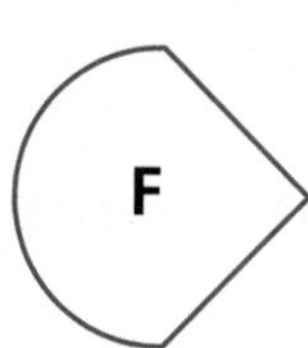

_______________ _______________ _______________

_______________ _______________ _______________

5 **Challenge** What are the similarities and differences of acute, right, and obtuse triangles?

____

____

____

____

____

Chapter 4
Lesson 4

Name ______________________ Date ____________

Classifying Triangles by Side Length

NCTM Standards 3, 4, 6, 7, 8, 9, 10

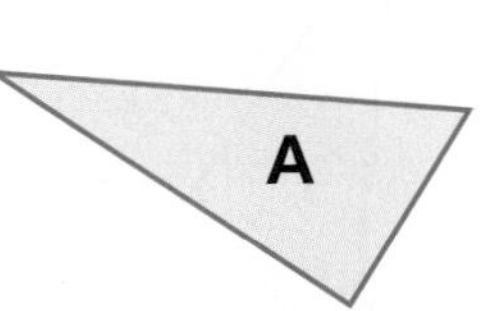

right and scalene

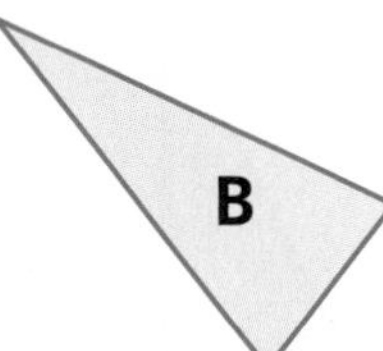

acute and isosceles

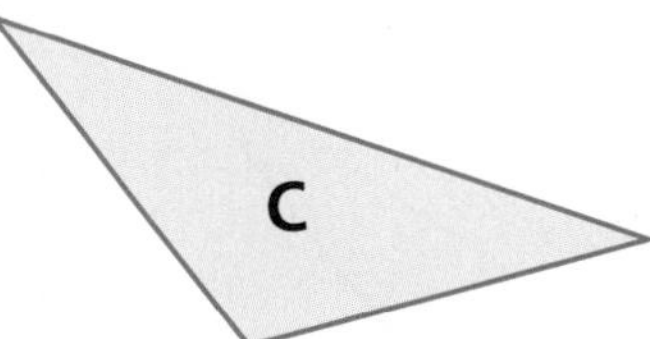

obtuse and isosceles

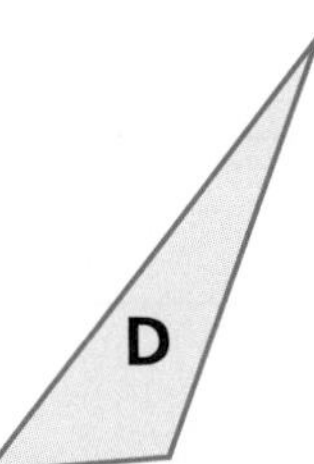

obtuse and scalene

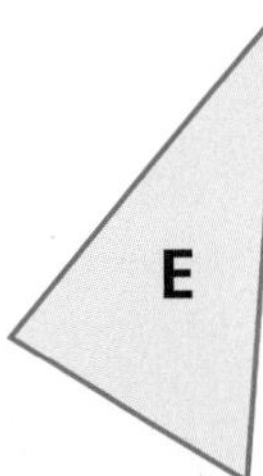

acute and scalene

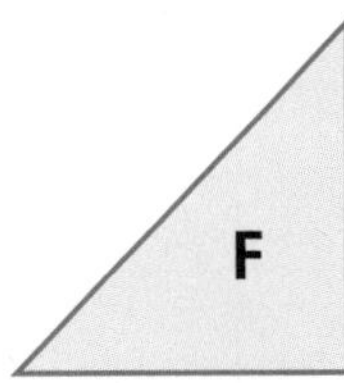

right and isosceles

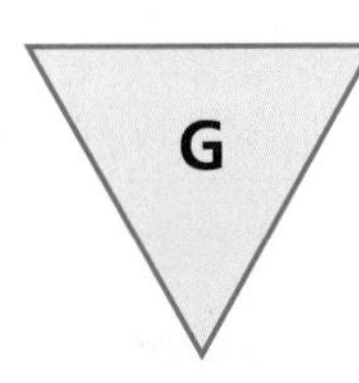

equilateral

1. I have 2 sides that are the same length and 1 right angle.

   I am triangle _____.

2. All of my sides are the same length. All of my angles are the same.

   I am triangle _____.

3. I have exactly 2 sides that are the same length and 3 acute angles.

   I am triangle _____.

4. I have no equal sides. All of my angles are acute.

   I am triangle _____.

5. All of my sides are different lengths. I have an obtuse angle.

   I am triangle _____.

6. Two of my sides are the same length. One of my angles is greater than a right angle.

   I am triangle _____.

Use a ruler and the corner of a piece of paper to help label each triangle with the 2 names that best describe it:

a. *acute, right,* or *obtuse;* and

b. *scalene, isosceles,* or *equilateral.*

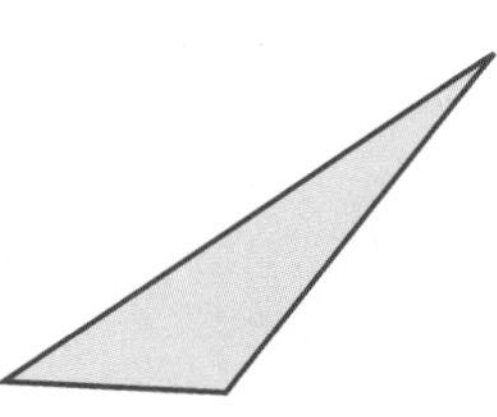

8

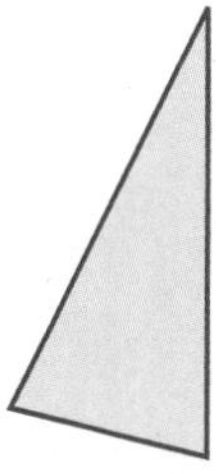

9

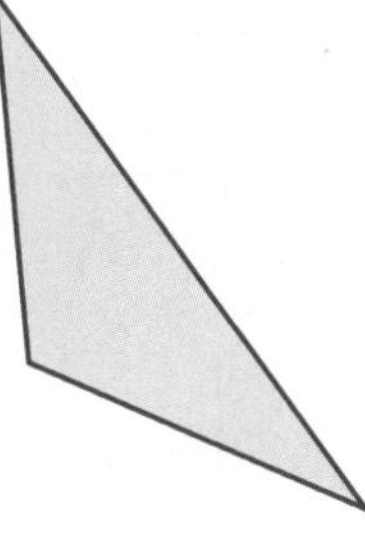

10

11

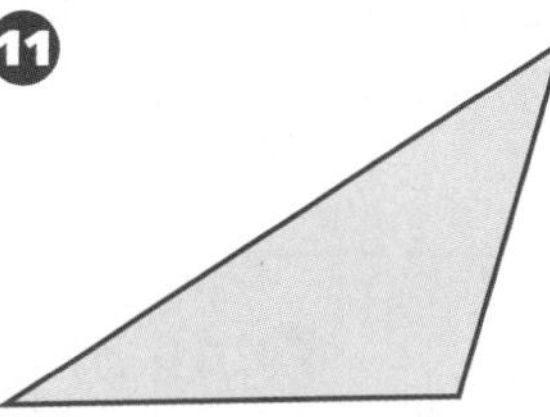

12

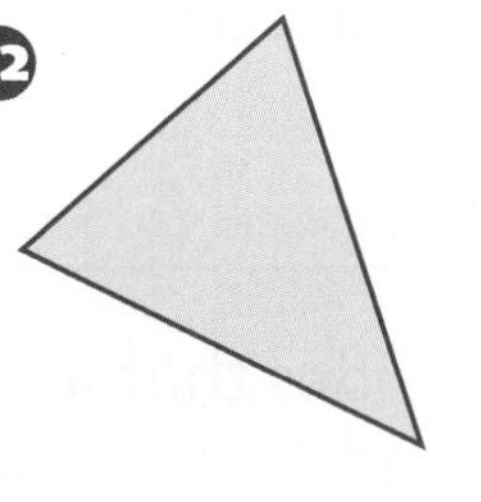

13 Challenge Draw a triangle and write clues to describe it. You might write about the number of equal sides, or the name of each angle.

Chapter 4
Lesson 5

Name ______________________ Date ____________

Introducing Perpendicular and Parallel Lines

NCTM Standards 3, 6, 7, 8, 9, 10

1. Imagine that the lines go on forever. Are they **intersecting** or are they **parallel?** If the lines are **perpendicular,** circle them.

A

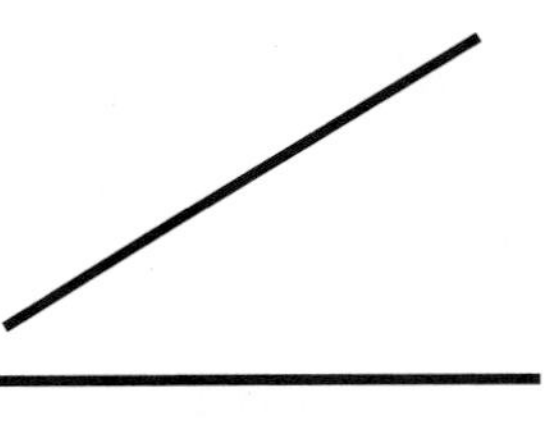

intersecting

B

____

C

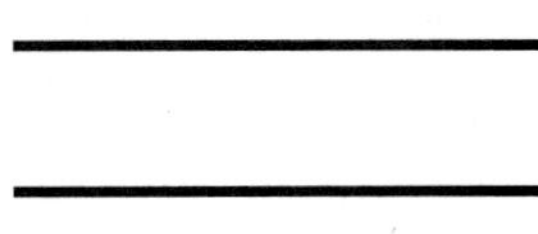

____

D

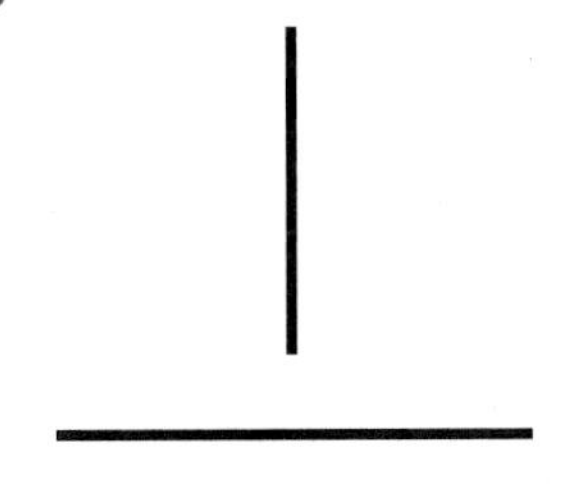

____

E

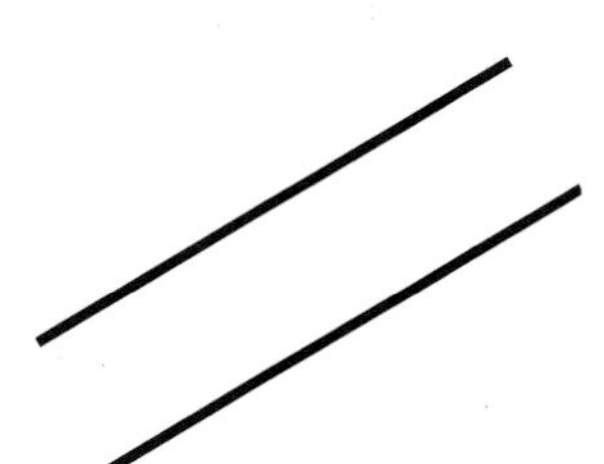

____

F

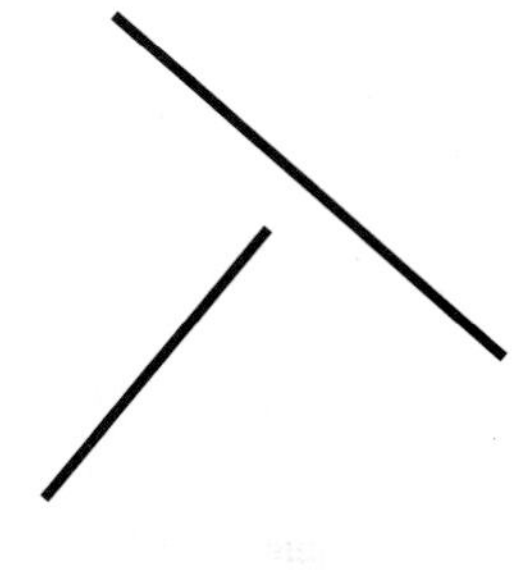

____

G

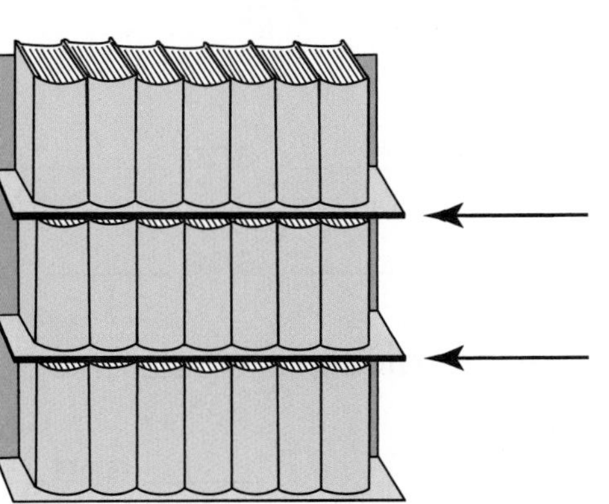

____

H

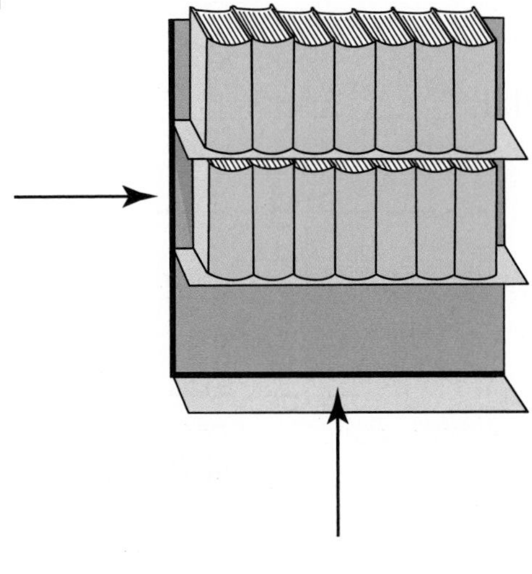

____

2 Identify the **parallel** and **perpendicular** lines in the figures. If there are no more, put an "x" on the answer line.

A

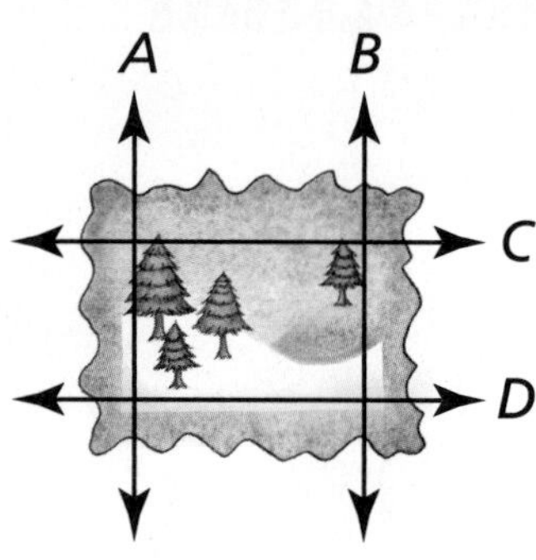

Parallel: ______ and ______

______ and ______

Perpendicular: ______ and ______

______ and ______

______ and ______

______ and ______

B

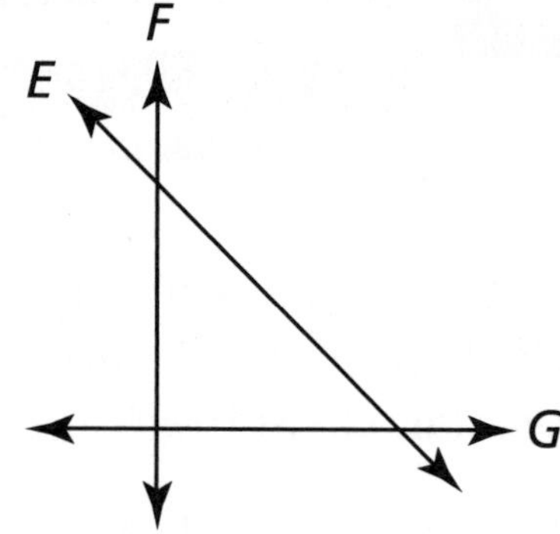

Parallel: ______ and ______

______ and ______

Perpendicular: ______ and ______

______ and ______

______ and ______

______ and ______

C

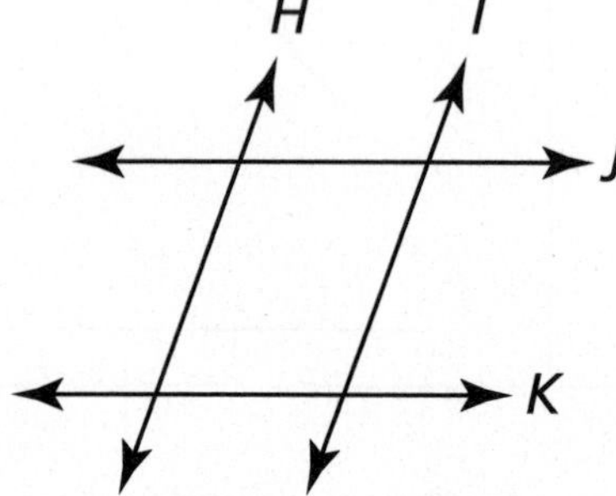

Parallel: ______ and ______

______ and ______

Perpendicular: ______ and ______

______ and ______

______ and ______

______ and ______

D Challenge

Parallel: ______ and ______

______ and ______

Perpendicular: ______ and ______

______ and ______

______ and ______

______ and ______

Name ______________________ Date __________

Chapter 4

Lesson 6

Classifying Quadrilaterals by the Number of Parallel Sides

NCTM Standards 3, 6, 7, 8, 9, 10

1 All of these belong.

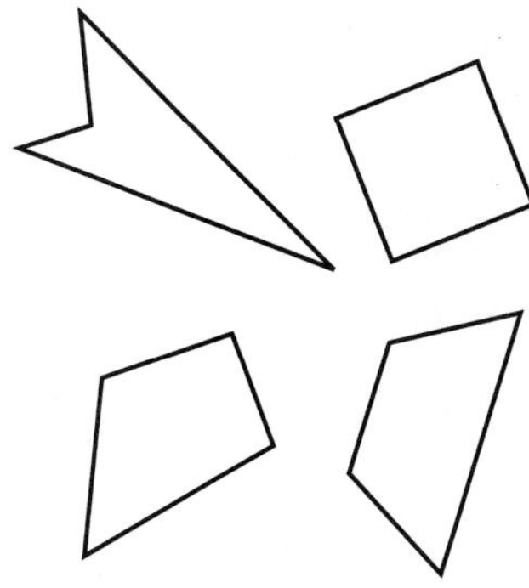

None of these belong.

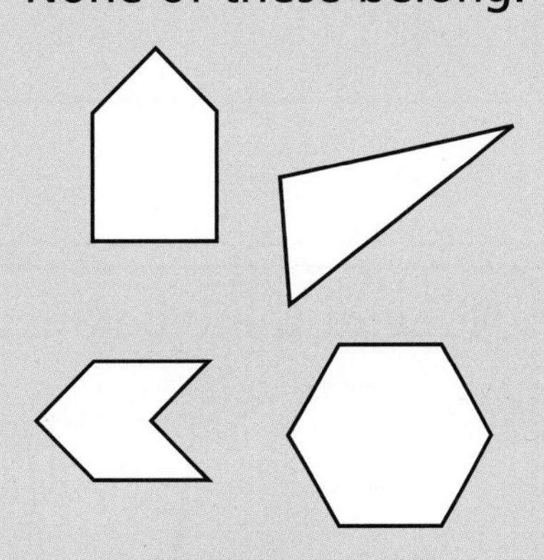

Which of these belong?

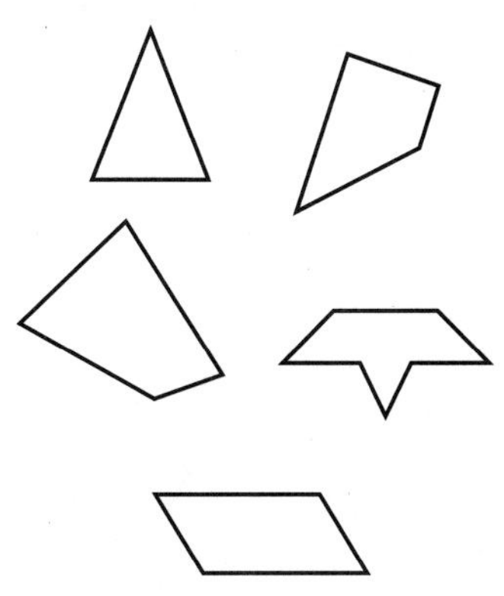

2 All of these belong.

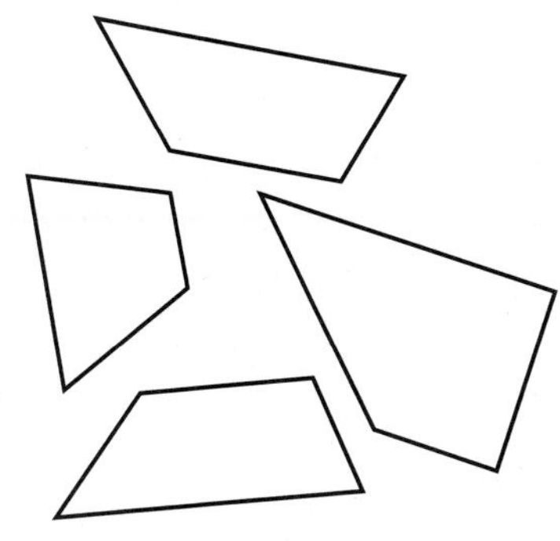

None of these belong.

Which of these belong?

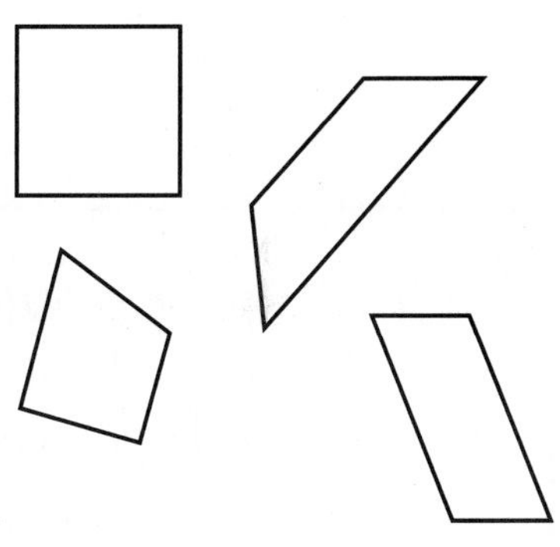

3 All of these belong.

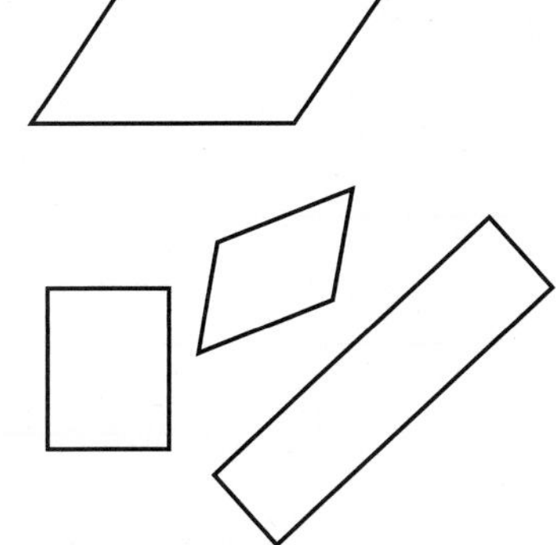

None of these belong.

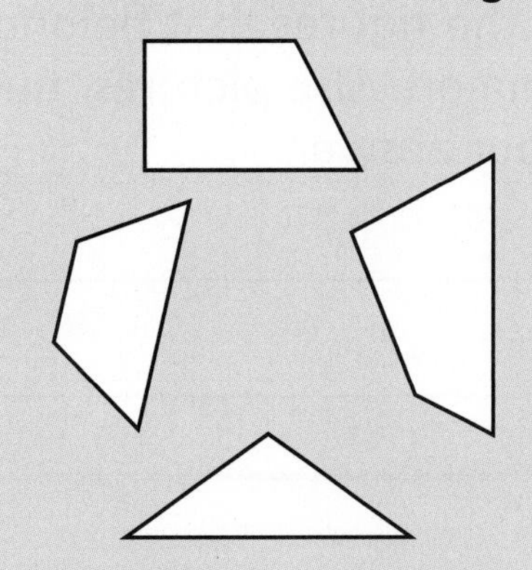

Which of these belong?

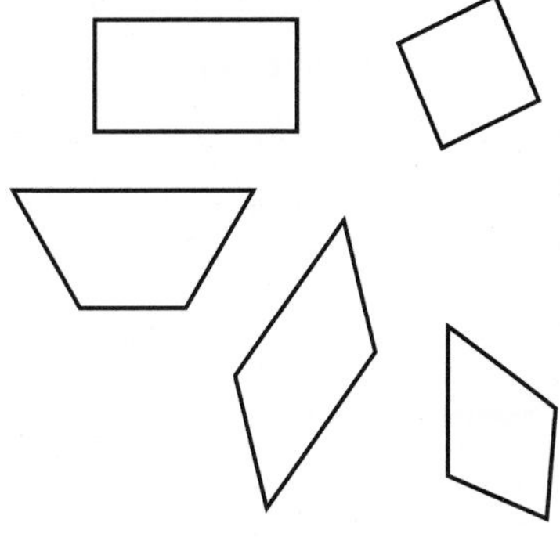

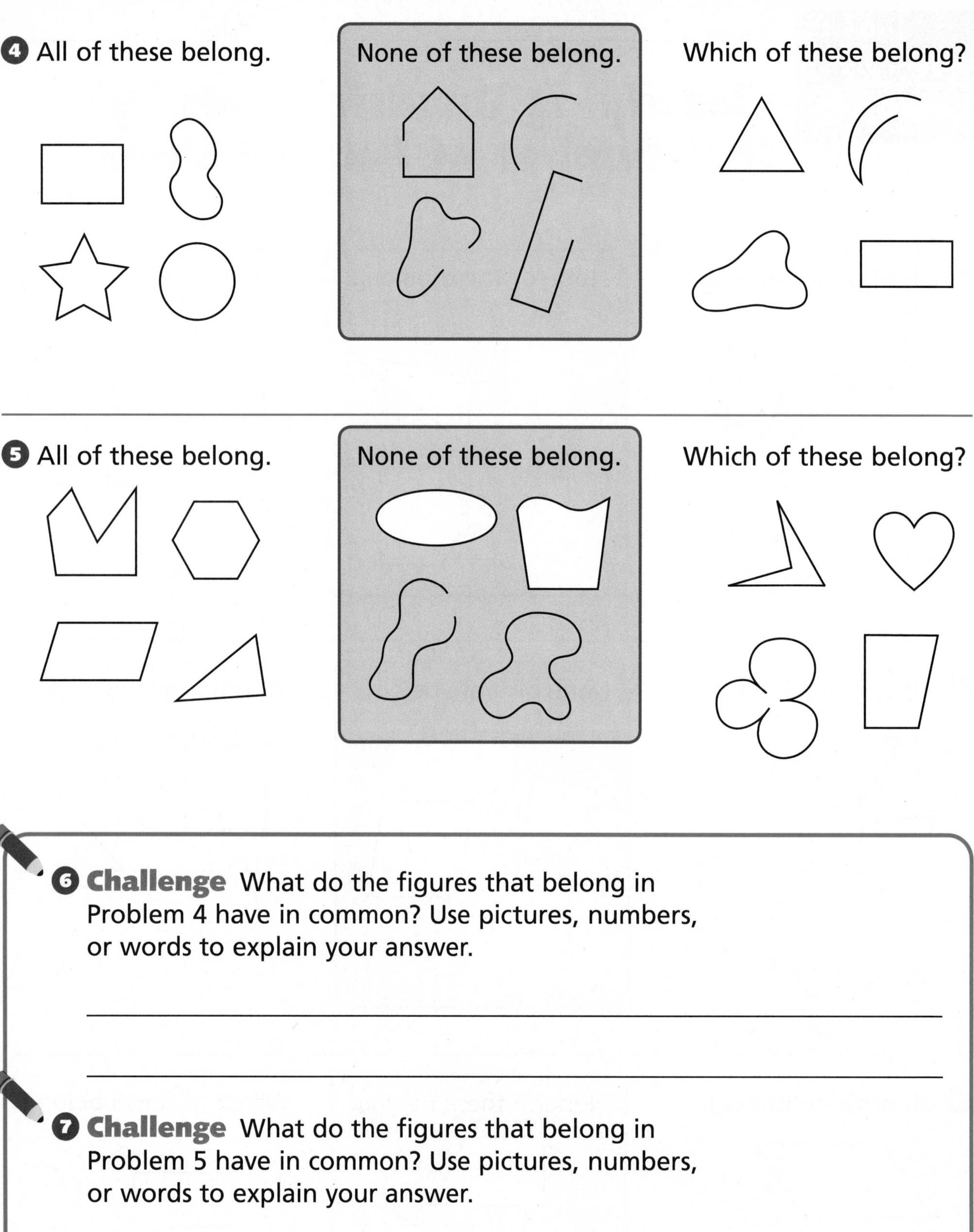

4 All of these belong. | None of these belong. | Which of these belong?

5 All of these belong. | None of these belong. | Which of these belong?

6 **Challenge** What do the figures that belong in Problem 4 have in common? Use pictures, numbers, or words to explain your answer.

____

____

7 **Challenge** What do the figures that belong in Problem 5 have in common? Use pictures, numbers, or words to explain your answer.

____

____

Chapter 4
Lesson 7

Name ____________________ Date __________

Classifying Parallelograms

NCTM Standards 3, 6, 7, 8, 9, 10

Each figure has at least one of these names:
parallelogram, rectangle, rhombus, square, trapezoid.

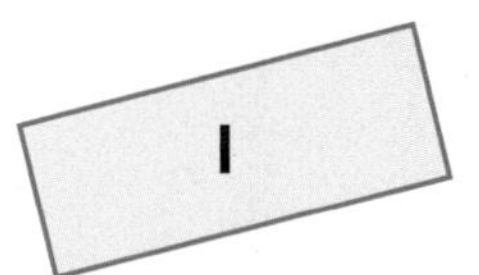

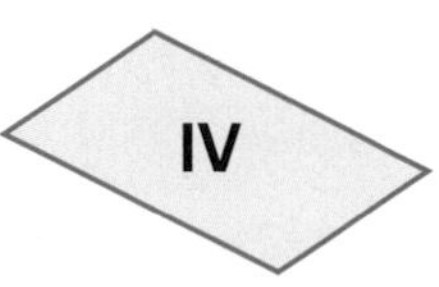

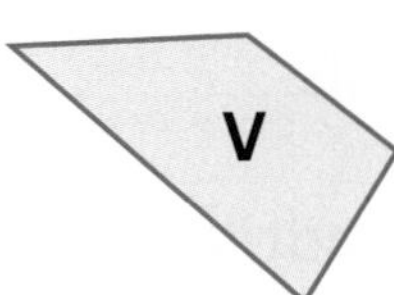

1. I have exactly one pair of parallel sides.

   I am quadrilateral _____.

   I am a ________________.

2. All of my sides are equal. All of my angles are equal.

   I am quadrilateral _____.

   I am a ________________.

3. I have 2 pairs of parallel sides.

   I am quadrilateral _____, _____,

   _____ or _____.

   I am a ________________.

   I am sometimes a ___________,

   a ___________ or a ___________.

4. All of my sides are the same length.

   I am quadrilateral _____ or _____.

   I am a ________________.

   I am sometimes a ___________.

5. I have 2 pairs of parallel sides. I have at least one right angle.

   I am quadrilateral _____ or _____.

   I am a ________________.

   I am sometimes a ___________.

6. I have more than 1 pair of parallel sides. My sides are not all the same length.

   I am quadrilateral _____ or _____.

   I am a ________________.

   I am sometimes a ___________.

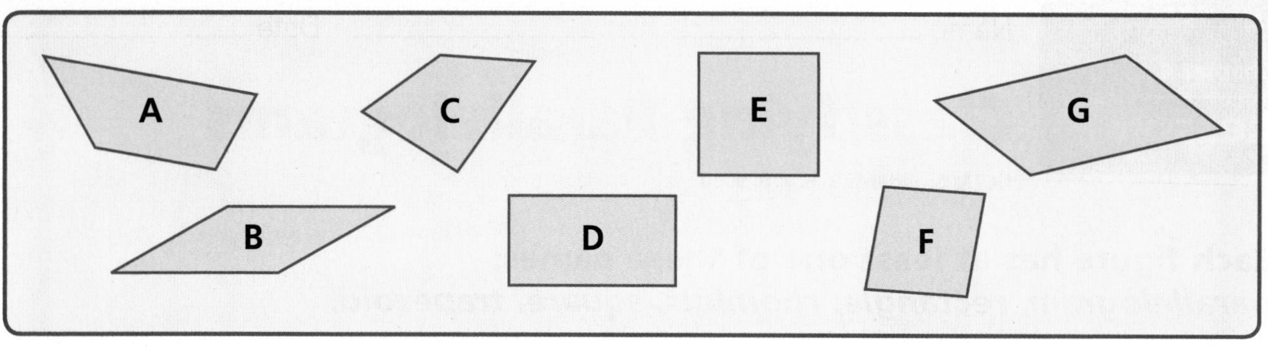

7 List all:

A quadrilaterals ______

B trapezoids ______

C parallelograms ______

D rhombuses ______

E rectangles ______

F squares ______

Write whether the statement is *true* or *false*.

8 Some quadrilaterals are parallelograms. true

9 All squares are parallelograms. ______

10 All parallelograms are squares. ______

11 All squares are rectangles. ______

12 All rectangles are squares. ______

13 All parallelograms are rectangles. ______

14 All quadrilaterals are either trapezoids or parallelograms. ______

Challenge

15 Some rhombuses are rectangles. ______

16 Some squares are trapezoids. ______

17 All squares are rhombuses. ______

Name ______________________ Date __________

Chapter 4

Lesson 8

Symmetry in Triangles and Quadrilaterals

NCTM Standards 3, 6, 7, 8, 9, 10

Sketch any lines of symmetry for these figures.

1

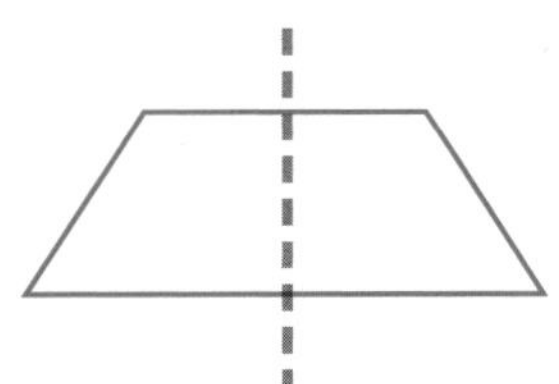

1 line(s) of symmetry

2

☐ line(s) of symmetry

3

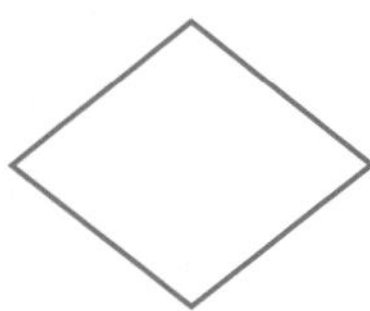

☐ line(s) of symmetry

4

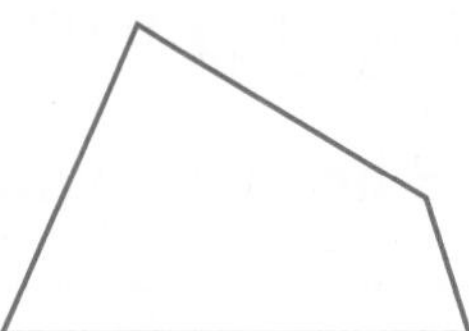

☐ line(s) of symmetry

Complete each figure by reflecting across the line of symmetry.

5

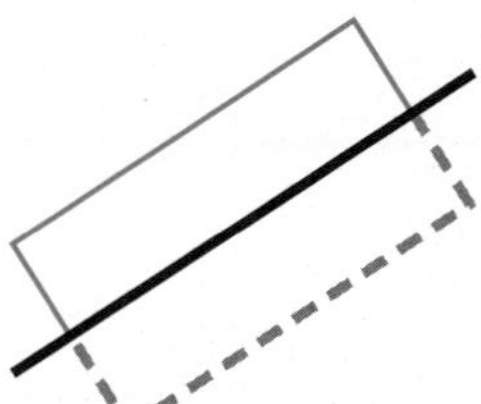

6

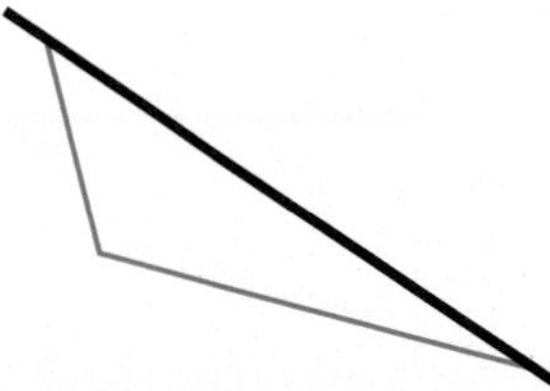

7

8

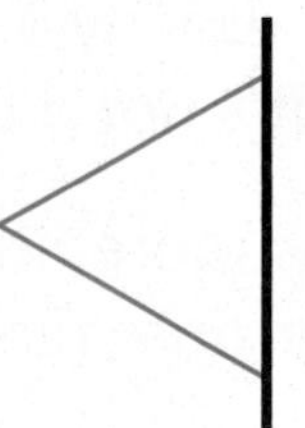

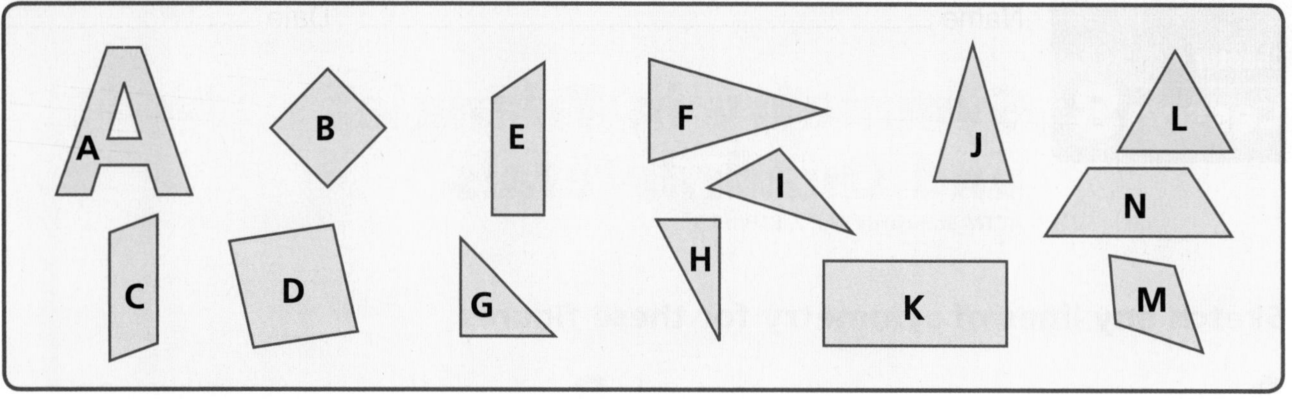

Draw the lines of symmetry for each figure and list all figures with:

9 no lines of symmetry ________________

10 exactly **1 line of symmetry** ________________

11 exactly **2 lines of symmetry** ________________

12 exactly **3 lines of symmetry** ________________

13 more than **3 lines of symmetry** ________________

Write whether the statement is *true* or *false*.

14 If a quadrilateral has exactly 1 line of symmetry, it is a rectangle. __________

15 If a triangle has more than **1** line of symmetry, it's equilateral. __________

16 If a triangle has **0** lines of symmetry, it's scalene. __________

Challenge

17 If a figure has exactly **2** lines of symmetry, it's not a triangle. __________

18 If a figure has exactly **3** lines of symmetry, it's not a quadrilateral. __________

19 A rhombus has more lines of symmetry than any other quadrilateral. __________

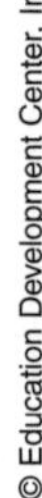

Chapter 4
Lesson 9

Name ______________________ Date ____________

Working with Transformations

NCTM Standards 3, 6, 7, 8, 9, 10

Perform each transformation.

1 Reflect across the dotted line.

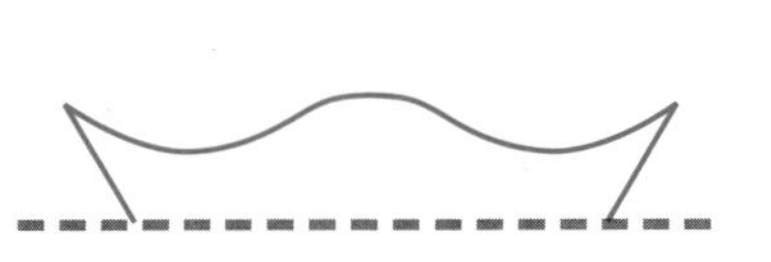

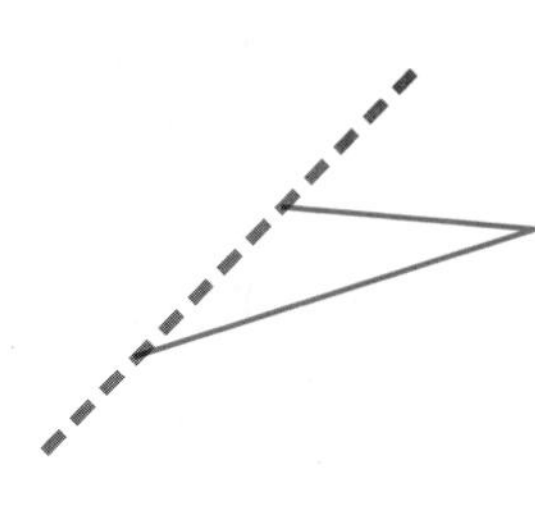

2 Translate in the direction of the arrow so that the resulting figure does not overlap with the original.

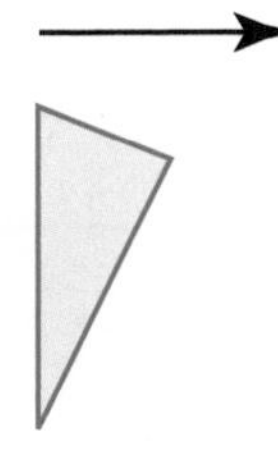

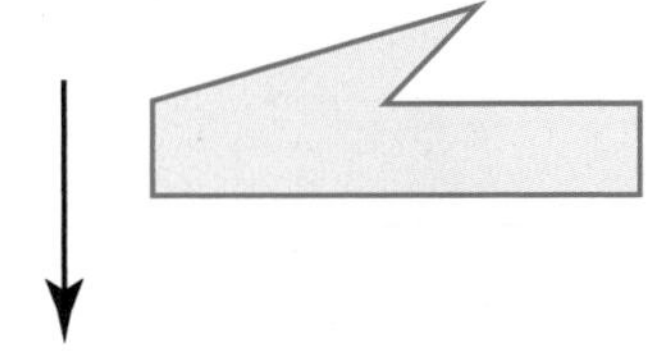

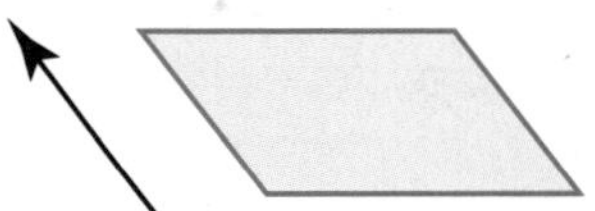

3 Rotate around the labeled point so that the resulting figure does not overlap with the original.

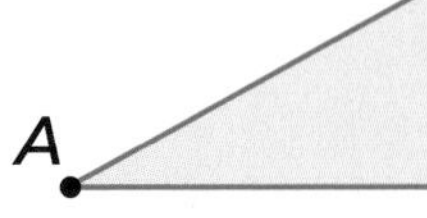

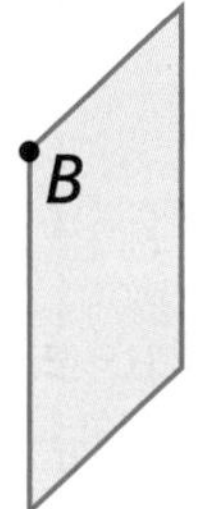

Show how to cut each figure into two congruent pieces.

Explain why the two pieces in each figure are congruent by circling all the terms that describe the transformation.

4

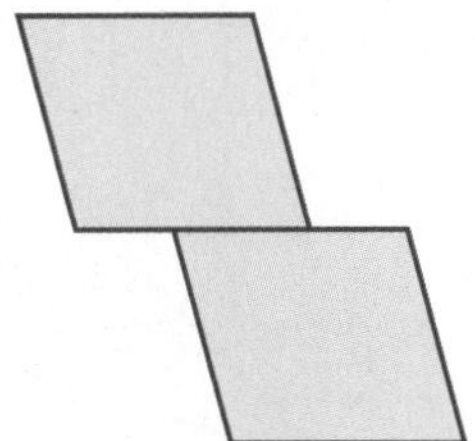

Rotation

Reflection

Translation

5

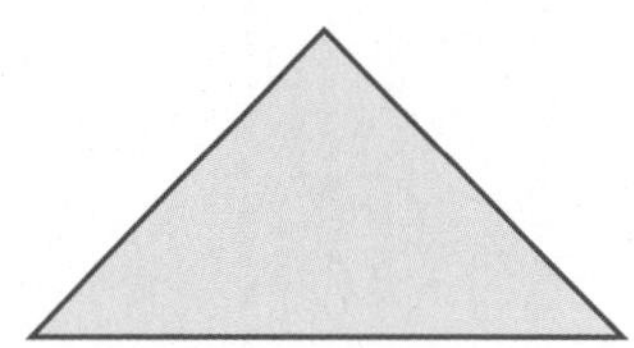

Rotation

Reflection

Translation

6

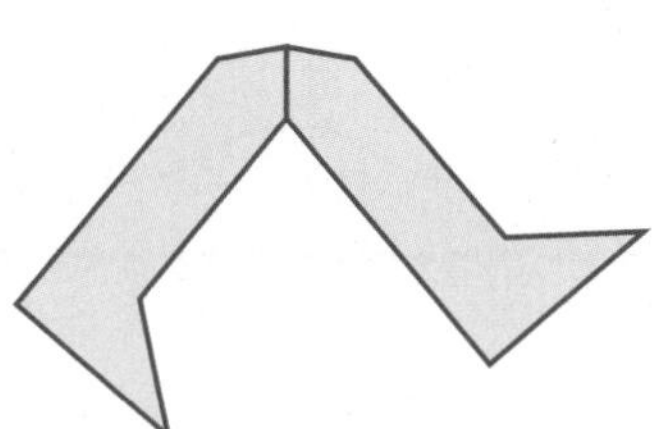

Rotation

Reflection

Translation

7

Rotation

Reflection

Translation

8

Rotation

Reflection

Translation

9 Challenge

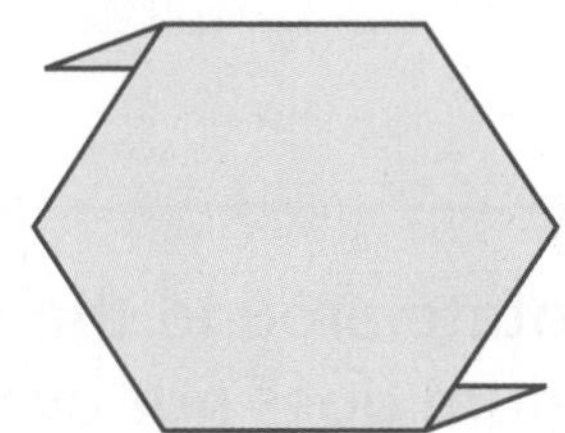

Rotation

Reflection

Translation

Chapter 4
Lesson 10

Name ______________________ Date ______________

Problem Solving Strategy
Look for a Pattern

NCTM Standards 3, 6, 7, 8, 9, 10

1. All of these belong.

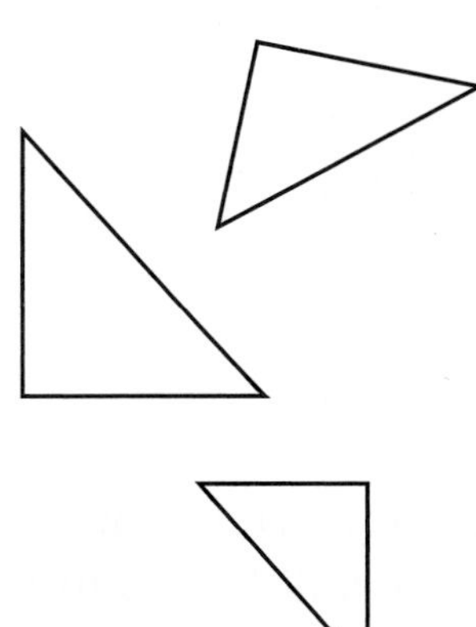

None of these belong.

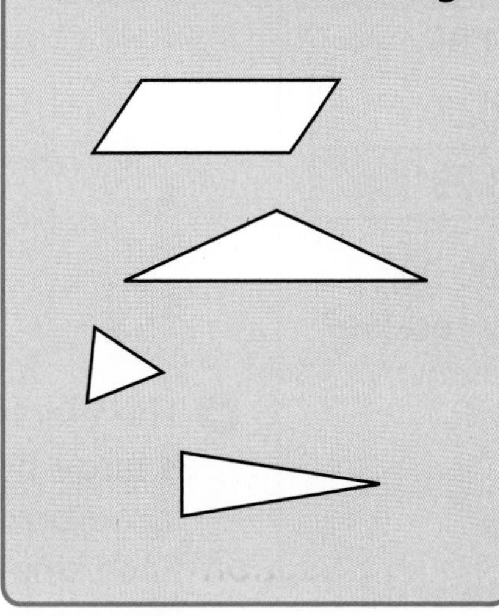

Circle the ones that belong.

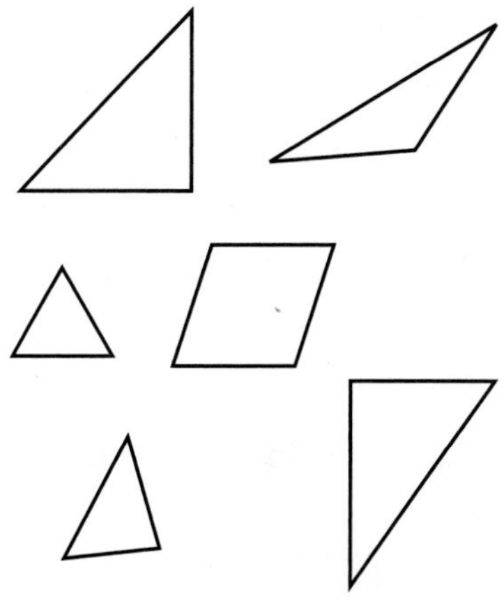

What is the same about all of the figures that belong?

____

2. Draw the next **4 figures** in the pattern below.

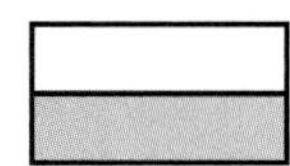
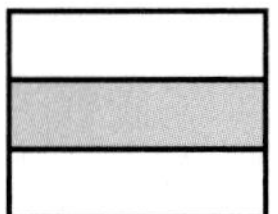
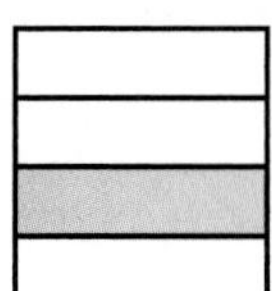

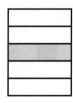

3. Describe this pattern and fill in the missing number:
1, 3, 9, ______, 81, 243. Explain.

____

____

Problem Solving Test Prep

Choose the correct answer.

1. The Wu family bought 2 adult, 1 child, and 3 student tickets.

AMUSEMENT PARK	
Ticket	**Price**
Adult	$11.95
Student	$10.50
Child (under 6)	$8.25

If they gave the cashier $100.00, how much change did they receive?

A. $35.35 **C.** $44.60
B. $36.35 **D.** $63.65

2. Cassie had 150 invitations to send. She sent 55 on Monday and 42 on Tuesday. How many invitations does Cassie still have to send?

A. 53 **C.** 108
B. 95 **D.** 247

3. Which fraction represents the part of the spinner labeled B?

A. $\frac{0}{6}$ **C.** $\frac{2}{6}$
B. $\frac{1}{6}$ **D.** $\frac{3}{6}$

4. The electronics store received 8 large boxes of batteries. Each large box had 16 small boxes in it. Each small box had 6 batteries in it. How many batteries did the store receive?

A. 30 batteries **C.** 128 batteries
B. 96 batteries **D.** 768 batteries

Show What You Know

Solve each problem. Explain your answer.

5. Mike's family bought 147 tickets for fair rides. Each ride takes 3 tickets. Do they have enough tickets to ride 50 rides? Explain.

6. What is the next figure in the pattern? Explain.

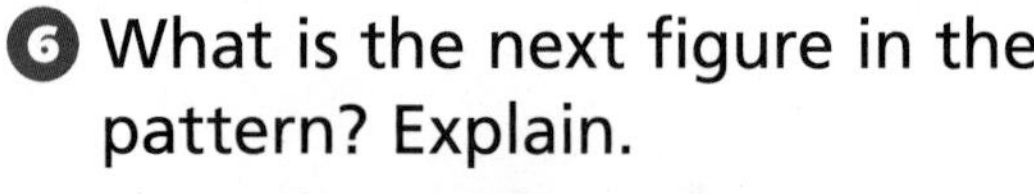

____

Name ____________________ Date ____________

Chapter 4

Review/Assessment

NCTM Standards 3, 6, 7, 8, 9, 10

Use the angles to answer the questions. Lesson 2

A B C D E

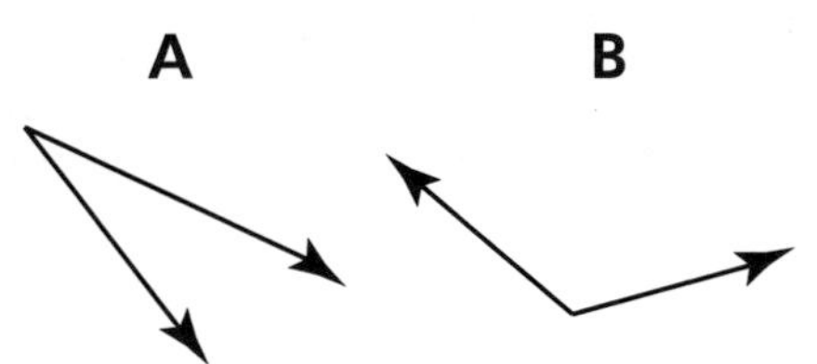

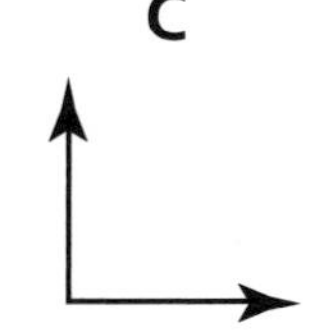

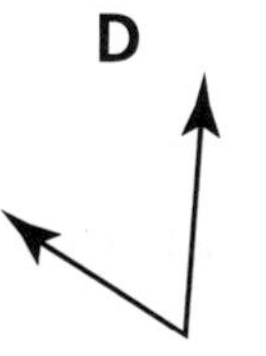

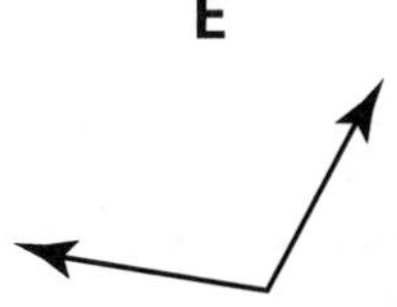

1. Order the angles from the largest to the smallest. ____, ____, ____, ____, ____

2. Compare each angle to a right angle.

   Which angles are acute angles? ____, ____

   Which angle is a right angle? ____

   Which angles are obtuse angles? ____, ____

Label each triangle as *acute, right,* or obtuse, and *scalene, isosceles,* or *equilateral.* Lesson 4

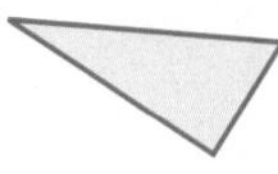

____

____

4. 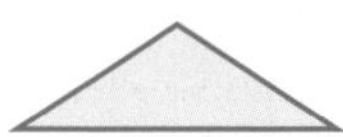

____

____

5. 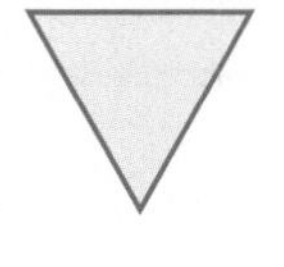

____

____

6. Identify the parallel and perpendicular lines in the figure.
   If there are no more, put an "X" on the answer line. Lesson 5

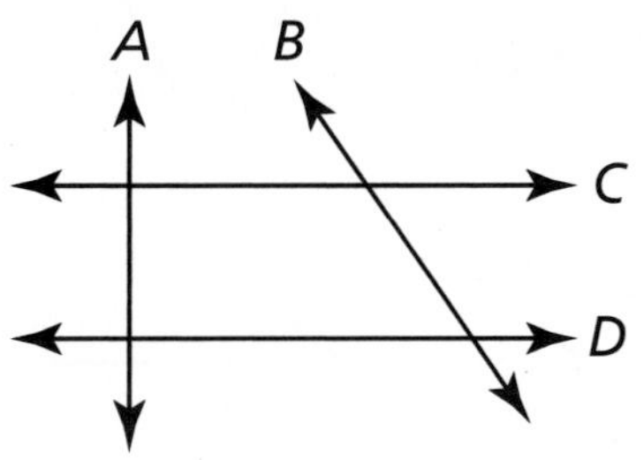

Parallel:

_____ and _____

_____ and _____

Perpendicular:

_____ and _____

_____ and _____

List all names for each figure: *parallelogram, rectangle, rhombus, square,* or *trapezoid.* Lesson 6

7  ______________________________

8 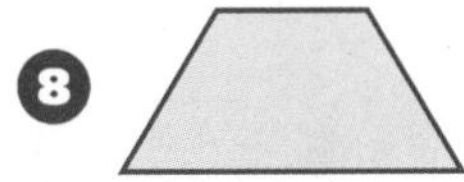 ______________________________

Write whether the statement is *true* or *false.* Lesson 8

9 If a triangle has exactly 1 line of symmetry, it is isosceles. __________

10 If a quadrilateral has exactly 4 lines of symmetry, it is a square. __________

Perform each transformation. Lesson 9

11 Translate in the direction of the arrow so that the resulting figure does not overlap with the original.

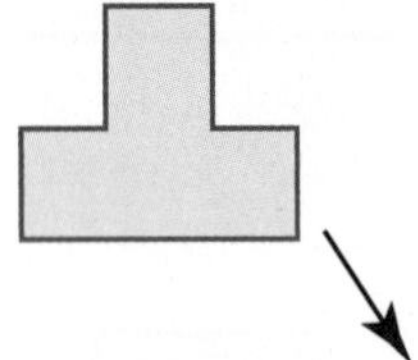

12 Reflect across the dotted line.

Solve the problem. Lesson 10

13 All of these belong.

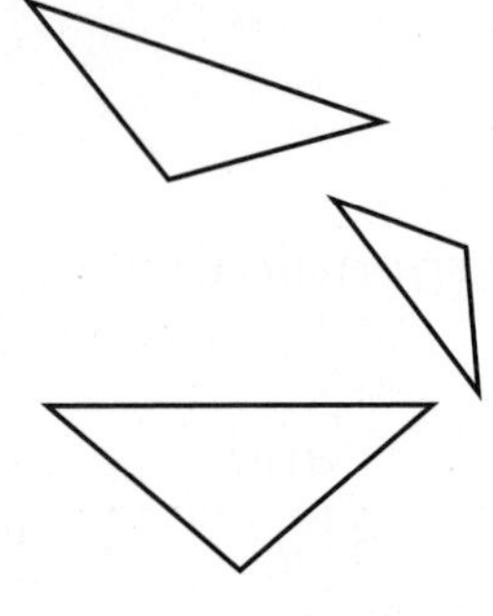

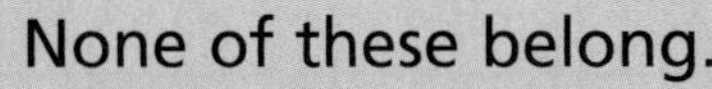
None of these belong.

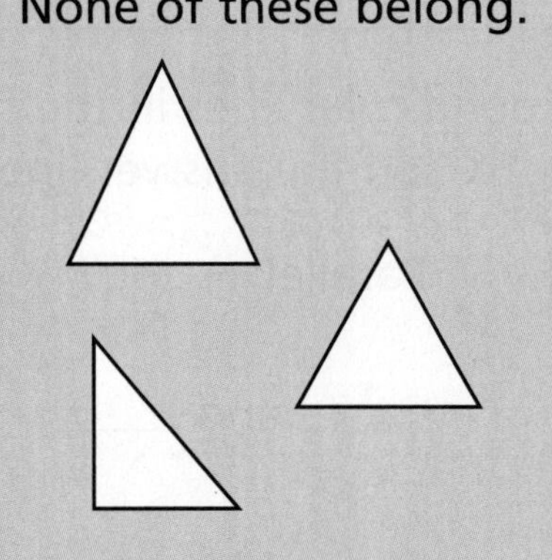

Circle the ones that belong.

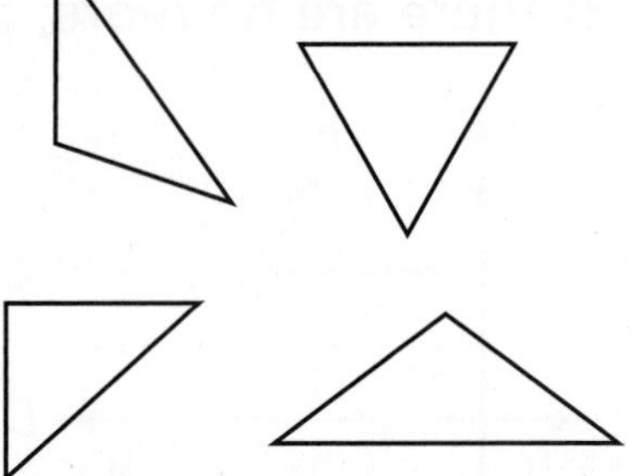

Chapter 5
Lesson 1

Name ______________________ Date ____________

Introducing Area

NCTM Standards 1, 2, 6, 7, 8, 9, 10

Find the area of each figure. How many square units is it?

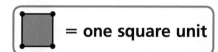

= one square unit

1. 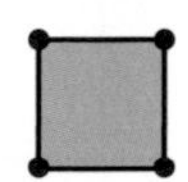

Area:	1

2. 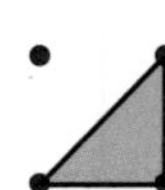

Area:	$\frac{1}{2}$

3. 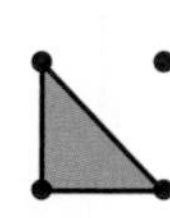

Area:	

4. 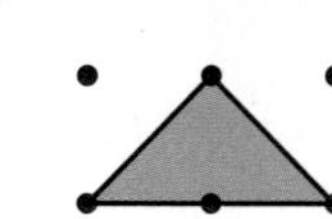

Area:	

5. 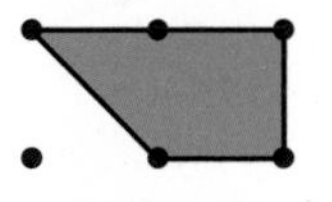

Area:	

6. 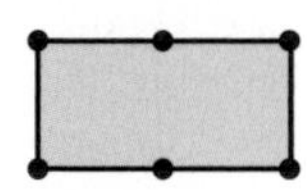

Area:	

7. 

Area:	

8.

Area:	

9. 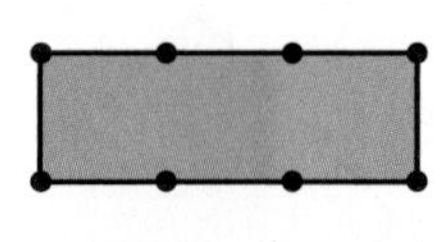

Area:	

10. 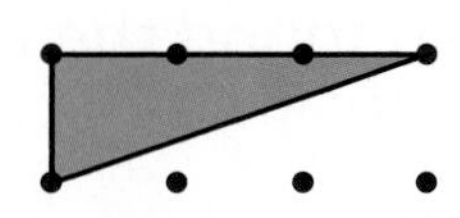

Area:	

11. 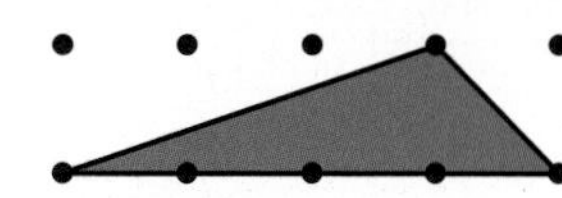

Area:	

12. 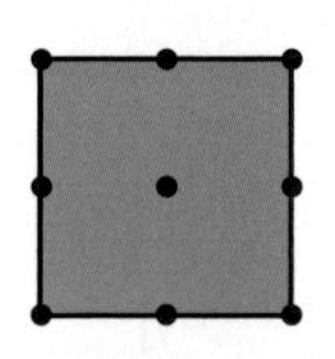

Area:	

13. 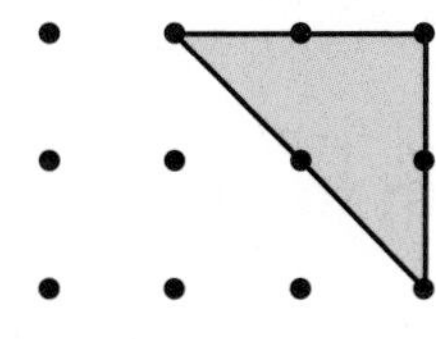

Area:	

14. 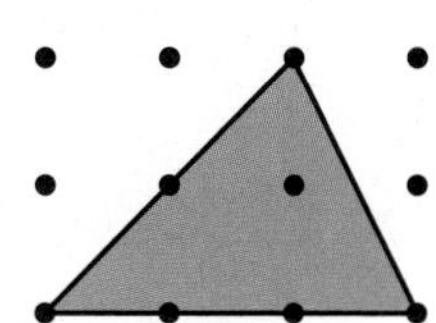

Area:	

Find the area of each figure. How many square units is it?

= one square unit

15

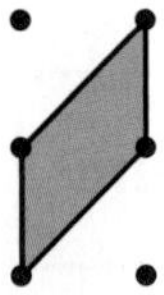

Area:

16

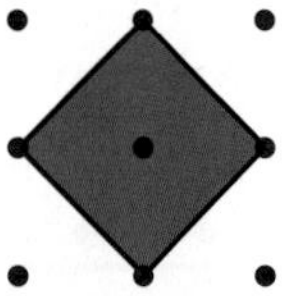

Area:

17

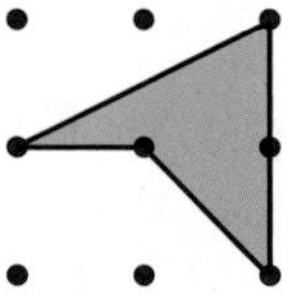

Area:

18

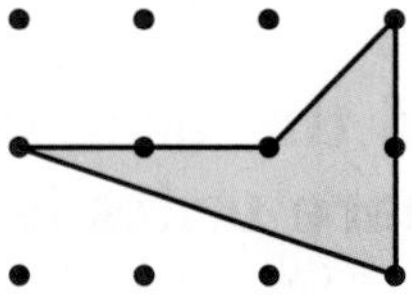

Area:

19

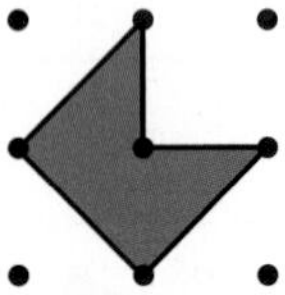

Area:

20

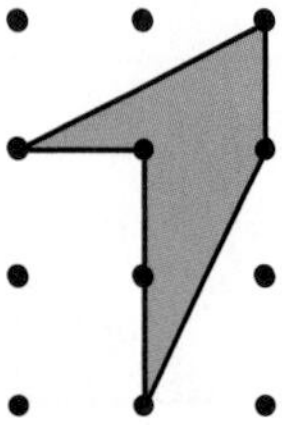

Area:

21

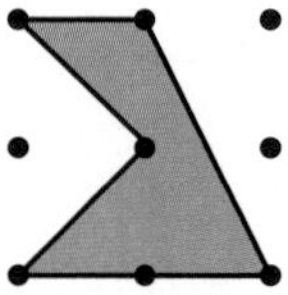

Area:

22

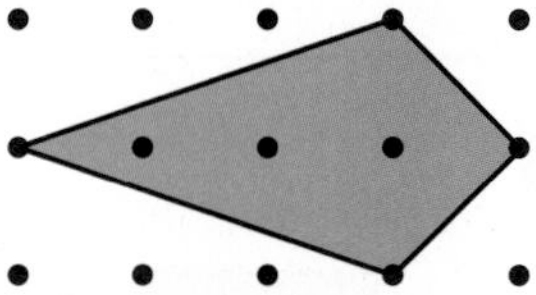

Area:

23 **Challenge** Explain how you found the area.

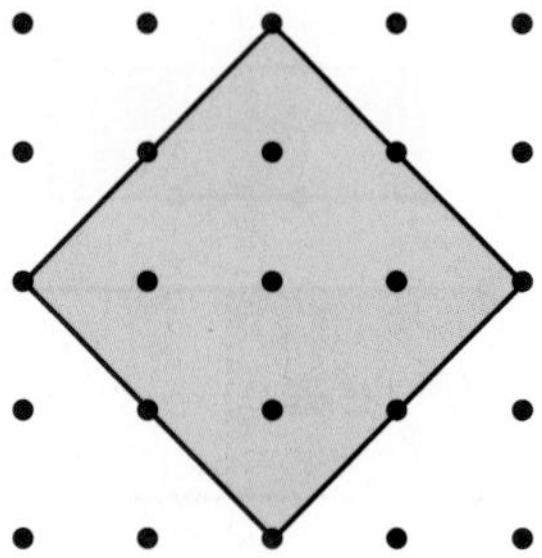

____

____

____

____

Area:

24 **Challenge** Use the diagram to find each area.

Purple area ______ White area ______

Yellow area ______ Total area ______

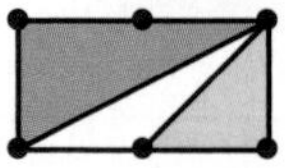

Chapter 5

Lesson 2

Name ______________________ Date ____________

Assembling Congruent Figures to Find Area

NCTM Standards 1, 2, 6, 7, 8, 9, 10

1 Quinlan's Quilt Shop makes quilts using pieces like these. Find the area of each piece in square units.

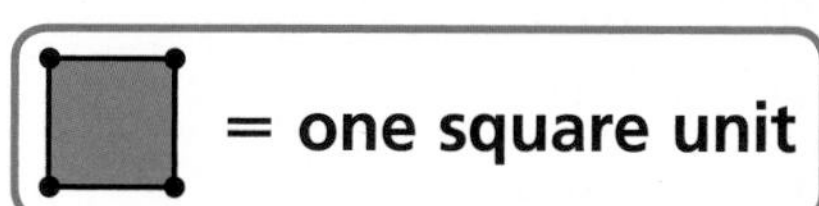

Piece W	Piece X	Piece Y	Piece Z
		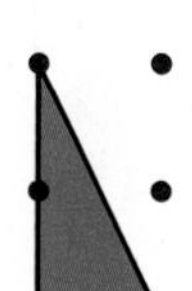	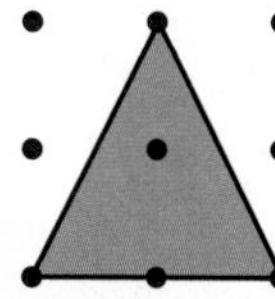
Area: ____	Area: ____	Area: ____	Area: ____

Find the area of these quilt designs in square units.

2

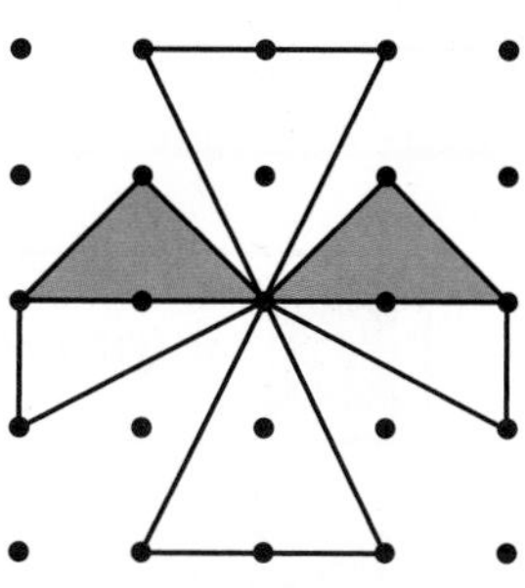

Area: ____

3

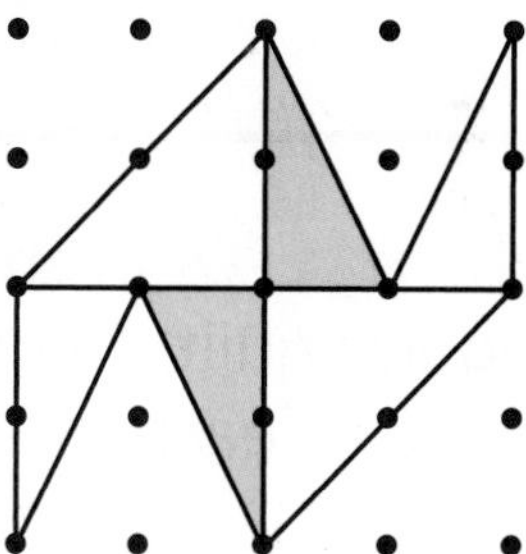

Area: ____

4 In Problem 2, would you **reflect**, **rotate**, or **translate** the left shaded piece to get the right shaded piece?

____

5 In Problem 3, would you **reflect**, **rotate**, or **translate** the upper shaded piece to get the lower shaded piece?

____

Use the quilt pieces for Problems 6–7.

Piece W

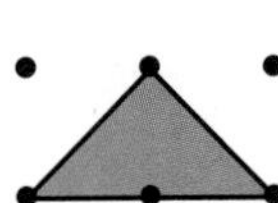

Piece X

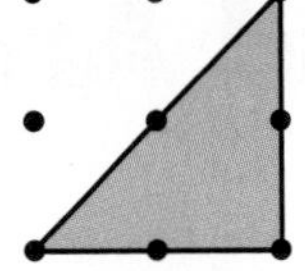

Piece Y

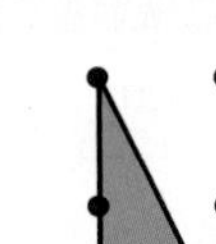

Piece Z

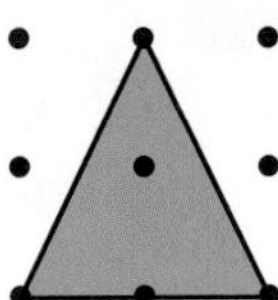

6 Quinlan's Quilt Shop sells the quilt shown at the right. On the blank grid, draw a figure congruent to the blue design and show how to make it using the 4 triangular pieces above.

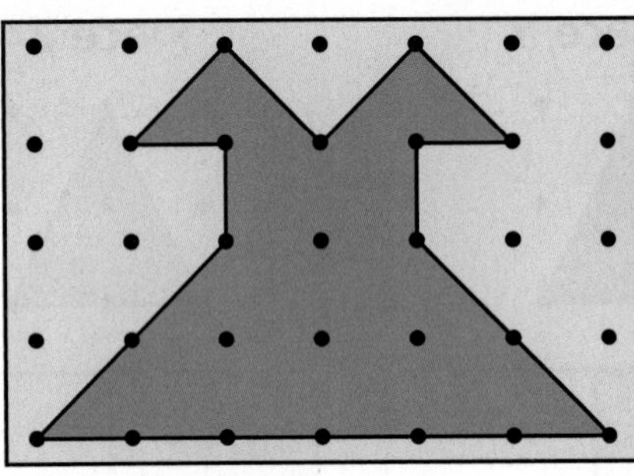

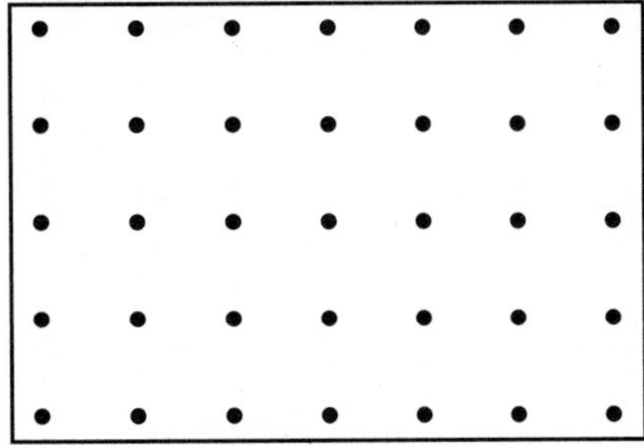

7 What is the area of the blue design? Explain how you found the answer.

____

____

____

8 **Challenge** Quinlan's Quilt Shop makes triangular quilts in different sizes. What is the area of each of these quilts?

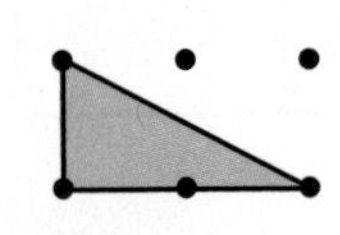

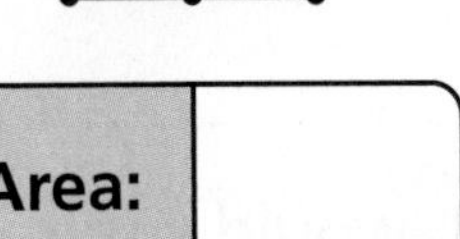

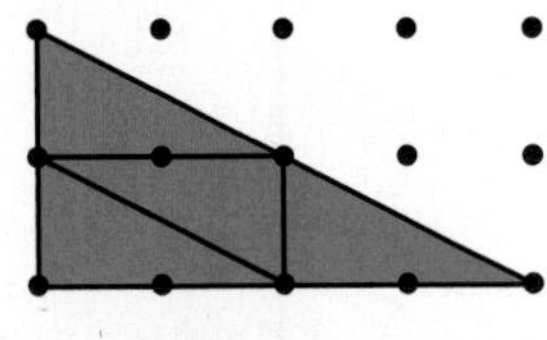

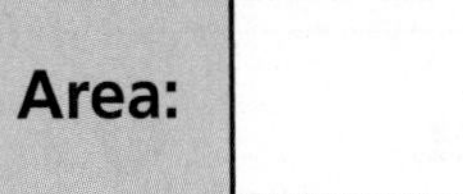

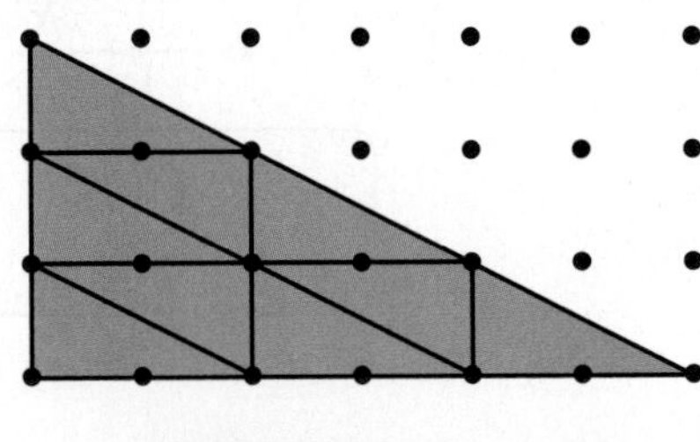

Area:

What would the area of the next largest quilt be? **Area:**

Chapter 5
Lesson 3

Name ______________________ Date ____________

Using Known Areas to Find Unknown Areas

NCTM Standards 1, 2, 6, 7, 8, 9, 10

Find the area of each region.

☐ has an area of one square unit.

1.

blue area	$\frac{1}{2}$
yellow area	
white area	
Total Area	1

2.

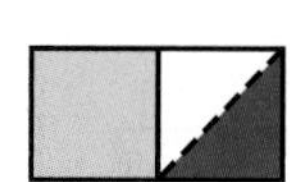

yellow area	
blue area	
white area	
Total Area	

3.

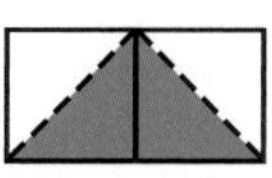

light blue area	
green area	
white area	
Total Area	

4.

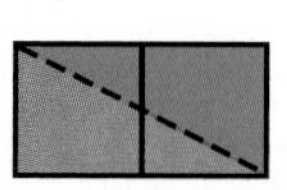

light blue area	
green area	
white area	
Total Area	

5.

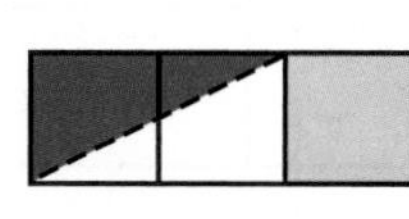

yellow area	
blue area	
white area	
Total Area	

6.

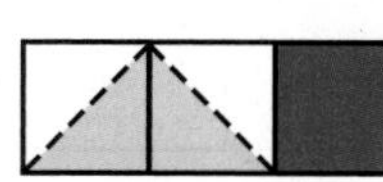

yellow area	
blue area	
white area	
Total Area	

7.

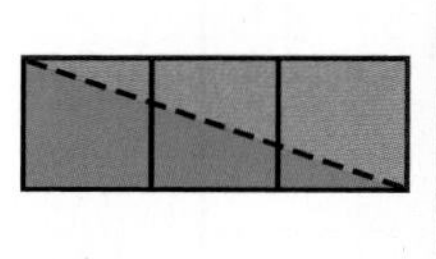

light blue area	
green area	
white area	
Total Area	

8.

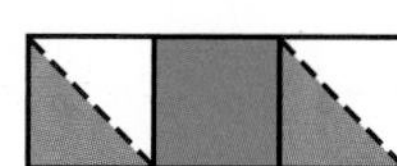

light blue area	
green area	
white area	
Total Area	

Find the area of each region.

▢ has an area of one square unit.

9

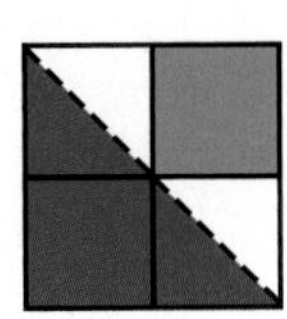

10

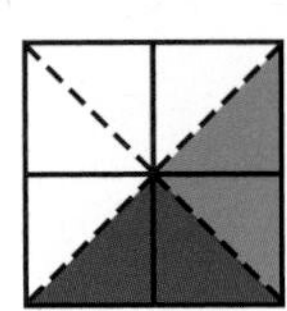

11

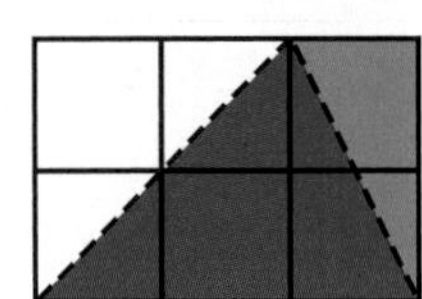

12

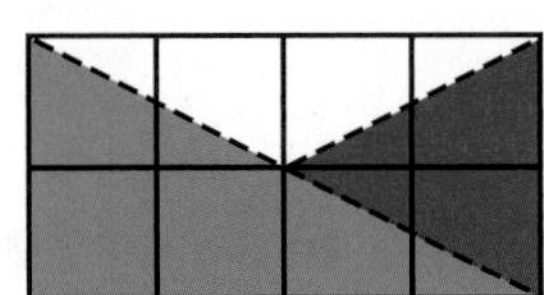

13

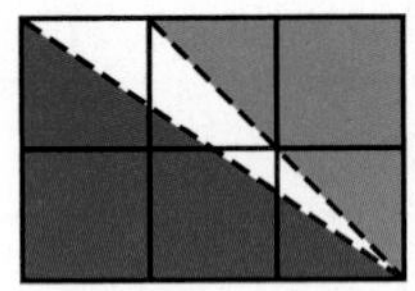

14

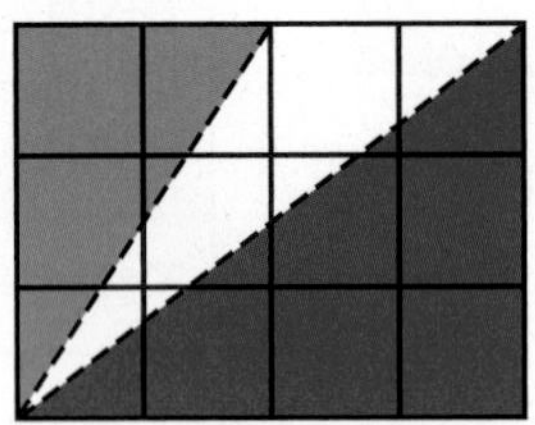

15

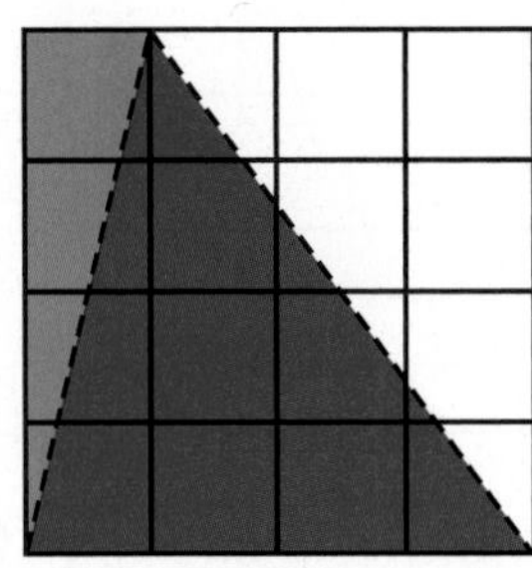

16

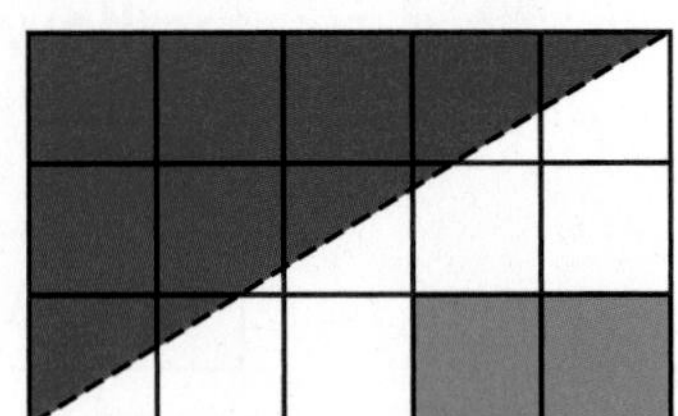

	9	10	11	12	13	14	15	16
blue area								
green area								
white area								
Total								

13 Challenge Color the grid to match the table.

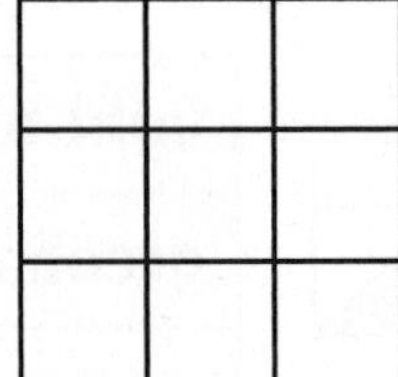

lighter shaded area	$1\frac{1}{2}$
darker shaded area	$4\frac{1}{2}$
white area	3
Total Area	9

Chapter 5
Lesson 4

Name ______________________ Date ____________

Introducing Standard Units for Measuring Area

NCTM Standards 1, 2, 6, 7, 8, 9, 10

Measure to find whether the unit of area for each figure is square inches, square centimeters, or neither. Then find the area of each region. Circle the correct area unit for each figure.

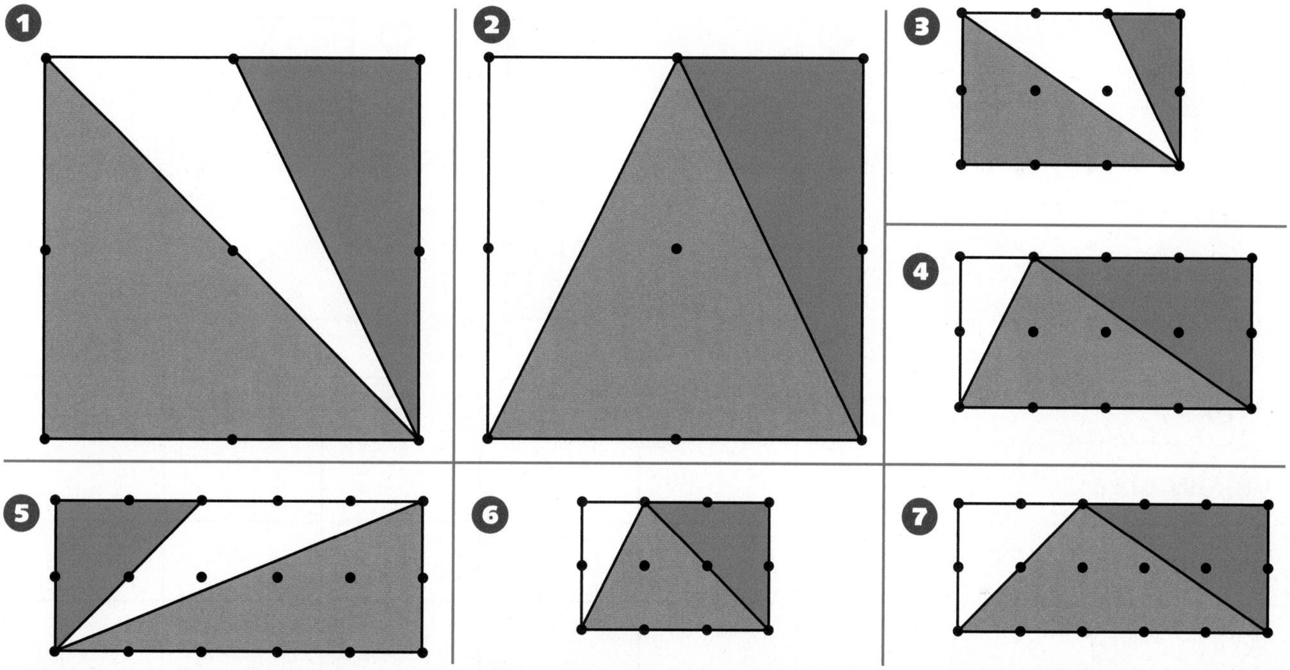

1

2

3

4

5

6

7

Area	1	2	3	4	5	6	7
green area							
purple area							
white area							
unit of area (circle one)	square in.	square in.	square in.	square in.	square in.	square in.	square in.
	square cm	square cm	square cm	square cm	square cm	square cm	square cm
	other unit	other unit	other unit	other unit	other unit	other unit	other unit

Find the area of each region and fill in the chart. Measure to identify the area unit.

8

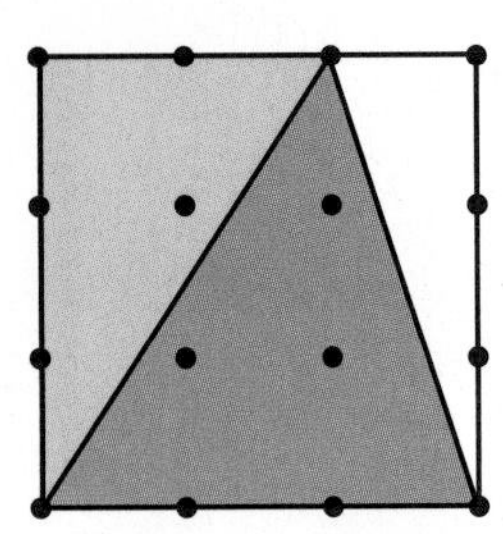

9

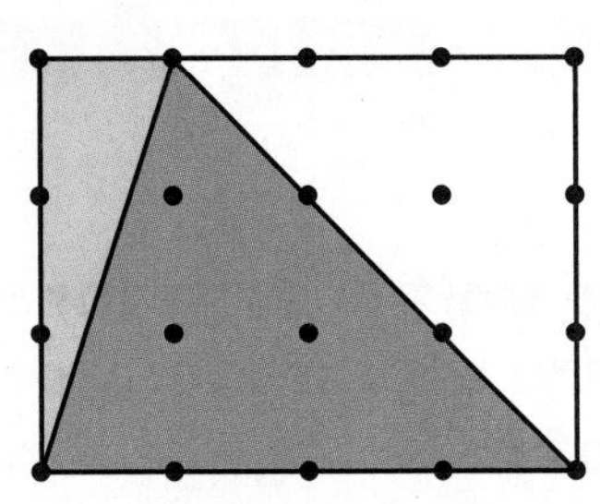

10

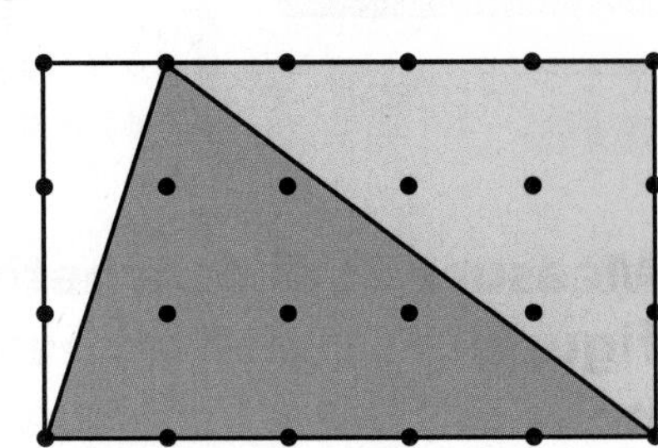

11

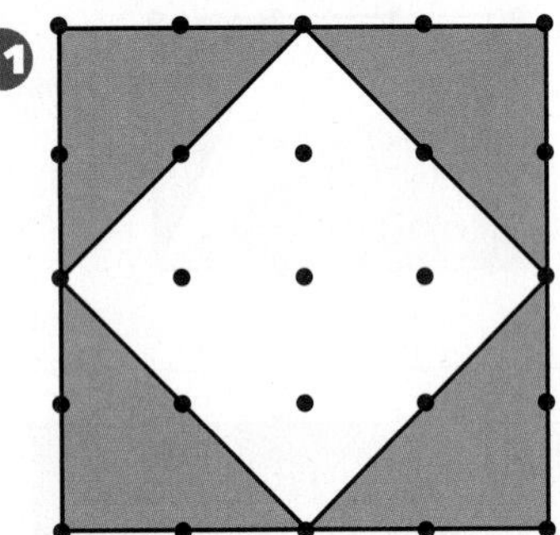

12

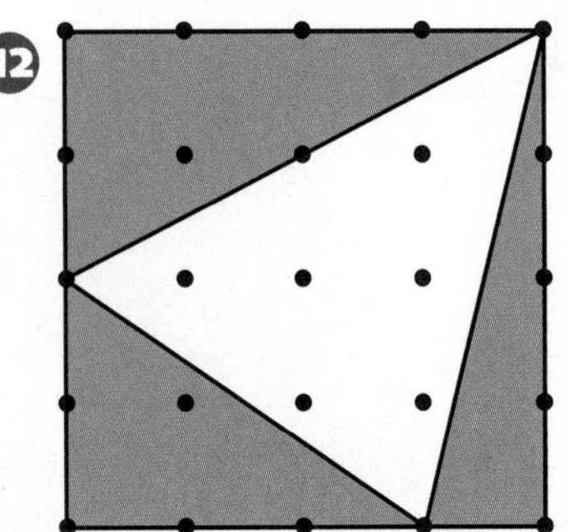

13

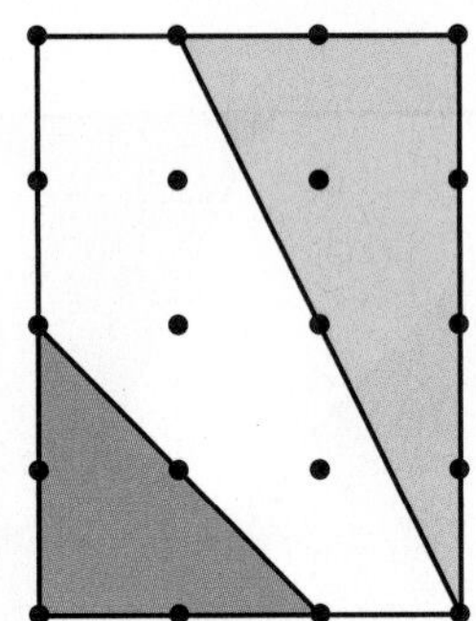

Area	8	9	10	11	12	13
yellow area	3					
purple area						
white area						
total area						
unit of area						

14 **Challenge** Color all the regions that have the same area with the same color.

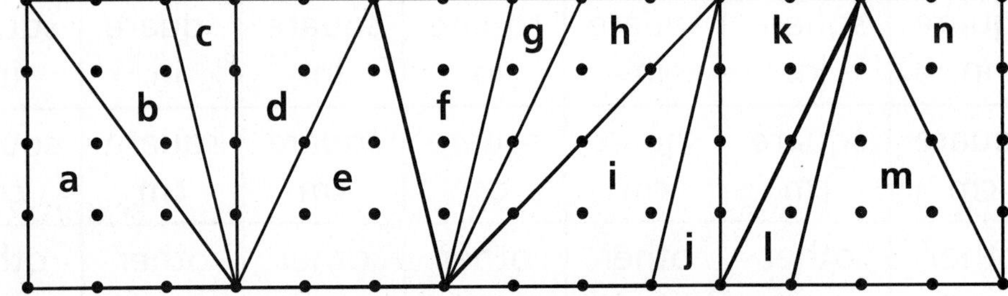

Chapter 5

Lesson 5

Name ______________________ Date ____________

Estimating Area in Standard Units

NCTM Standards 1, 2, 6, 7, 8, 9, 10

Estimate the area of each figure in square centimeters.

1

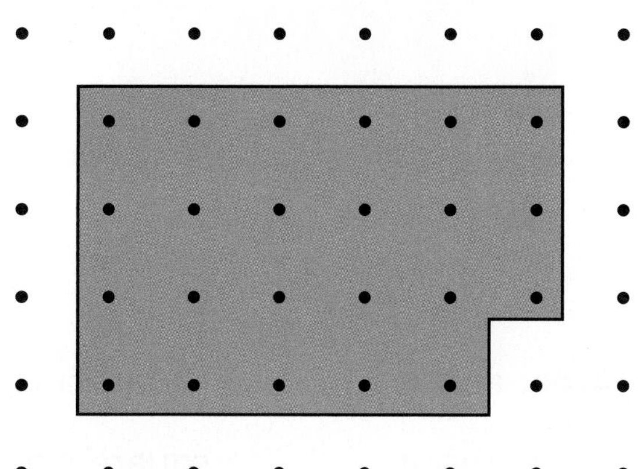

Area: about ________ square cm

2

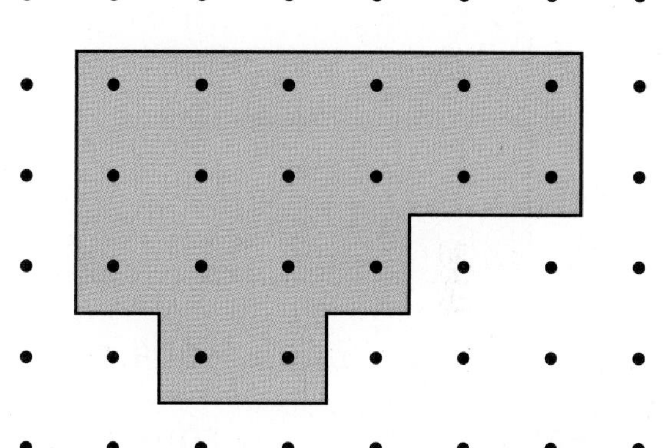

Area: about ________ square cm

3

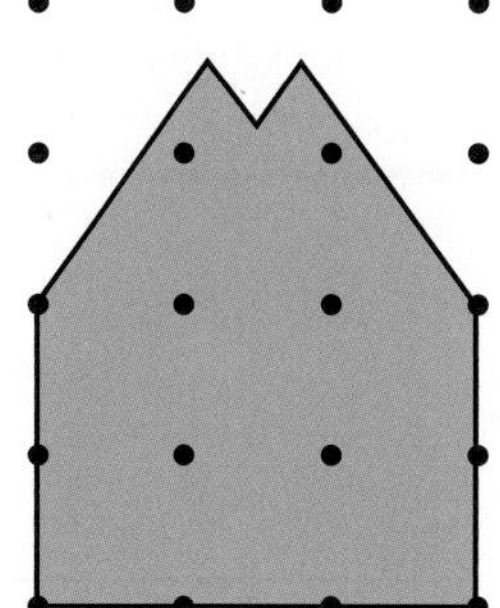

Area: about

________ square cm

4

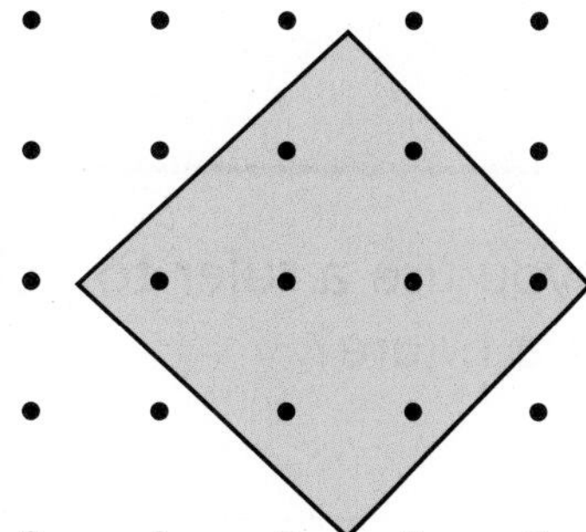

Area: about

________ square cm

5

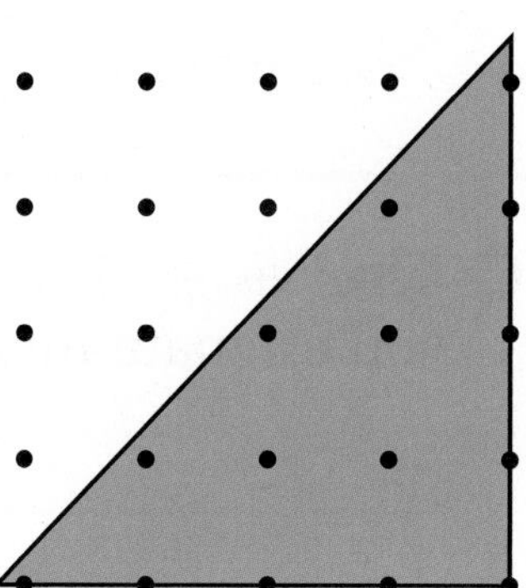

Area: about

________ square cm

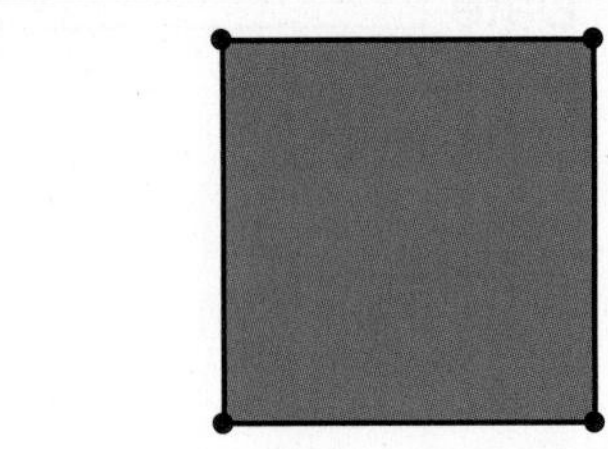
= 1 square inch

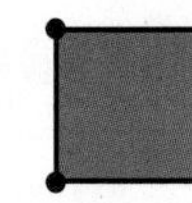
= 1 square centimeter

Estimate the area of each figure in square inches and in square centimeters.

6

Area: about ________ square inches

Area: about ________ square cm

7

Area: about ________ square inches

Area: about ________ square cm

8

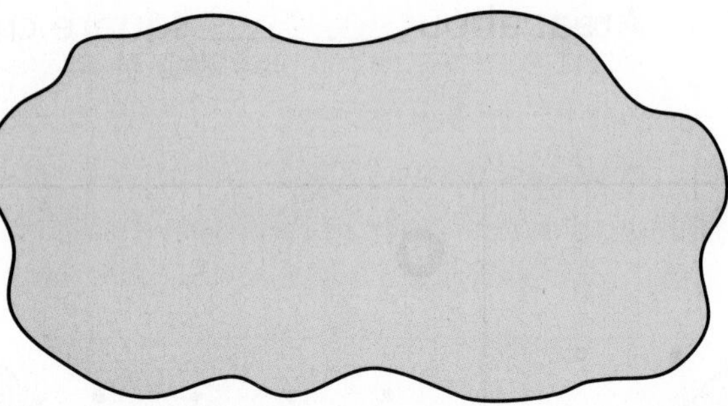

Area: about ________ square inches

Area: about ________ square cm

9 Challenge How could you use a ruler to help you estimate the area of a figure?

____

____

____

____

Name ____________________ Date ____________

Chapter 5

Lesson 6

Introducing Perimeter

NCTM Standards 1, 2, 6, 7, 8, 9, 10

1

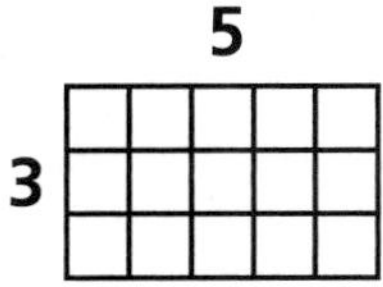

length	5
width	3

area	
perimeter	16

2

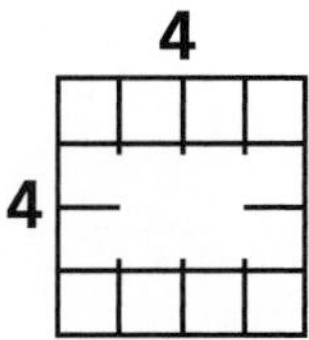

length	4
width	4

area	
perimeter	

3

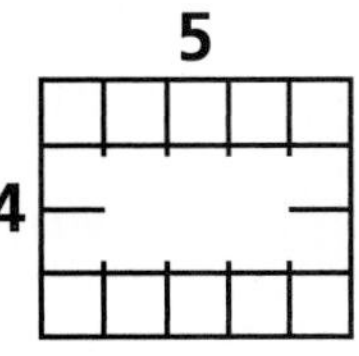

length	5
width	4

area	
perimeter	

4

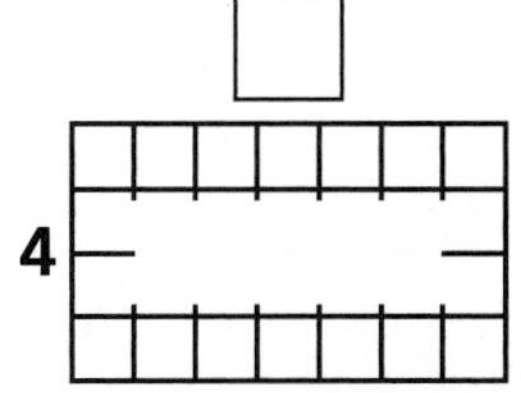

length	
width	4

area	28
perimeter	

5

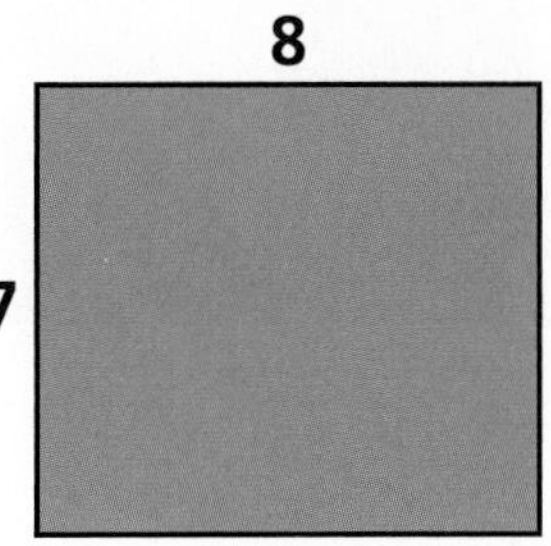

length	8
width	7

area	
perimeter	

6

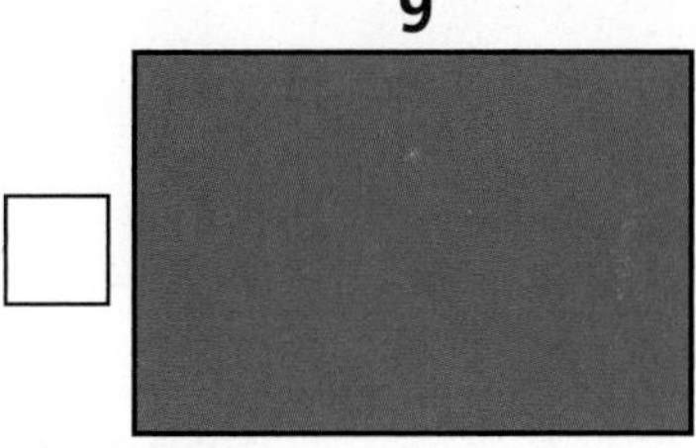

length	9
width	

area	54
perimeter	

7

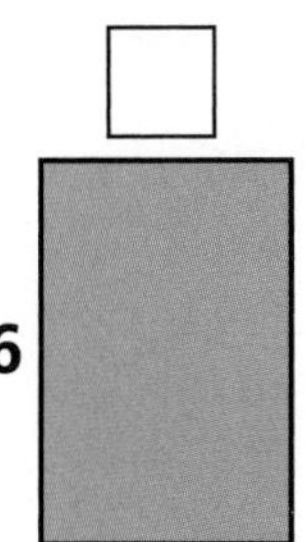

length	
width	6

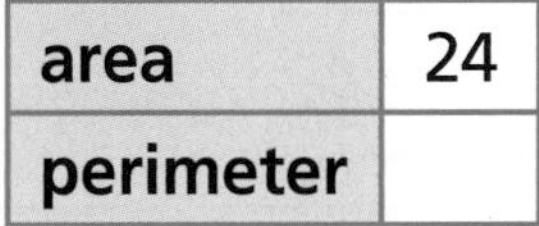

area	24
perimeter	

8

length	8
width	

area	24
perimeter	22

Measure to find the length, width, and perimeter of the rectangle.

9

length	inches
width	inches
perimeter	inches

10

length	centimeters
width	centimeters
perimeter	centimeters

11

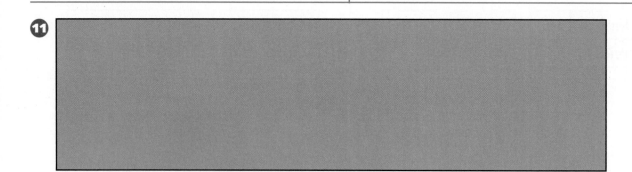

length	centimeters
width	centimeters
perimeter	centimeters

12 **Challenge** Find the areas of the rectangles on this page. Include the units in your answers.

9	
10	
11	

Chapter 5
Lesson 7

Name ____________________ Date __________

Connecting Perimeter and Area

NCTM Standards 1, 2, 6, 7, 8, 9, 10

1 7 × 3 (grid rectangle, 7 across, 3 down)

perimeter		area	

2 10 × 3

perimeter		area	

3 6 × 5

perimeter		area	

4 9 × 4

perimeter		area	

5 7 × 8

perimeter		area	

6 9 × 9

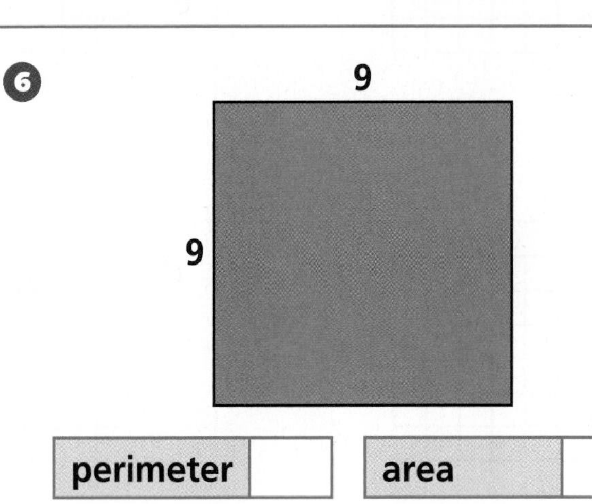

perimeter		area	

Quinlan's Quilt Shop sold a quilt that was 5 feet wide and 7 feet long.

7 What was the perimeter of the quilt? How did you find the answer?

____

____

8 The quilt was made out of squares whose sides were 1 foot long. How many squares were in the quilt? __________

9 What was the area of the quilt? __________

For each column in the table, draw a figure with the given area or perimeter. The figure does not have to be a rectangle. Fill in the rest of the table based on the figures you drew.

	10	11	12	13	14	15
area	12	12				15
perimeter			16	18	20	16

10 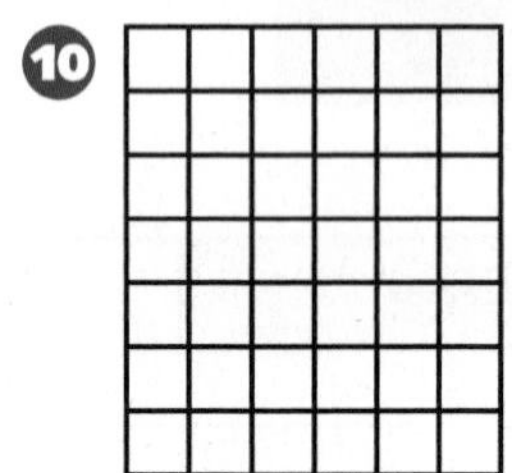

11 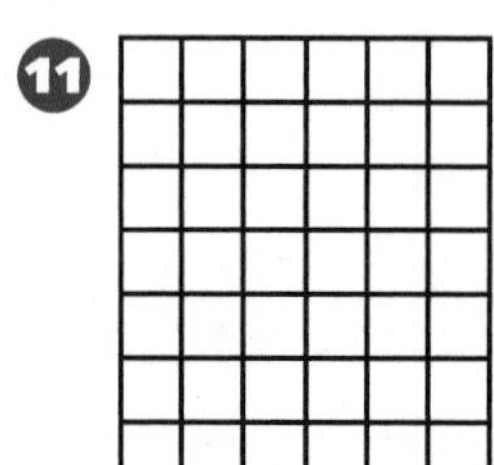

12 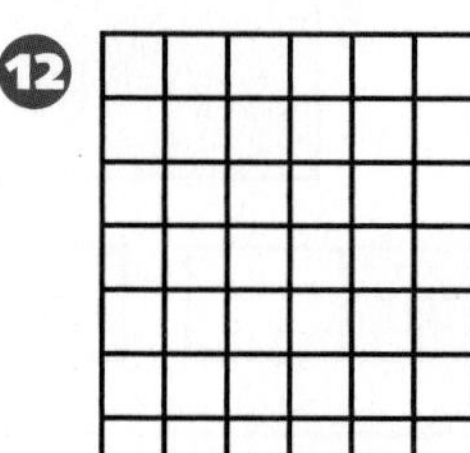

13 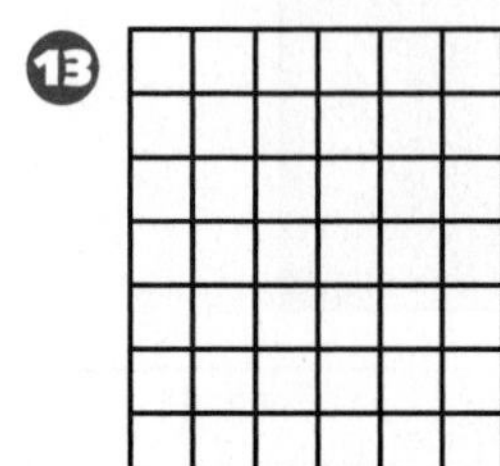

14 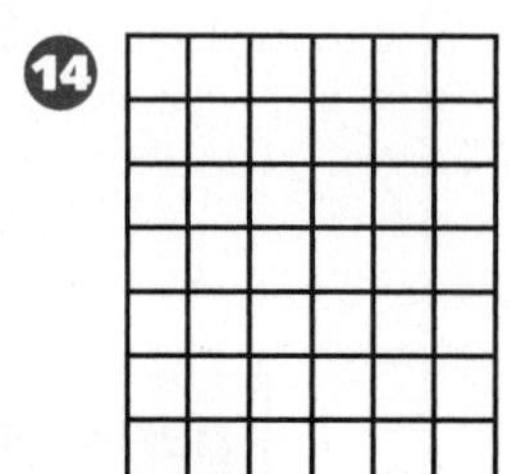

15 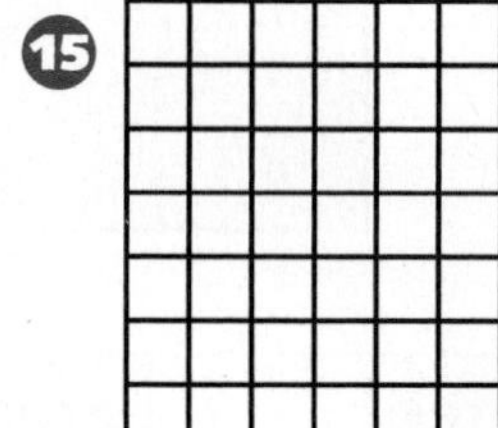

Challenge **Kathleen has 28 meters of wire fence to put around her garden.**

16 What is the largest rectangular area she can enclose inside the fence? ____________

17 What would be the length and width of her garden? ____________

Chapter 5
Lesson 8

Name ____________________ Date ____________

Problem Solving Strategy

Solve a Simpler Problem

NCTM Standards 1, 2, 6, 7, 8, 9, 10

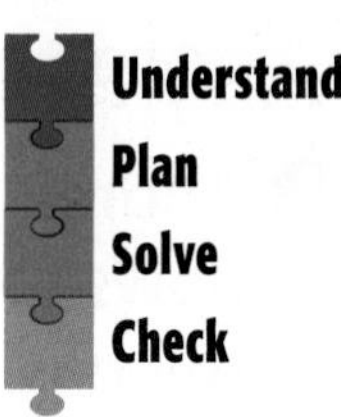

Solve each problem.

1. A diagram of Hong Lin's swimming pool is shown at the right.

   She measured some of the sides. Use her measurements to find the perimeter and area of her pool.

   perimeter: ____________________

   area: ____________________

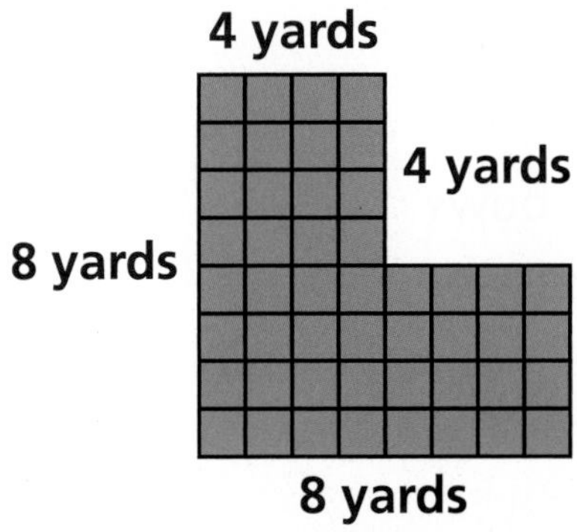

2. A diagram of Maria's garden is shown at the right.

   What is the area of the garden?

   ____

   How long is the fence around the garden?

   ____

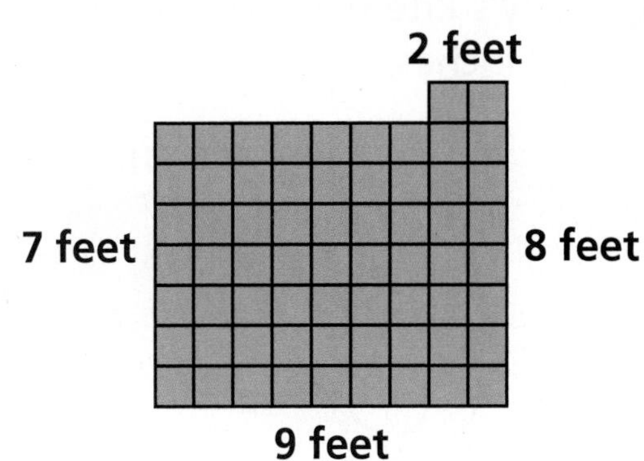

3. A diagram of Tony's kitchen is shown at the right.

   What is the perimeter of his kitchen?

   ____

   What is the area of the kitchen?

   ____

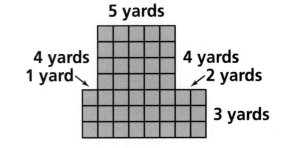

5 yards
4 yards
1 yard
4 yards
2 yards
3 yards

Problem Solving Test Prep

Choose the correct answer.

1. Andrea has a roll of ribbon to make bows for bags of cookies. If the roll has 248 inches of ribbon and Andrea uses 8 inches of ribbon to make each bow, how many bows can she make?

   A. 30 bows
   B. 31 bows
   C. 34 bows
   D. 40 bows

2. Timon's dad is figuring out how many posts he needs for a fence around a garden. He draws the three plans below. If he continues the pattern, how many posts will he use in his next plan?

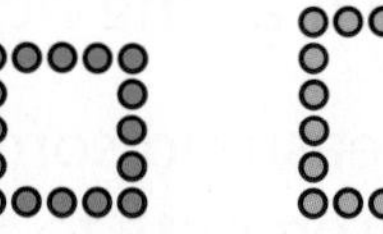

12 posts 16 posts 20 posts

   A. 22 posts **C.** 26 posts
   B. 24 posts **D.** 28 posts

Show What You Know

Solve each problem. Explain your answer.

3. Holly's kite has a perimeter of 108 inches.

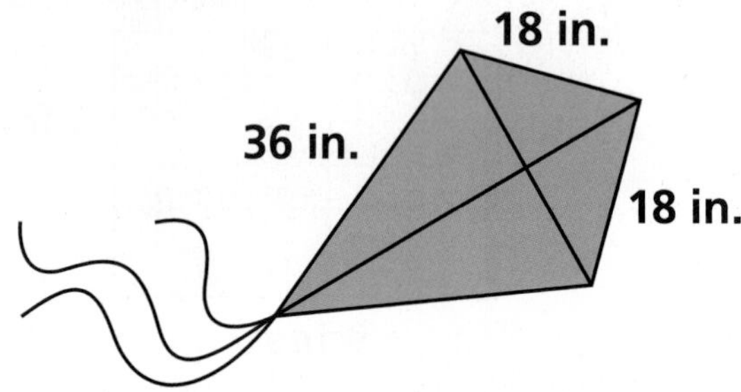

   How long is the fourth side of Holly's kite? Explain how you know your answer is correct.

   ____
   ____
   ____
   ____
   ____

4. Will transformed this figure from Position 1 into Position 2.

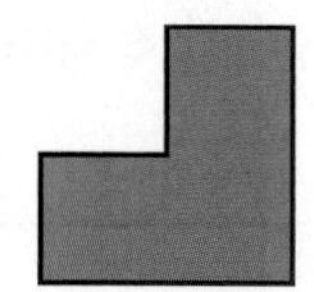
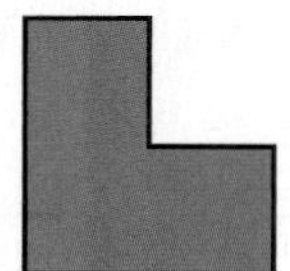

Position 1 Position 2

   Name a transformation that Will could have used to move the figure. Explain how you know.

   ____
   ____
   ____
   ____
   ____
   ____

Chapter 5

Name ____________________ Date ____________

Review/Assessment

NCTM Standards 1, 2, 6, 7, 8, 9, 10

Use the figure for Problems 1–3. Lessons 1, 2

1. What is the area of the yellow piece? Dots are 1 centimeter apart.

   ________ square cm

2. Would you **reflect**, **rotate**, or **translate** the yellow piece to get each of the other pieces?

   X: __________ **Y:** __________ **Z:** __________

3. What is the total area of the shape? ________ square cm

Measure the perimeter of each figure in inches. Estimate the area of each figure in square inches. Lessons 4, 5, 6, 7

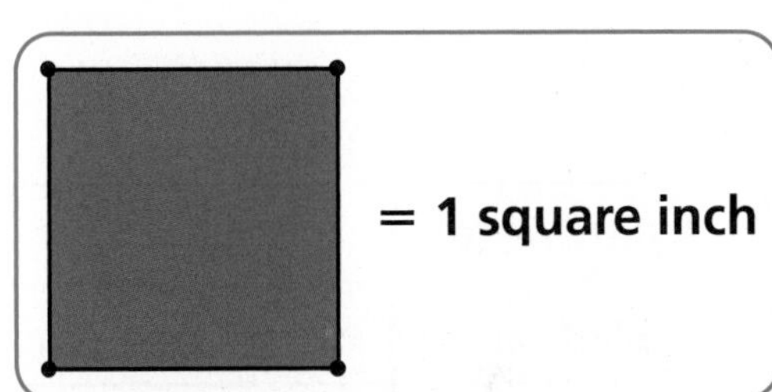

4.

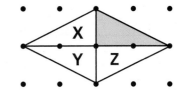

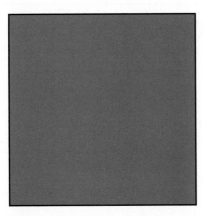

perimeter	inches
area (estimated)	square inches

5.

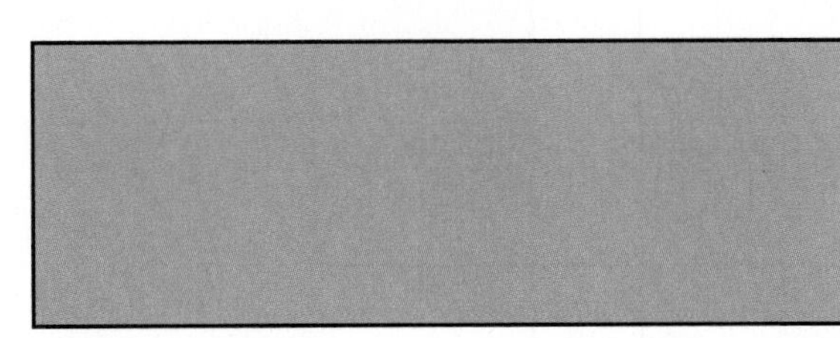

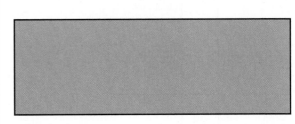

perimeter	inches
area (estimated)	square inches

6 How many small triangles would you need to make a figure congruent to the big triangle? ________

7 Show how you would arrange the small triangles.

8 What is the area of the small triangle?

________ square cm

9 What is the area of the big triangle?

________ square cm Lesson 2

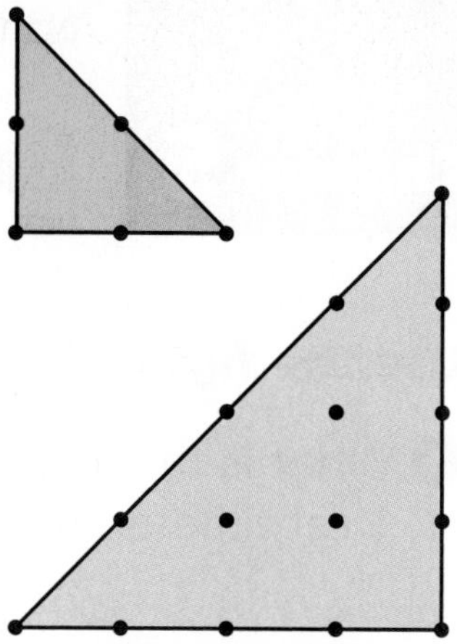

For 10–12, find the length of the missing sides in centimeters. Then find the area and perimeter. Lesson 6

10

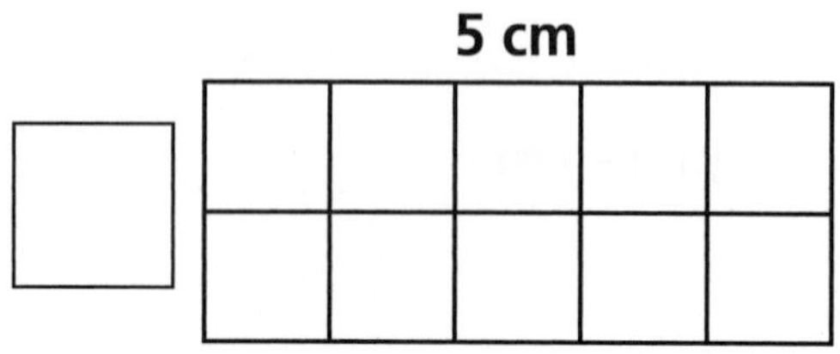

5 cm

perimeter	cm
area	square cm

11

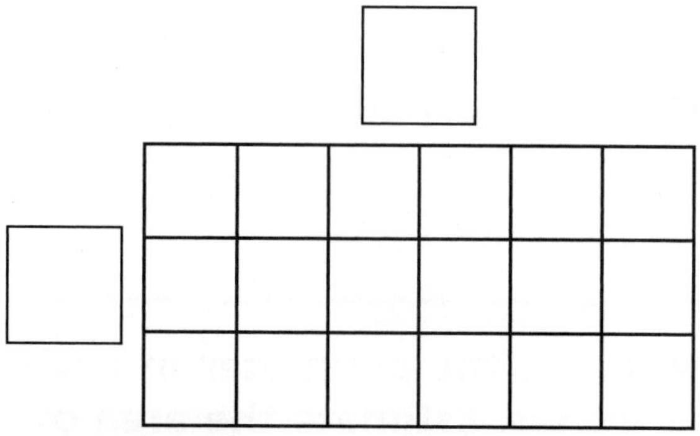

perimeter	
area	

12

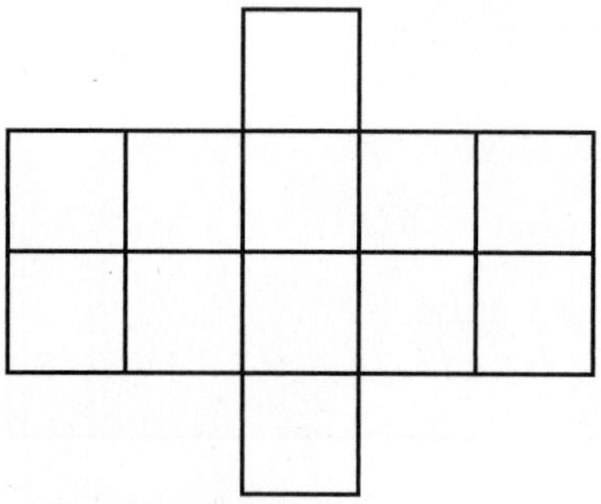

perimeter	
area	

13 What simpler problem could you solve to help you find the area in Problem 12?

____

____

____

____

____

____

____

Chapter 6
Lesson 1

Name ______________________ Date ____________

Multiplication Puzzles

NCTM Standards 1, 2, 6, 7, 8, 9, 10

Complete each puzzle.

1.

×	3
	5

2.

	3
×	
	8

3.

	9
×	
2	

4.

×	6
2	

5.

	7
×	
	9

6.

×	4
2	0

7.

×	4
4	8

8.

×	
2	5

9.

×	8
5	

10.

×	9
	1

11.

1	0
×	
7	

12.

	9
×	
	3

13

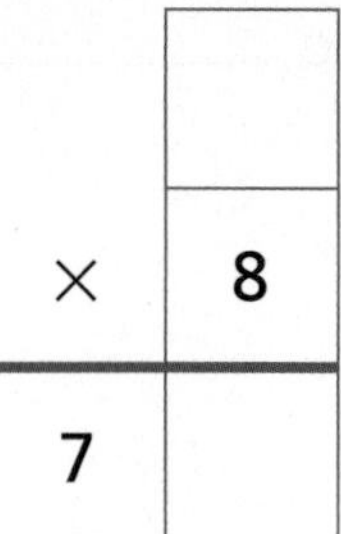

14

8
×
3

15

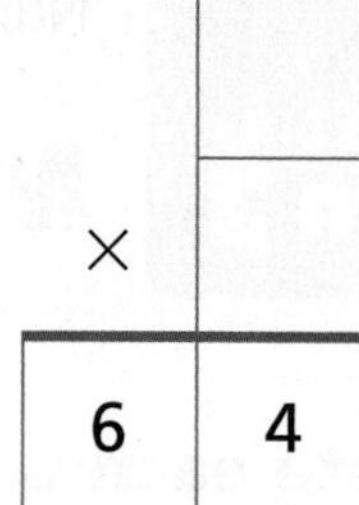

16

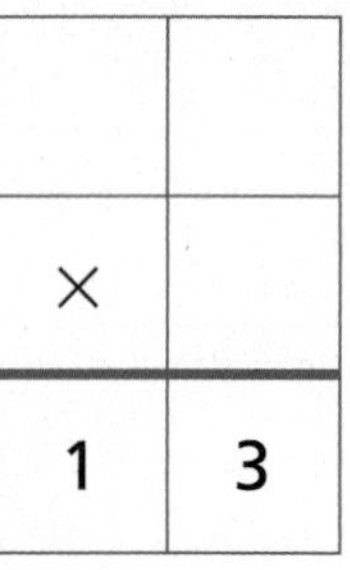

17

3
×
1 5 0

18

7
×
1 1 9

19

5
×
2 0 0

20

3
×
2 1 2

21

5
×
1 7 0

Challenge

22

2 | 2 4 2

23

4
| 9 2 2

24

1 1
5 | 9 0

Name ____________________ Date ____________

Chapter 6
Lesson 2

Multiples of 10 and 100

NCTM Standards 1, 2, 6, 7, 8, 9, 10

Remember the Eraser Store?
They sell erasers, and package 10 erasers in a pack, 10 packs in a box, and 10 boxes in a crate.

Find the number of erasers.

1. 6 packs

5 × 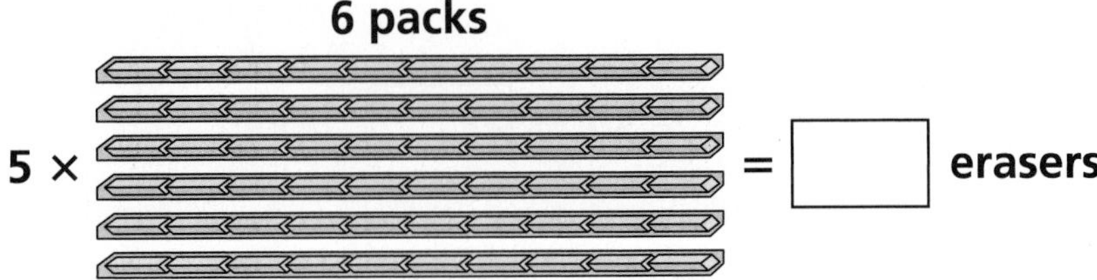 = ☐ erasers

2. 3 packs

8 × ☐ = ☐ erasers

3. 4 packs

4 × ☐ = ☐ erasers

4. ☐ packs

3 × ☐ = 270 erasers

5. 5 packs

☐ × 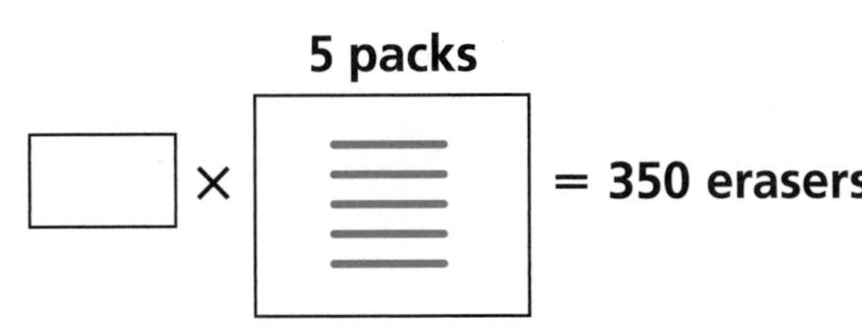 = 350 erasers

6. 7 boxes

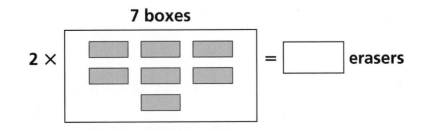

2 × ☐ = ☐ erasers

Find the area of each rectangle.

7. 12 by 10: $10 \times 12 = \square$

8. 15 by 10: $10 \times 15 = \square$

9. 30 by 9: $9 \times 30 = \square$

Find the missing length.

10. 10 by $\square$: $\square \times 10 = 70$

11. $\square$ by 6: $6 \times \square = 120$

12. $\square$ by 10: $10 \times \square = 180$

13. $\square$ by 10: $10 \times \square = 200$

14. **Challenge**

100 by 10: $10 \times 100 = \square$

15. **Challenge**

200 by 20: $20 \times 200 = \square$

Chapter 6
Lesson 3

Name ____________________ Date ____________

Using Arrays to Model Multiplication

NCTM Standards 1, 2, 6, 7, 8, 9, 10

Complete each chart to find the number of squares in each array.

1 3 × 12 = ☐

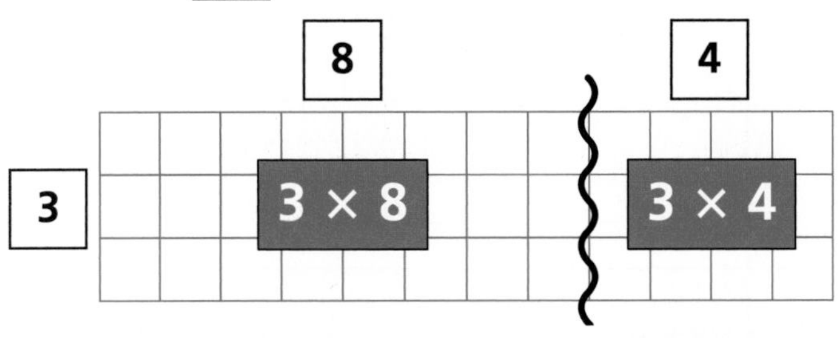

×	8	4	12
3		12	

2 5 × 16 = ☐

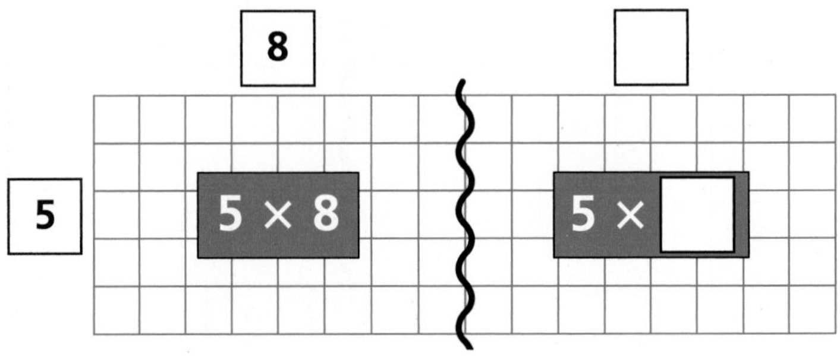

×	8	8	
5			

3 14 × 6 = ☐

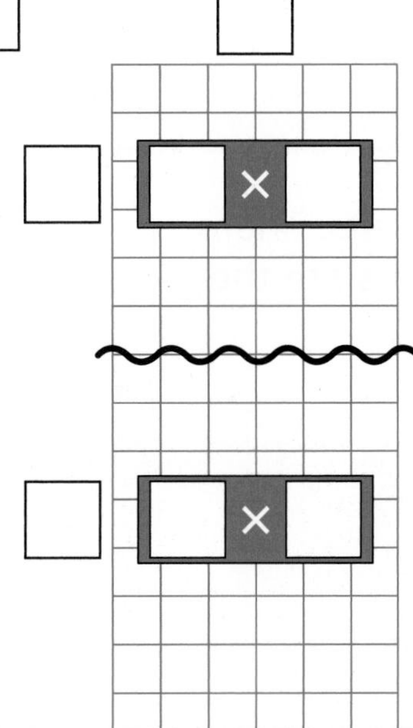

×	6
6	
8	

4 $15 \times 7 =$ ☐

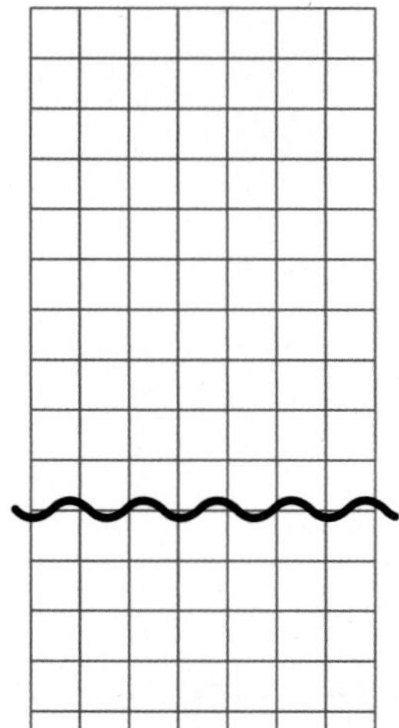

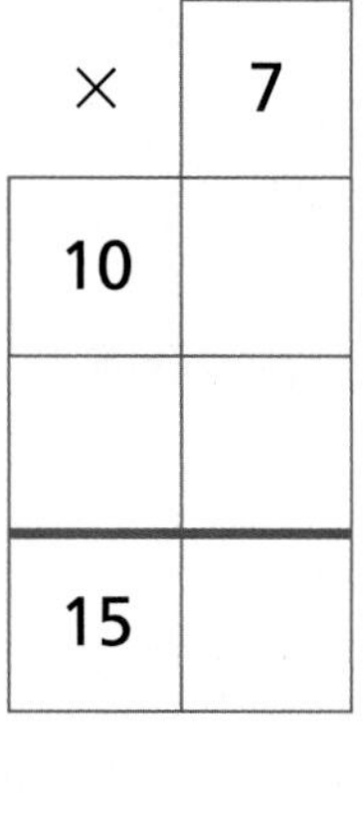

5 $17 \times 9 =$ ☐

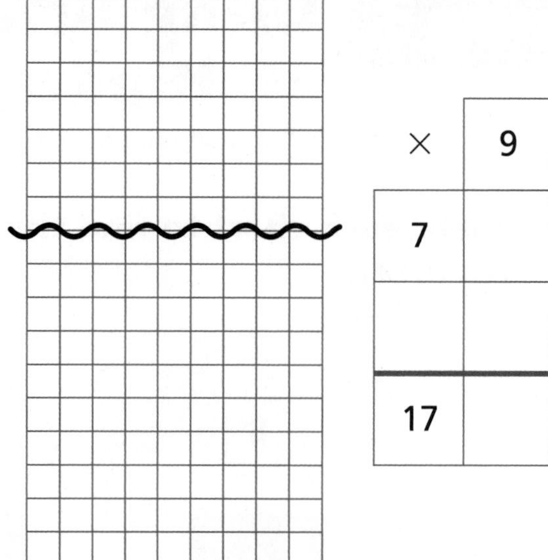

6 $8 \times 13 =$ ☐

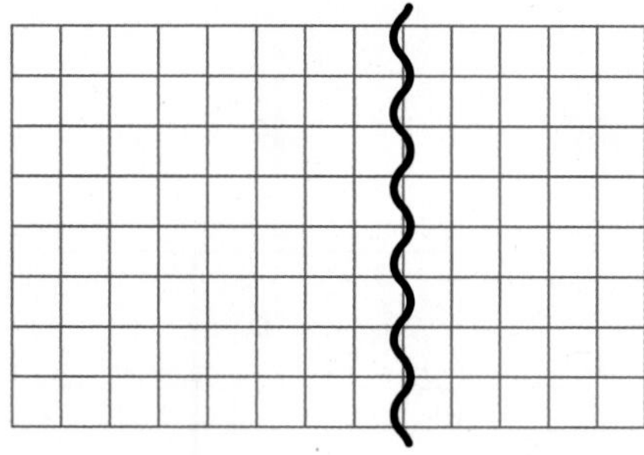

×			13
8			

7 $7 \times 16 =$ 112

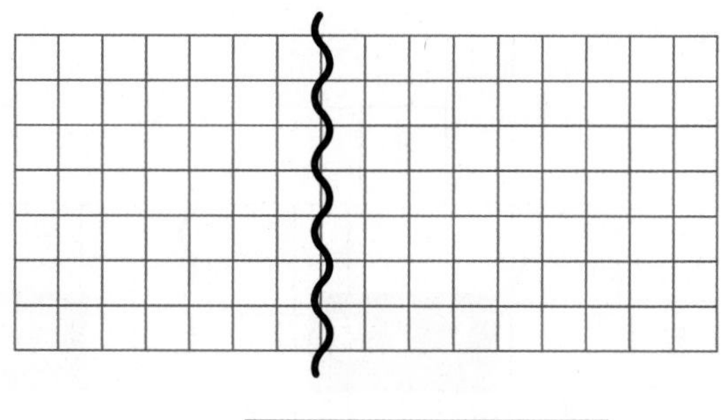

×			16
7			

8 **Challenge** A theater has 12 rows of seats. There are 18 seats in each row. How many seats are there?

☐ seats

Name ______________________ Date ____________

Chapter 6

Lesson 4

Splitting Larger Arrays

NCTM Standards 1, 2, 6, 7, 8, 9, 10

Use the arrays and charts to solve the multiplication problems.

1. $9 \times 8 = \square$

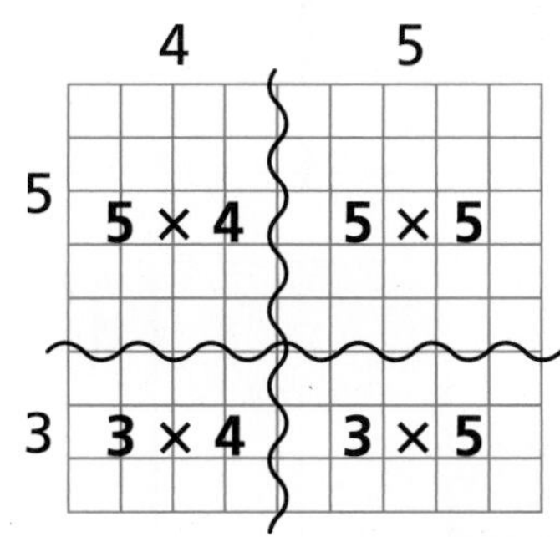

×	4	5	9
5	20		
3			
8			

2. $15 \times 7 = \square$

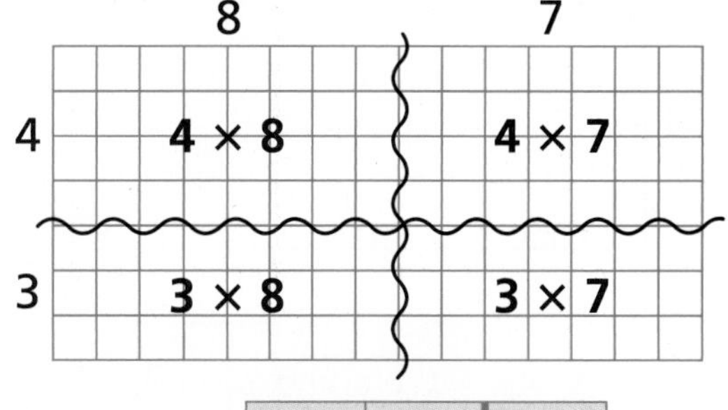

×	8	7	
4			
3			
7			

3. $17 \times 6 = \square$

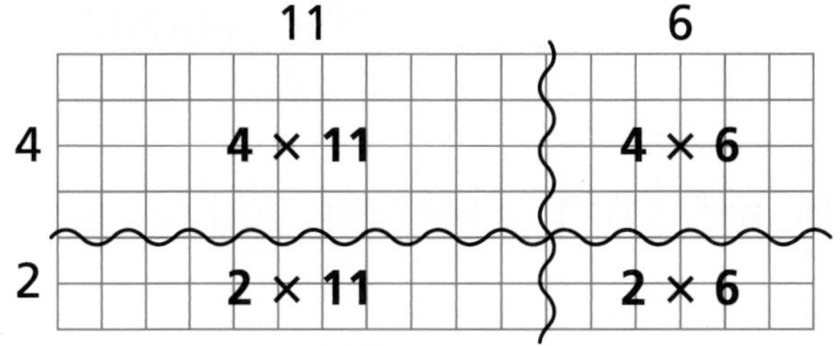

×	11	6	
4			
2			

4. $19 \times 9 = \square$

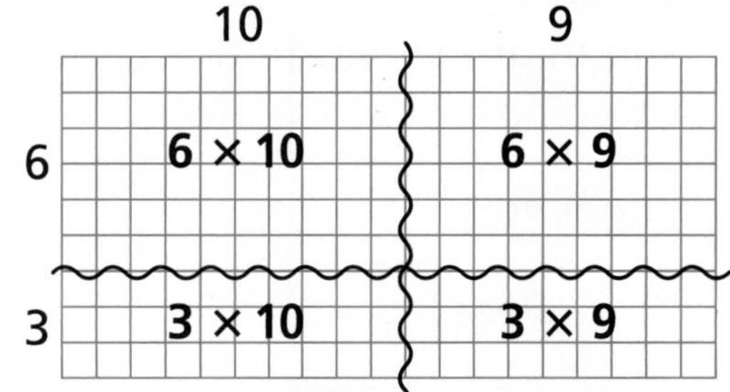

×	10	9	
6			
3			

5 $19 \times 18 =$ ☐

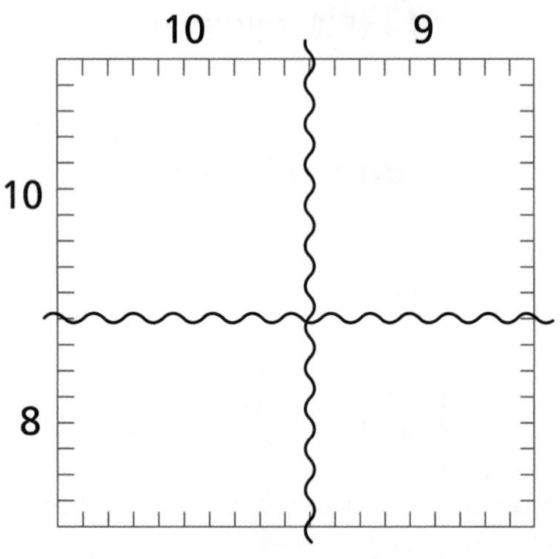

×		9	19
8			
18			

6 $16 \times 14 =$ ☐

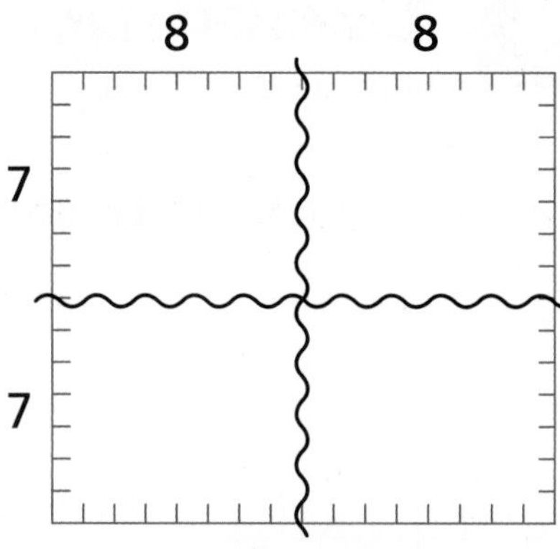

×		8	16
7			
14			

7 Challenge Jenna is planting a garden that is 11 feet long and 18 feet wide. She wants to plant peas, tomatoes, melons, and onions in separate rectangular sections. Suggest a way she might separate the garden to match the diagram at the right.

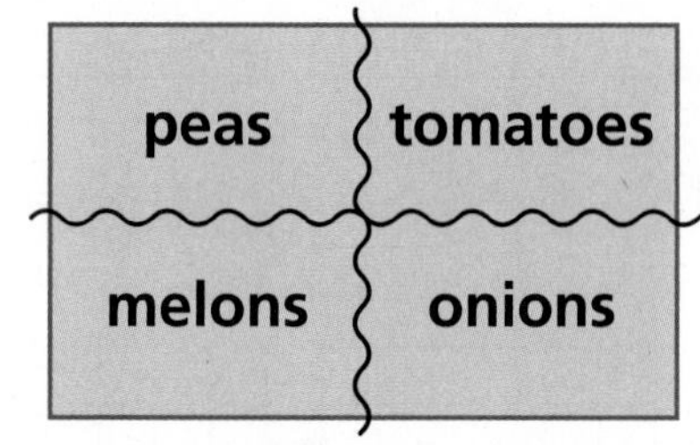

Find the areas of the sections you suggest.

Areas for:

Peas ☐

Tomatoes ☐

Melons ☐

Onions ☐

Total ☐

×			18
11			

Chapter 6
Lesson 5

Name ______________________ Date ____________

Choosing Simpler Problems

NCTM Standards 1, 2, 6, 7, 8, 9, 10

Solve the multiplication problems.

$19 \times 11 = \square$

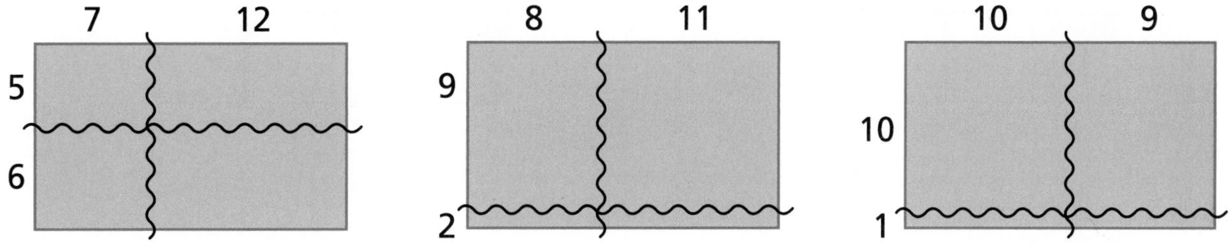

7, 12; 5, 6

8, 11; 9, 2

10, 9; 10, 1

1

×	7	12	19
5	35		
6			
11			

2

×	8	11	19
9			
2			
11			

3

×	10	9	19
10			
1			

$17 \times 16 = \square$

4

×	11	6	17
8			

5

×	10	7	
6			
16			

6

×	9	8	
9			
7			

7 $16 \times 16 = \square$

×			16
16			

8 $13 \times 19 = \square$

×			

9 $14 \times 17 = \square$

×			

10 $17 \times 18 = \square$

×			

11 **Challenge** Explain why you decided to fill in the chart in Problem 10 the way you did.

____

____

____

____

Chapter 6
Lesson 6

Name ______________________ Date ____________

From Charts to Vertical Records

NCTM Standards 1, 2, 6, 7, 8, 9, 10

Fill in the boxes to complete each problem.

1 $18 \times 6 =$ ☐

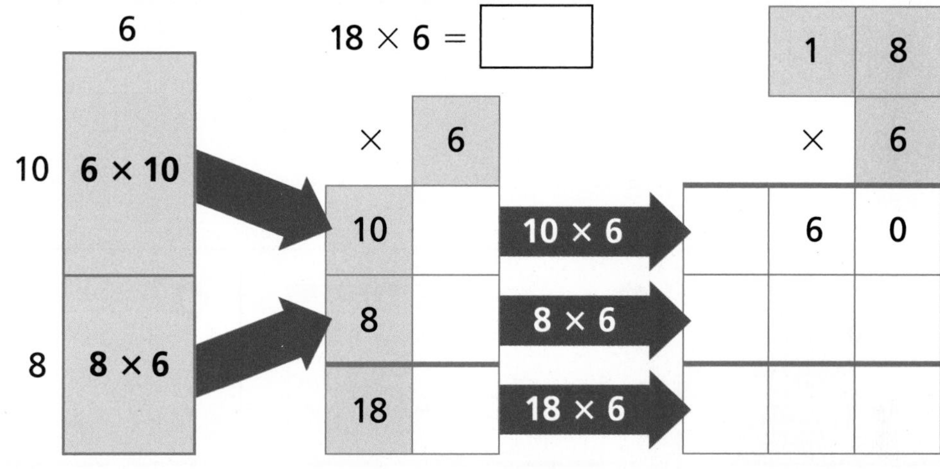

2 $30 \times 14 =$ ☐

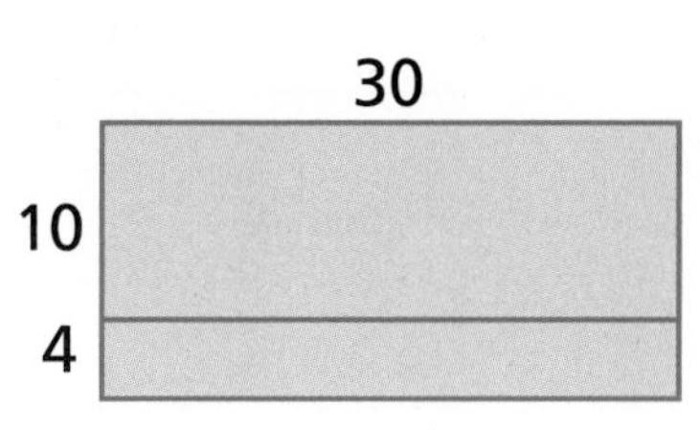

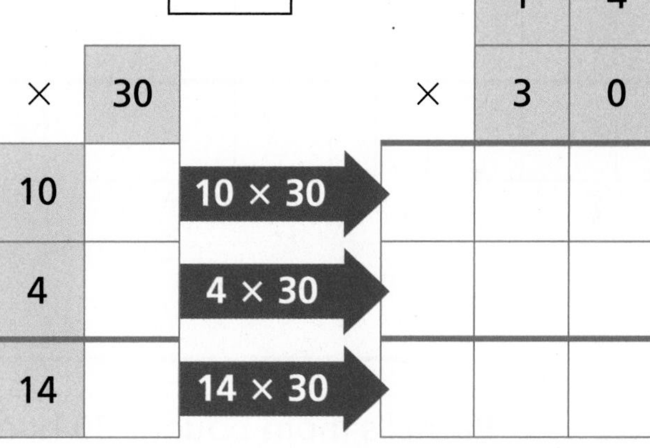

3 $18 \times 60 =$ ☐

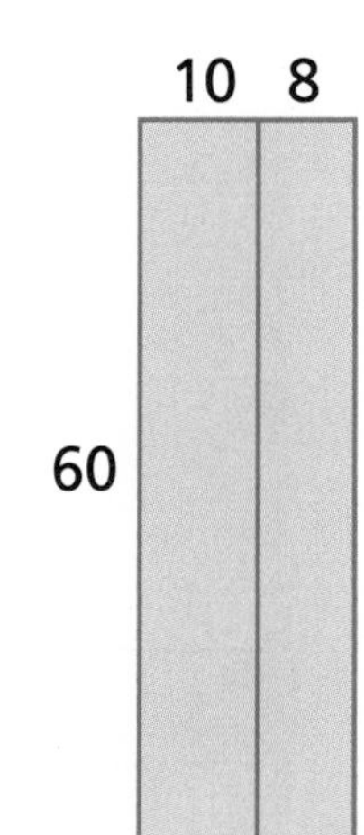

×	10	8	18
60			

		1	8
	×	6	0

4

		1	6
	×	2	0

5

		4	0
	×	1	7

6

		2	5
	×	6	0

7

		5	0
	×	3	8

8

		8	0
	×	1	9

9

		4	1
	×	9	0

10 Challenge Rachel's mom bought 30 books at the book fair. Ten of the books cost \$12 each, and the rest of the books cost \$11 each. How much did she spend?

\$

Name ______________________ Date __________

Chapter 6

Lesson 7

Recording Your Process of Multiplication

NCTM Standards 1, 2, 6, 7, 8, 9, 10

Use the chart and vertical record to help you complete each problem.

1. 13 × 18 = ☐

×	10	3	13
10	100		
8			
18			

		1	3
	×	1	8
10 × 10 →	1	0	0
3 × 10 →			
10 × 8 →			
3 × 8 →			
13 × 18 →			

2. 23 × 14 = ☐

×	20	3	23
4			
10			
14			

		2	3
	×	1	4
20 × 4 →			
→			
→			
→			
23 × 14 →			

Find the products. Record your work in the boxes below each problem.

3

		2	7
×		1	6

4

		3	8
×		4	3

5

		2	6
×		5	4

6

		6	7
×		6	8

7

		6	8
×		6	8

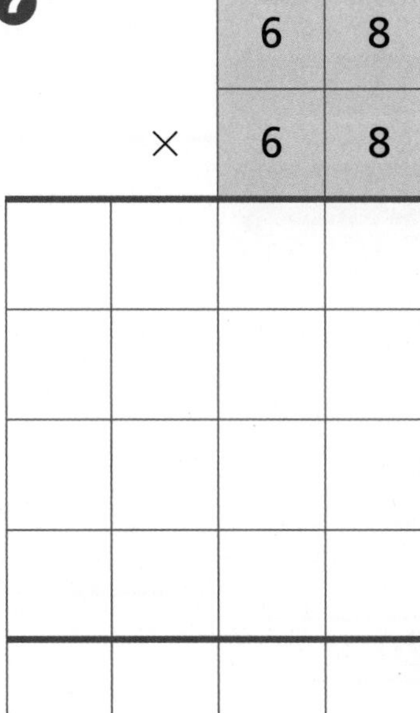

8

		6	7
×		6	9

9 Challenge 86 people came to the school car wash. The charge for having your car washed was $12. The students spent $150 on supplies. How much money did they make, after paying for supplies?

$ ______

Chapter 6
Lesson 8

Name ______________________ Date ____________

Checking for Reasonable Answers

NCTM Standards 1, 2, 6, 7, 8, 9, 10

Look for ways to make the multiplication easier. Record as much of your work as you need.

1. 67×23

2. 35×26

3. 32×65

4. 52×18

5. 84×76

6. 76×84

7

		6	7
	×	3	8

8

		6	7
	×	4	8

9

		6	7
	×	5	8

10

		8	4
	×	8	7

11

		1	8	4
		×	8	7

12 **Challenge** Amy tried 1,904 × 21 and got 70,085 as the answer. Describe one quick way to show this is NOT correct, without doing the whole problem.

____

____

____

Name ______________________ Date __________

Chapter 6
Lesson 9

Multiplication Situations

NCTM Standards 1, 2, 6, 7, 8, 9, 10

All of these problems can be solved using the same numbers. Fill in the missing numbers.

1. The kitchen floor is 25 tiles long 16 tiles wide.

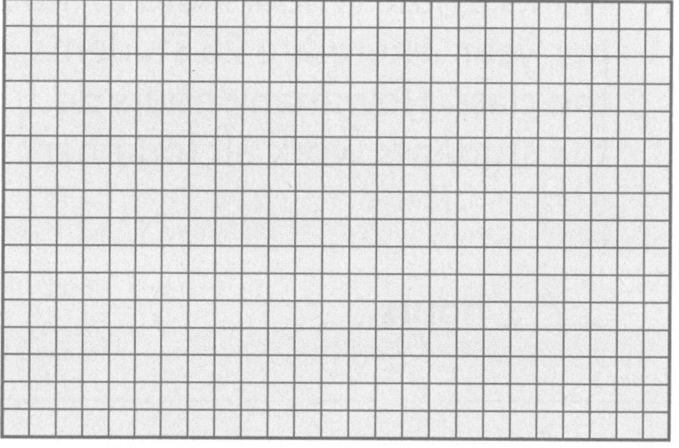

[ ] tiles are on the kitchen floor.

2. I have 16 quarters. How much money do I have?

[ ]

3. There are 400 ounces in _____ pounds.
   16 ounces = 1 pound

4. A bakery made _____ cakes and cut each cake into 25 pieces. There were 400 pieces to sell.

5. There are 16 classes in the school. Each class has [ ] students. There are 400 students in the school.

6. Write another problem that can be solved using $16 \times 25 = 400$.

____

____

____

Ms. Johnson's students raise money for charity at the school store. They sell school supplies to the other students. Solve these problems about the store.

SCHOOL STORE	
Eraser ....19¢	Pencil ....34¢
Black Pen ......47¢	Red Pen ....96¢

7 A box of markers costs 24 times as much as one eraser. How much does a box of markers cost?

____

8 Each student in Ms. Johnson's class works at the school store 27 hours per year. There are 26 students in the class. How many hours do the students work all together?

_____ hours

9 Ms. Yee bought 37 pencils and 26 erasers. How much did she pay?

____

10 Red pens come in packs of 48 pens. How much would an entire pack cost?

____

11 **Challenge** One morning, **17 students** each bought **one black pen**. How much money did they spend all together?

____

12 **Challenge** The school store earned **$28** this week. The store is open **34 weeks** per year. If the store earns this much money every week, how much money will it earn?

____

Name ______________________ Date ____________

Chapter 6
Lesson 10

Problem Solving Strategy

Guess and Check

NCTM Standards 1, 2, 6, 7, 8, 9, 10

Understand
Plan
Solve
Check

1. The sum of two numbers is 25, and their product is 156. What are the numbers?

☐ and ☐

2. All of Laura's 105 books are on 3 shelves. Each shelf has 5 more books than the shelf above it. How many books are on each shelf?

3. Eight friends shared $192 equally. How much money did each friend get?

☐

Problem Solving Test Prep

Choose the correct answer.

1. What is the weight of box X on the scale?

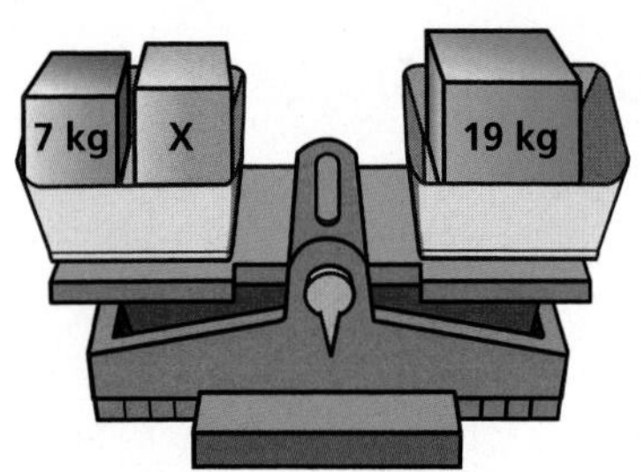

A. 26 kg **C.** 12 kg
B. 25 kg **D.** 11 kg

2. What product can you find using the array?

×		9	
10	100	90	
	20	18	

A. 10×9 **C.** 12×19
B. 10×12 **D.** 19×28

3. Which number completes the magic square?

4	20	9
16	11	6
13	2	■

A. 18 **C.** 15
B. 17 **D.** 14

4. Which set of measures is ordered correctly from least to greatest?

A. 3 pints, 2 quarts, 5 cups
B. 1 gallon, 6 quarts, 11 cups
C. 2 gallons, 9 quarts, 24 cups
D. 1 gallon, 5 quarts, 21 cups

Show What You Know

Solve each problem. Explain your answer.

5. Ralph has 20 coins. He makes 4 stacks so that each stack has a different number of coins. What is the largest number of coins he could put in any stack? Explain.

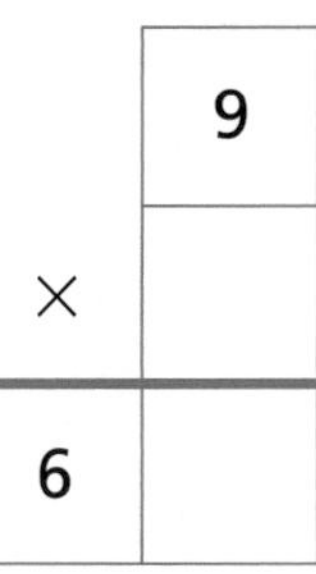

Name ______________________ Date ____________

Review/Assessment

NCTM Standards 1, 2, 6, 7, 8, 9, 10

Solve. Lessons 1 and 2

1.

	9
×	
6	

2.

	7
×	
3	

3. $6 \times 7 = \square$

$6 \times 70 = \square$

$60 \times 7 = \square$

$60 \times 70 = \square$

4. Use the array and the chart to solve the problem. Lessons 3, 4, and 5

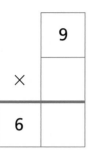

$18 \times 26 = \square$

	20			
10				

×			

	1	8
×	2	6

Find the product. Lessons 6, 7, and 8

5

		4	3
	×	4	3

6

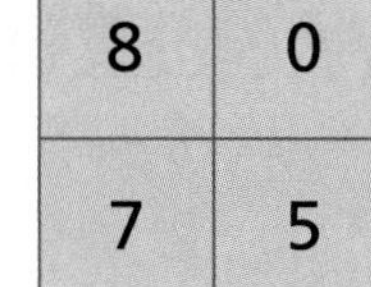

7

	2	3
×	1	3

Solve. Lesson 9

8 Stephen read for 30 minutes each night. He read 13 pages per night. How many pages had he read after 14 nights?

__________ pages

9 Julie unpacked 22 boxes of library books. Evan unpacked 19 boxes of library books. Each box held 28 books. How many books did they unpack?

__________ books

10 Mr. Myer's class is planning a field trip to the science center. Twelve students and six adults will be on the trip. The total cost for tickets will be $216. Each adult ticket costs $3 more than each student ticket. How much is each student tickets? Explain your answer.

____

____

Chapter 7
Lesson 1

Name ______________________ Date ____________

Exploring Fractions

NCTM Standards 1, 2, 6, 7, 8, 9, 10

Make the pictures and fractions match.
Each whole rectangle = 1.

1
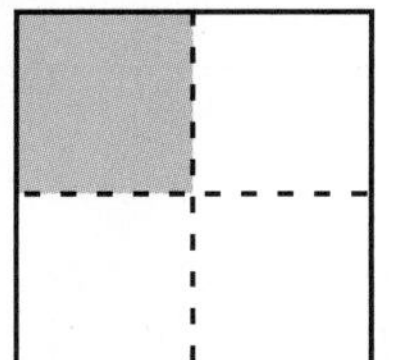

$\frac{1}{\square}$

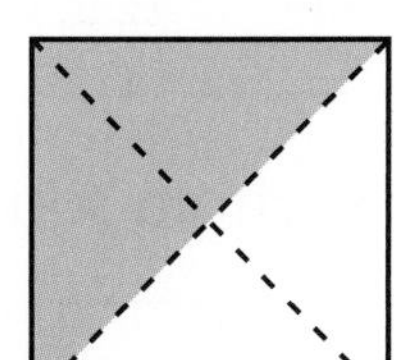

$\frac{\square}{4}$

$\frac{1}{2}$

2
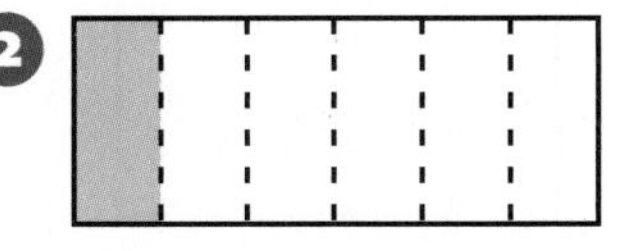

$\frac{1}{6}$

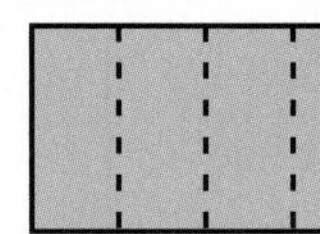

$\frac{\square}{\square}$

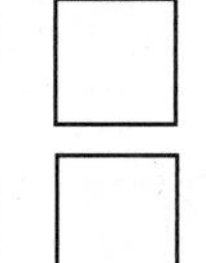

$\frac{6}{6}$

$\frac{1}{2}$

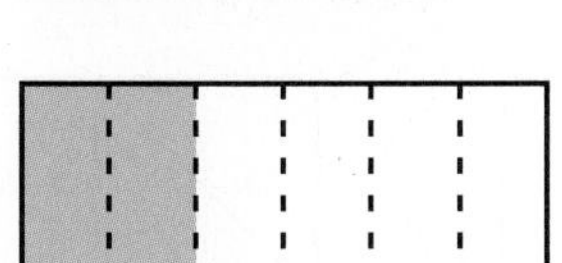

$\frac{\square}{3}$

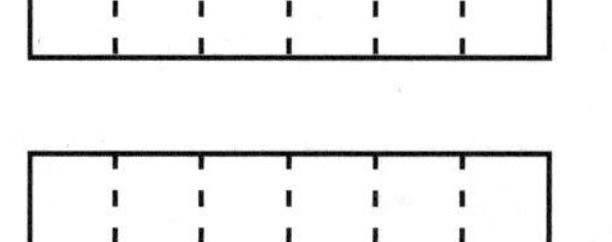

$\frac{2}{3}$

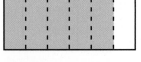

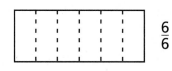

3 Separate each picture into **thirds.**

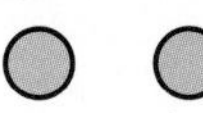

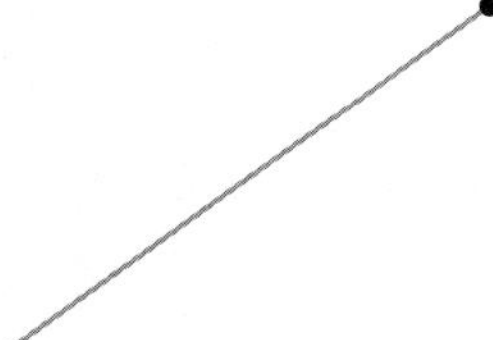
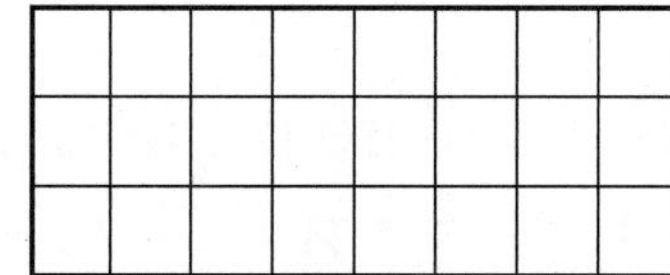

4 Separate each picture into **fourths.**

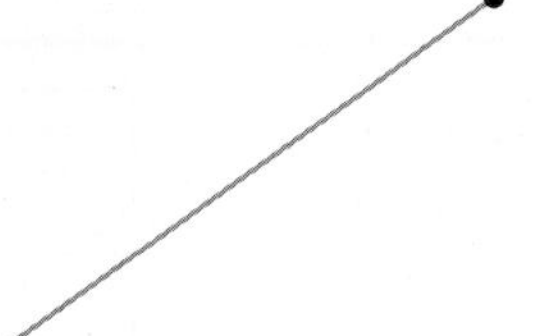
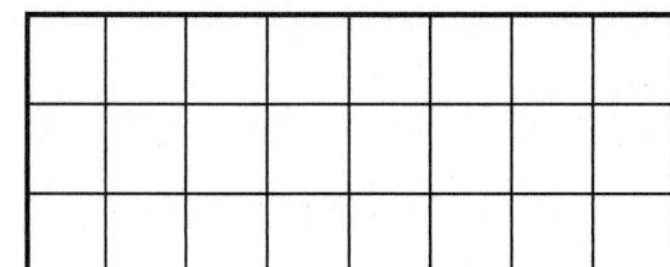

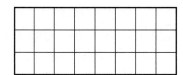

5 Separate each picture into **sixths.**

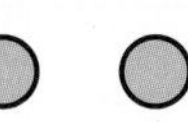
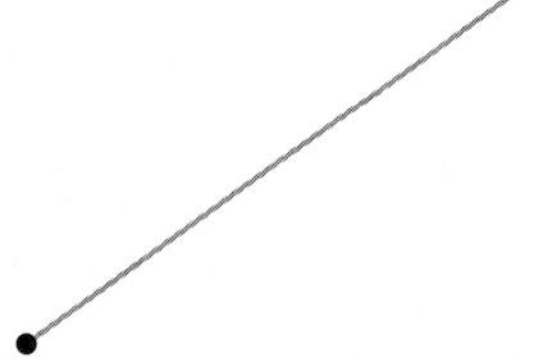

6 Make the pictures and fractions match.

$\frac{1}{2}$ $\frac{1}{3}$ $\frac{\square}{\square}$ $\frac{2}{3}$

7 Name the fraction for each part. Each whole square = 1.

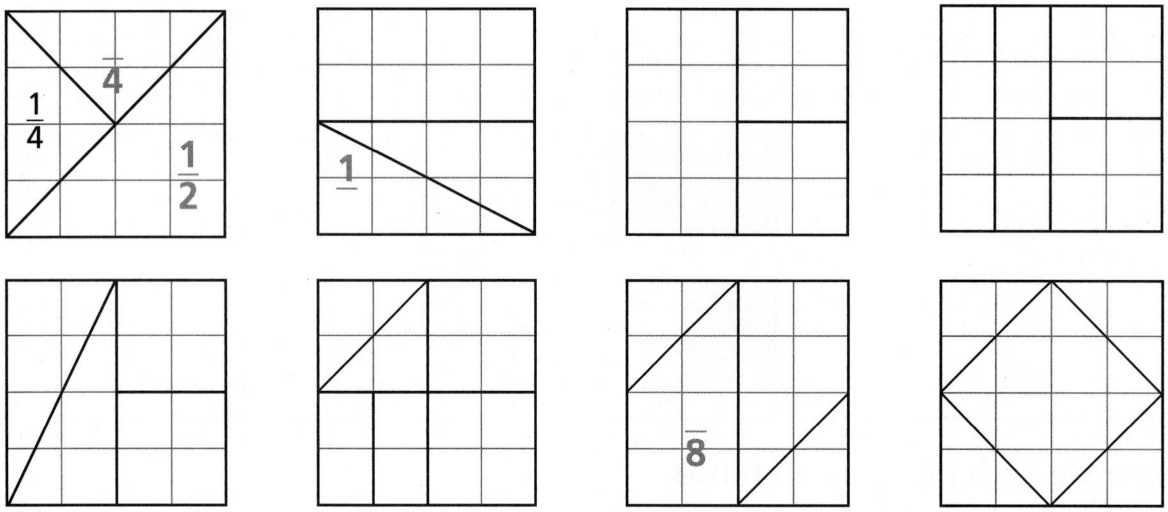

$\frac{1}{4}$ $\frac{}{4}$ $\frac{1}{2}$

$\frac{1}{}$

$\frac{}{8}$

8 Two of these pictures are not cut into quarters. Cross them out.

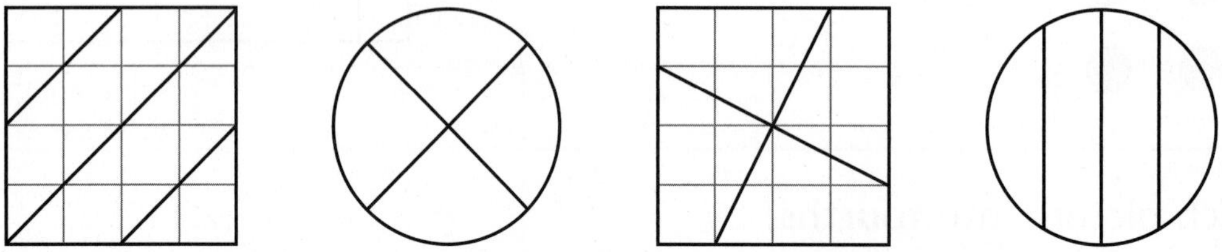

9 **Challenge** Use a picture to show which fraction is greater, $\frac{3}{8}$ or $\frac{1}{2}$. Explain how you decided.

$\frac{\square}{\square}$ is greater than $\frac{\square}{\square}$

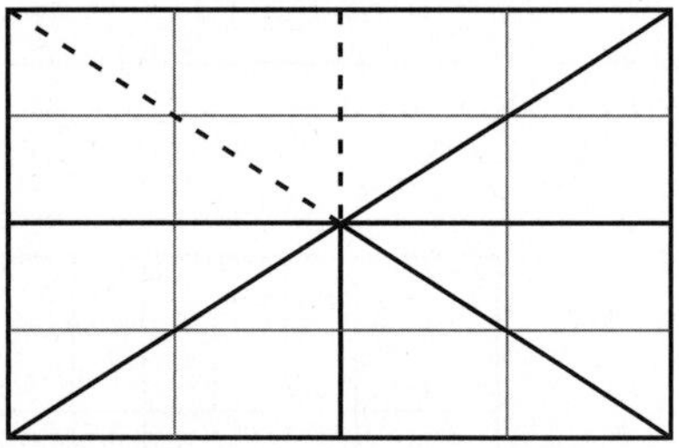

Chapter 7
Lesson 2

Name ______________________ Date ______________

Exploring Fractions Greater than 1

NCTM Standards 1, 2, 6, 7, 8, 9, 10

To solve the problems on this page, use these four pattern block shapes.

R

1 If  is 1

then  is ______

 is ______

 is ______

2 If B is 1

then  is ______

Y is ______

R is ______

3 If  is 1

then  is ______

R is ______

Y is ______

4 If R is 1

then  is ______

B is ______

Y is ______

For the problems on this page,  **is 1.**

Use pattern blocks if you like.

5  is $\frac{1}{2} + \frac{1}{3}$ is $\frac{\square}{6}$

6 B B is $\frac{\square}{\square} + \frac{\square}{\square}$ is $\frac{\square}{\square}$

7 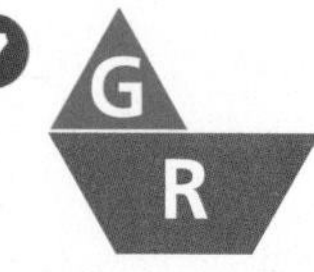

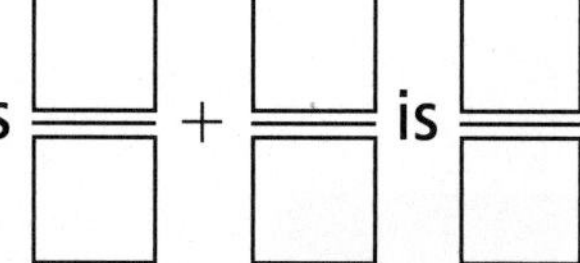

8 

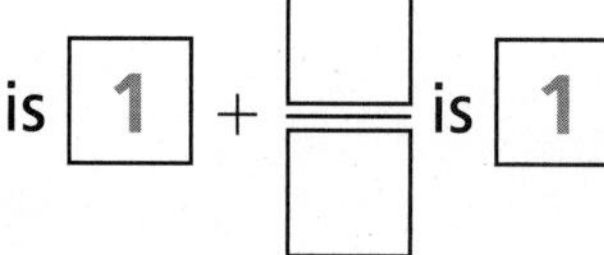

9 

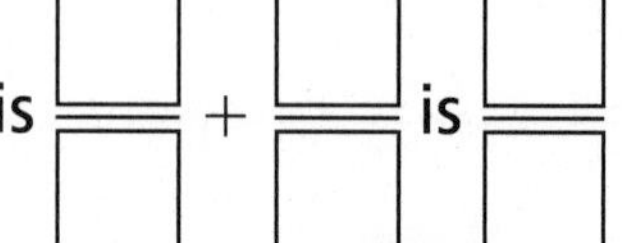

10 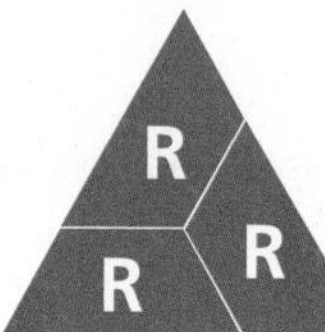

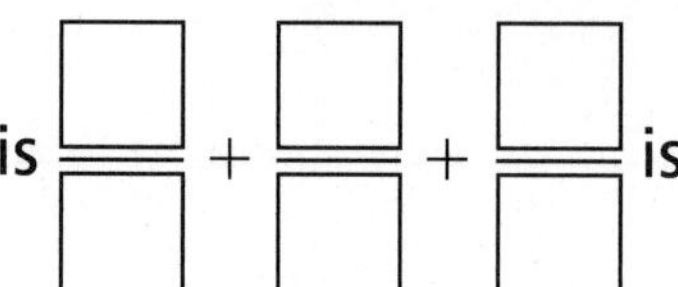

11 Challenge Create your own design that is equal to $3\frac{1}{2}$, or $\frac{7}{2}$.

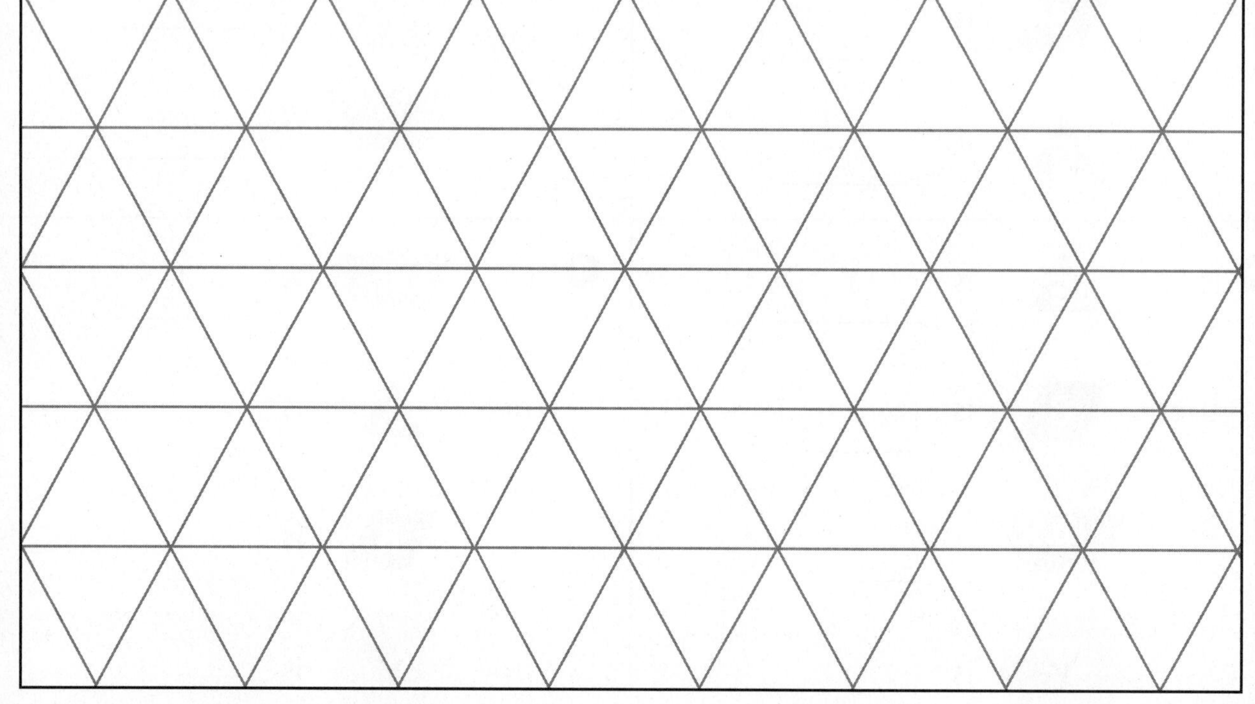

Chapter 7
Lesson 3

Name ______________________ Date ____________

Exploring Fractions with Cuisenaire® Rods

NCTM Standards 1, 2, 6, 7, 8, 9, 10

All the problems on this page involve Cuisenaire® Rods.

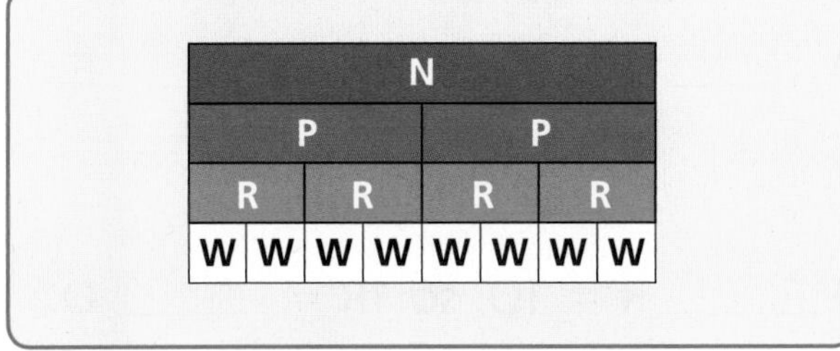

D
G G
R R R
W W W W W W

1 If N is 1, then

P is ______.

R is ______.

W is ______.

2 If P is 1, then

R is ______.

W is ______.

N is ______.

3 If G is 1, then

W is ______.

R is ______.

D is ______.

4 If D is 1, then

G is ______.

W is ______.

R is ______.

5 If R is 1, then

W is ______.

R is ______.

G is ______.

P is ______.

Y is ______.

D is ______.

K is ______.

N is ______.

E is ______.

O is ______.

W
R
G
P
Y
D
K
N
E
O

All the problems on this page involve Cuisenaire® Rods.

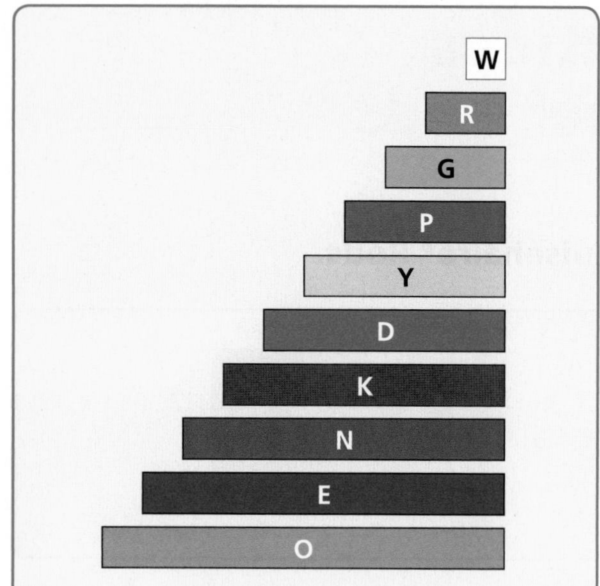

6. $\frac{1}{2}$ of R = 1W, so 1R = _______ W.

7. $\frac{1}{3}$ of G = 1W, so 1G = _______ W.

8. $\frac{1}{2}$ of D = 1G, so 1D = _______ G.

9. $\frac{1}{4}$ of P = 1W, so 1P = _______ W.

10. _______ R = 1N, so 1R = $\frac{1}{4}$ N.

11. _______ N = 1P, so 1N = _______ P.

12. _______ G = 1E, so 1G = _______ E.

13. _______ R = 1O, so 1R = _______ O.

14. 1W = _______ P, so 3W = _______ P.

15. 1R = _______ D, so 2R = _______ D.

16. _______ G = $\frac{1}{3}$ E, so 2G = $\frac{2}{3}$ E.

17. 1R = _______ O, so 3R = _______ O.

18. **Challenge** Find a rod that is exactly $\frac{2}{5}$ of another rod. Explain how you found your answer.

____

____

____

____

Name ______________________ Date ____________

Chapter 7

Lesson 4

Reasoning About Cuisenaire® Rod Fractions

NCTM Standards 1, 2, 6, 7, 8, 9, 10

All the problems on this page involve Cuisenaire® Rods.

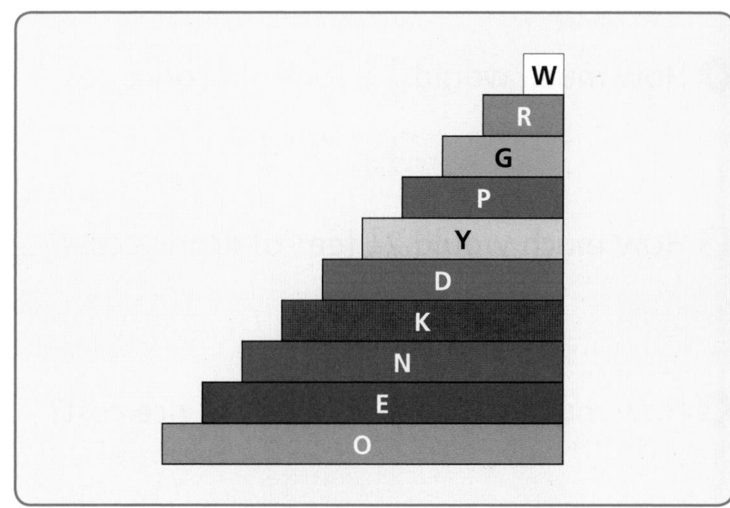

1. If W is $1\frac{1}{2}$, then

   R is ________.

   G is ________.

   P is ________.

   N is ________.

   E is ________.

   O is ________.

   G + O is ________.

   P + E is ________.

2. If G is $1\frac{1}{2}$, then

   W is ________.

   R is ________.

   P is ________.

   Y is ________.

   D is ________.

   K is ________.

   O is ________.

   Y × 2 is ________.

3. If D is 2, then

   W is ________.

   R is ________.

   G is ________.

   P is ________.

   Y is ________.

   O is ________.

   R + N is ________.

   G + K is ________.

Use the price chart to answer the questions below.

2 feet of licorice	**$1.00**	**$2\frac{1}{2}$ feet of string**	**$1.50**
2 pounds of rice	**$2.00**	**3 bags of peanuts**	**$0.99**

4 How much would $\frac{1}{2}$ a foot of licorice cost? ________

5 How much would $2\frac{1}{2}$ feet of licorice cost? ________

6 How much would $1\frac{1}{2}$ pounds of rice cost? ________

7 How much would 3 feet of string cost? ________

8 How much would 4 bags of peanuts cost? ________

9 **Challenge** Licorice is on sale!

If you buy at least 3 feet of licorice, every $1\frac{1}{2}$ feet costs only 60¢.

How much would 7 feet of licorice cost? Explain how you found the answer.

____

____

____

Chapter 7

Lesson 5 Fractions of a Foot

Name ______________________ Date ____________

NCTM Standards 1, 2, 6, 7, 8, 9, 10

What fraction of each picture is shaded?
What fraction is not shaded?

1

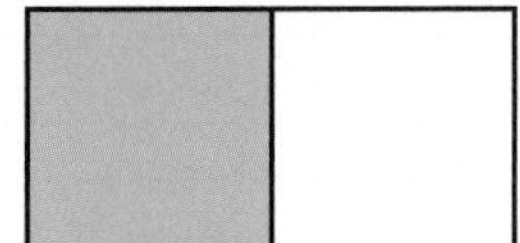

shaded not shaded

$\frac{\square}{2}$ $\frac{\square}{\square}$

2

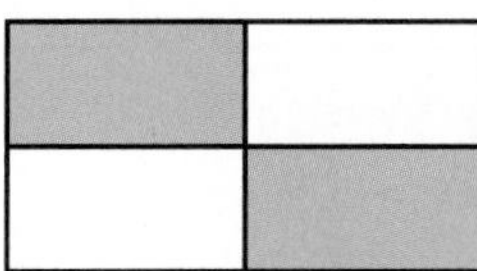

shaded not shaded

$\frac{\square}{4}$ $\frac{\square}{\square}$

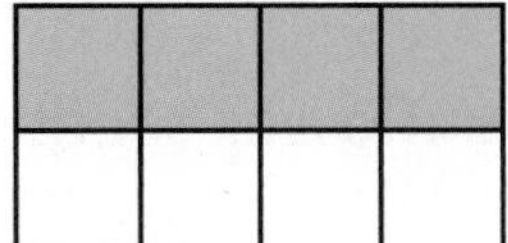

shaded not shaded

$\frac{\square}{8}$ $\frac{\square}{\square}$

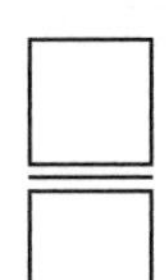

4

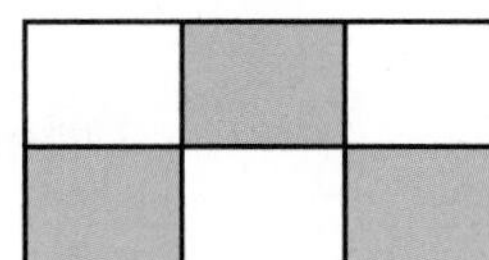

shaded not shaded

$\frac{3}{\square}$ $\frac{\square}{\square}$

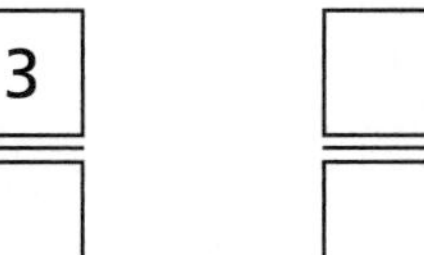

5

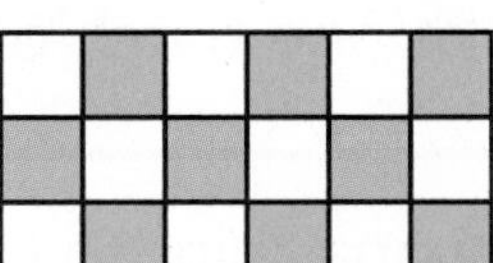

shaded not shaded

$\frac{\square}{\square}$ $\frac{\square}{\square}$

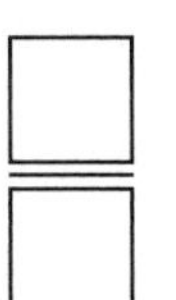

6

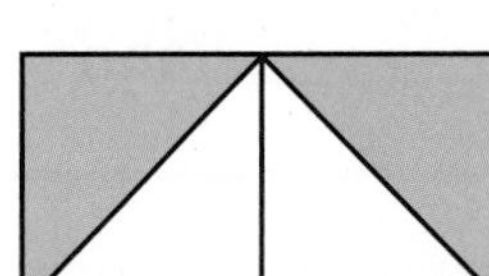

shaded not shaded

$\frac{\square}{\square}$ $\frac{\square}{\square}$

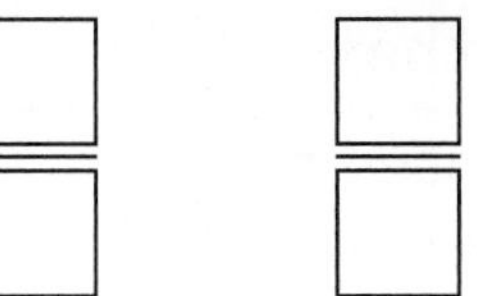

7 Record all of the fractions above, and complete the others so that they all represent one half.

$\frac{1}{2}$ $\frac{2}{4}$ $\frac{3}{\square}$ $\frac{\square}{8}$ $\frac{10}{\square}$ $\frac{9}{\square}$ $\frac{\square}{40}$ $\frac{\square}{100}$ $\frac{\square}{98}$

8 Nick is going to make some trail mix, but he's not sure how many batches he wants to make. Complete this table for him to use:

Number of Batches	1	$\frac{1}{2}$	2	3	4	$4\frac{1}{2}$
Granola	1 c	$\frac{1}{2}$ c	c	c	c	c
Dried Apricots	$\frac{1}{2}$ c	c	c	c	c	c
Sunflower Seeds	$\frac{2}{3}$ c	c	c	c	c	c
Raisins	$\frac{1}{4}$ c	c	c	c	c	c
Chocolate Chips	$\frac{1}{3}$ c	c	c	c	c	c

9 Nick decided to make just **one** batch of trail mix. Here is what he has in his kitchen:

Granola . . . $\frac{9}{10}$ c **Dried apricots** . . . $\frac{8}{16}$ c **Sunflower seeds** . . . $\frac{4}{6}$ c
Raisins . . . $\frac{7}{8}$ c **Chocolate chips** . . . $\frac{1}{5}$ c

Nick has enough ____________, ____________, and ____________ to make one batch of trail mix. He needs to buy more ____________ and ____________ to make one batch of trail mix.

10 Challenge Nick decided to add **10** ounces of banana chips to each batch.

Number of Batches	1	$\frac{1}{2}$	2	4		$\frac{1}{10}$			$3\frac{1}{2}$
Ounces of Banana Chips	10				30		100	70	

How could you use this chart to figure out how many ounces of banana chips Nick should add to $1\frac{1}{2}$ batches of trail mix?

____

____

Chapter 7
Lesson 6

Name ______________________ Date ______________

Comparing Fractions with $\frac{1}{2}$

NCTM Standards 1, 2, 6, 7, 8, 9, 10

1 Complete each fraction so that it equals $\frac{1}{2}$.

$\frac{1}{2}$ $\frac{2}{4}$ $\frac{\_\_}{10}$ $\frac{\_\_}{50}$

$\frac{6}{\_\_}$ $\frac{\_\_}{16}$

$\frac{3}{\_\_}$ $\frac{4}{\_\_}$ $\frac{\_\_}{20}$

Use <, >, or = to compare each fraction with $\frac{1}{2}$.

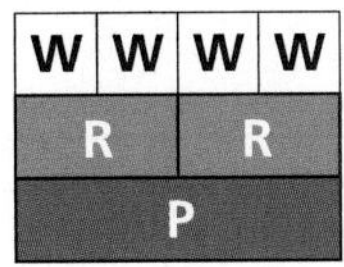

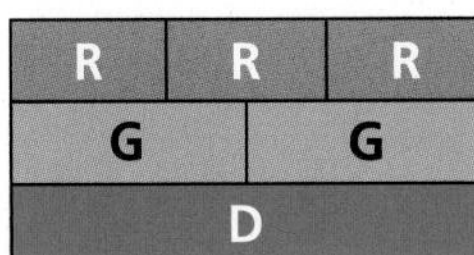

2 $\frac{1}{2} \bigcirc \frac{3}{4}$ (<)

3 $\frac{1}{2} \bigcirc \frac{2}{4}$

4 $\frac{1}{2} \bigcirc \frac{0}{4}$

5 $\frac{1}{2} \bigcirc \frac{2}{3}$

6 $\frac{1}{2} \bigcirc \frac{1}{2}$

7 $\frac{1}{2} \bigcirc \frac{3}{3}$

8 $\frac{15}{16}$ ◯ $\frac{1}{2}$

9 $\frac{8}{16}$ ◯ $\frac{1}{2}$

10 $\frac{1}{2}$ ◯ $\frac{7}{16}$

11 $\frac{14}{28}$ ◯ $\frac{1}{2}$

12 $\frac{2}{5}$ ◯ $\frac{1}{2}$

13 $\frac{5}{8}$ ◯ $\frac{1}{2}$

14 On Monday, $\frac{5}{9}$ inch of rain fell. On Tuesday, $\frac{2}{3}$ inch of rain fell. On Wednesday, $\frac{1}{2}$ inch of rain fell. On which day did the most rain fall? Use Cuisenaire® Rods to help you solve this problem. Explain your answer.

____

____

____

____

____

____

____

15 **Challenge** Show three different ways to shade $\frac{5}{10}$ of the rectangle.

Chapter 7

Lesson 7

Name ______________________ Date ______________

Comparing Fractions

NCTM Standards 1, 2, 6, 7, 8, 9, 10

Compare the fractions using <, =, or >.
Use Cuisenaire® Rods or pattern blocks if you like.

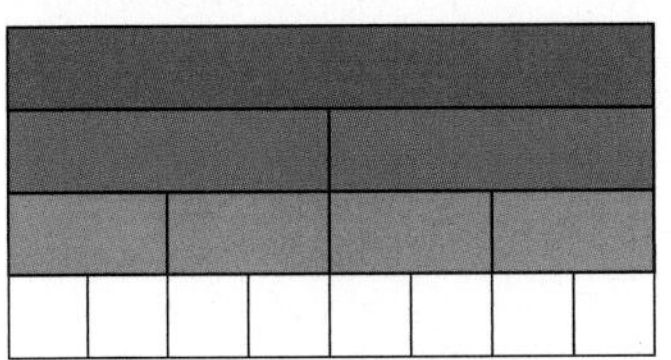

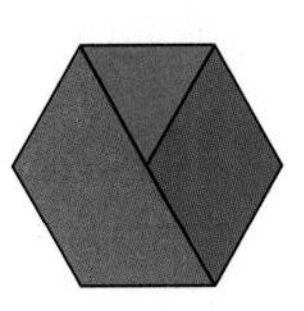

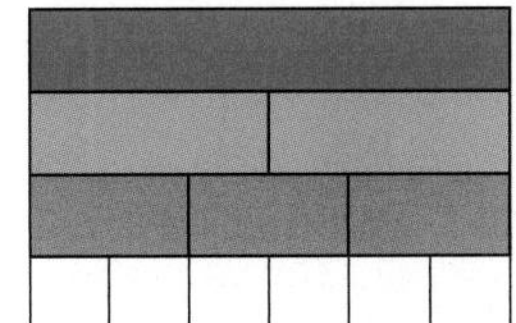

1

$\frac{1}{2}$ ◯ $\frac{1}{4}$

$\frac{2}{4}$ ◯ $\frac{1}{2}$

$\frac{3}{4}$ ◯ $\frac{1}{2}$

$\frac{1}{4}$ ◯ $\frac{0}{4}$

$\frac{1}{4}$ ◯ $\frac{3}{4}$

$\frac{3}{8}$ ◯ $\frac{2}{4}$

$\frac{1}{2}$ ◯ $\frac{4}{8}$

$\frac{5}{8}$ ◯ $\frac{3}{4}$

2

$\frac{1}{3}$ ◯ $\frac{3}{3}$

$\frac{2}{3}$ ◯ $\frac{1}{2}$

$\frac{2}{3}$ ◯ $\frac{4}{6}$

$\frac{3}{6}$ ◯ $\frac{1}{2}$

$\frac{1}{3}$ ◯ $\frac{1}{2}$

$\frac{4}{6}$ ◯ $\frac{1}{2}$

$\frac{2}{6}$ ◯ $\frac{1}{6}$

$\frac{3}{3}$ ◯ $\frac{6}{6}$

3 Which is greater: $\frac{3}{5}$ or $\frac{4}{10}$? Use words or a drawing to show your answer.

4 Compare these fractions using $<$, $=$, or $>$.

$\frac{1}{2}$ (>) $\frac{1}{5}$	$\frac{2}{5}$ ◯ $\frac{1}{10}$	$\frac{1}{2}$ ◯ $\frac{4}{10}$
$\frac{1}{5}$ ◯ $\frac{3}{10}$	$\frac{1}{2}$ ◯ $\frac{5}{10}$	$\frac{5}{10}$ ◯ $\frac{2}{5}$
$\frac{3}{5}$ ◯ $\frac{1}{2}$	$\frac{5}{10}$ ◯ $\frac{4}{5}$	$\frac{2}{10}$ ◯ $\frac{1}{5}$
$\frac{7}{10}$ ◯ $\frac{2}{5}$	$\frac{2}{5}$ ◯ $\frac{3}{5}$	$\frac{6}{10}$ ◯ $\frac{3}{5}$

5 **Challenge** Which is greater, $\frac{1}{5}$ or $\frac{1}{10}$? Explain how you know.

____

____

____

____

____

6 **Challenge** Fill in the missing numbers to make the fractions equal. Use Cuisenaire® Rods to help.

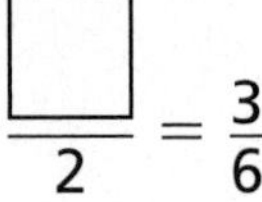

$\frac{\square}{2} = \frac{3}{6}$	$\frac{2}{5} = \frac{\square}{10}$	$\frac{\square}{2} = \frac{3}{6}$
$\frac{5}{5} = \frac{\square}{4}$	$\frac{6}{8} = \frac{\square}{4}$	$\frac{1}{3} = \frac{\square}{9}$
$\frac{1}{2} = \frac{2}{\square}$	$\frac{3}{3} = \frac{7}{\square}$	$\frac{0}{4} = \frac{\square}{8}$

Chapter 7
Lesson 8

Name ____________________ Date ____________

Finding Equivalent Fractions

NCTM Standards 1, 2, 6, 7, 8, 9, 10

Complete the fractions to make the sentences true.

1 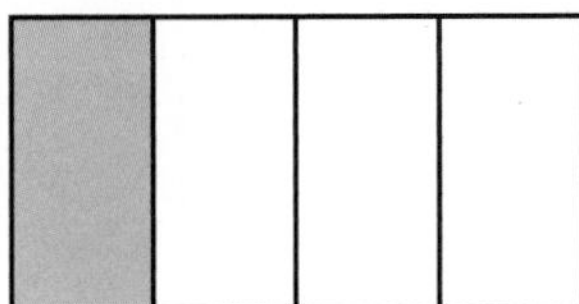

$\frac{1}{4} = \frac{2}{\square}$ $\frac{1}{4} = \frac{\square}{20}$

$\frac{1}{4} = \frac{4}{\square}$ $\frac{1}{4} = \frac{\square}{32}$

$\frac{1}{4} = \frac{6}{\square}$ $\frac{1}{4} = \frac{\square}{40}$

2 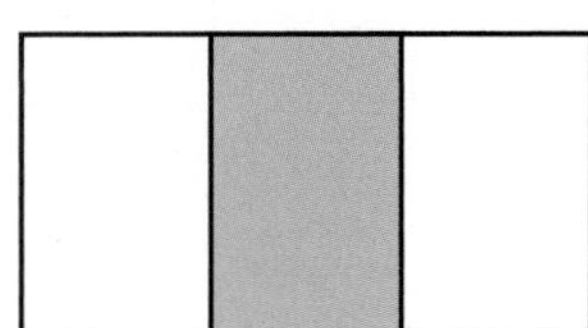

$\frac{1}{3} = \frac{2}{\square}$ $\frac{1}{3} = \frac{3}{\square}$

$\frac{1}{3} = \frac{\square}{15}$ $\frac{1}{3} = \frac{6}{\square}$

$\frac{1}{3} = \frac{\square}{30}$ $\frac{1}{3} = \frac{8}{\square}$

3 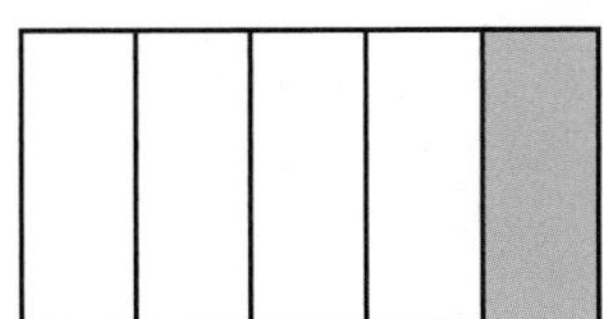

$\frac{1}{5} = \frac{2}{\square}$ $\frac{1}{5} = \frac{\square}{15}$

$\frac{1}{5} = \frac{6}{\square}$ $\frac{1}{5} = \frac{\square}{25}$

$\frac{1}{5} = \frac{10}{\square}$ $\frac{1}{5} = \frac{\square}{40}$

4 How do you know that $\frac{1}{4}$ and $\frac{3}{12}$ are the same portion of the rectangle in Problem 1?

____

____

____

____

____

Use = or ≠ to show whether the fractions are equal or not.

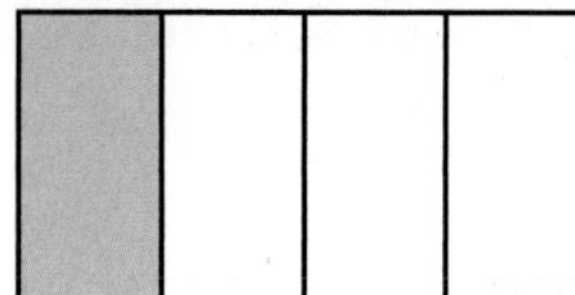

$\frac{1}{3}$ (≠) $\frac{1}{2}$ $\frac{3}{4}$ ◯ $\frac{15}{20}$

$\frac{3}{4}$ ◯ $\frac{6}{8}$ $\frac{9}{10}$ ◯ $\frac{3}{4}$

6

$\frac{6}{6}$ ◯ $\frac{8}{8}$ $\frac{4}{4}$ ◯ $\frac{9}{8}$

$\frac{100}{100}$ ◯ $\frac{3}{3}$ $\frac{7}{8}$ ◯ $\frac{13}{13}$

7 Write 3 fractions that are equivalent to $\frac{1}{6}$.

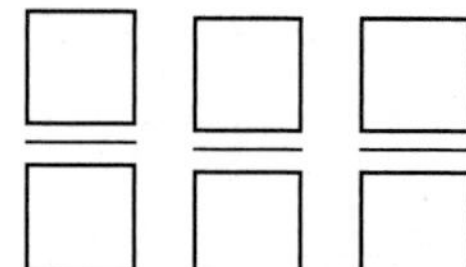

8 Write 3 fractions that are equivalent to $\frac{1}{8}$.

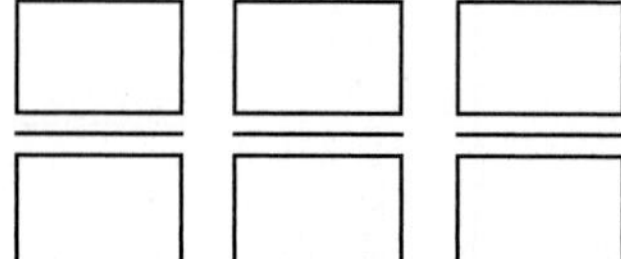

9 Challenge Find a rule. Then complete the fractions.

$\frac{7}{49}$ $\frac{2}{14}$ $\frac{10}{70}$ $\frac{1}{\square}$ $\frac{5}{\square}$ $\frac{\square}{21}$ $\frac{8}{\square}$ $\frac{\square}{63}$ $\frac{b}{\square}$

Chapter 7

Lesson 9

Name ______________________ Date ____________

Making Equivalent Fractions

NCTM Standards 1, 2, 6, 7, 8, 9, 10

Complete the fractions to make the sentences true. Draw pictures to help you complete Problems 3 and 4, if it will help.

1

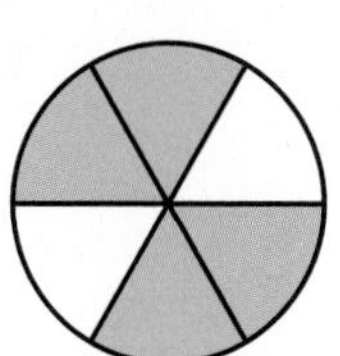

$\frac{4}{6} = \frac{2}{\square}$ $\frac{4}{6} = \frac{\square}{18}$

$\frac{4}{6} = \frac{8}{\square}$ $\frac{4}{6} = \frac{\square}{60}$

2

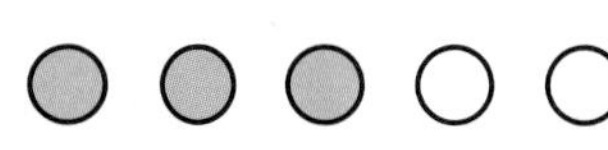

$\frac{3}{5} = \frac{6}{\square}$ $\frac{3}{5} = \frac{9}{\square}$

$\frac{3}{5} = \frac{\square}{30}$ $\frac{3}{5} = \frac{\square}{25}$

3

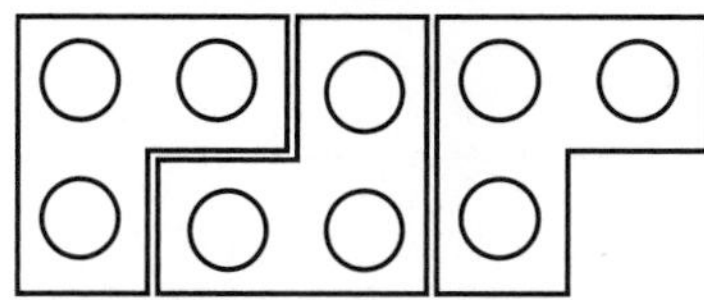

$\frac{2}{3} = \frac{\square}{6}$ $\frac{2}{3} = \frac{20}{\square}$

$\frac{2}{3} = \frac{10}{\square}$ $\frac{2}{3} = \frac{\square}{21}$

4

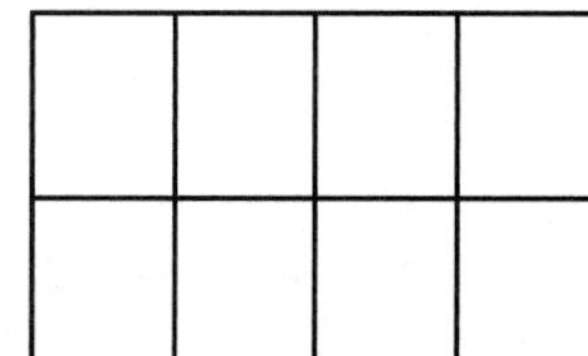

$\frac{5}{8} = \frac{\square}{16}$ $\frac{5}{8} = \frac{15}{\square}$

$\frac{5}{8} = \frac{25}{\square}$ $\frac{5}{8} = \frac{\square}{80}$

5 Write 3 fractions that are equivalent to $\frac{4}{5}$.

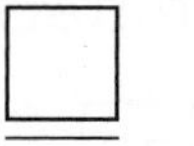
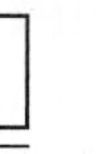

$\frac{\square}{\square}$ $\frac{\square}{\square}$ $\frac{\square}{\square}$

Use = or ≠ to show whether the fractions are equal or not.

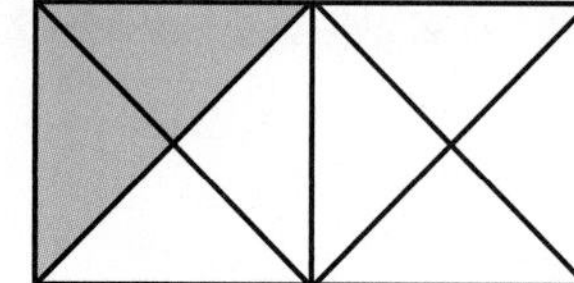

$\frac{2}{8} \bigcirc\!\!\!\!= \; \frac{1}{4}$ (=) $\qquad \frac{2}{8} \bigcirc \frac{3}{8}$

$\frac{2}{8} \bigcirc \frac{1}{2} \qquad \frac{1}{2} \bigcirc \frac{4}{8}$

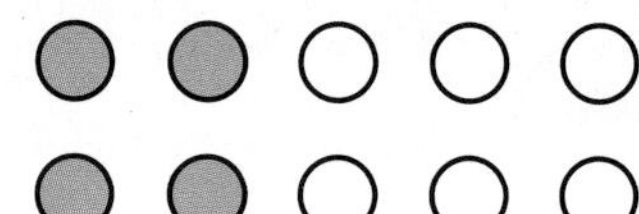

$\frac{4}{10} \bigcirc \frac{2}{5} \qquad \frac{4}{10} \bigcirc \frac{4}{5}$

$\frac{1}{2} \bigcirc \frac{5}{10} \qquad \frac{3}{5} \bigcirc \frac{1}{4}$

8 In the fourth grade, $\frac{1}{5}$ of the students were absent on Monday and $\frac{2}{10}$ were absent on Tuesday. Were the numbers of absent students on the two days the same or different? Explain how you found the answer.

____

____

____

____

9 Challenge Find a rule. Then complete the fractions.

2	10	1	3	8	☐	☐	☐	n
12	60	6	☐	☐	24	54	120	☐

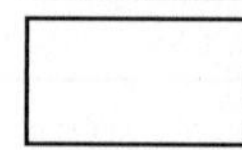

10 Challenge Find a rule. Then complete the fractions.

6	15	3	9	☐	☐	30	☐	$3 \times n$
16	40	8	☐	56	32	☐	160	☐

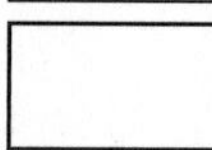

Name ______________________ Date ______________

Chapter 7
Lesson 10

Fractions in Measurement

NCTM Standards 1, 2, 6, 7, 8, 9, 10

1 Record the lengths of these lines.

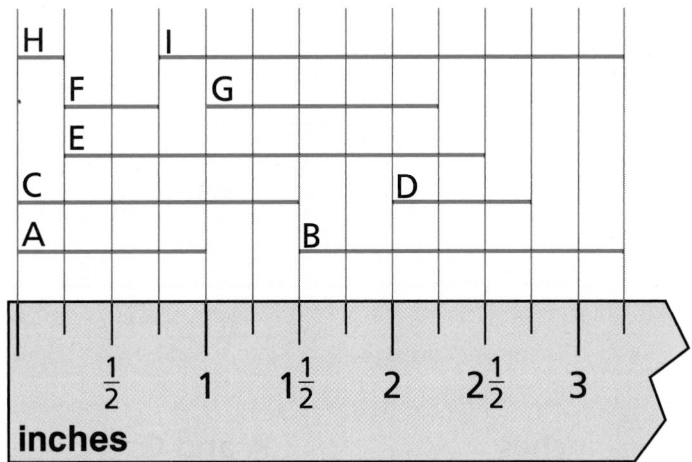

Lengths:

A: __________ inches D: __________ inches G: __________ inches

B: __________ inches E: __________ inches H: __________ inches

C: __________ inches F: __________ inches I: __________ inches

2 Put all of the lengths above in order from least to greatest.

_____ _____ _____ _____ _____ _____ _____ _____ _____

3 Locate each measurement from above on the number line below.

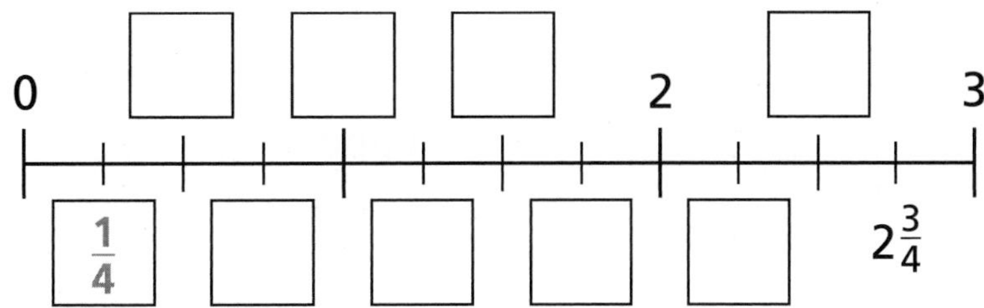

Use this drawing of the lines from the previous page to answer the questions below.

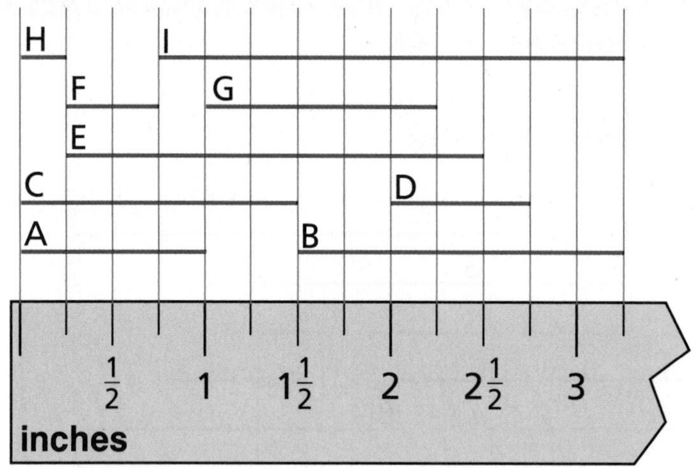

❹ Sum of lengths:

H and **F**: ___________ inches

A and **G**: ___________ inches

F and **I**: ___________ inches

C and **B**: ___________ inches

H and **E**: ___________ inches

A and **I**: ___________ inches

---

❺ Differences between lengths:

I and **B**: ___________ inches

C and **A**: ___________ inches

A and **H**: ___________ inches

C and **H**: ___________ inches

E and **F**: ___________ inches

I and **G**: ___________ inches

Name ______________________ Date ____________

Chapter 7
Lesson 11

Modeling Addition of Fractions

NCTM Standards 1, 2, 6, 7, 8, 9, 10

1. 1 sixth + 3 sixths = _____ sixths

2. 4 sixths + 1 sixth = _____ sixths

3. 4 sixths + 2 sixths = _____ sixths

4. 3 sixths + _____ sixths = 5 sixths

5. $\frac{1}{2} + \frac{1}{2} = \frac{\square}{\square}$

6. $\frac{2}{6} + \frac{\square}{6} = \frac{3}{6}$

7. $\frac{1}{6} + \frac{1}{6} = \frac{\square}{\square}$

8. $\frac{4}{6} + \frac{3}{6} = \frac{\square}{6}$

9. 4 sixths − 2 sixths = _____ sixths

10. 5 sixths − 1 sixth = _____ sixths

11. 6 sixths − 3 sixths = _____ sixths

12. 8 sixths − _____ sixths = 1 sixth

13. $\frac{5}{6} - \frac{2}{6} = \frac{\square}{6}$

14. $\frac{2}{6} - \frac{0}{6} = \frac{2}{\square}$

15. $\frac{\square}{6} - \frac{1}{6} = \frac{3}{6}$

16. $\frac{6}{6} - \frac{\square}{6} = \frac{1}{6}$

Use these fractional pieces of a foot to complete the number sentences below.

$\frac{1}{4}$ 3 inches	$\frac{1}{6}$ 2 inches	$\frac{1}{12}$ 1 inch
$\frac{1}{3}$ 4 inches		
$\frac{1}{2}$ 6 inches		

17

$\frac{1}{4}$	$\frac{1}{12}$
___	

$\frac{1}{12} + \frac{1}{4} = \frac{\square}{\square}$

18

$\frac{1}{4}$	___	___
___		

$\frac{1}{4} + \frac{\square}{\square} + \frac{\square}{\square} = \frac{\square}{\square}$

19 Challenge Count by $\frac{2}{7}$ to fill in the missing numbers.

0, $\frac{2}{7}$, $\frac{4}{7}$, $\frac{\square}{7}$, $1\frac{1}{7}$, $1\frac{\square}{7}$,

$1\frac{5}{7}$, $\square$, $2\frac{2}{7}$, $\square$, $\square$, . . .

Name ______________________ Date __________

Chapter 7

Lesson 12

Problem Solving Strategy

Draw a Picture

NCTM Standards 1, 2, 6, 7, 8, 9, 10

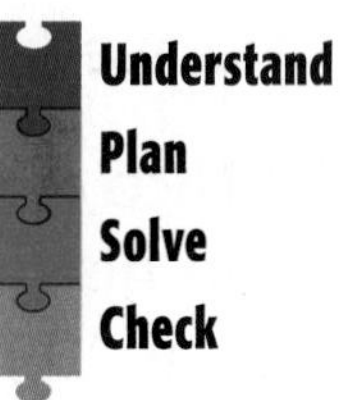

Use the large white space to draw pictures if you want.

1. 1 lb

1 pound = 16 ounces

$\frac{1}{2}$ of a pound = __________ ounces

$\frac{1}{4}$ of a pound = __________ ounces

$\frac{3}{4}$ of a pound = __________ ounces

$\frac{1}{8}$ of a pound = __________ ounces

$\frac{5}{8}$ of a pound = __________ ounces

2. Ben and Jasmine shared a small cake that was cut into 6 equal pieces. Jasmine ate $\frac{1}{2}$ of the cake. Ben ate $\frac{1}{3}$ of the cake. What fraction of the cake was left?

____

3. Three kids divided 4 small pizzas equally. How much pizza did each kid get?

____

Problem Solving Test Prep

Choose the correct answer.

1. Nico is planting a pattern of plants in his flower garden. The first row has 10 plants, the second row has 15 plants, and the third row has 20 plants. If this pattern continues, how many plants will Nico need in all to plant six rows of plants?

   A. 35 plants **C.** 125 plants

   B. 60 plants **D.** 135 plants

2. Kiki is putting a fence around a rectangular part of her backyard that measures 14 feet by 9 feet. What is the area of the fenced part of the backyard?

   A. 23 square feet

   B. 46 square feet

   C. 126 square feet

   D. 276 square feet

3. Melanie is drawing a figure with 4 sides and 4 angles. She wants her figure to have at least one acute angle. Which figure could Melanie draw?

   A. right triangle **C.** square

   B. trapezoid **D.** rectangle

4. Below is a diagram of Jenny's backyard. What is the perimeter of Jenny's backyard?

20 feet

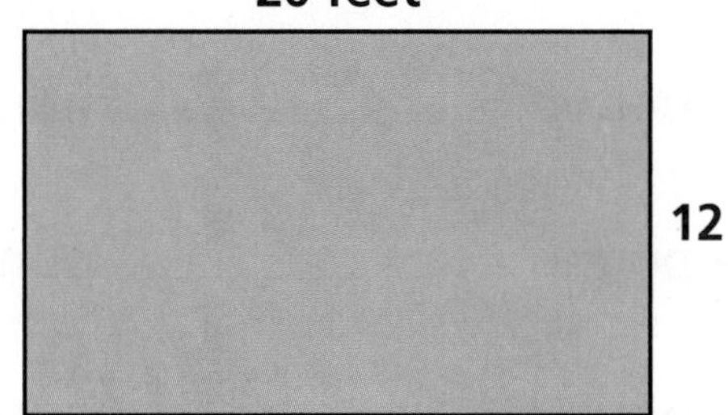

12 feet

   A. 64 feet **C.** 32 feet

   B. 40 feet **D.** 24 feet

Show What You Know

Solve each problem. Explain your answer.

5. Julio measured the length of a piece of yarn to be 3 feet long. How long is the piece of yarn in inches?

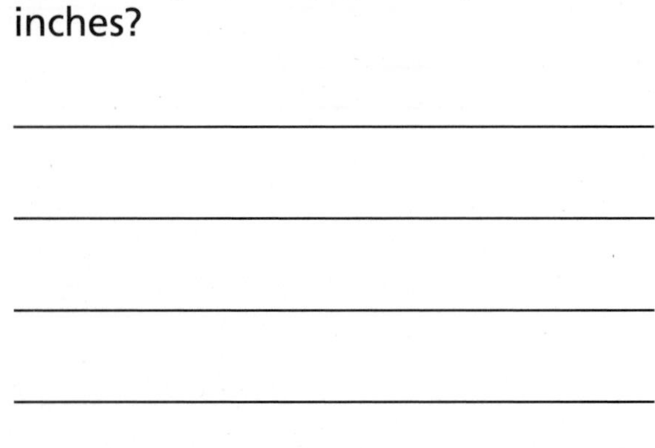

6. Draw a picture to find $\frac{3}{8} + \frac{2}{8}$.

Name ______________________ Date ____________

Chapter 7

Review/Assessment

NCTM Standards 1, 2, 6, 7, 8, 9, 10

Use these pictures to answer the questions below. Lessons 1, 2, 3, 4, and 11

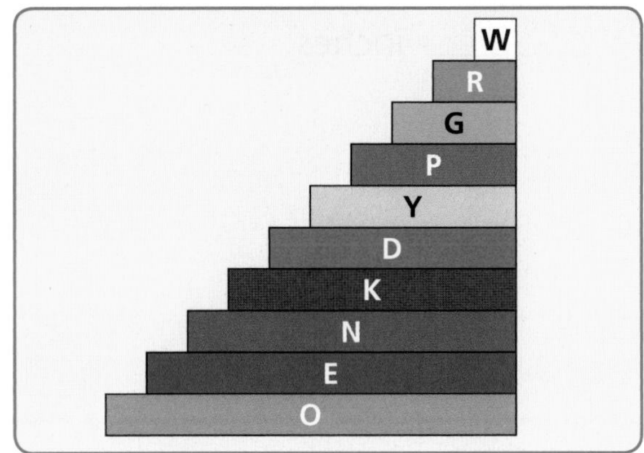

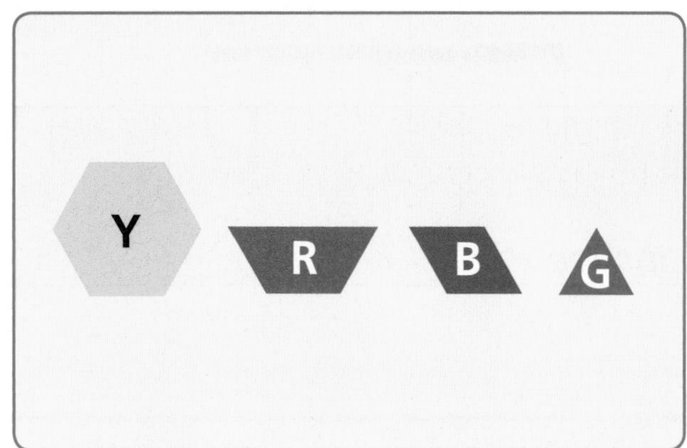

1. If O = 1, then Y = ________
2. If R = $\frac{1}{2}$, then D = ________
3. If ______ = $\frac{1}{2}$, then N = 1
4. If E = 1, then O = ________
5. If Y = 1, then B = ________
6. If R = 1, then G = ________
7. If R = $1\frac{1}{4}$, then Y = ________
8. If G = $\frac{1}{4}$, then B = ________

Cross out the one or two fractions that do not represent the shaded portion of each picture. Lessons 8 and 9

Example

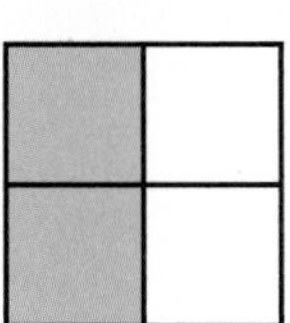

$\frac{1}{2}$ ~~$\frac{2}{2}$~~ $\frac{2}{4}$ ~~$\frac{1}{3}$~~

9.

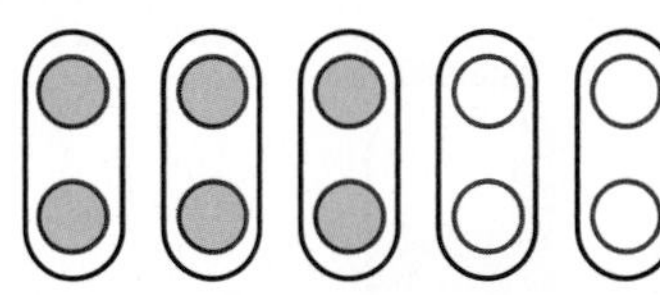

$\frac{3}{5}$ $\frac{6}{4}$ $\frac{6}{10}$ $\frac{4}{6}$

10.

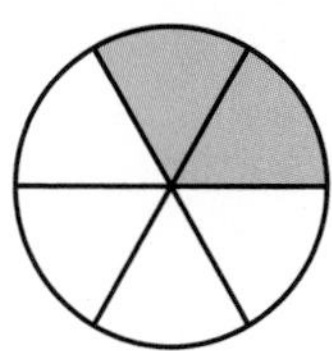

$\frac{2}{4}$ $\frac{1}{3}$ $\frac{2}{6}$ $\frac{1}{6}$

11.

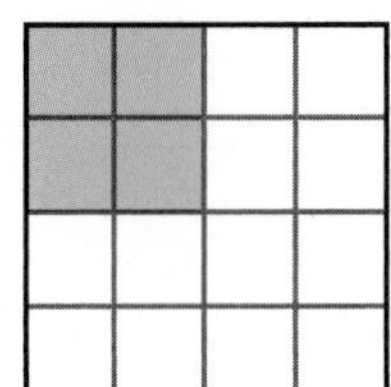

$\frac{1}{4}$ $\frac{2}{8}$ $\frac{4}{12}$ $\frac{4}{16}$

How long is each piece of string? Lessons 5 and 10

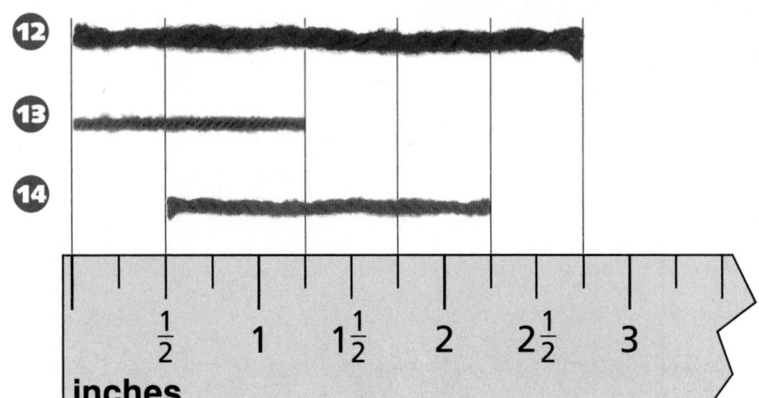

12. _______ inches

13. _______ inches

14. _______ inches

Write <, >, or = to make each statement true. Lessons 6 and 7

15 $\frac{2}{7} \bigcirc \frac{5}{7}$	16 $\frac{2}{3} \bigcirc \frac{1}{2}$	17 $\frac{1}{4} \bigcirc \frac{1}{10}$
18 $\frac{3}{8} \bigcirc \frac{7}{8}$	19 $\frac{1}{2} \bigcirc \frac{8}{16}$	20 $\frac{3}{4} \bigcirc \frac{1}{3}$

Use the space to draw pictures if you want. Lesson 12

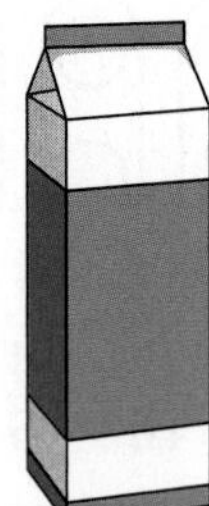

1 quart = 32 ounces

21. $\frac{1}{2}$ of a quart = _______ ounces

22. $\frac{1}{4}$ of a quart = _______ ounces

23. $\frac{5}{8}$ of a quart = _______ ounces

Chapter 8
Lesson 1

Name ______________________ Date ____________

Place Value

NCTM Standards 1, 2, 6, 7, 8, 9, 10

Write the number.

1. three hundred sixty thousand, two hundred seven ☐

2. six million, fifty-four thousand, nine ☐

3. two million, one hundred eight thousand, seventy-six ☐

4. My tens digit is **9.** My ones digit is **7.** My thousands digit is **5.**

   My millions digit is **1.** My hundred millions digit is **7.**

   All of my other digits are **0.** ☐

5. 8,000,000 + 500,000 + 7,000 + 900 + 4 = ☐

6. ☐00,000 + ☐0,000 + ☐,000 + ☐00 + ☐0 + ☐ = 793,065

7. Write the value of each digit.

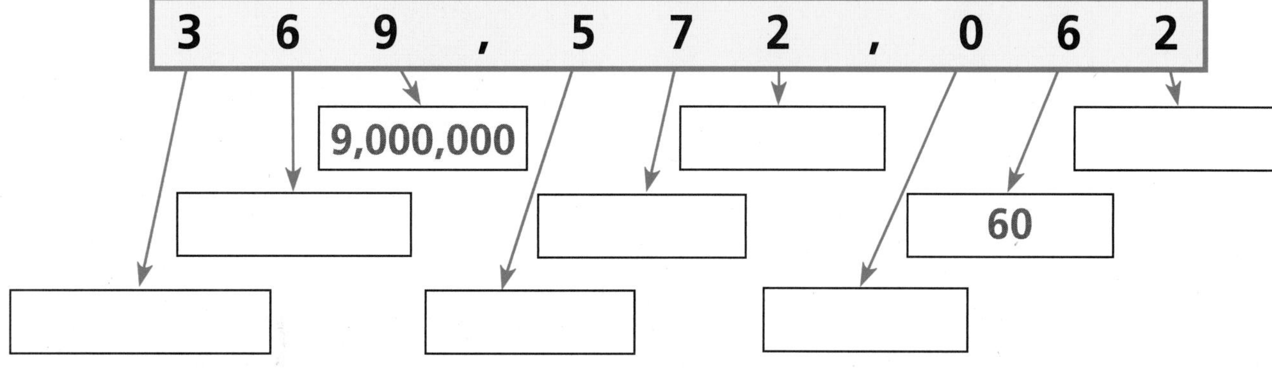

Fill in <, =, or >.

8	1,250 ◯ 1,520	9	787,099 ◯ 787,100
10	6,135,000 ◯ 6,153,000	11	2,005,607 ◯ 2,010,580
12	989,000 ◯ 979,956	13	1,650,207 ◯ 1,506,720

Put these numbers in order from smallest to largest:

1,702,000 10,702,000 6,503 2,999 70,000

2,500 905,608 859,990 70,030

14 ☐	15 ☐	16 ☐
17 ☐	18 ☐	19 ☐
20 ☐	21 ☐	22 ☐

23 **Challenge** Explain how you decided on the order of the numbers in Problems 14–22.

Chapter 8
Lesson 2

Name ______________________ Date ____________

Introducing Decimals

NCTM Standards 1, 2, 6, 7, 8, 9, 10

Shade part of each number line to show the space between two numbers where each number belongs.

1. 4 ☐ ☐

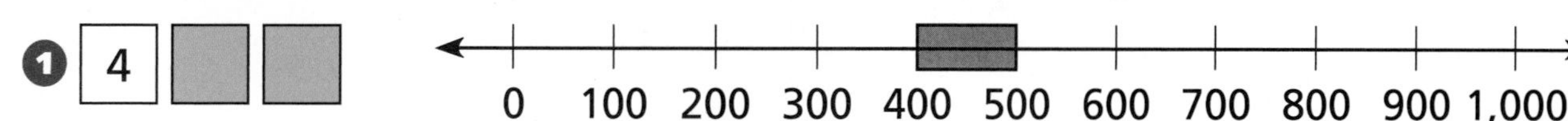

2. 3 ☐ ☐

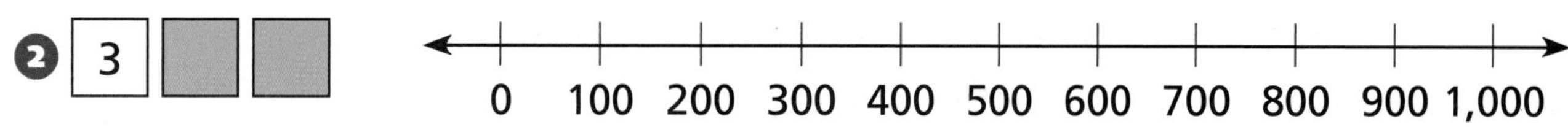

3. 3 5 ☐

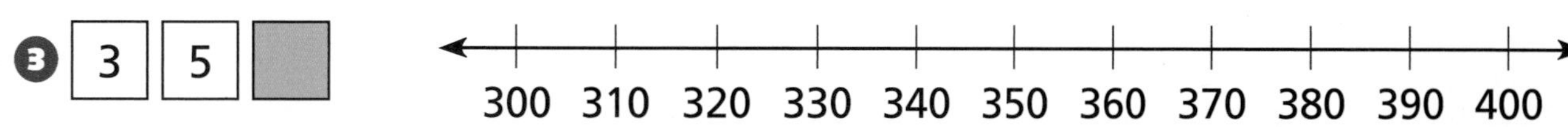

4. 3 ☐

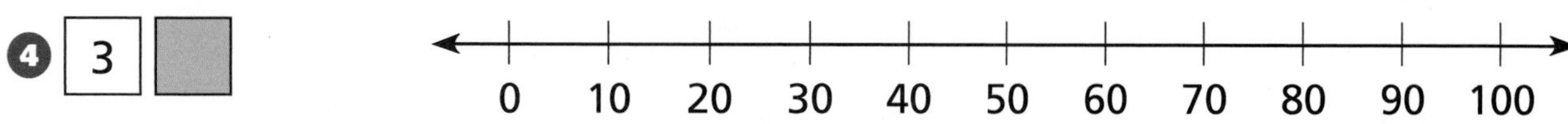

5. 5 ☐

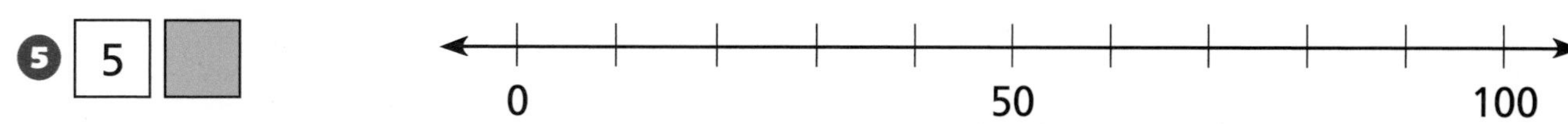

6. 5 . ☐

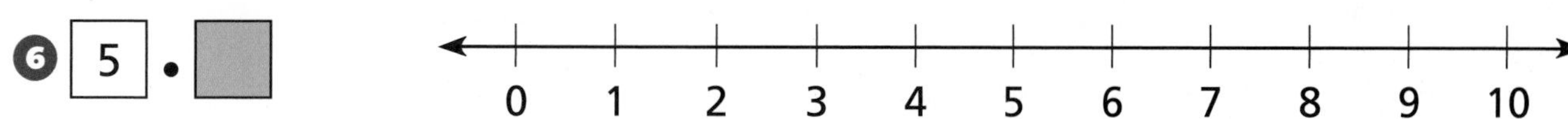

7. 8 . ☐

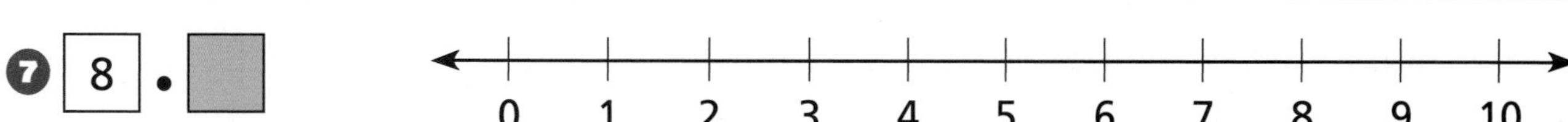

8. 1 8 . ☐

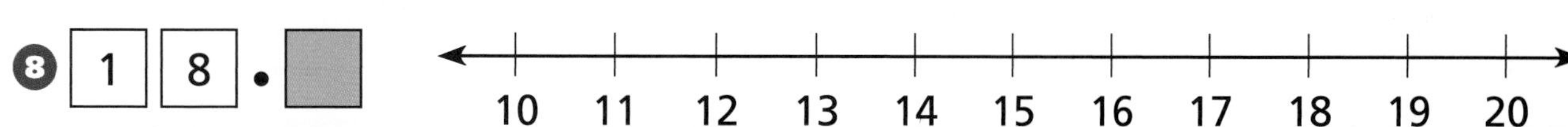

9. Now use the shading on the number line to find the tens digit and the ones digit in the number.

☐ ☐ . ☐

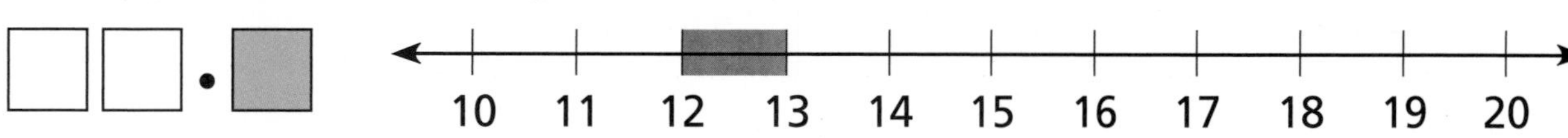

10 Use a calculator to multiply these numbers between **4** and **5.**

Numbers between 4 and 5 →	Numbers multiplied by themselves
4	
4.1	
4.2	
4.3	
5	

Fran multiplied a number by itself and got 20. Her number must be between two numbers in the left column above.

Her number must be between _____ and _____.

How do you know? ____

____

11 **Challenge** Name 2 numbers that are between 1 and 2.

_____ and _____

12 **Challenge** Name 2 numbers that are between the numbers you wrote in the problem to the left.

_____ and _____

Chapter 8
Lesson 3

Name ______________________ Date ____________

Zooming in on the Number Line

NCTM Standards 1, 2, 6, 7, 8, 9, 10

Fill in the missing numbers.

1

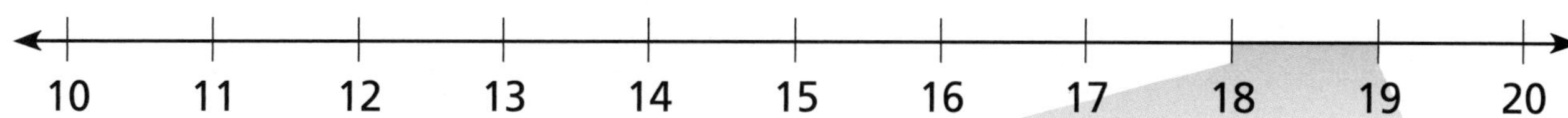

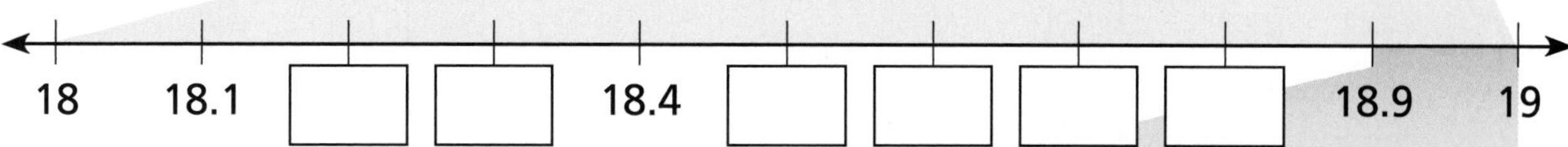

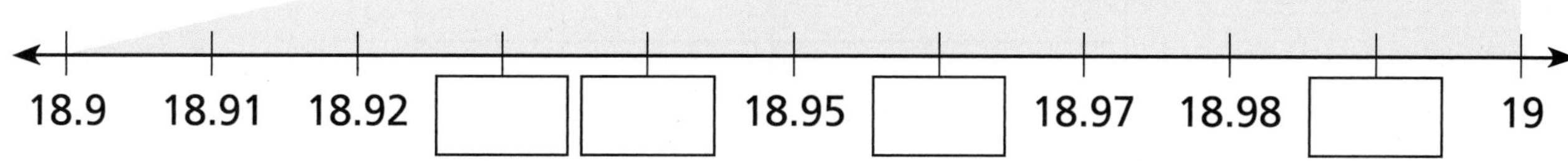

2

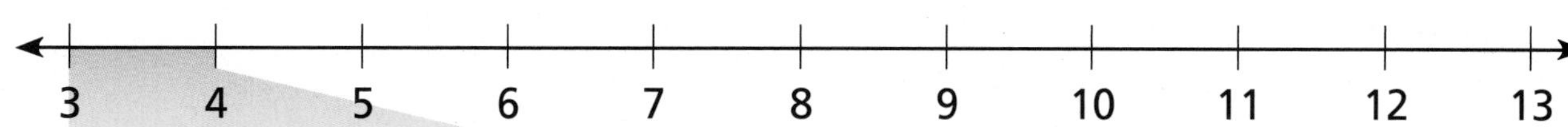

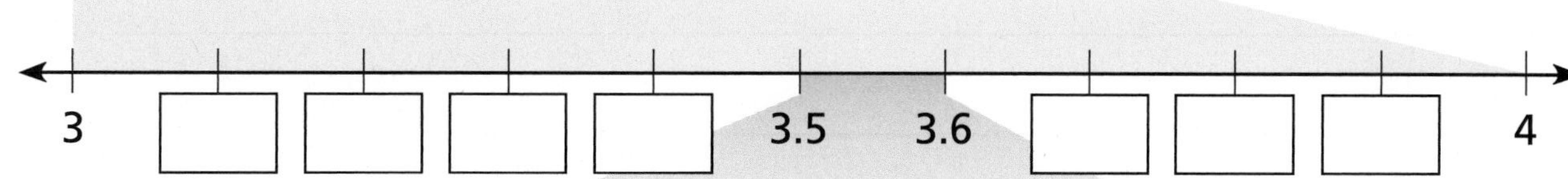

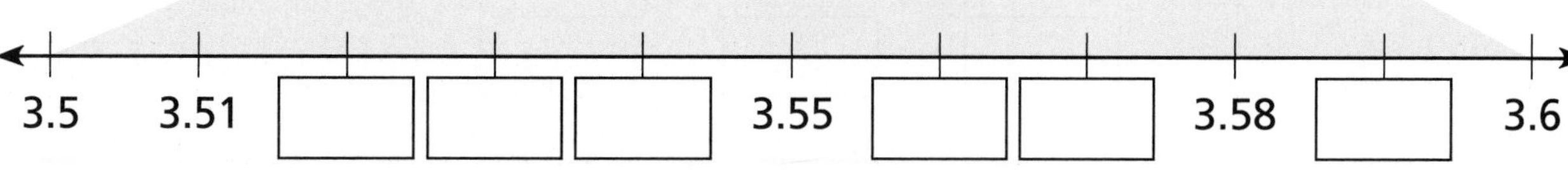

3 Use a calculator to multiply these numbers between **6.5** and **6.6.**

Numbers between 6.5 and 6.6 →	Numbers multiplied by themselves
6.5	
6.51	
6.52	
6.6	

Paul multiplied a number by itself and got 43. His number must be between two numbers in the left column.

His number must be between ______ and ______.
How do you know?

____

____

4 Challenge Name three numbers between 3.65 and 3.66.

[ ] [ ] [ ]

Chapter 8

Lesson 4

Name ______________________ Date ____________

Decimals on the Number Line

NCTM Standards 1, 2, 6, 7, 8, 9, 10

Fill in the missing numbers.

1

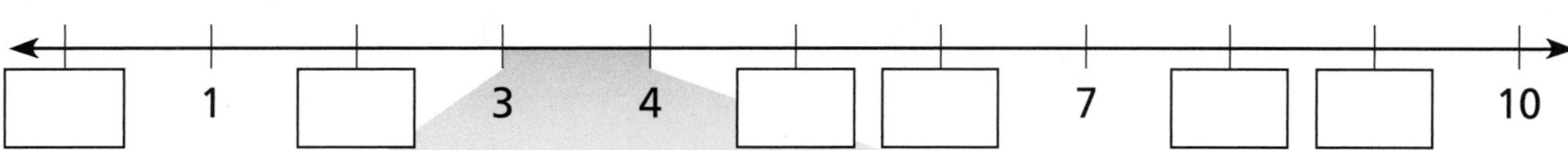

2

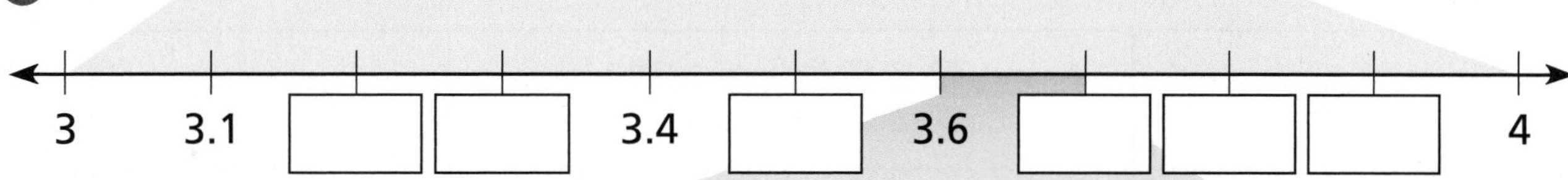

3

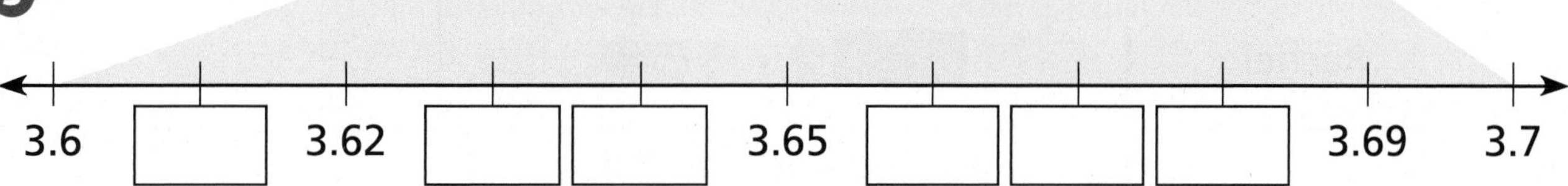

---

4 Use the number lines to compare the numbers. Write < or >.

8 (>) 5	3.7 ○ 3	3.62 ○ 3.7
3.2 ○ 3.6	3.7 ○ 3.09	3.64 ○ 3.69
3.1 ○ 3.4	3.7 ○ 4	3.64 ○ 3.66
3.8 ○ 3.1	3.7 ○ 7	3.69 ○ 3.6
3.7 ○ 3.6	3.68 ○ 3.7	3.69 ○ 3
3.5 ○ 4	3.64 ○ 3.8	3.64 ○ 4

Write an ✕ to mark each number on the number line.

5 4.6

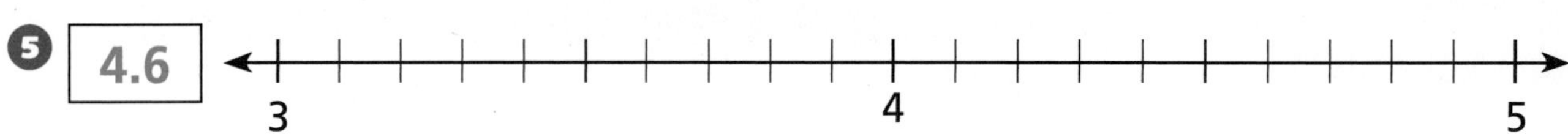

6 98.6

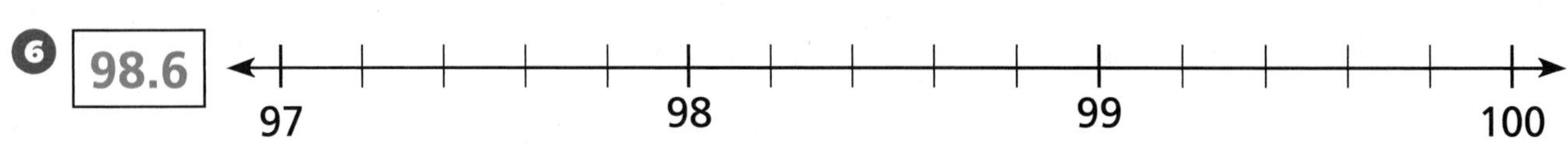

7 Abby, Julie, Rachel and Sam were saving money for tickets to a movie. Here is the money each boy or girl saved. Count the money and write the amount using decimals.

Abby		______
Julie		______
Rachel		______
Sam		______

Circle the correct answer.

Who saved more money? Abby or Julie

Who saved less money? Rachel or Sam

Who saved the most money of all? Abby Julie Rachel Sam

Who saved the amount closest to $1.00? Rachel or Julie

8 Challenge

What number is halfway between 4 and 5? ______

What number is halfway between 4.2 and 4.3? ______

What number is halfway between 4.87 and 4.88? ______

Chapter 8

Lesson 5

Name ______________________ Date ____________

Connecting Fractions and Decimals

NCTM Standards 1, 2, 6, 7, 8, 9, 10

Label these number line points with both fractions and decimals.

1

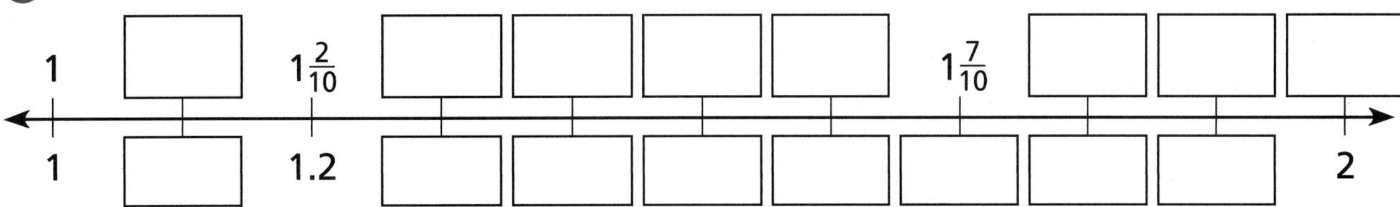

2

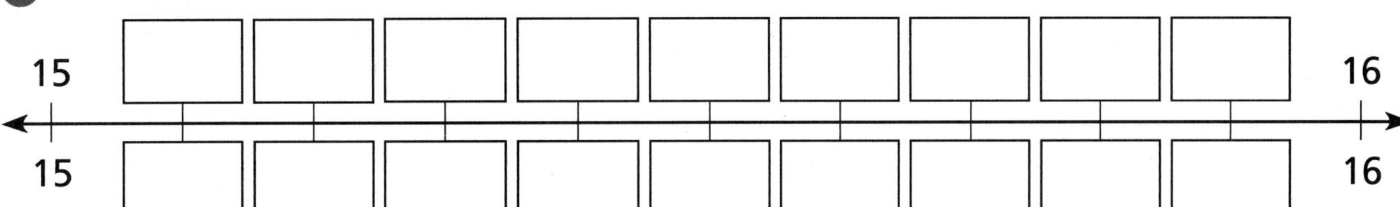

3

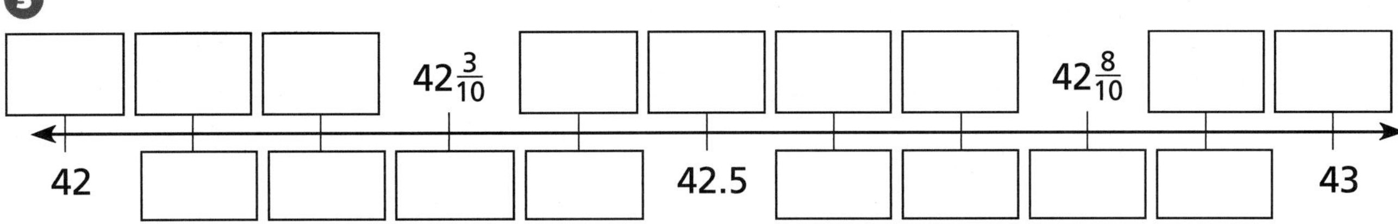

4 James and Ge earned $13 doing yard work together. James said his half of the money was $6.50. Ge said his half of the money was six and a half dollars. Who was right? Explain your answer.

____

____

5 Write the decimals and matching fractions.

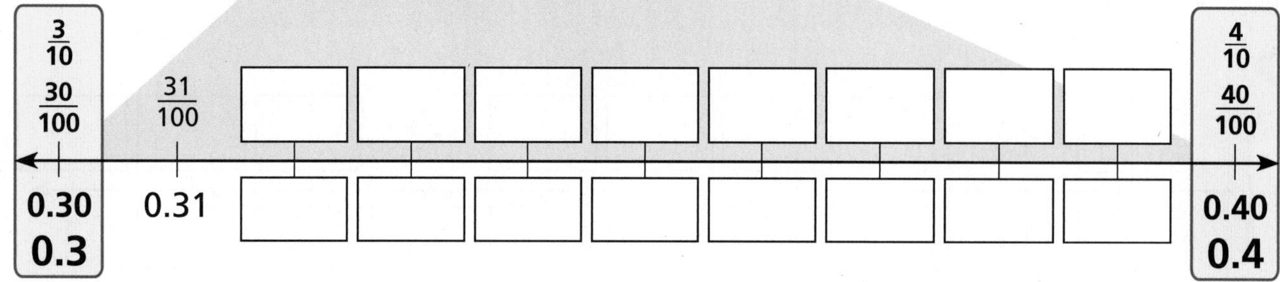

6 Which is bigger, $\frac{4}{10}$ or 0.38? How do you know?

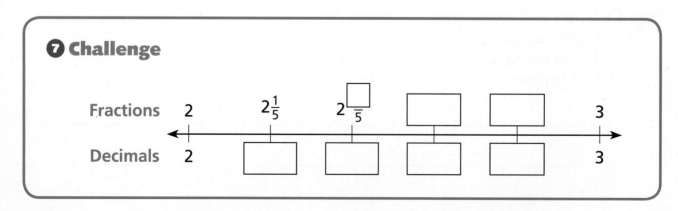

____

____

____

7 Challenge

Fractions 2 $2\frac{1}{5}$ $2\frac{\square}{5}$ ☐ ☐ 3

Decimals 2 ☐ ☐ ☐ ☐ 3

Chapter 8
Lesson 6

Name ______________________ Date ____________

Representing Decimals Using a Grid

NCTM Standards 1, 2, 6, 7, 8, 9, 10

Write the decimal to show what parts of the square are shaded.

1

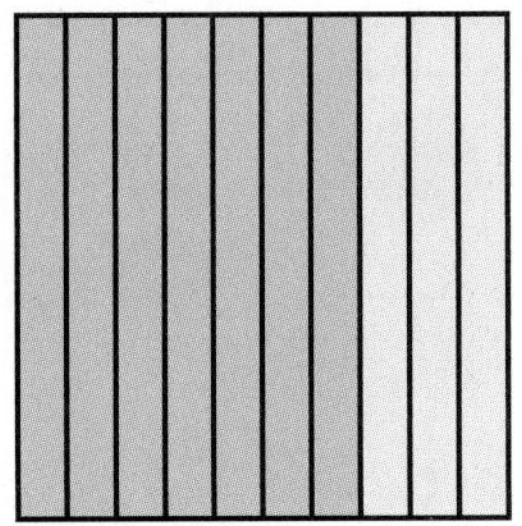

dark	0.7
light	

2

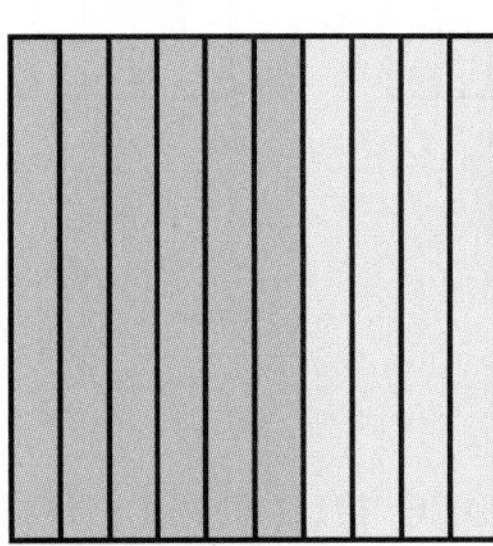

dark	
light	

3

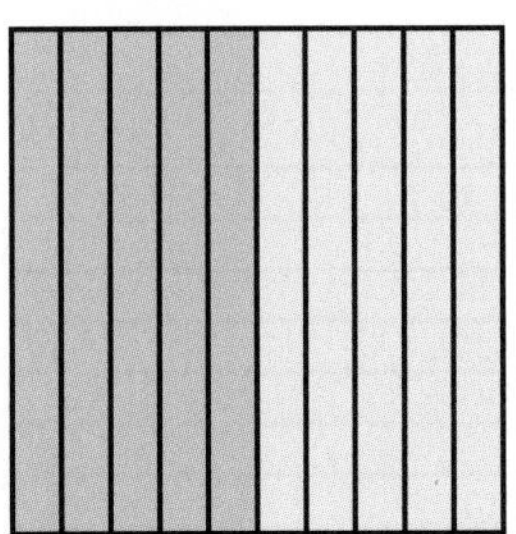

dark	
light	

4

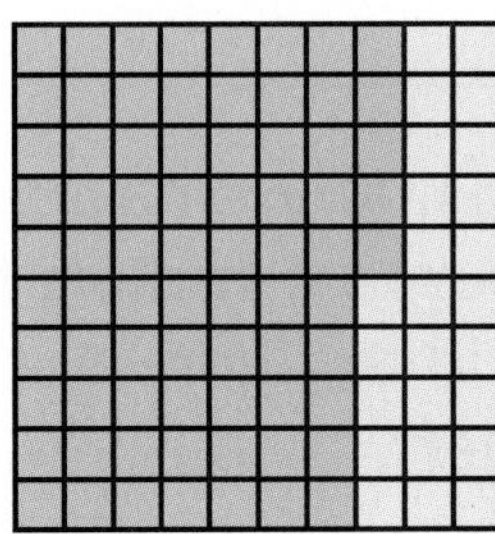

dark	
light	0.25

5

dark	
light	

6

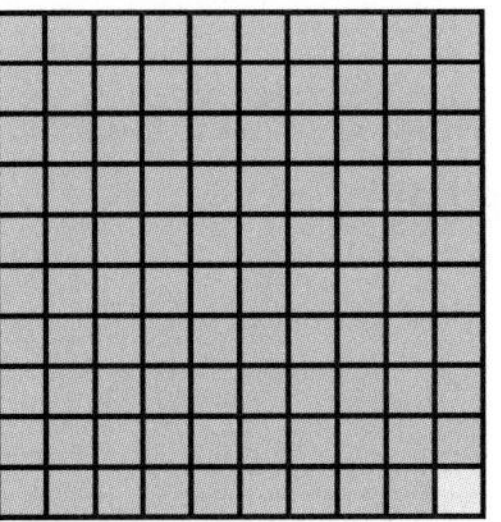

dark	
light	

Shade each diagram to match the money amounts.

7
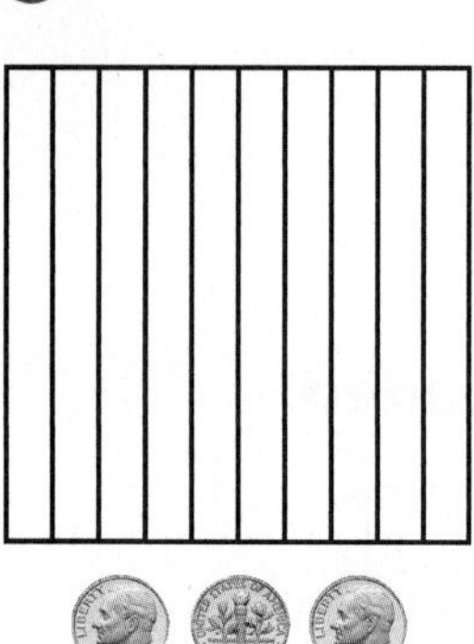

8
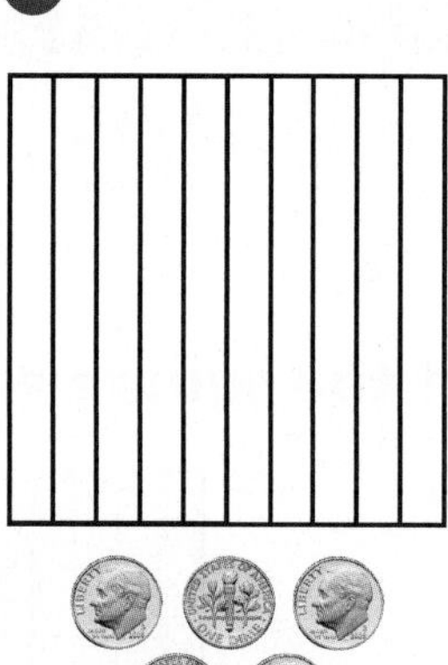

9
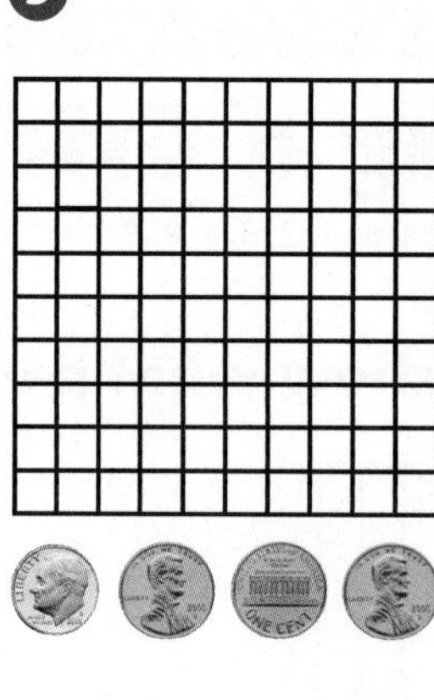

10
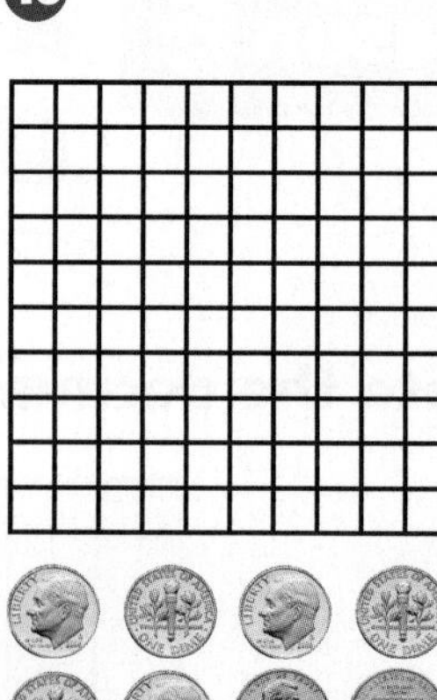

Write the above numbers in order from least to greatest.

______ ______ ______ ______

11 Keith has $1.00. He gave 53¢ to Connie, and he bought 4 stickers that cost 7¢ each. Use the grid to figure out how much money Keith has left.

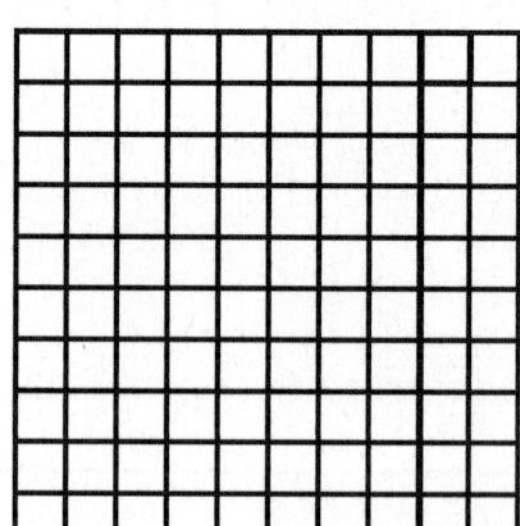

$0.

12 **Challenge** Put these numbers in order from least to greatest.

$\frac{1}{3}$ 0.5 0.97 $\frac{3}{4}$ 0.01 0.1 $\frac{2}{5}$

______ ______ ______ ______ ______ ______ ______

Chapter 8
Lesson 7

Name ______________________ Date ____________

Representing Decimals Using Base-Ten Blocks

NCTM Standards 1, 2, 6, 7, 8, 9, 10

Use the clues to complete the tables.

1 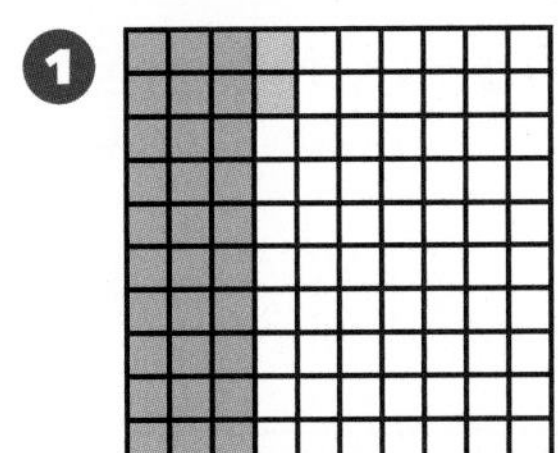

	Dark Shading	Light Shading	Total Shaded	Total Unshaded
Decimal	0.3	0.02		0.68
Fraction	$\frac{3}{10}$	$\frac{2}{100}$	$\frac{32}{100}$	

2 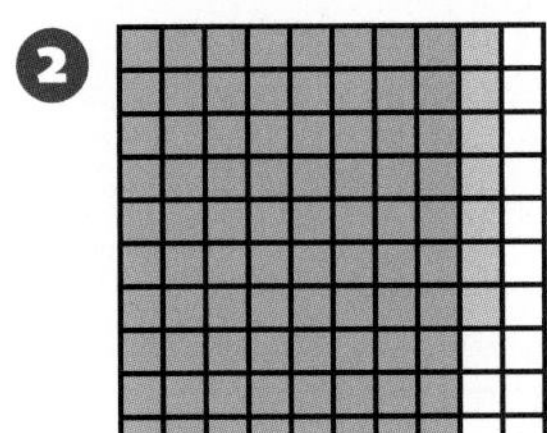

	Dark Shading	Light Shading	Total Shaded	Total Unshaded
Decimal	0.8			
Fraction				

3 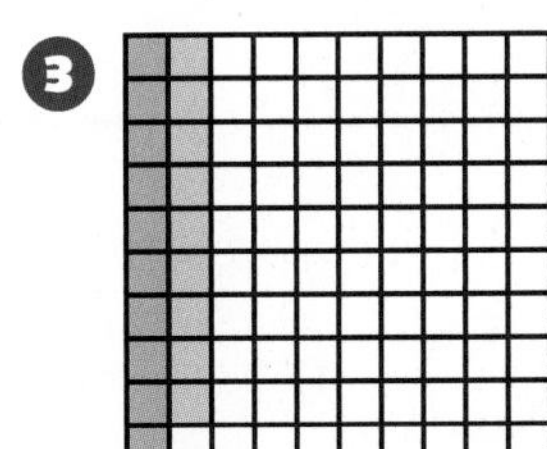

	Dark Shading	Light Shading	Total Shaded	Total Unshaded
Decimal				
Fraction				

4 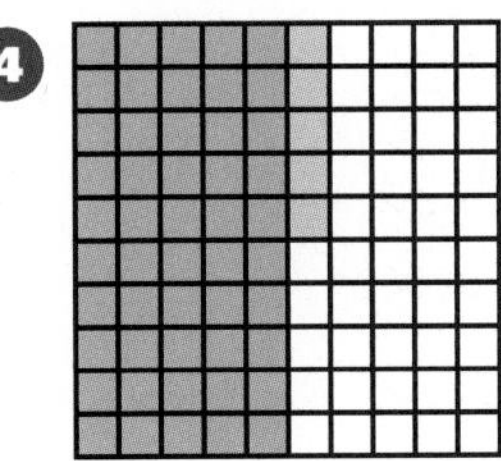

	Dark Shading	Light Shading	Total Shaded	Total Unshaded
Decimal				
Fraction				

Fill in the missing numbers.

5. 0.12 + 0.01 = 0.13 + 0.02 = ☐ + 0.04 = ☐

6. 0.28 − 0.02 = ☐ − 0.01 = ☐ − 0.03 = ☐

7. 1.73 + 0.04 = ☐ − 0.05 = ☐ + 0.01 = ☐

Use the clues to complete the table.

8

	Dark Shading	Light Shading	Total Shaded	Total Unshaded
Decimal				
Fraction	$\frac{9}{10}$	$\frac{4}{100}$		

9

	Dark Shading	Light Shading	Total Shaded	Total Unshaded
Decimal	0.6	0.07		
Fraction				

10

	Dark Shading	Light Shading	Total Shaded	Total Unshaded
Decimal	0.4		0.46	
Fraction				

Compare the decimals. Write <, >, or =.

11 0.6 ◯ 0.62

0.79 ◯ 0.7

0.43 ◯ 0.4

0.5 ◯ 0.50

12 0.2 ◯ 0.19

0.36 ◯ 0.2

0.47 ◯ 0.8

0.06 ◯ 0.1

13 0.11 ◯ 0.1

0.01 ◯ 0.1

0.01 ◯ 0.10

0.10 ◯ 0.1

14 **Challenge** Write the numbers from problem 12 in order from smallest to largest.

______, ______, ______, ______, ______, ______, ______

Name ________________________ Date ____________

Chapter 8

Lesson 8 Adding Decimals

NCTM Standards 1, 2, 6, 7, 8, 9, 10

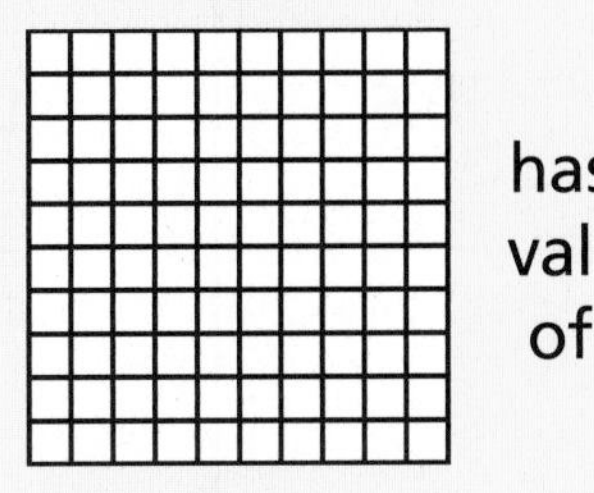

has a value of 1

Use the clues to fill in the missing numbers. Use blocks to help you.

1

		0.24
0.5		

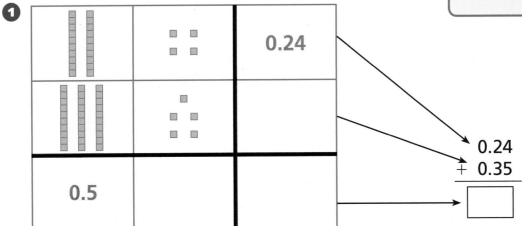

$$\begin{array}{r} 0.24 \\ +\ 0.35 \\ \hline \square \end{array}$$

2

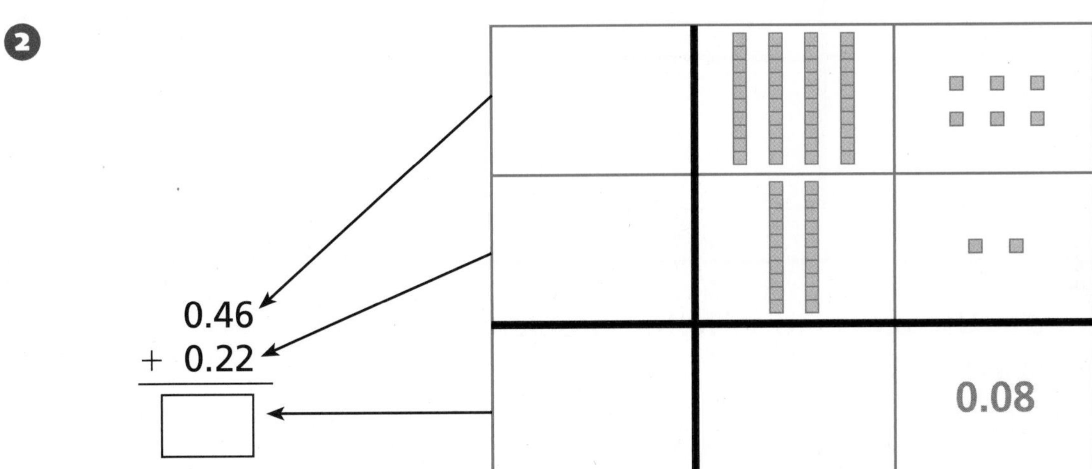

3

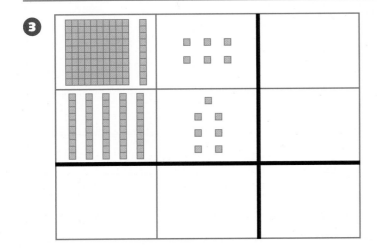

$$\begin{array}{r} 1.16 \\ +\ \square \\ \hline \square \end{array}$$

Use the clues to fill in the missing numbers.

4

0.6	0.03	
		0.54
1.1		

[ ] has a value of 1

$$\begin{array}{r} \square \\ +\ 0.54 \\ \hline \square \end{array}$$

5

		0.48
0.9	0.13	

$$\begin{array}{r} 0.48 \\ +\ \square \\ \hline \square \end{array}$$

6 Challenge Use blocks to solve this problem. Show how you found your answer.

Frania's mom told her she could buy 3 pounds of candy for her party at the Secret Sweets store. Frania bought 1.28 pounds of malted milk balls, $\frac{53}{100}$ of a pound of gummy bears, and $\frac{2}{10}$ of a pound of licorice. How much did her candy weigh? Will she need to put some back? Explain.

____

____

____

____

Chapter 8
Lesson 9

Name ______________________ Date __________

Subtracting Decimals

NCTM Standards 1, 2, 6, 7, 8, 9, 10

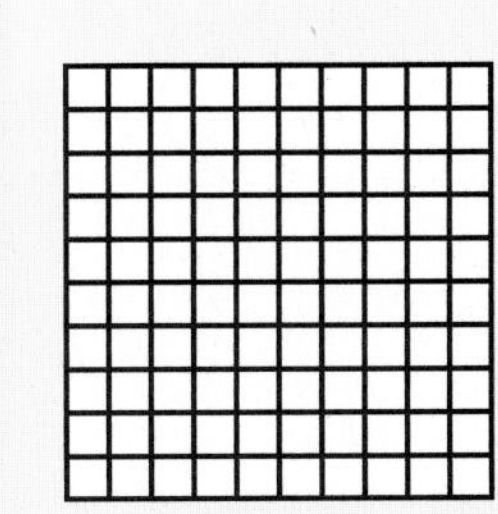
has a value of 1.

Subtract.

1 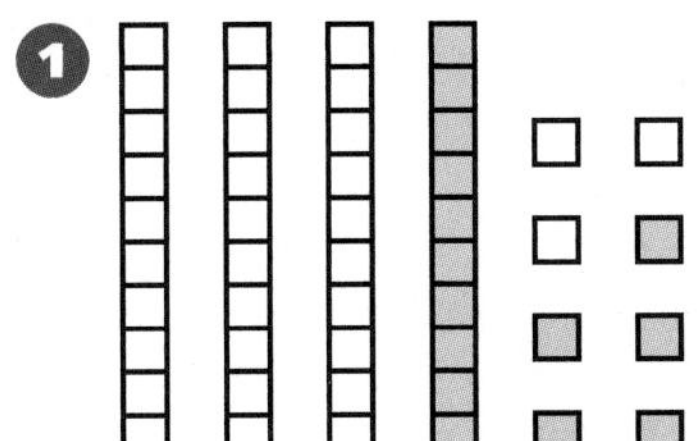

0.48
− 0.15
0.33

2 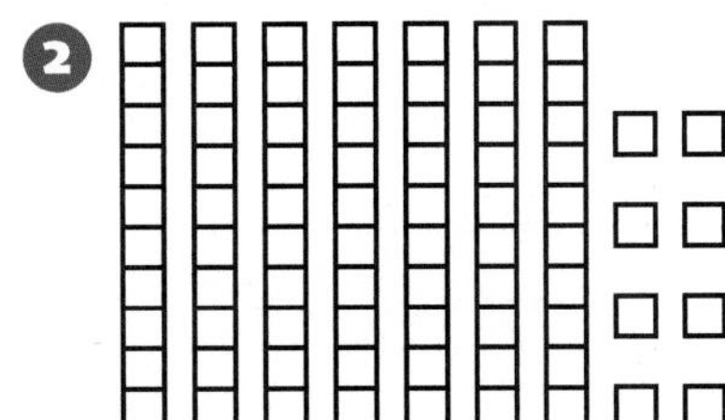

0.78
− 0.36

3 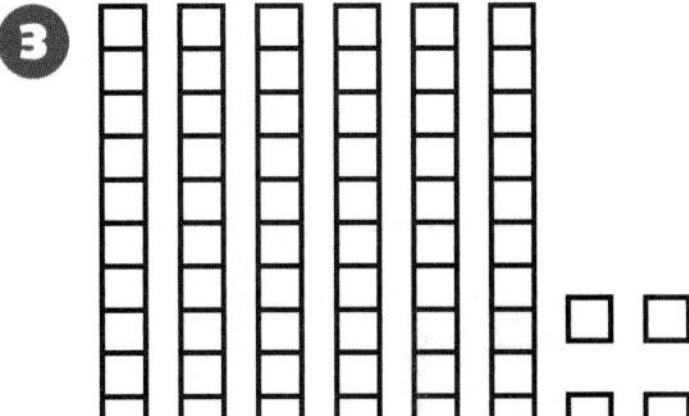

0.64
− 0.29

4 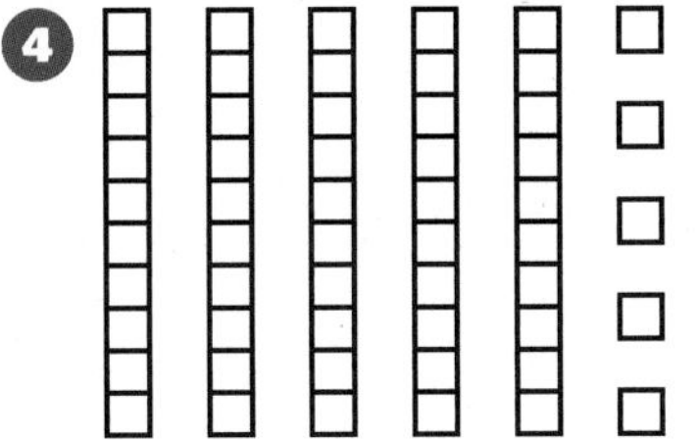

0.55
− 0.48

5 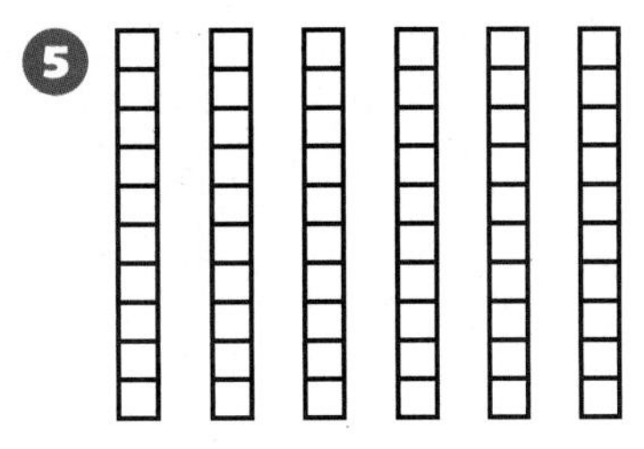

0.6
− 0.24

6 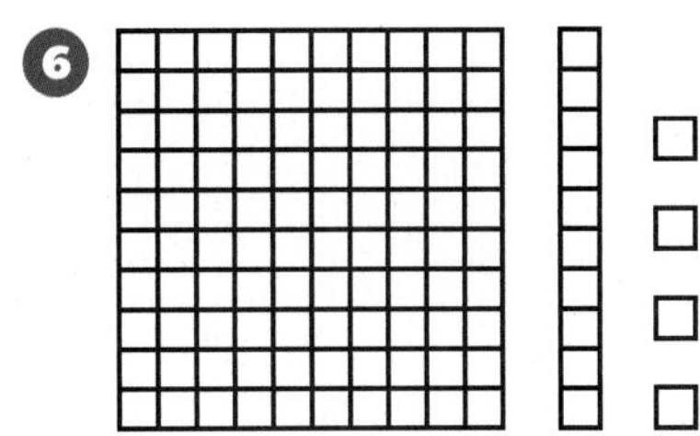

1.14
− 0.73

7 Stanley and Jeffrey earned $9.50 mowing lawns. They used the money to buy 2 ice cream cones that each cost $3.25. The remaining money they shared evenly. How much money will each of them get? Use blocks and pictures to help you. Explain how you found your answer.

______

8 2.25 − 1.13 = ☐

9 0.72 − 0.44 = ☐

10 1.35 − 0.41 = ☐

11 0.8 − 0.73 = ☐

12 0.11 − 0.03 = ☐

13 1.48 − 0.96 = ☐

14 **Challenge**

1.03 − ☐ = 0.18

2.3 − ☐ = 0.71

11.24 − ☐ = 4.89

Chapter 8
Lesson 10

Name ______________________ Date ____________

Representing Decimals Using Money

NCTM Standards 1, 2, 6, 7, 8, 9, 10

Use the clues to fill in the missing numbers.

1

Number of dimes	1	3			4	11		19	27	36
Decimal	0.10		0.90	0.80			1.30			

2

Number of pennies	37			1	8		119		207	
Decimal	0.37	0.49	0.18			0.36		1.93		6.35

3

Number of nickels	1			15	20	21			49	59
Decimal	0.05	0.25	0.45		1		1.50	1.65		

4 $0.51
+ $0.49
[ ]

5 $0.96
+ $0.04
[ ]

6 $0.83
+ $0.17
[ ]

7

$$\begin{array}{r} \$1.00 \\ -\ \$0.73 \\ \hline \square \end{array}$$

8

$$\begin{array}{r} \$1.00 \\ -\ \$0.89 \\ \hline \square \end{array}$$

9

$$\begin{array}{r} \$1.00 \\ -\ \$0.92 \\ \hline \square \end{array}$$

10

$$\begin{array}{r} \$1.30 \\ +\ \square \\ \hline \$2.00 \end{array}$$

11

$$\begin{array}{r} \$1.03 \\ +\ \square \\ \hline \$2.00 \end{array}$$

12

$$\begin{array}{r} \$0.71 \\ +\ \square \\ \hline \$2.00 \end{array}$$

13

$$\begin{array}{r} \$10.00 \\ -\ \square \\ \hline \$7.28 \end{array}$$

14

$$\begin{array}{r} \$20.00 \\ -\ \square \\ \hline \$12.72 \end{array}$$

Challenge **Use words, pictures, and numbers to show how you found your answers.**

15 Letitia is collecting money for her youth group. Her goal is to have $13.50 by Sunday. She's set aside $6.73 of her own money, and her brother said he'd contribute the rest. How much will he need to give her? ________

16 Joneau and Sonya are having a contest to see who can save the most money. Joneau has $15.68 saved up. When Sonya counts her money, she finds out that Joneau has $3.29 more than she does. How much money has Sonya saved? ________

Name ______________________ Date ____________

Chapter 8
Lesson 11

Problem Solving Strategy

Act It Out

NCTM Standards 1, 2, 6, 8, 9, 10

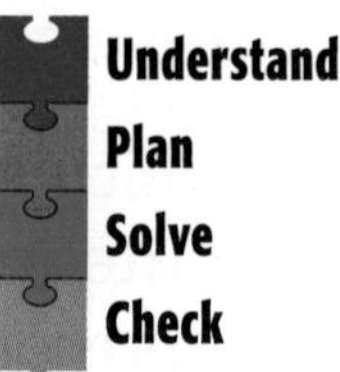

1. Andy gave the cashier a $5 bill to pay for a bag of chips that cost $1.18 and a bottle of juice that cost $0.97. How much change did the cashier give him?

______

2. Loni dealt out 100 cards to her 7 friends so that the friends could play a game. How many cards did each friend get, and how many cards were left over?

Each friend got ______ cards. There were ______ cards left over.

3. Four students lined up from shortest to tallest. Their heights were 4.17 feet, 4.1 feet, 4.71 feet, and 4.7 feet. Celia was taller than Mora but shorter than Soong. Huong was 4.17 feet tall. What was each student's height?

Celia: ____________

Mora: ____________

Soong: ____________

Huong: ____________

Problem Solving Test Prep

Choose the correct answer.

1. Which number sentence can be represented by the picture?

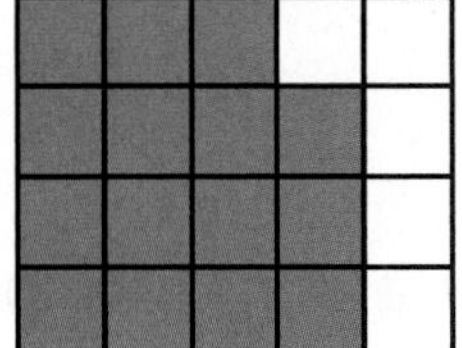

A. $(3 \times 3) + 3 = 12$

B. $(3 \times 4) + 3 = 15$

C. $(4 \times 4) + 3 = 19$

D. $(4 \times 5) + 3 = 23$

2. Which quadrilateral has more than one line of symmetry?

A. 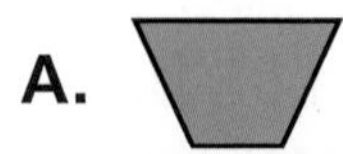

B.

C.

D.

3. Irina begins making a fair spinner by drawing the figure shown here. Which could NOT be the final number of sections on the spinner if she continues to divide the sections equally?

A. 6

B. 8

C. 12

D. 16

4. What is the volume of the box in cubic units?

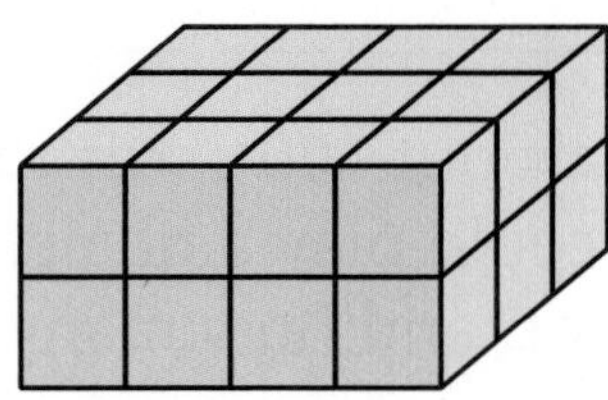

A. 12 cubic units

B. 18 cubic units

C. 24 cubic units

D. 30 cubic units

Show What You Know

Solve each problem. Explain your answer.

5. Ms. Ford buys 6 packages of hamburger rolls. Each package costs \$1.49. She pays with a \$10 bill. The clerk gives her \$2.06 in change. Is the clerk correct? Explain.

6. Ramon folds a square sheet of paper in half, in half again, and then in half one more time. Then he unfolds it. What fraction of the paper is each of the smallest sections? Explain.

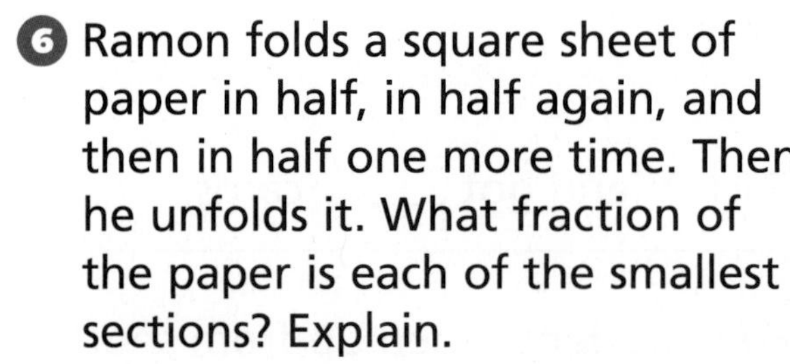

Chapter 8

Name ______________________ Date __________

Review/Assessment

NCTM Standards 1, 2, 6, 7, 8, 9, 10

Write the letter that matches each number's location on the number line. Lessons 1–4

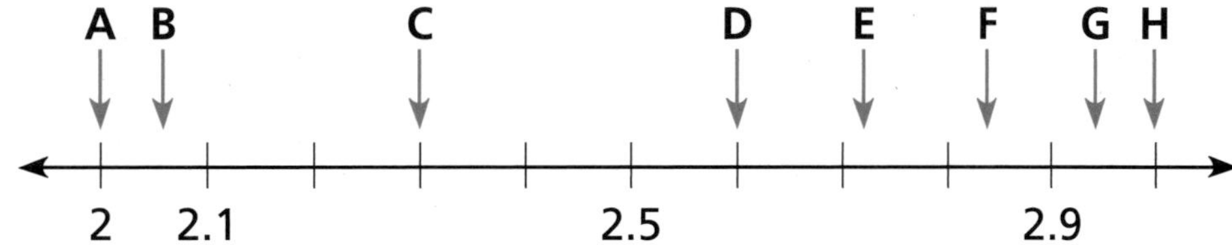

1. 2.3 ______
2. 2.06 ______
3. 2.72 ______
4. 2.94 ______

Complete the table. Lesson 5

	5	6	7
Fraction		$4\frac{48}{100}$	
Decimal	0.3		5.03

Add or subtract. Lessons 8, 9

8. 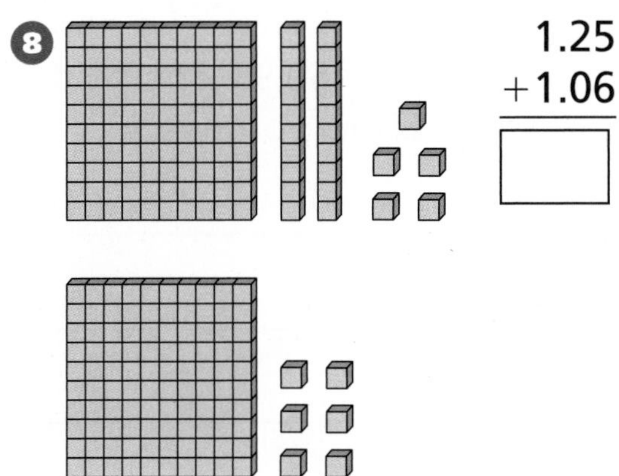

$$\begin{array}{r} 1.25 \\ +1.06 \\ \hline \end{array}$$

9. 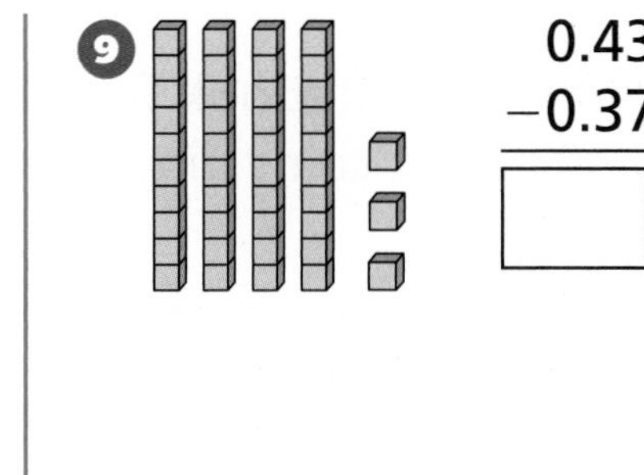

$$\begin{array}{r} 0.43 \\ -0.37 \\ \hline \end{array}$$

Solve. Lessons 3–7, 10

10 Four students ran 100 yards. Their times, in seconds, are 12.17, 12.1, 12.71, and 12.70. Write their times in order from fastest to slowest.

_______ _______ _______ _______

least greatest

11 Luis spent $9.47 at the grocery store. He paid for his items with a $20 bill. How much change did he receive?

____

Compare the numbers. Lessons 3–7

12 9,908,302 ◯ 9,980,302

13 3.78 ◯ 3.7

14 1,301,000 ◯ 1,300,792

15 0.2 ◯ 0.20

Solve. Lessons 8, 10

16 Kaitlyn bought two watermelons. One weighed 6.37 pounds and the other weighed 8.58 pounds. What was the total weight of the two watermelons?

____

17 Latoria bought a new notebook for $2.59 and a new pen for $0.95. She paid the cashier $4.00. What coins did she receive as change? Show your work.

____

____

____

Name ______________________ Date ____________

Chapter 9
Lesson 1

Computing with Time and Money

NCTM Standards 1, 2, 6, 7, 8, 9, 10

Complete the tables and number sentences.

1

Weeks	1	2	3	4	5
Days	7				

2

Hours	1	2	3	4	5
Minutes	60				

3

Dimes	1	2	3	4	5
Nickels	2				

4

Dollars	1	2	3	4	5
Quarters	4				

5   +      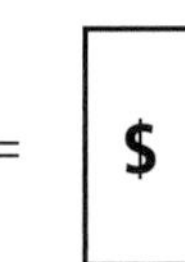 = 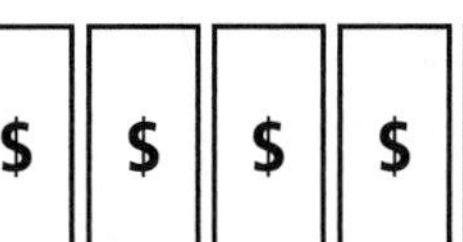

$1.50 + ______ = ______

6     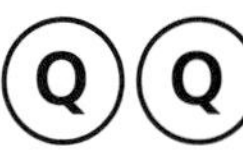

______ − ______ = ______

7. 4 nickels + 3 dimes = ____¢

8. 2 weeks × 3 = ____ days

9. 13 days + 8 days = ____ weeks

10. 1 nickel × 4 = ____¢

11. 2 weeks − 9 days = ____ days

12. 30 minutes × 4 = ____ hours

13. 7 nickels + 9 nickels = ____ dimes

14. 1 hour ÷ 2 = ____ minutes

15. 80 minutes + 40 minutes = ____ hours

16. 1 hour ÷ 4 = ____ minutes

Find the missing numbers.

17 9¢ + 18¢ = ______

18 $1.18 + ______ = $1.93

19 $3.00 − $2.50 = ______

20 ______ − ______ = 27¢

21 ______ + 27¢ = $1.00

22 25¢ × 7 = ______

23 75¢ + ______ = $1.50

24 50¢ × 2 = ______

25 $2.00 − $1.25 = ______

26 25¢ × 3 = ______

27 86¢ − ______ = 59¢

28 $2.00 ÷ 4 = ______

29 $2.50 + ______ = $7.00

30 75¢ × 2 = ______

31 ______ + ______ = 86¢

32 ______ ÷ 2 = 75¢

How many cents?

33 13¢ + 1 quarter = ______

34 13¢ × 4 = ______

35 13¢ + 7 nickels = ______

36 13¢ × 5 = ______

37 13¢ + 3 quarters = ______

38 13¢ × 6 = ______

39 13¢ + 12 dimes = ______

40 13¢ × 7 = ______

41 Challenge

7 + _____ = 2 dozen

_____ min + 48 min = 1 ______

317 days + _____ days = 1 ______

_____ min + __________ = 1 day

Name ______________________ Date ______________

Chapter 9
Lesson 2

Measuring Temperature

NCTM Standards 1, 2, 6, 7, 8, 9, 10

Use the table to answer the questions below.

	Temperature at 7:00 A.M.	Temperature at noon	Temperature at 7:00 P.M.
Monday	60°F	82°F	71°F
Wednesday	53°F	70°F	65°F
Friday	49°F	76°F	69°F

1. On what day and at what time was the coldest temperature measured?

   On ______________ at 7:00 A.M.

2. On what day and at what time was the hottest temperature measured?

   On ______________ at ______________

3. Which day had the greatest change in temperature from 7:00 A.M. to noon?

   ____

4. Which day had the least change in temperature from 7:00 A.M. to noon?

   ____

5. By how many degrees did the temperature change from noon to 7:00 P.M. on Monday?

   ________°F

Solve.

6. If today's weather forecast is a low of 68°F and a high of 87°F, by how many degrees is the temperature expected to change?

_______°F

7. The temperature dropped 16°F overnight. The temperature in the morning was 45°F. What was the temperature the previous night?

_______°F

8. Joey has a fever of 101.3°F. By how many degrees must his temperature drop to reach the normal body temperature of 98.6°F?

_______°F

9. **Challenge** Erin is going on a trip to visit her aunt. The weather where her aunt lives is always 23°F cooler than it is where Erin lives. Complete the table with the correct temperatures to help Erin decide what to bring on her trip.

	Monday	Tuesday	Wednesday	Thursday	Friday
Erin's Town	61°F			84°F	72°F
Aunt's Town		35°F	46°F		

Name ______________________ Date ____________

Chapter 9
Lesson 3

Measuring Length

NCTM Standards 1, 2, 6, 7, 8, 9, 10

Measurement Scavenger Hunt

Use a ruler to find things in your classroom that match these descriptions. Write the length of each object below its name.

1. something longer than your foot

   Object: ____________

   Length: ____________

2. something shorter than 2 inches

   Object: ____________

   Length: ____________

3. something a little longer than 6 inches

   Object: ____________

   Length: ____________

4. something about 1 inch wide

   Object: ____________

   Length: ____________

5. something about 2.5 centimeters wide

   Object: ____________

   Length: ____________

6. something shorter than your pinkie finger

   Object: ____________

   Length: ____________

7. something longer than 1 foot but shorter than 2 feet

   Object: ____________

   Length: ____________

8. something longer than 20 centimeters but shorter than 25 centimeters

   Object: ____________

   Length: ____________

9. something about the length of your thumb

   Object: ____________

   Length: ____________

Use a ruler and estimate to find things in your classroom that match these descriptions.

10. something taller than you

Object: ____________

11. something taller than your teacher

Object: ____________

12. something a little shorter than 2 feet

Object: ____________

13. something about 10 centimeters long

Object: ____________

14. something about 1 foot long

Object: ____________

15. something longer than 5 feet

Object: ____________

16. something about 1 yard long

Object: ____________

17. something about 100 centimeters long

Object: ____________

18. something about 3 feet long

Object: ____________

19. **Challenge**

something longer than 1 foot but shorter than 100 centimeters

Object: ________

20. **Challenge**

something longer than 2 centimeters but shorter than 1 foot

Object: ________

21. **Challenge**

something longer than 1 meter but shorter than 3 yards

Object: ________

Name ______________________ Date ____________

Chapter 9

Lesson 4

Measuring in Inches, Feet, and Yards

NCTM Standards 1, 2, 6, 7, 8, 9, 10

Complete the tables and number sentences.

1

Feet	$\frac{1}{2}$	1	2	3	4
Inches					

Weeks	1	2	3	4	5
Days					

Hours	$\frac{1}{2}$	1	2	3	4
Minutes					

Yards	$\frac{1}{3}$	1	2	3	4
Feet					

2 2 feet = ______ inches

2 feet + 8 inches = ______ inches

3 1 foot = ______ inches

1 foot ÷ 2 = ______ inches

4 1 yard = ______ feet

1 yard − 1 foot = ______ feet

5 5 yards = ______ feet

5 yards − 9 feet = ______ feet

Estimate the length of each line. Then measure each line with a ruler to find the exact length.

6 Estimate: ______ inches

Exact: ______ inches

7 Estimate: ______ inches

Exact: ______ inches

Complete the tables and number sentences.

8

Yards	0	1	2	3	4
Feet	0	3			

Feet	0	1	2	3	4
Inches					

Yards	2	4	6	10	16
Feet					

Feet	2		12	3	20
Inches		120			

9

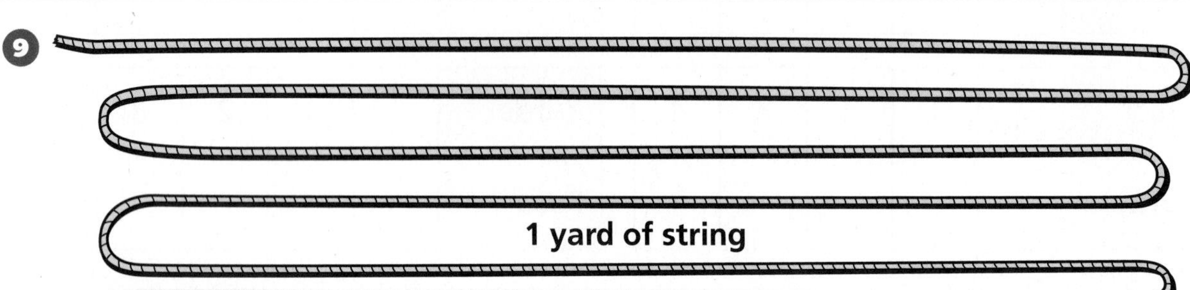

1 yard + 2 feet = ______ feet

1 yard + 4 inches = ______ inches

1 yard − 1 inch = ______ inches

1 yard − 6 inches = ______ inches

1 yard + 1 foot = ______ inches

1 yard × 3 = ______ feet

1 yard × 2 = ______ feet

1 yard ÷ 3 = ______ feet

1 yard ÷ 3 = ______ inches

1 yard ÷ 6 = ______ inches

10 Challenge

Dimes	10	20	25	30	40
Dollars					

Chapter 9
Lesson 5

Name ______________________ Date ______________

Measuring Length in Centimeters

NCTM Standards 1, 2, 6, 7, 8, 9, 10

1 Complete the table.

Cuisenaire® Rod										
Length in Centimeters	1									

Measure each line with the Cuisenaire® Rod shown. Then, find the length of the line in centimeters.

2

7 red rods ______ centimeters

3

______ light green rods ______ centimeters

4

______ yellow rods ______ centimeters

5

______ purple rods ______ centimeters

Estimate the length of each line with the units shown. Then, estimate each length in centimeters. The paper clip is about 3 cm long.

6

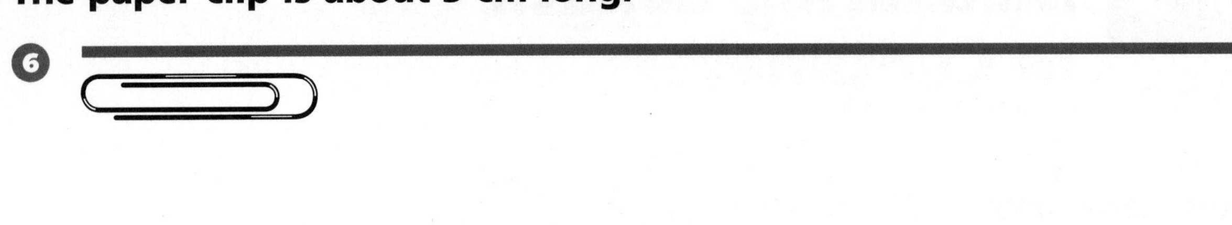

______ paper clips ______ centimeters

7

______ paper clips ______ centimeters

8

______ paper clips ______ centimeters

9

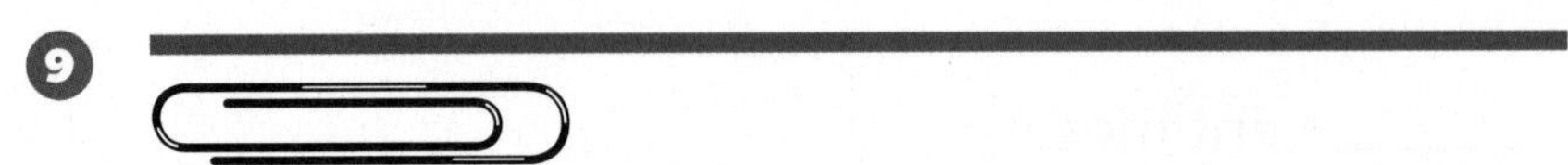

______________ paper clips ______ centimeters

10 Challenge

2 ____________ rods 14 centimeters

Name ______________________ Date ____________

Chapter 9
Lesson 6

Measuring Capacity in Cups, Pints, and Quarts

NCTM Standards 1, 2, 6, 7, 8, 9, 10

Compare the amounts. Write <, >, or = in each ◯.

1. 1 quart ◯ 1 pint
2. 2 cups ◯ 1 pint
3. 1 cup ◯ 1 quart
4. 1 quart ◯ 3 pints
5. 1 pint ◯ 1 cup
6. 3 cups ◯ 1 quart

Write the missing number to make each statement true.

7. 1 pint = _____ cups
8. 1 quart = _____ pints
9. 1 quart = _____ cups
10. _____ pints = 4 cups
11. 6 pints = _____ quarts
12. _____ cups = 3 pints

Solve.

13 Howie filled a pint container halfway. How many more cups does he need to fill the container completely?

_____ cup(s)

14 Sharon poured 3 cups of water out of a filled 2-pint container. How many cups were left?

_____ cup(s)

15 Rebecca used a pint container to fill a quart container with water. How many times did she fill the pint container?

_____ times

16 Carl needed a quart of milk for his special smoothies. He had 3 cups of milk. Did he have enough?

yes no

17 Jen bought a pint of juice at the store and shared it equally with a friend. How much did each child get?

____

18 Lizzie gave each of her 6 friends a cup of milk. How many pints is that?

_____ pints

19 **Challenge** Peter poured 6 cups of water into a 2-quart container. Did he fill the container?

yes no

20 **Challenge** James emptied half of a 2-quart container into pint containers. He poured the rest into cups. How many cups did he fill?

_____ cups

Chapter 9
Lesson 7

Name ____________________ Date ____________

Measuring Capacity in Gallons and Liters

NCTM Standards 1, 2, 6, 7, 8, 9, 10

1 cup

1 pint

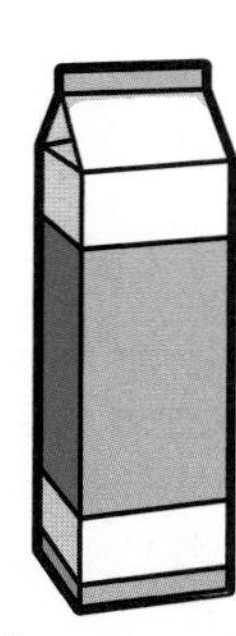
1 quart

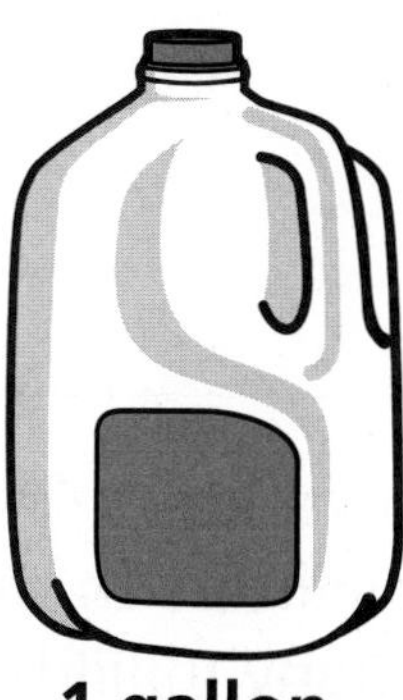
1 gallon

Fill in the missing numbers.

1. 1 gallon = _____ quarts

2. 1 gallon = _____ pints

3. 1 gallon = _____ cups

4. _____ cups = 1 pint

5. 2 pints = _____ quart

6. 8 quarts = _____ gallons

7. 8 quarts = _____ pints

8. _____ gallons = 16 pints

Solve.

9 Evan poured a cup of water into a quart container. How many more cups are needed to fill the container?

_____ cups

10 Elsie filled a gallon container with water using a pint container. How many times did she fill the pint container?

_____ times

11 Pat had a liter of milk. He used 300 milliliters to make pancakes. How many milliliters did he have left?

_____ milliliters

12 Stephanie poured 18 cups of water into a gallon container. Did the container overflow?

yes no

13 Josh bought a gallon of milk at the store and gave a pint to each of his 8 friends. Was there any milk left for him?

yes no

14 Matt filled a quart container halfway. How many more cups did he need to fill the container completely?

_____ cups

15 **Challenge** Cindy had 2 gallons of milk to make smoothies. Each smoothie used 2 cups of milk. How many smoothies could she make?

_____ smoothies

16 **Challenge** June needed 7 quarts of juice, but the store sold only liter containers. How many liters should she buy?

_____ liters

Chapter 9

Lesson 8

Name ______________________ Date ____________

Computing Amounts of Liquid

NCTM Standards 1, 2, 6, 7, 8, 9, 10

Complete the table.

1.

Gallons	0	1	2	3	4	5
Quarts	0	4	8			

2.

Quarts	1	2	3	5	8	13
Pints	2	4				

3.

Quarts	$\frac{1}{2}$	1	$1\frac{1}{2}$	2	$2\frac{1}{2}$	3
Cups		4				

Fill in the blanks. Use the above tables to help you.

4. 2 quarts + 2 quarts = _____ quarts

   2 quarts + 2 quarts = _____ gallon

5. 3 pints + 1 pint = _____ pints

   3 pints + 1 pint = _____ quarts

6. 1 gallon = _____ quarts

   1 gallon − 1 quart = _____ quarts

7. 1 quart × 8 = _____ quarts

   1 quart × 8 = _____ gallons

8. 2 quarts = _____ pints

   2 quarts − 1 pint = _____ pints

9. 1 gallon × 3 = _____ gallons

   1 gallon × 3 = _____ quarts

Complete the table.

10

Gallons	1	2	3	4	5	6
Quarts	4					
Pints	8					
Cups	16					

11 Write a word problem that can be solved using the table above. Then solve it.

____

____

____

Fill in the blanks. Use the above table to help you.

12 $\frac{1}{2}$ gallon = ______ quarts

$\frac{1}{2}$ gallon = ______ pints

2 cups × 4 = ______ pints

2 pints ÷ 2 = ______ cups

5 pints − 2 cups = ______ cups

$\frac{1}{2}$ quart = ______ pint

8 quarts ÷ 2 = ______ gallon

1 gallon − 1 cup= ______ cups

13

Liters	$\frac{1}{2}$	1	$1\frac{1}{2}$	2	$2\frac{1}{2}$	3
Milliliters		1,000				

14 **Challenge**

1 liter − $\frac{1}{2}$ liter = ______ mL

15 **Challenge**

2,500 mL + 1 liter = ______ mL

16 **Challenge**

3 liters ÷ 2 = ______ mL

17 **Challenge**

2,000 mL × 2 = ______ liters

Chapter 9
Lesson 9

Name ______________________ Date ______________

Measuring Weight in Ounces, Pounds, and Tons

NCTM Standards 1, 2, 6, 7, 8, 9, 10

Complete the tables.

1.

Pounds	1	2	3	4	5	6	7	8	9	10
Ounces	16									

2.

Pounds	0	$\frac{1}{2}$	1	$1\frac{1}{2}$	2	$2\frac{1}{2}$	3	$3\frac{1}{2}$	4	$4\frac{1}{2}$
Ounces	0	8								

3.

Pounds	0	$\frac{1}{4}$	$\frac{1}{2}$	$\frac{3}{4}$	1	$1\frac{1}{4}$	$1\frac{1}{2}$	$1\frac{3}{4}$	2	$2\frac{1}{4}$
Ounces	0	4								

4.

Tons	1	2	3	4	5	6	7	8	9	10
Pounds	2,000									

5.

Tons	0	$\frac{1}{2}$	1	$1\frac{1}{2}$	2	$2\frac{1}{2}$	3	$3\frac{1}{2}$	4	$4\frac{1}{2}$
Pounds										

6.

Tons	0	$\frac{1}{4}$	$\frac{1}{2}$	$\frac{3}{4}$	1	$1\frac{1}{4}$	$1\frac{1}{2}$	$1\frac{3}{4}$	2	$2\frac{1}{4}$
Pounds										

7 Decide whether you would measure the weight of each item in ounces, pounds, or tons. Then write the name of the item in the correct column below.

Pencil	Lamp	Package
Statue of Liberty	Car	Dog
Apple	Light bulb	Pad of paper
Whale	Chair	Desk
Refrigerator	Newspaper	Fire truck

Ounces	Pounds	Tons
Pencil		

8 **Challenge** Explain how you chose where to write package.

____

____

____

____

Chapter 9
Lesson 10

Name ______________________ Date ____________

Measuring Weight in Grams and Kilograms

NCTM Standards 1, 2, 6, 7, 8, 9, 10

Complete the tables.

1

Kilograms	1	2	3	5	8	10	12	15
Grams	1,000							

2

Kilograms	0	$\frac{1}{2}$	1	$1\frac{1}{2}$	2	$2\frac{1}{2}$	3	$3\frac{1}{2}$
Grams	0	500						

3

Kilograms		$\frac{1}{4}$	$\frac{1}{2}$	$\frac{3}{4}$			$3\frac{3}{4}$	
Grams	0			750	1,000	2,250		5,500

4

Yards	1	2	3	5	10		$\frac{5}{6}$	$1\frac{1}{6}$
Feet	3					$4\frac{1}{2}$		
Inches	36						30	42

5

Hours	0	$\frac{1}{2}$	1	$1\frac{1}{2}$	2	$2\frac{1}{2}$	3	$3\frac{1}{2}$
Minutes	0		60					
Seconds	0		3,600					

Solve.

6. If a paper clip weighs about 1 gram, about how much do 273 paper clips weigh?

____

7. If 3,016 large paper clips weigh about 6 kilograms, about how much does 1 large paper clip weigh?

____

8. There are 250 paper clips in a box. Each box weighs $\frac{1}{4}$ of a kilogram.

How many boxes weigh $3\frac{1}{2}$ kilograms? _______________

How many boxes weigh 7 kilograms? _______________

How many boxes weigh 70 kilograms? _______________

9. Could a car weigh 5 kilograms?

____

10. Could a book weigh 5 kilograms?

____

11. **Challenge** A kilogram is a little heavier than 2 pounds. Write <, >, or =.

2 kilograms ◯ 4 pounds

3 kilograms ◯ 10 pounds

3 kilograms ◯ 3 pounds

$5\frac{1}{2}$ kilograms ◯ 10 pounds

Name ______________________ Date ______________

Chapter 9
Lesson 11

Problem Solving Strategy

Look for a Pattern

NCTM Standards 1, 2, 6, 7, 8, 9, 10

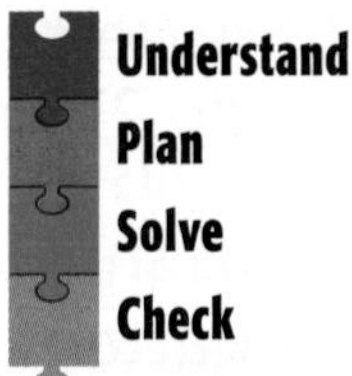

1. Rita measured the temperature in degrees Fahrenheit (°F) for several days. Her teacher, Mr. Chang, changed her measurements to a made-up unit called degrees Zonk (°Z). Complete the table.

°F	32	50	68	86	
°Z	0	10	20		40

How did you complete the table?

____

____

____

____

____

____

2. Wendy invented her own unit of measurement called the gool. She made a table of some measurements, and then converted them into inches. Complete the table.

	Paper	Crayon	Pencil	Water Bottle	Finger
Gools	104	52	65		39
Inches	8		5	9	3

Problem Solving Test Prep

Choose the correct answer.

1. Rolls at the bakery are priced as shown in the table. If the pattern continues, how much would 10 rolls cost?

Rolls	1	2	3	4
Cost	$0.50	$0.75	$1.00	$1.25

A. $2.00   C. $2.50
B. $2.25   D. $2.75

2. How many more faces does a rectangular prism with a square base have than a pyramid with a square base?

A. 1
B. 2
C. 3
D. 4

Show What You Know

Solve each problem. Explain your answer.

3. There are 10 sandwiches on a plate. They have either turkey or salami or both. Four of the sandwiches have turkey, and 8 have salami. How many have both? Explain how you found your answer.

____

____

____

____

____

____

____

____

____

4. In the pattern shown below, you can find the sum of each row.

			1				Row 1
		1		1			Row 2
	1		2		1		Row 3
1		3		3		1	Row 4

Describe the pattern you see in the sums of the first 4 rows. If the pattern continues, what will be the sum of Row 8? Explain how you decided.

____

____

____

____

____

Name ______________________ Date ____________

Review/Assessment

NCTM Standards 1, 2, 6, 7, 8, 9, 10

1. Write the temperatures. Lesson 2

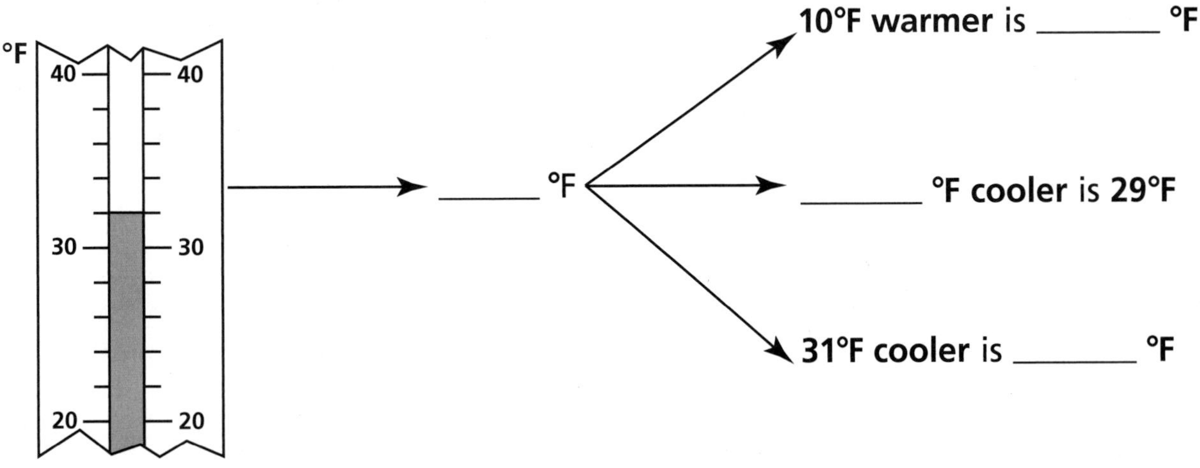

Measure each length. Lesson 3

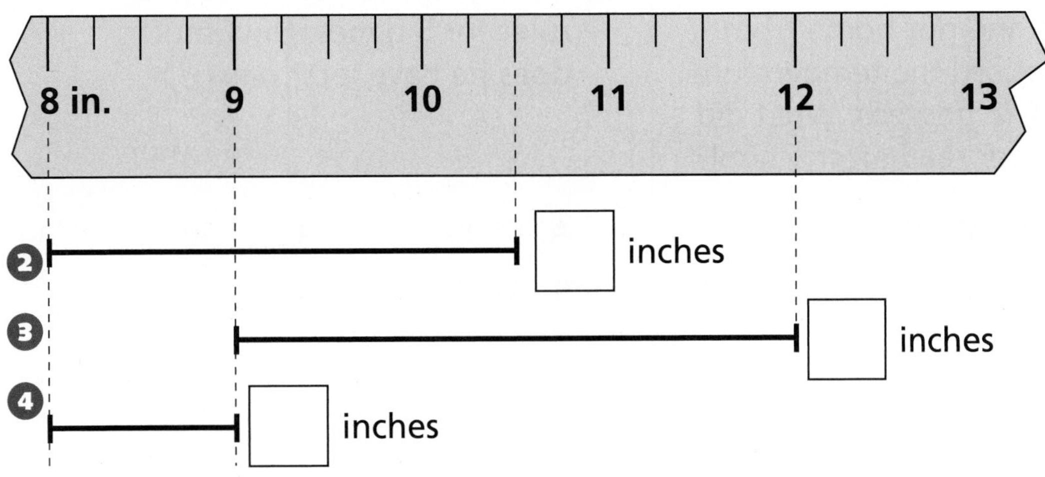

5. Complete the table. Lesson 5

Centimeters		300			600		250	10,000
Meters	1	3	5	10		$1\frac{1}{2}$		

Find the missing numbers to make each statement true. Lessons 1, 4, 6, 9

6. $3.00 ÷ 3 = _____ quarters

7. 3 weeks = _____ days

   3 weeks − 9 days = _____ days

8. 4 inches × 3 = _____ inches

   4 inches × 3 = _____ foot

9. 9 inches × 4 = _____ inches

   9 inches × 4 = _____ yard(s)

10. 2 kilograms = _______ grams

    2 kilograms ÷ 2 = _______ grams

11. 25 centimeters × 12 = _____ cm

    25 centimeters × 12 = _____ meters

12. It was 56°F when Erin got up for school. When she got home from school, she noticed the temperature had increased 12 degrees. What did the thermometer read after school? Lesson 2

    A. 12°F
    B. 44°F
    C. 70°F
    D. 68°F

13. Manny has $2.10. He buys a ruler for 5 dimes. How much does he have left? Lesson 1

    A. $1.00
    B. $1.50
    C. $1.60
    D. $1.70

14. A brick wall has 40 bricks on the first layer, 36 bricks on the second layer and 32 in the third layer. If the pattern continues, how many bricks will be on the fifth layer? Lesson 11

    A. 44 bricks
    B. 28 bricks
    C. 24 bricks
    D. 20 bricks

Chapter 10
Lesson 1

Name ______________________ Date ____________

Finding Combinations of Attributes

NCTM Standards 1, 2, 6, 7, 8, 9, 10

Describe all the cards that could be made for each setting. You might not need all the spaces.

1. Figure = [parallelogram]

_______________ _______________
_______________ _______________
_______________ _______________

2. Color = green

_______________ _______________
_______________ _______________
_______________ _______________

3. Shading = [shaded diamond]; Figure = [triangle]

_______________ _______________
_______________ _______________
_______________ _______________

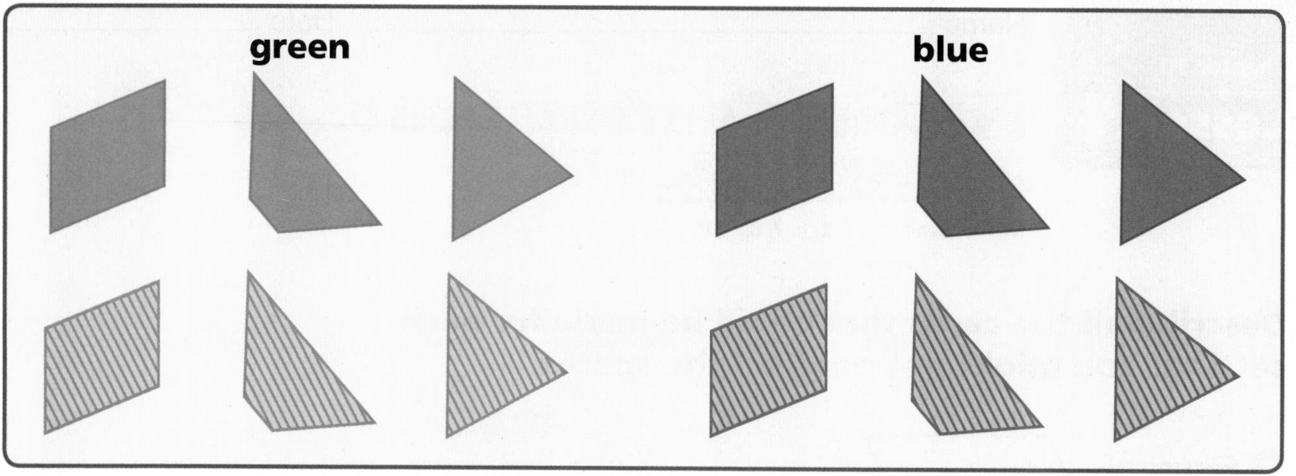

Answer the questions about the cards.

4 What portion of the cards

are green? ____ out of ____

What portion of the cards

have a triangle? ____ out of ____

What portion of the cards have

a green triangle? ____ out of ____

5 What portion of the cards

have polka dots? ____ out of ____

What portion of the cards

have a trapezoid? ____ out of ____

What portion of the cards have a

polka-dot trapezoid? ____ out of ____

6 What portion of the cards have a parallelogram? ____ out of ____

What portion of the cards have a solid blue figure? ____ out of ____

What portion of the cards have at least one of these attributes: a parallelogram or a solid blue figure? ____ out of ____

7 Challenge

What portion of the cards do not have a triangle? ____ out of ____

What portion of the cards are not green? ____ out of ____

What portion of the cards are green and do not have a triangle? ____ out of ____

What portion of the cards have at least one of these attributes: green or no triangle? ____ out of ____

Chapter 10

Lesson 2

Name ______________________ Date ____________

Describing the Likelihood of an Event

NCTM Standards 1, 2, 6, 7, 8, 9, 10

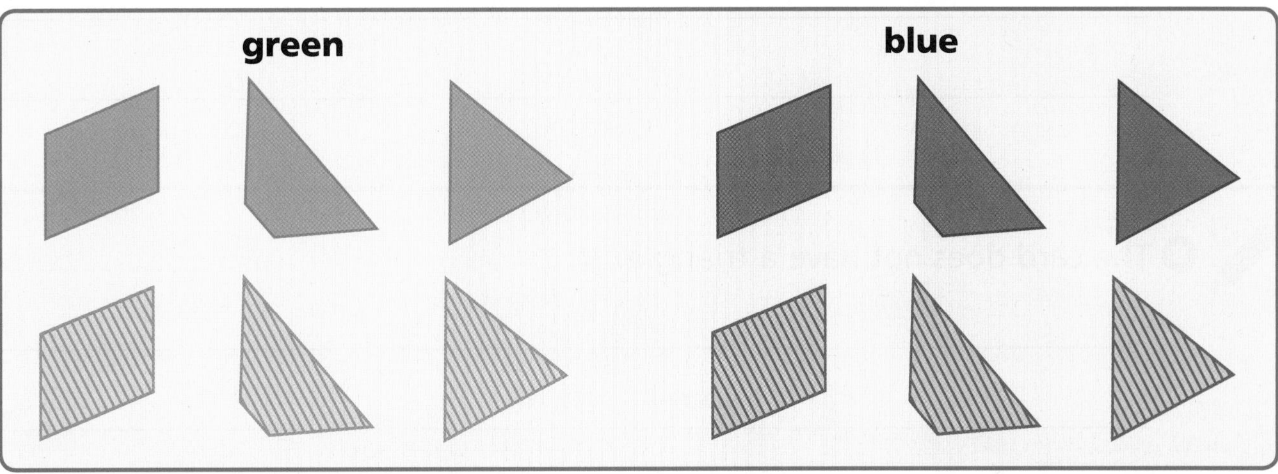

1. What portion of the cards have parallelograms? ____ out of ____

   Write your answer as a fraction. ______

2. What portion of the cards are blue or green? ____ out of ____

   Write your answer as a fraction. ______

3. What portion of the cards are blue or solid-colored or both? ____ out of ____

   Write your answer as a fraction. ______

Label these possibilities *certain, likely, unlikely,* or *impossible,* using your answers to the above questions.

4. choosing a card with a parallelogram ____________

5. choosing a card that is blue or green ____________

6. choosing a card that is blue or solid or both ____________

Label these possibilities *certain, likely, unlikely,* or *impossible* and explain why you chose each answer.

7 The card has a striped trapezoid. ______

______

______

______

8 The card does not have a triangle. ______

______

______

______

Give an example of a possibility that fits each label.

9 Impossible The card ______

10 Likely The card ______

11 Unlikely The card ______

12 **Challenge** Michaela has a bag of marbles. $\frac{1}{3}$ of the marbles are red, $\frac{1}{6}$ of the marbles are blue, and $\frac{1}{2}$ of the marbles are yellow.

If Michaela picks a marble without looking, what color is she most likely to pick? ______

Explain your reasoning.

______

______

Name ________________________ Date ____________

Introducing Probability

NCTM Standards 1, 2, 6, 7, 8, 9, 10

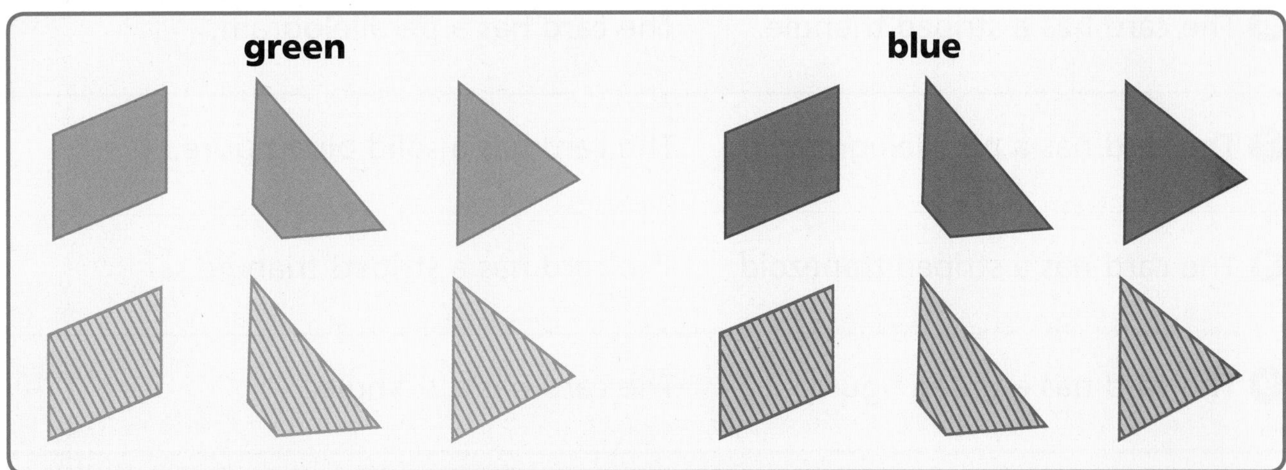

In the answer boxes on the right side of the page, write a fraction to show the probability of getting a card like the named card if you draw one card without looking.

What portion of the cards . . .

1. . . . have a solid green trapezoid? ____ out of ____ ______

   . . . do NOT have a solid green trapezoid? ____ out of ____ ______

2. . . . are red? ____ out of ____ ______

   . . . are NOT red? ____ out of ____ ______

3. . . . have a solid blue figure? ____ out of ____ ______

   . . . do NOT have a solid blue figure? ____ out of ____ ______

4. . . . have a trapezoid? ____ out of ____ ______

   . . . are blue? ____ out of ____ ______

   . . . have a blue trapezoid? ____ out of ____ ______

   . . . are a trapezoid or blue or both? ____ out of ____ ______

For each pair, circle the outcome that is more likely. Circle both if they are equally likely.

5. The card has a parallelogram. The card does NOT have a parallelogram.

6. The card has a striped triangle. The card has a parallelogram.

7. The card has a parallelogram. The card has a solid blue figure.

8. The card has a striped trapezoid. The card has a striped triangle.

9. The card has a green figure. The card has a triangle.

10. Explain why you chose your answers for Problems 5–9.

11. The card has an orange figure. The card does NOT have a parallelogram.

12. Explain why you chose your answer for Problem 11.

13. **Challenge** Imagine that you choose one card from the deck, look at it, put it back, shuffle, and then repeat 30 times. About how many times do you expect to see a card with a blue figure on it? ________

Is it certain, likely, unlikely, or impossible that you will see at least one card more than once? ________

Name ______________________ Date ____________

Chapter 10
Lesson 4

Drawing From a Deck of Attribute Cards

NCTM Standards 1, 2, 6, 7, 8, 9, 10

Trapezoid Experiment

Draw an attribute card from the deck 30 times, replacing the card and shuffling the deck after each draw. How many times did you pick a card with a trapezoid on it?

Data

For each draw, mark whether the card has a trapezoid or not by writing **YES** or **NO** in the column on the right.

Draw	Trapezoid?
1	
2	
3	
4	
5	
6	
7	
8	
9	
10	

Draw	Trapezoid?
11	
12	
13	
14	
15	
16	
17	
18	
19	
20	

Draw	Trapezoid?
21	
22	
23	
24	
25	
26	
27	
28	
29	
30	

What portion of the cards you drew were trapezoids? _____ out of 30

In several classrooms, students drew a card 30 times and recorded the number of triangles they picked. The results for three of the classes are given below.

A

Number of triangles picked	5	6	7	8	9	10	11	12	13	14	15
Number of students	0	0	0	8	4	8	7	2	1	0	0

B

Number of triangles picked	5	6	7	8	9	10	11	12	13	14	15
Number of students	0	0	1	6	6	11	5	1	0	0	0

C

Number of triangles picked	5	6	7	8	9	10	11	12	13	14	15
Number of students	1	0	3	5	7	6	3	1	2	0	2

Label each graph with the set of data it matches.

1

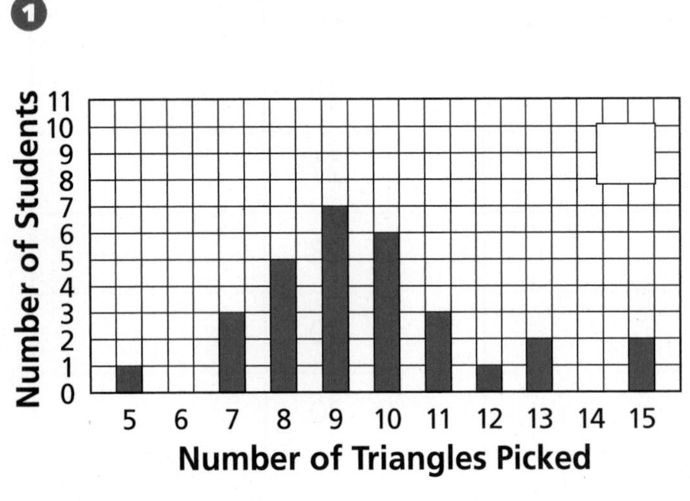

2 Challenge

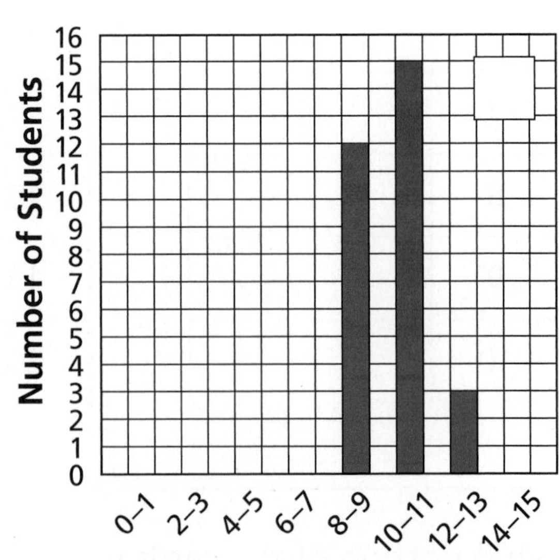

Chapter 10

Lesson 5

Name ______________________ Date ____________

Drawing Blocks

NCTM Standards 1, 2, 6, 7, 8, 9, 10

In the 9-block experiment, your class drew one of these blocks at random, 27 times. Use your class's graph of the data from the experiment to answer these questions.

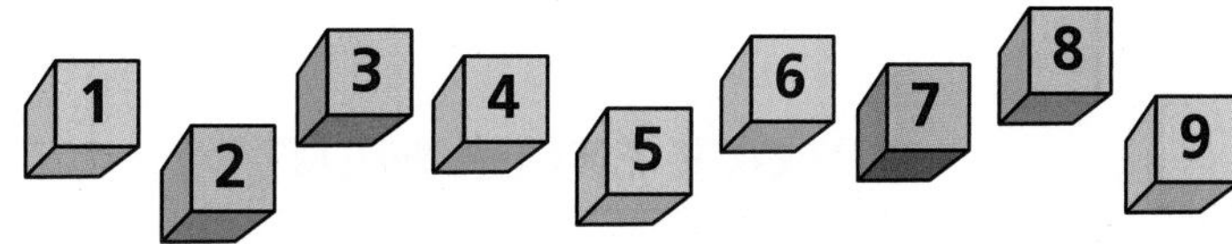

1. Which block or blocks was picked most frequently? ____________

2. Which block or blocks was picked least frequently? ____________

3. What portion of the blocks picked were even-numbered? _____ out of _____

4. What portion of the blocks picked were numbered with multiples of 3? _____ out of _____

5. What portion of the blocks picked were numbered with square numbers? _____ out of _____

6. What portion of the blocks picked were numbered 5 or higher? _____ out of _____

7. Were there any blocks that didn't get picked at all? ____________

Mrs. Garabedian's class did the 9-block experiment. Each student picked a block from the bag. Here are their results:

❽ Graph the data.

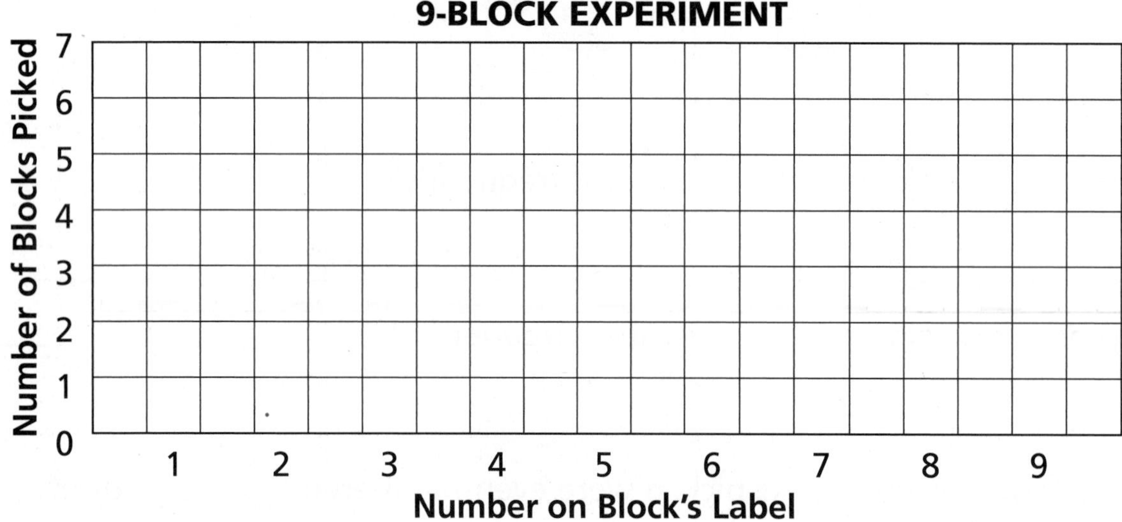

❾ What portion of the blocks picked were even-numbered? _____ out of _____

❿ What portion of the blocks picked were numbered with multiples of 3? _____ out of _____

⓫ **Challenge** Choose one thing about this class's results that surprises you. Explain why it surprises you.

____

____

____

Chapter 10
Lesson 6

Name ____________________ Date ____________

Collecting and Analyzing Survey Data

NCTM Standards 1, 2, 6, 7, 8, 9, 10

Ms. Ramiro's class made a graph of the number of books each student read during summer vacation.

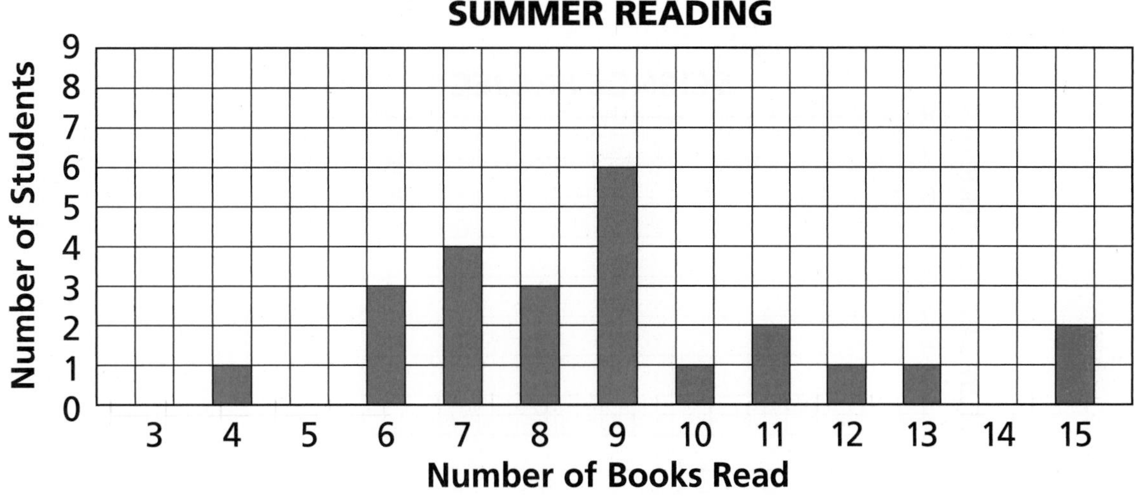

1. What was the most common number of books read? ____

2. What was the largest number of books read? ____

3. What portion of the students read at least 8 books? ____ out of ____

4. What portion of the students read 6, 7, 8, or 9 books? ____ out of ____

Mr. Tan surveyed his students to find out how long it took them to finish a science project. Here is the data:

3 hours	5 hours	$5\frac{1}{2}$ hours	4 hours	3 hours
5 hours	$4\frac{1}{2}$ hours	4 hours	$4\frac{1}{2}$ hours	$3\frac{1}{2}$ hours
$3\frac{1}{2}$ hours	4 hours	3 hours	$3\frac{1}{2}$ hours	3 hours
4 hours	$3\frac{1}{2}$ hours	6 hours	3 hours	5 hours

5 Graph the data.

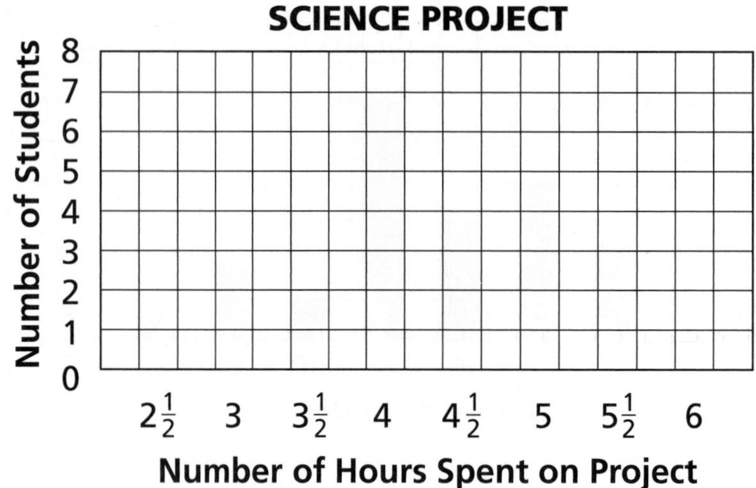

6 About half the class spent at least _____ hours on the project.

7 The amount of time the most students spent was _____ hours.

8 **Challenge** The students who took at least 5 hours to finish their project included graphs. Mr. Tan now wants all of his students to include graphs in their next project. Predict how much extra time it will take the students to include graphs in their next project. Explain how you found your answer.

____

____

____

____

Chapter 10
Lesson 7

Name ______________________ Date ____________

Collecting Measurement Data

NCTM Standards 1, 2, 6, 7, 8, 9, 10

Collecting Data
Measure the length of your arm to the nearest quarter inch.

Measurement: ____________ Round to the nearest inch: ____________

Here are the arm lengths in a fourth-grade class.
Record your own arm length on the graph.

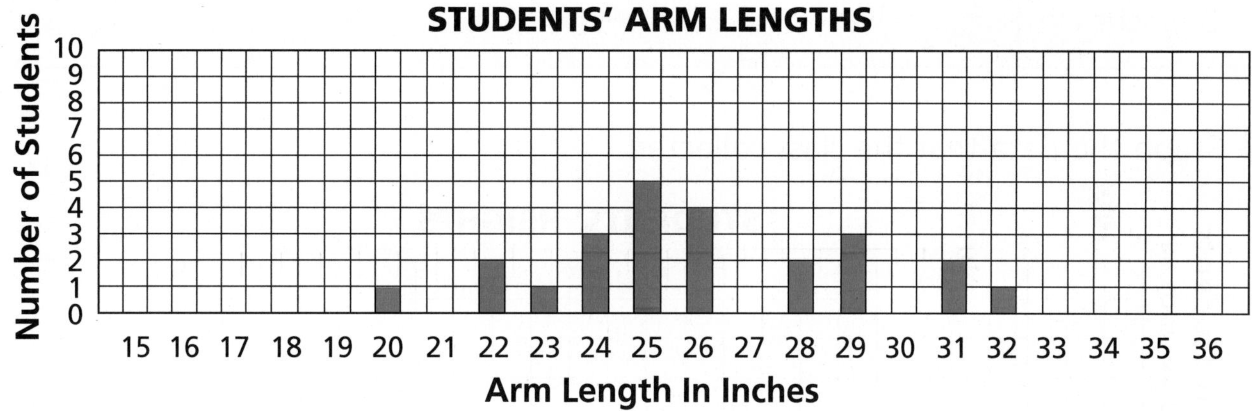

1. If you picked a student at random from this class, what is the likelihood that the student's arms would be at least 1 inch longer than yours? Circle your answer.

   Certain Likely Unlikely Impossible

   Explain your answer. ______________________________

2. If you picked a student at random from this class, what is the likelihood that the student's arms would be at least 5 inches longer than yours? Circle your answer.

   Certain Likely Unlikely Impossible

   Explain your answer. ______________________________

Height Measurements

A third grade class measured the height of each student.

50 inches	54 inches	52 inches	51 inches	51 inches
56 inches	58 inches	54 inches	54 inches	55 inches
51 inches	52 inches	53 inches	55 inches	52 inches
54 inches	51 inches	55 inches	52 inches	54 inches
50 inches				

3 Graph the data that the class collected.

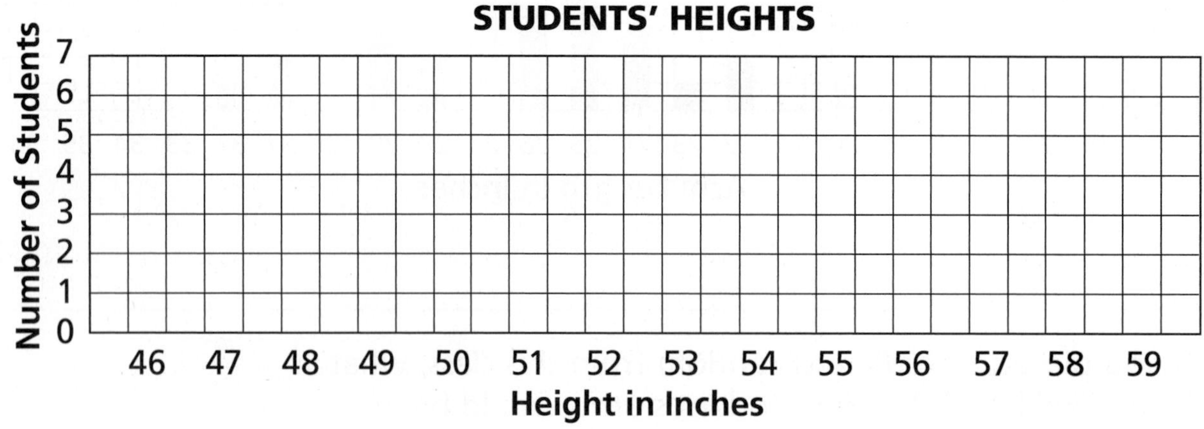

4 What is the most common height in the class? ____________

5 **Challenge** Shawn is a student in the class. Half the students are shorter than he is and half are taller. How tall is Shawn? ____________

Chapter 10
Lesson 8

Name ______________________ Date ______________

Analyzing Measurement Data

NCTM Standards 1, 2, 6, 7, 8, 9, 10

Now that your class has collected and graphed data about the lengths of students' arms, use the graph to answer these questions about the data.

1. What is the shortest arm length in your class? _______ inches

2. What is the longest arm length in your class? _______ inches

3. Which arm lengths showed up most frequently in your measurement data? _______ inches

4. What is the range of arm lengths in your class? _______ in. to _______ in.

5. How many students are in your class? _______ students

6. How many students have arms that are 20 inches long? _______ students

7. If you picked a student at random from your class, what is the probability that the student's arms would be exactly 20 inches long? _______

8. How many students have arms that are 40 inches long? _______ students

9. If you picked a student at random from your class, what is the probability that the student's arms would be 40 inches long? _______

Use these graphs to compare the data from two classrooms.

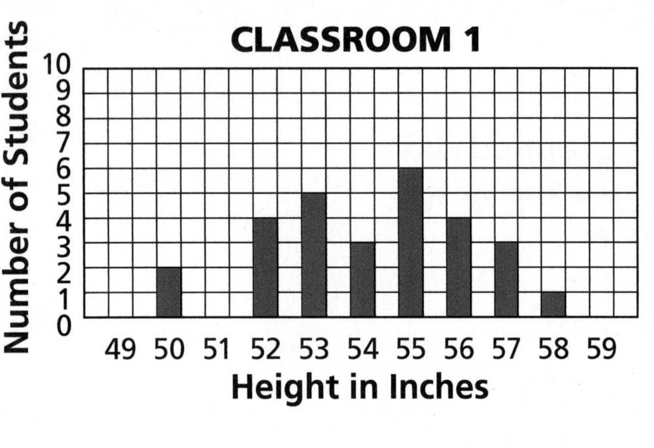

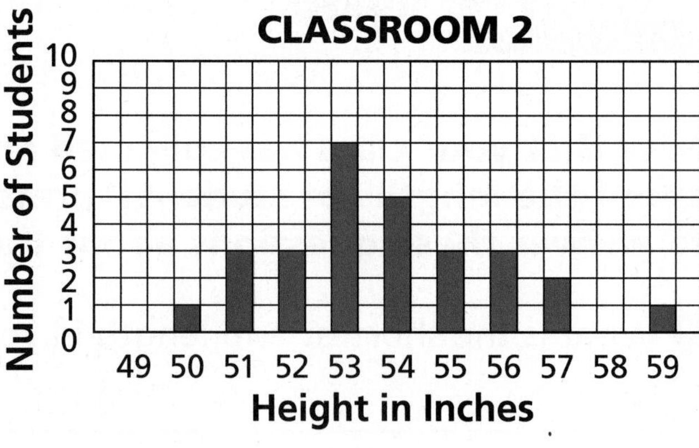

10. How many students are in each classroom? ______ students

---

11. How tall is the shortest student in each classroom?

Classroom 1 ____________ Classroom 2 ____________

---

12. In each classroom, half the students are as tall or taller than what height?

Classroom 1 ____________ Classroom 2 ____________

---

13. If you picked a student at random from each class, what is the probability that the student would be 53 inches tall?

Classroom 1 ____________ Classroom 2 ____________

14. **Challenge** You measure the height of a student in one of the classrooms. What can you be certain will be true about the measurement?

____

____

Chapter 10
Lesson 9

Name ______________________ Date __________

Problem Solving Strategy

Make a Graph

NCTM Standards 1, 2, 6, 7, 8, 9, 10

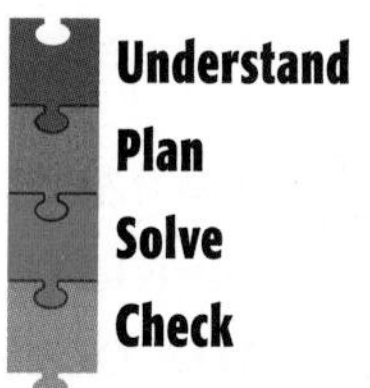

Solve each problem. Helga's Hat Shop can afford to keep only 3 sizes of hats in stock. Helga measured the heads of 20 customers to get an idea of which sizes are most common.

1. Graph the data to find the 3 most common sizes.

18 inches	24 inches	22 inches	25 inches	19 inches
22 inches	20 inches	19 inches	20 inches	19 inches
21 inches	19 inches	21 inches	21 inches	20 inches
21 inches	20 inches	25 inches	21 inches	20 inches

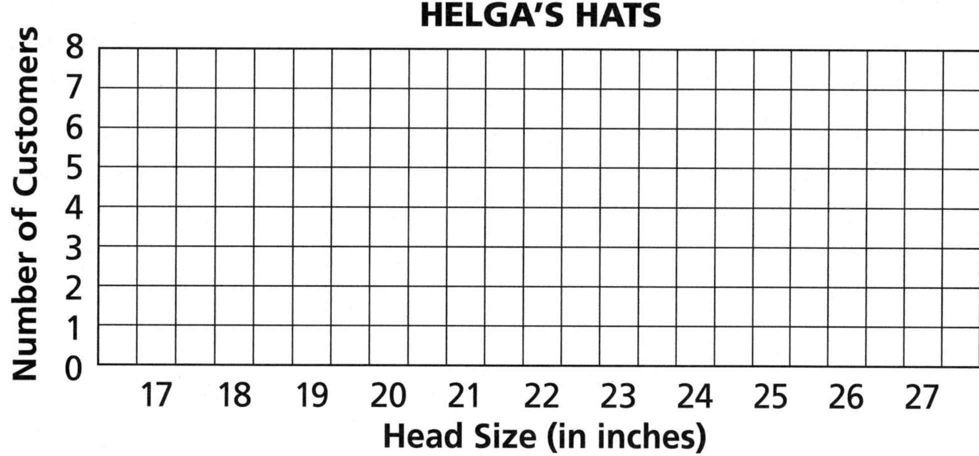

2. The 3 most common head sizes are:

_______ inches

_______ inches

_______ inches

3. One of the 20 customers wants to buy a hat. What is the probability that one of the 3 sizes you chose will fit the customer? _______

Problem Solving Test Prep

Choose the correct answer.

1. Samantha glues 8 cubes together to make a larger cube and paints the outside. When she takes the large cube apart, how many of the original 8 cubes will have exactly 3 faces painted?

   A. 0 C. 4

   B. 2 D. 8

2. In a board game, Tim begins at 0. He moves forward 3 spaces and back 1. If he makes that move a total of 12 times, how many spaces will he have advanced after the 12 moves?

   A. 6 C. 9

   B. 8 D. 24

Show What You Know

Solve each problem. Explain your answer.

3. Jenny brought 36 pieces of fruit to class. Of the 36 pieces of fruit, $\frac{1}{3}$ are oranges, $\frac{1}{3}$ are apples, and the rest are bananas. At the end of the school day, there are 5 bananas. How many bananas were eaten? Explain how you solved the problem.

   ____
   ____
   ____
   ____
   ____
   ____
   ____
   ____

4. Four girls compare their heights. Only one girl is shorter than Abby. Halley is shorter than Ellen. Jesse is shorter than Halley. From this information, can the girls be put in order from shortest to tallest? If so, explain your solution. If not, explain what other information you would need.

   ____
   ____
   ____
   ____
   ____
   ____
   ____
   ____

Name ______________________ Date ______________

Chapter 10 Review/Assessment

NCTM Standards 1, 2, 6, 7, 8, 9, 10

1 Nona has 2 pairs of pants, 2 shirts, and 2 pairs of shoes. Lesson 1

Pants		**Shirts**		**Shoes**	

blue	**green**	**yellow**	**purple**	**black**	**red**

How many different outfits can she wear? ______ outfits

List all the outfits here:

____

____

____

____

____

There are 3 coins in a bag, a penny, a dime, and a nickel. You reach in and pull out one coin. Lesson 2

2 Label the events *certain, likely, unlikely,* or *impossible.*

You pull a coin that is worth **25¢**

____

You pull a coin that is worth at least 5¢

____

You pull a coin that is worth at least 1¢

____

3 Circle the event that is more likely. If they are equally likely, circle them both.

You pull a coin that is worth 10¢.

You pull a coin that is worth less than 10¢.

You spin each spinner once. Write the probabilities that you'll land on green (G) or blue (B). Lessons 3, 4, and 5

4

green sections =	____ out of ____
blue sections =	____ out of ____

Probability of landing = on green	
Probability of landing = on blue	

5

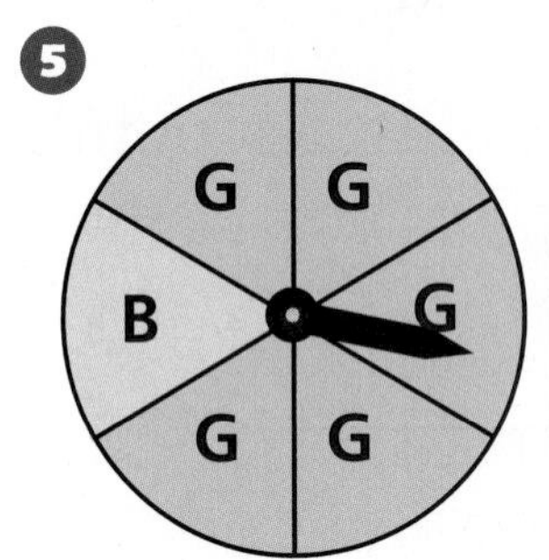

Probability of landing = on green	
Probability of landing = on blue	

6

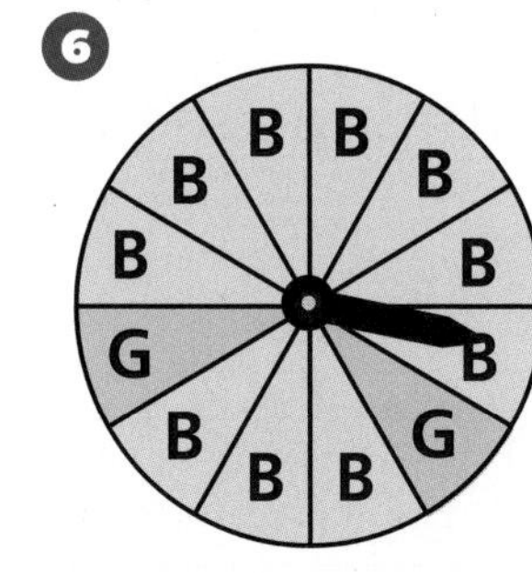

Probability of landing = on green	
Probability of landing = on blue	

7 Each student in a class of 28 students tossed a coin 30 times. Here are two graphs. One is NOT correct. Lessons 6, 7, 8, and 9

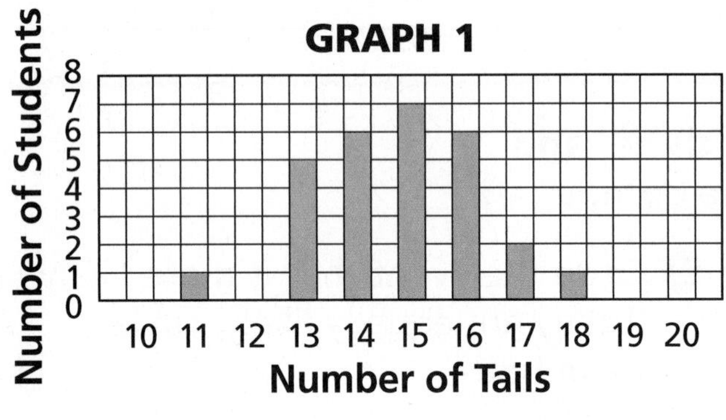

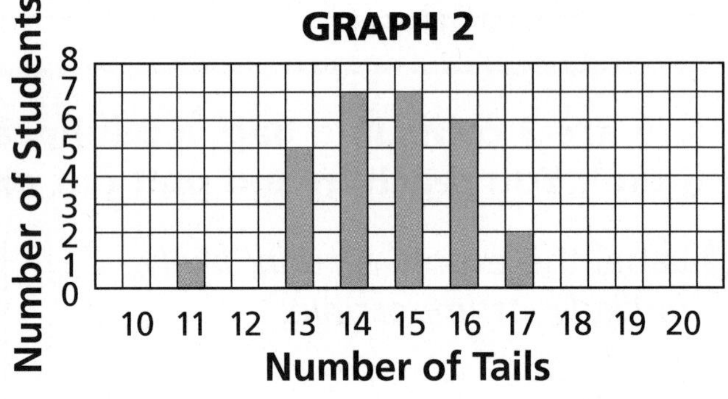

Here is a table of the original data.

Number of tails	10	11	12	13	14	15	16	17	18	19	20
Number of students	0	1	0	5	7	7	6	2	0	0	0

Which graph matches the data? ____________

Chapter 11
Lesson 1

Name ______________________ Date ____________

Making a Figure Zoo

NCTM Standards 3, 6, 7, 8, 9

Use the picture or the actual polyhedron to answer these questions.

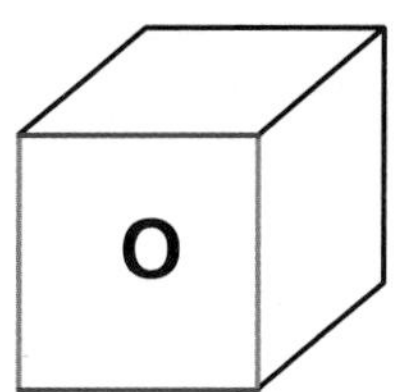

The polyhedron has six square faces.

1. Look at face O.

   The two blue edges are: parallel or perpendicular

   The blue edges are: parallel or perpendicular to the green edges.

   An angle formed by a blue and green edge is: acute or right or obtuse

---

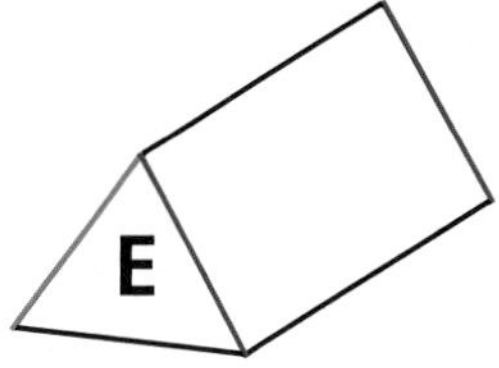

This polyhedron has five faces.

Three of them are rectangles

2. What shape is face E on the figure?

   ____

3. The angle formed by a blue and green edge of face E is:

   acute or right or obtuse

Use your previous experience with figures or refer to a polyhedron in the figure zoo to help you answer these questions. Think about the sides and angles of each figure while you answer.

4 Describe the features that make a figure a square.

5 Describe the features that make a figure a triangle.

6 **Challenge** Describe the features that make a figure a trapezoid.

Name ______________________ Date ____________

Chapter 11

Lesson 2

Describing Three-Dimensional Figures

NCTM Standards 3, 6, 7, 8, 9, 10

Attach a copy of your net here.

1. Describe the faces of your figure.

____

____

____

2. Does your figure have two faces that don't share an edge?

☐ Yes ☐ No

If you answered yes, shade one pair of those faces on the net.

3. Does your figure have two faces that appear to be perpendicular to each other?

☐ Yes ☐ No

If you answered yes, circle them on the net.

4 The quadrilateral on this net is a square. Find two parallel edges on the three-dimensional figure. Circle them on the net.

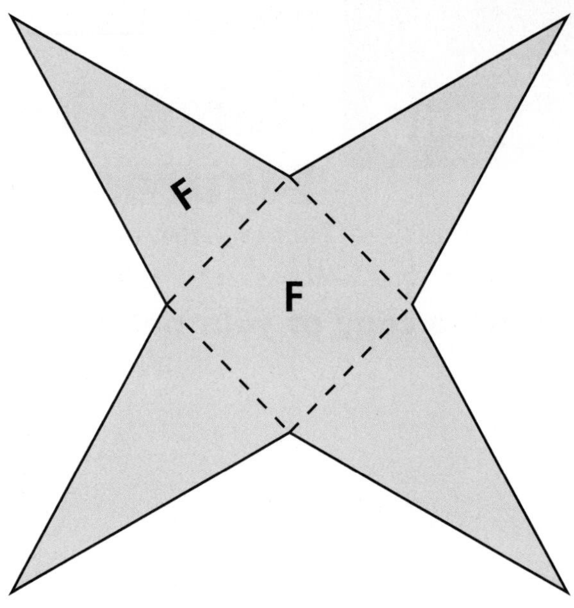

5 All of the figures on this net are rectangles. Find two perpendicular faces on the three-dimensional figure. Shade them on the net.

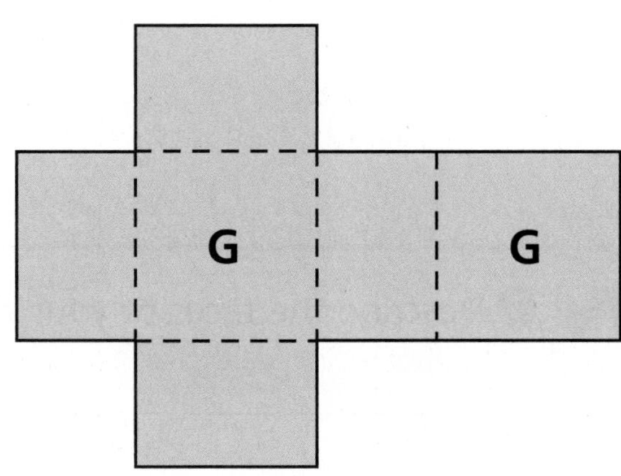

6 **Challenge** Find two vertices that are not connected by an edge. Circle them on the net.

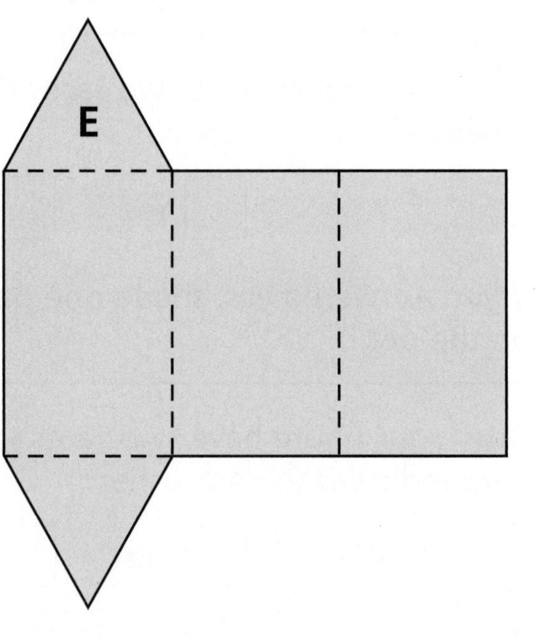

Chapter 11
Lesson 3

Name ______________________ Date ____________

Going On a Figure Safari

NCTM Standards 3, 6, 7, 8, 9, 10

For each puzzle, look through all the polyhedra and list the letters of those that appear to match the clues. Try standing each figure on different faces to see if there is any way the figure might fit the clues.

Clues	Answers
1 ☑ All of my faces are rectangles. ☑ At least 2 of my faces are squares.	
2 ☑ I have at least 2 faces that are parallel to each other.	
3 ☑ All of my angles are right. ☑ All of my faces are congruent.	
4 ☑ I have the same number of faces as vertices. ☑ At least 3 of my faces are congruent.	
5 ☑ I have more vertices than faces. ☑ At least one of my faces is not a rectangle. ☑ None of my faces is perpendicular to another face.	

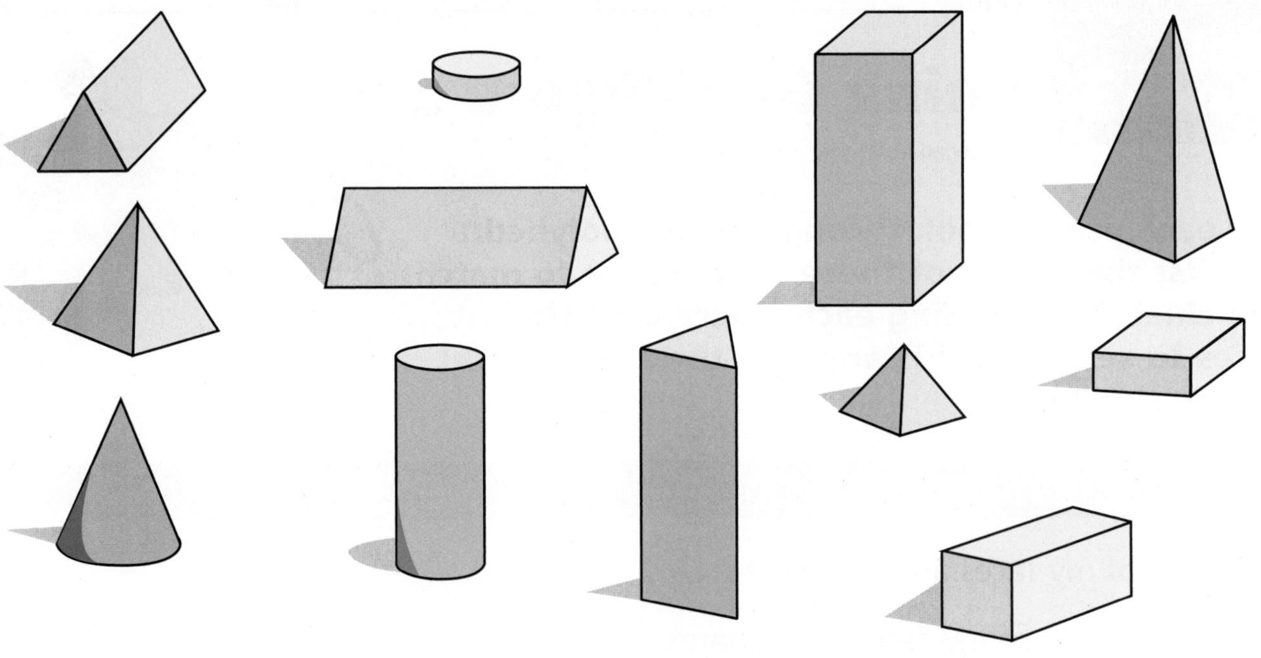

Write the name of the figure that matches each puzzle. Use pyramid, prism, cone, or cylinder.

Clues	Answers
6 ☑ All of my faces are polygons. ☑ None of my faces is parallel to another face.	
7 ☑ Two of my faces are congruent and parallel to each other. ☑ All of my other faces are parallelograms.	
8 ☑ All of my faces are polygons. ☑ I have the same number of faces and vertices.	

9 Challenge

☑ I have exactly two congruent surfaces.

☑ The two surfaces are not polygons.

Name ______________________ Date ______________

Chapter 11
Lesson 4

Finding the Areas of Faces on Three-Dimensional Figures

NCTM Standards 1, 3, 4, 6, 7, 8, 9, 10

Attach a small copy of the net for your three-dimensional figure here:

1. Label your picture to show the full size measurements of each edge of your polyhedron. See the example at the right.
2. Based on your measurements, label your picture to show the area of each face or surface of your polyhedron.
3. What is the total area of the faces or surfaces of your polyhedron?

____

Example

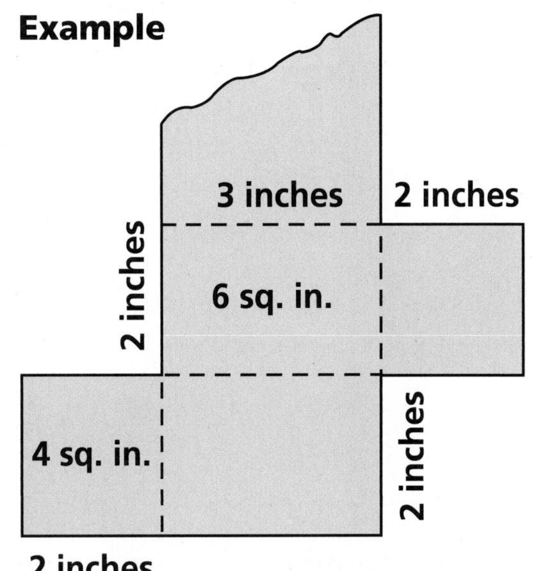

These small copies of nets are labeled with the measurements of the three-dimensional figure. Find the total area of the faces of each three-dimensional figure. All the figures whose areas are not given are rectangles.

4

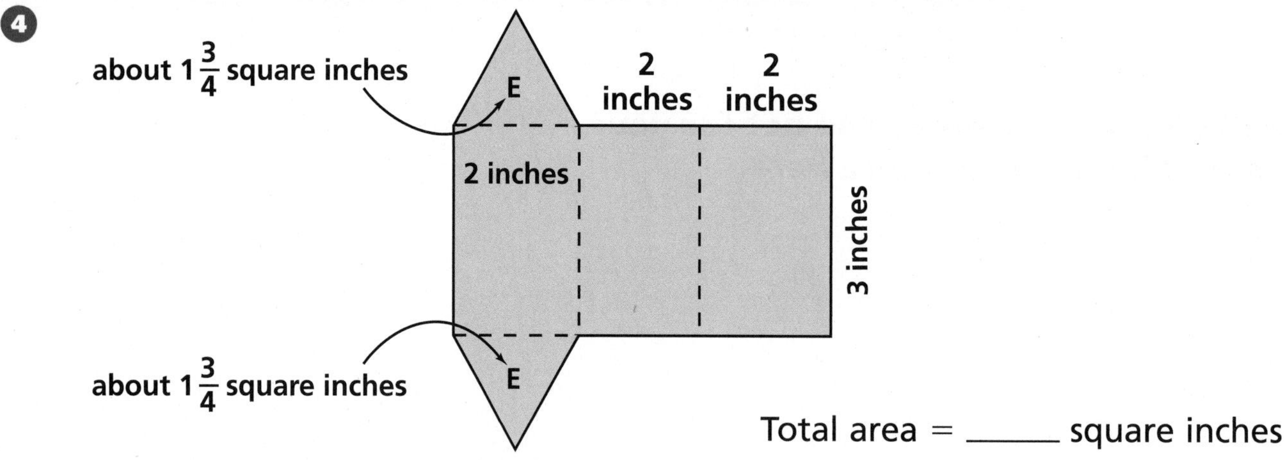

Total area = _____ square inches

5

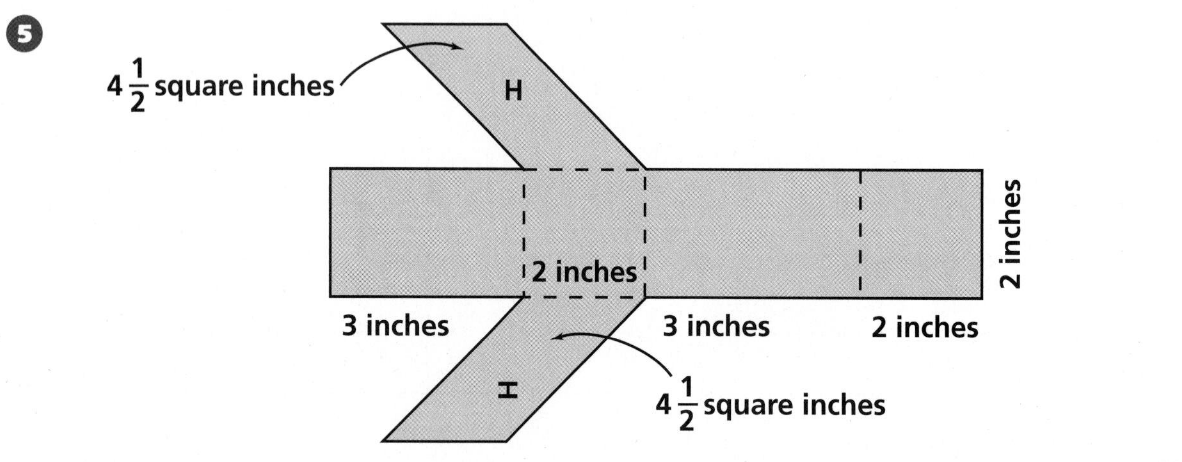

Total area = _____ square inches

6 Challenge The trapezoids are congruent.

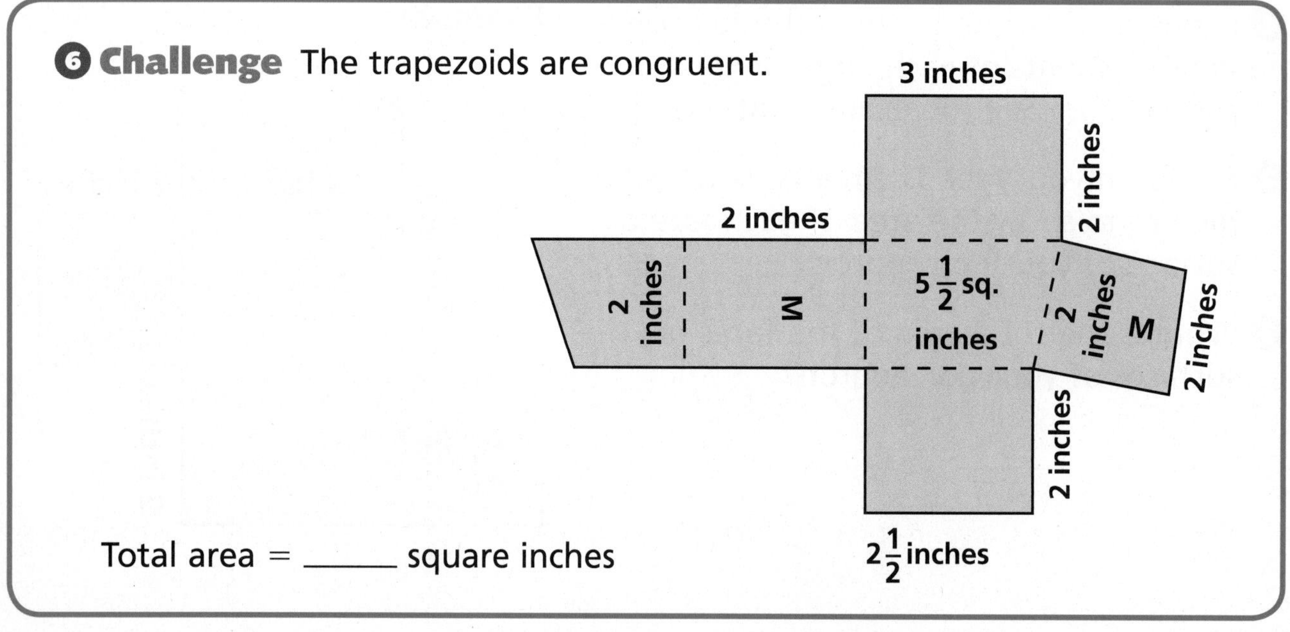

Total area = _____ square inches

Chapter 11
Lesson 5

Name ____________________ Date ____________

Finding Volumes of Three-Dimensional Figures

NCTM Standards 1, 3, 4, 6, 7, 8, 9, 10

Attach a small copy of the net for your three-dimensional figure here:

Place your three-dimensional figure on the desk so that its bottom and top surfaces are congruent. Build the figure with cube blocks.

1. How many cubes are in the model? ________ cubes

2. How many cubes are in each layer? ________ cubes

3. How many layers of cubes are there? ________ layers

4. What is the volume of your three-dimensional shape? ________ cubic inches

5

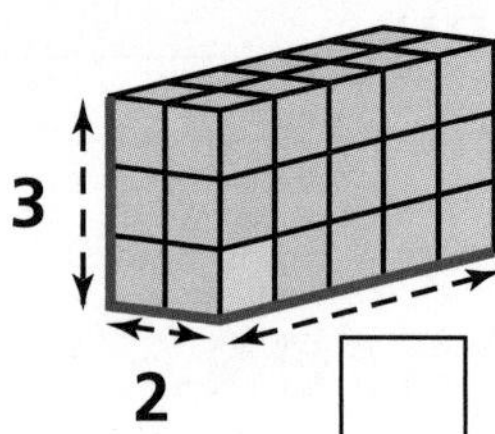

Number of cubes in each layer: ______ cubes

Volume: ______ cubes

6

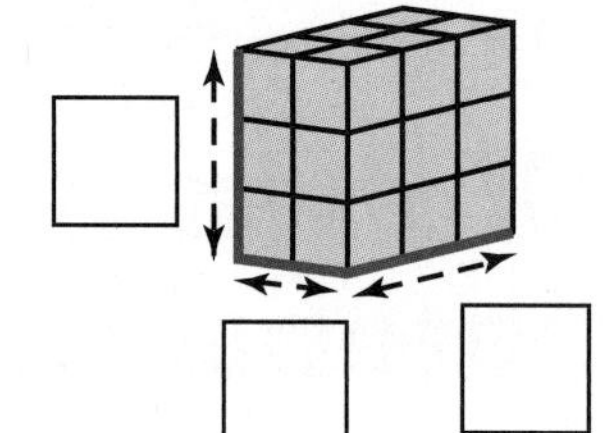

Number of cubes in each layer: ______ cubes

Volume: ______ cubes

7

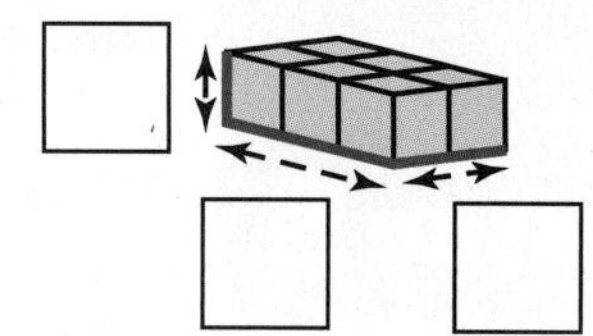

Number of cubes in each layer: ______ cubes

Volume: ______ cubes

8

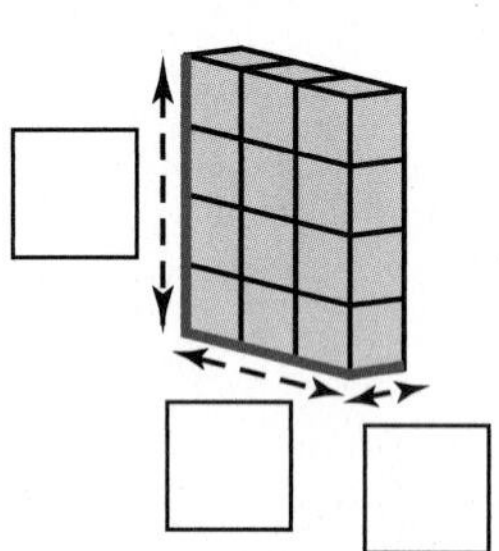

Number of cubes in each layer: ______ cubes

Volume: ______ cubes

9

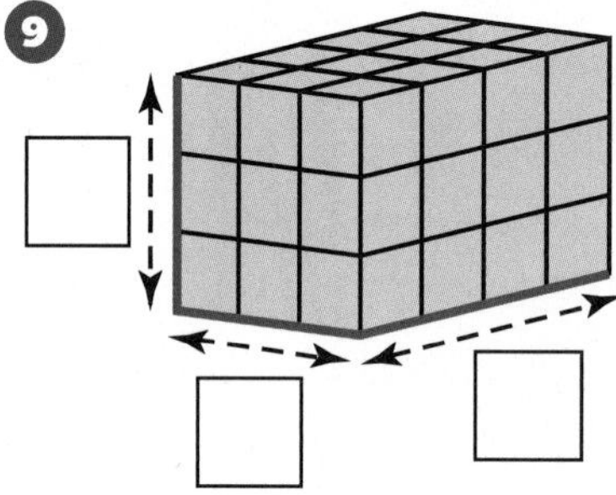

Number of cubes in each layer: ______ cubes

Volume: ______ cubes

10

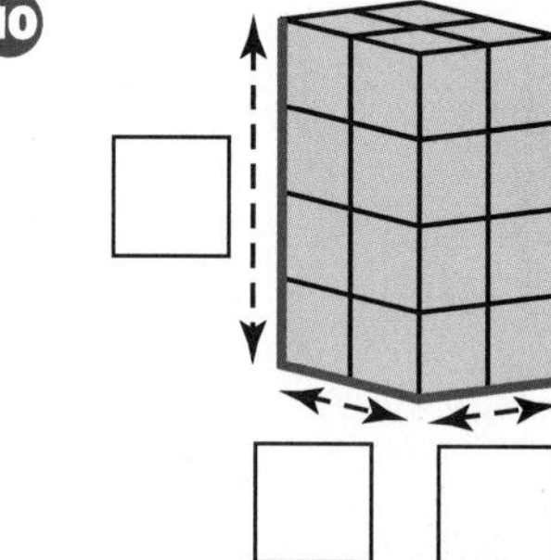

Number of cubes in each layer: ______ cubes

Volume: ______ cubes

11 **Challenge**

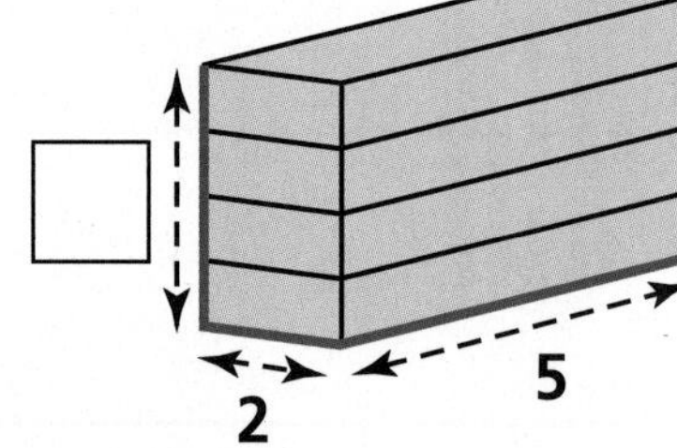

Number of cubes in each layer: ______ cubes

Volume: ______ cubes

12 **Challenge**

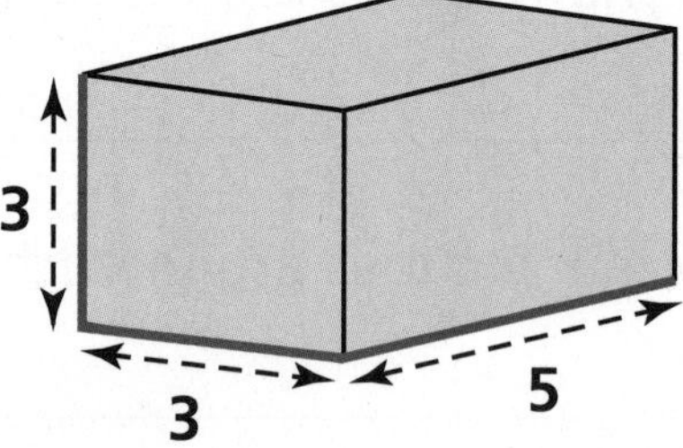

Number of cubes in each layer: ______ cubes

Volume: ______ cubes

Chapter 11
Lesson 6

Name ______________________ Date ____________

More Volumes of Three-Dimensional Figures

NCTM Standards 1, 3, 4, 6, 7, 8, 9, 10

What is the volume of each three-dimensional figure? Each cube is 1 cubic inch.

1

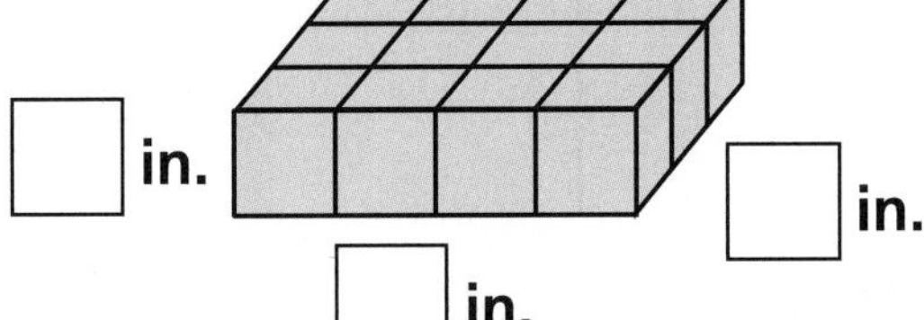

Volume: _____ cubic inches

2

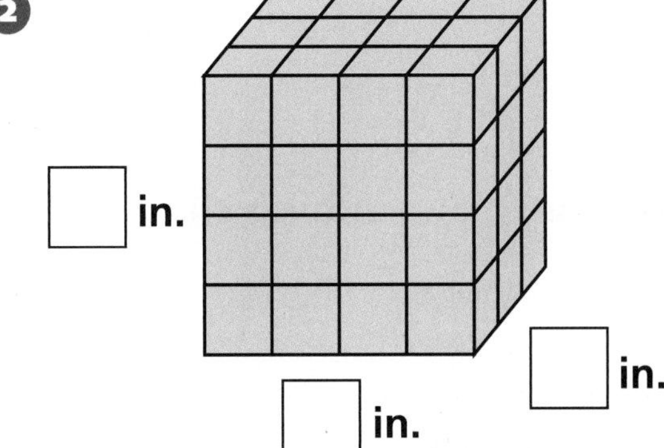

Volume: _____ cubic inches

3

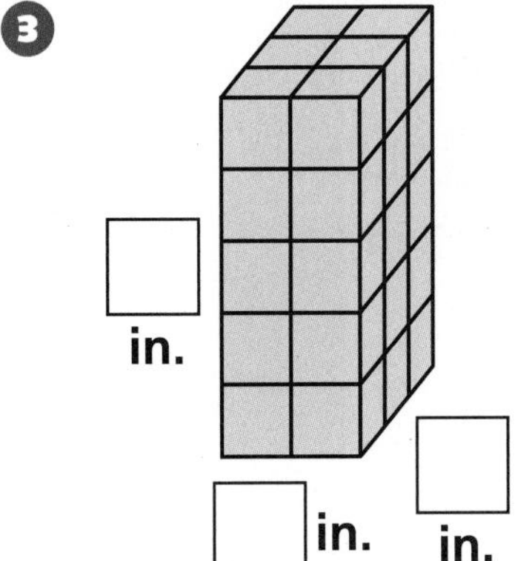

Volume:

_____ cubic inches

4

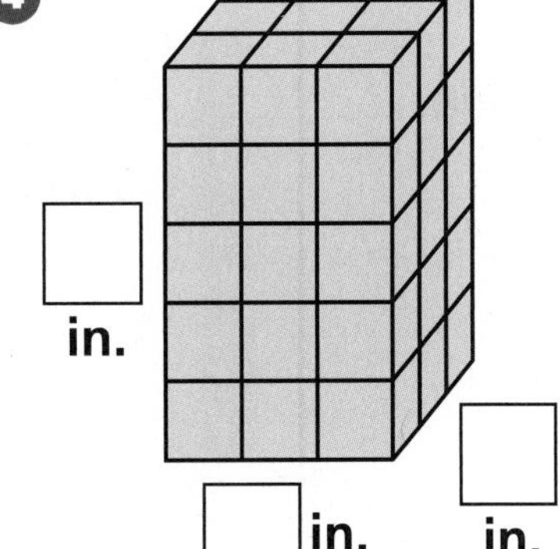

Volume:

_____ cubic inches

5

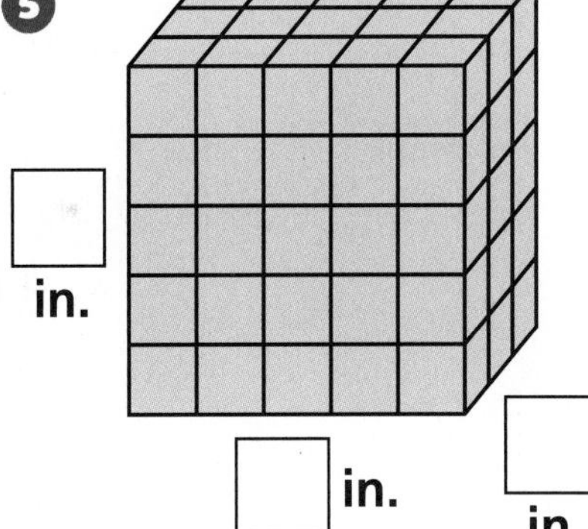

Volume:

_____ cubic inches

6 Explain how you found the volume of the figure in Problem 5.

____

____

____

Find the volumes of these rectangular prisms in cubic inches.

7

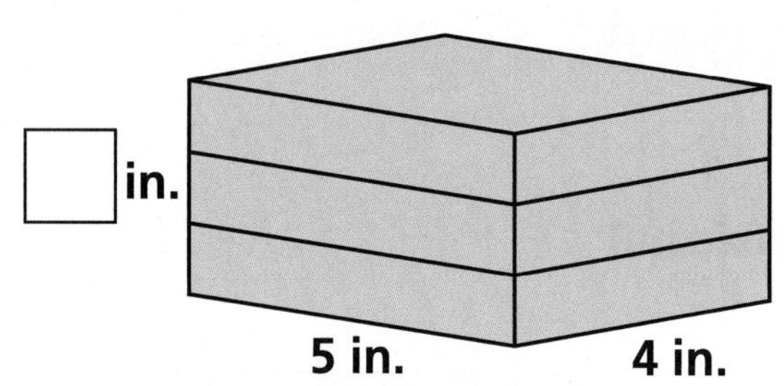

Volume: _____ cubic inches

8

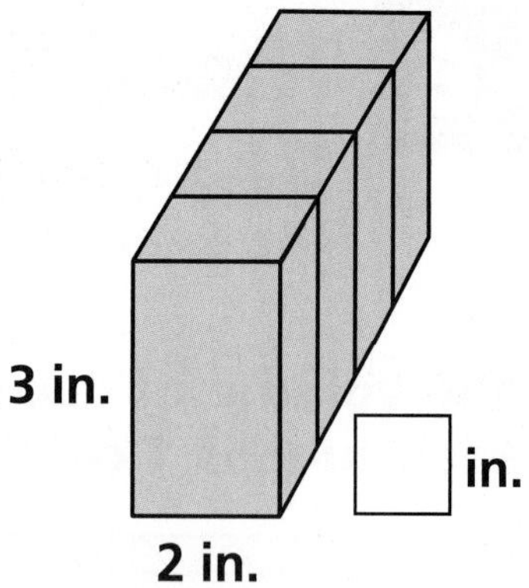

Volume: _____ cubic inches

9

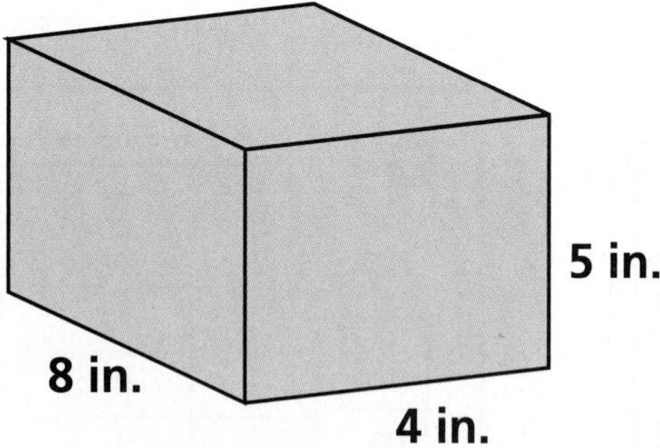

Volume: _____ cubic inches

10

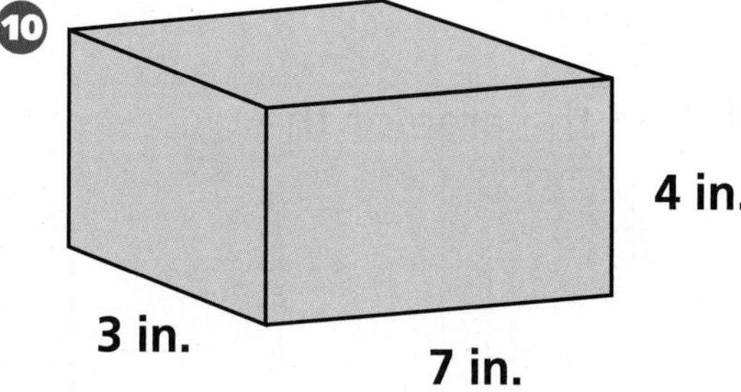

Volume: _____ cubic inches

11 **Challenge** Think of a prism with a volume of 30 cubic inches. What are the dimensions of the prism you thought of?

☐ in. × ☐ in. × ☐ in.

Name ______________________ Date ____________

Chapter 11

Lesson 7

Problem Solving Strategy

Act It Out

NCTM Standards 1, 2, 6, 7, 8, 9, 10

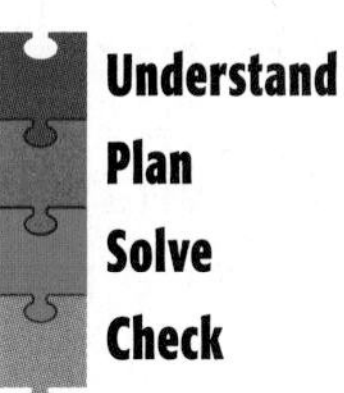

1. A cardboard box has a volume of 48 cubic feet. Give four possible sets of measurements that could be its dimensions.

   ☐ feet × ☐ feet × ☐ feet   ☐ feet × ☐ feet × ☐ feet

   ☐ feet × ☐ feet × ☐ feet   ☐ feet × ☐ feet × ☐ feet

2. Melissa folded a net and made a cube. She measured one of the edges as 4 inches long. How much paper did she use to make the cube? ______________

3. The Gangulis are painting their bedroom walls. To figure out how much paint they need, they will find the area of the walls in the rectangular room without worrying about windows and doors. One wall is 10 feet long and the other wall is 12 feet long. Both walls are 8 feet high.

   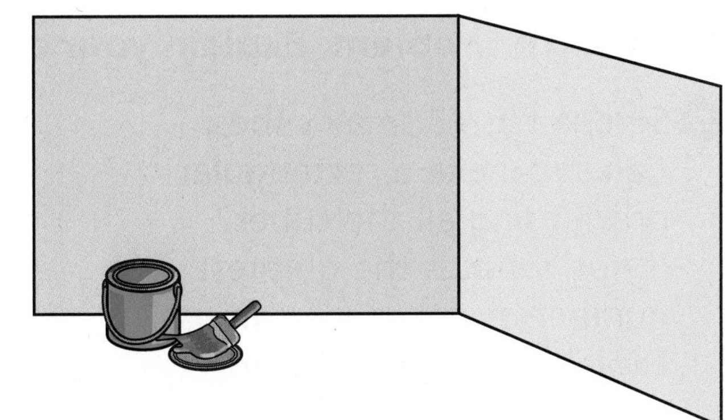

   An estimate of the total area of the room's four walls is ________ sq ft.

   The actual area of the room's four walls is ________ sq ft.

4. Cory is mailing some books that are each 1 inch by 4 inches by $5\frac{1}{2}$ inches. He uses a box that is 4 inches by 3 inches by $5\frac{1}{2}$ inches. How many books can he send in the box?

   ______ books

Problem Solving Test Prep

Choose the correct answer.

1. What are the length and width of a rectangle that has the same perimeter as the figure?

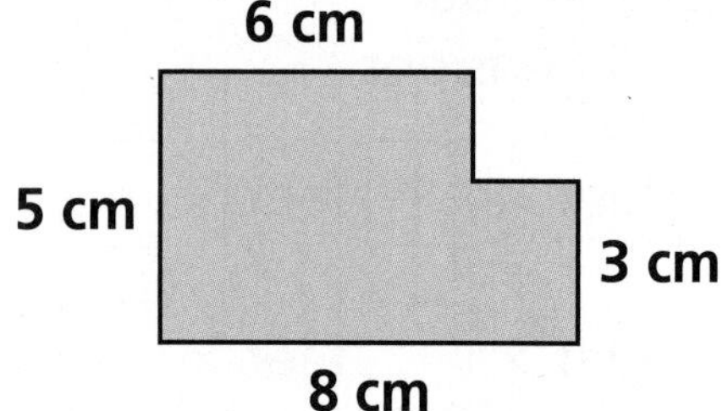

A. 3 cm by 6 cm C. 8 cm by 5 cm

B. 3 cm by 8 cm D. 8 cm by 6 cm

2. Which is the best estimate of 391×42?

A. 1,200 C. 12,000

B. 1,600 D. 16,000

3. Which pair of equivalent fractions matches the shaded area of the figure below?

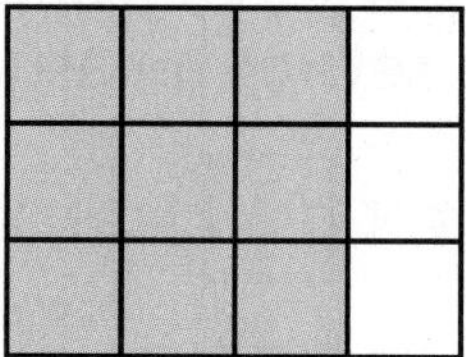

A. $\frac{3}{4} = \frac{8}{12}$ C. $\frac{1}{4} = \frac{3}{12}$

B. $\frac{3}{4} = \frac{9}{12}$ D. $\frac{2}{3} = \frac{8}{12}$

4. Which is the only number that is NOT between 21.8 and 21.9?

A. 21.81 C. 21.89

B. 21.88 D. 21.91

Show What You Know

Solve each problem. Explain your answer.

5. Serena has 43 small cubes. Can she make a rectangular prism using all the cubes? If not, what is the greatest number of cubes she can use? Explain how you decided.

____

____

____

____

____

____

6. Alex has 35 small cubes. He begins building a staircase in which the first step has 1 cube, the next has 2 cubes, and so on. Can he use all 35 cubes? If not, how many will he have left? Explain.

____

____

____

____

____

____

Chapter 11

Name ______________________ Date ____________

Review/Assessment

NCTM Standards 1, 2, 6, 7, 8, 9, 10

All of the faces of this polyhedron are rectangles. Lessons 1, 2, and 3

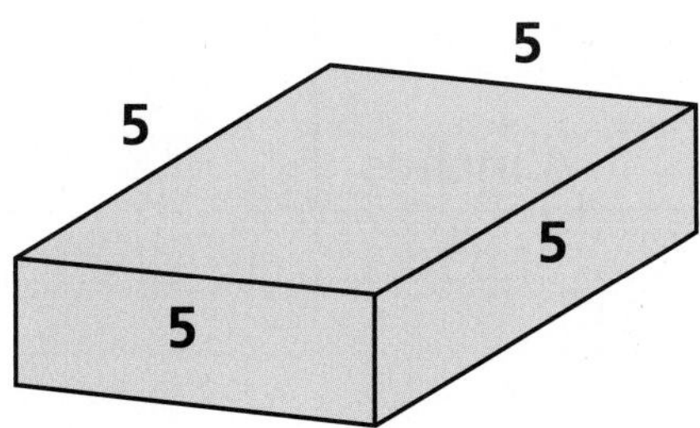

1. The polyhedron is a: Pyramid or Prism or Cone

2. How many of the polyhedron's faces are squares?

   ________ faces

3. Circle a pair of parallel edges.

4. Put on "X" on an edge that is perpendicular to one of the edges you just circled.

What figures make each tower?

Use Pyramid, Prism, Cone, and Cylinder. Lesson 3

5. 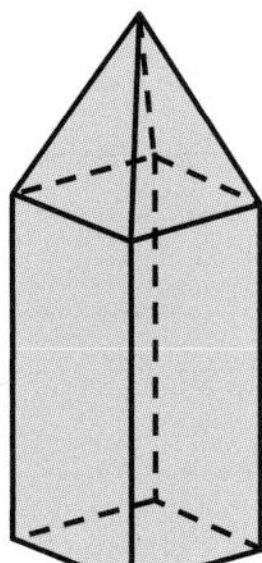

   ____

6. 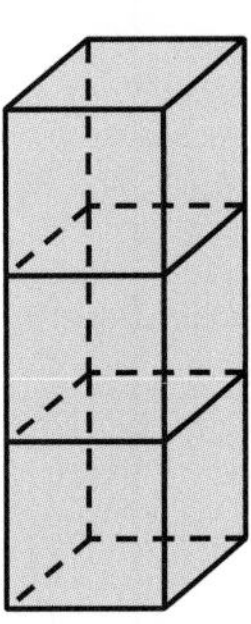

   ____

7. 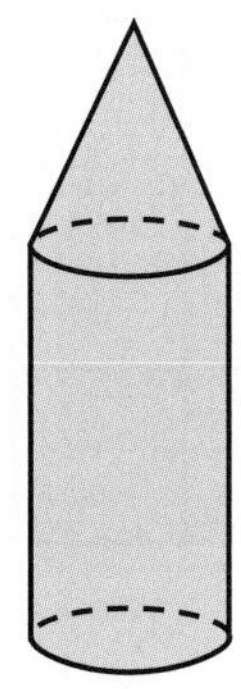

   ____

8. Here is a small copy of a net. All of the figures are rectangles. It is marked with the actual dimensions of the three-dimensional figure. What is the total area of the faces of the three-dimensional figure? Lesson 4

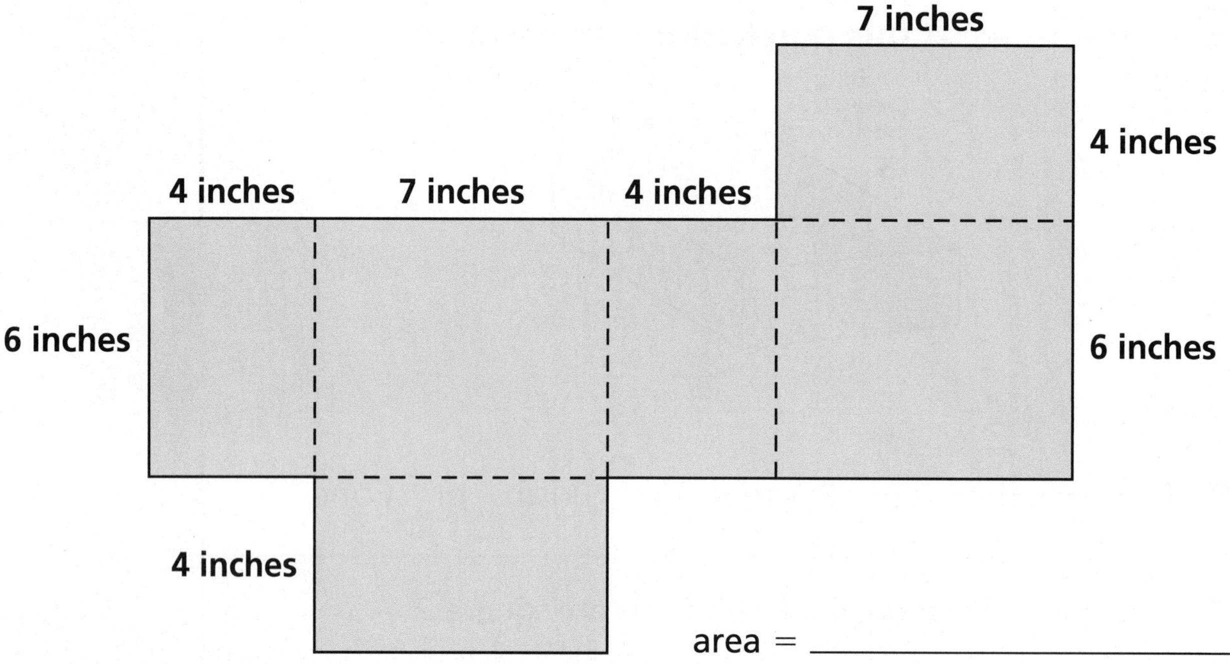

area = ______________________

9. What is the volume of this rectangular prism? Lessons 5 and 6

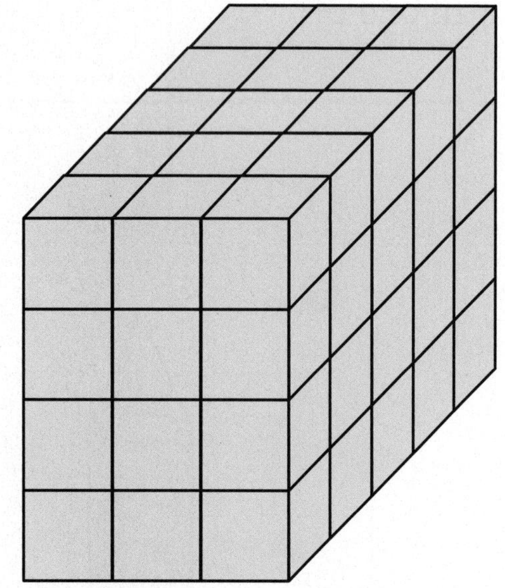

Volume = _____ cubes

10. Alexia is packing her baby sister's toys. There are 27 blocks to pack. After Alexia puts them all into one box, there is no extra space in the box for anything else. What size might the box be? Explain. Lesson 7

____

____

____

____

____

____

____

Chapter 12
Lesson 1

Name ______________________ Date ____________

Introducing Negative Numbers

NCTM Standards 1, 4, 6, 7, 8, 9, 10

Brrr! It's very cold this week. Every day at 6 A.M. Nina went outside and measured the temperature. Here's the information that she recorded. Fill in the missing information.

1

Monday

0° C

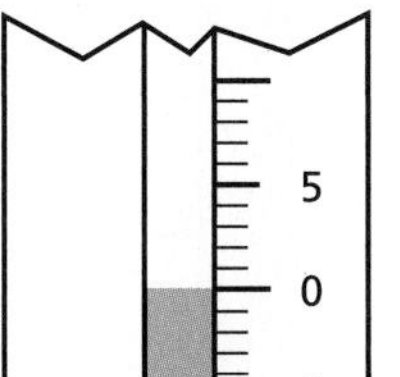

2

Tuesday

____

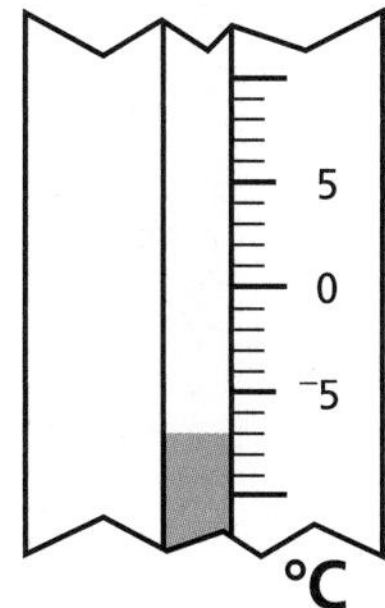

Change from Monday 7° lower

3

Wednesday

____

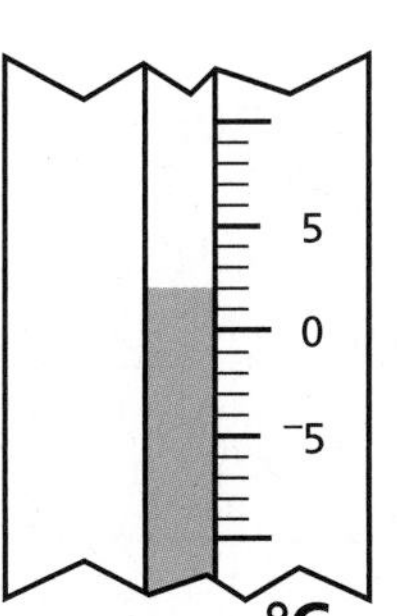

Change from Tuesday __________

4

Thursday

____

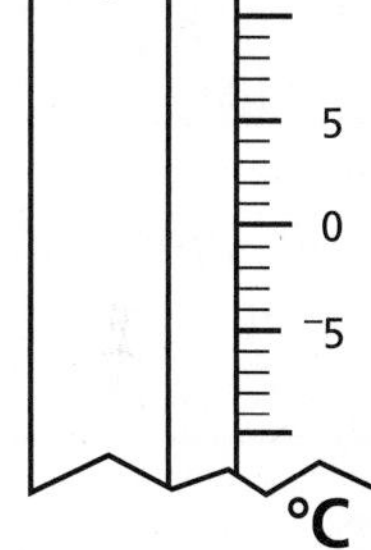

Change from Wednesday 6° higher

5

Friday

⁻3° C

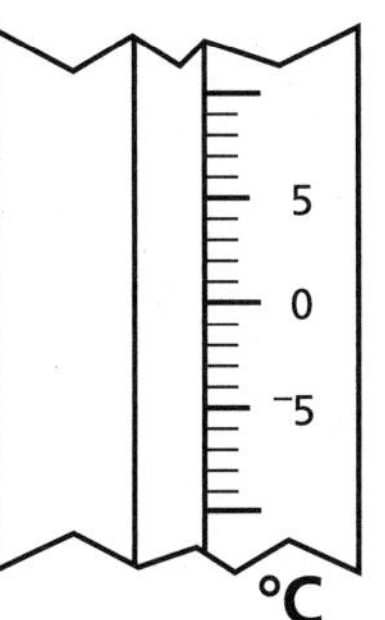

Change from Thursday __________

6

Saturday

⁻8° C

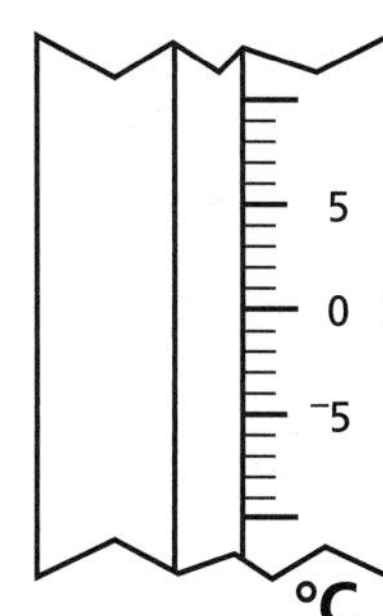

Change from Friday __________

Fill in the missing temperatures on each thermometer.

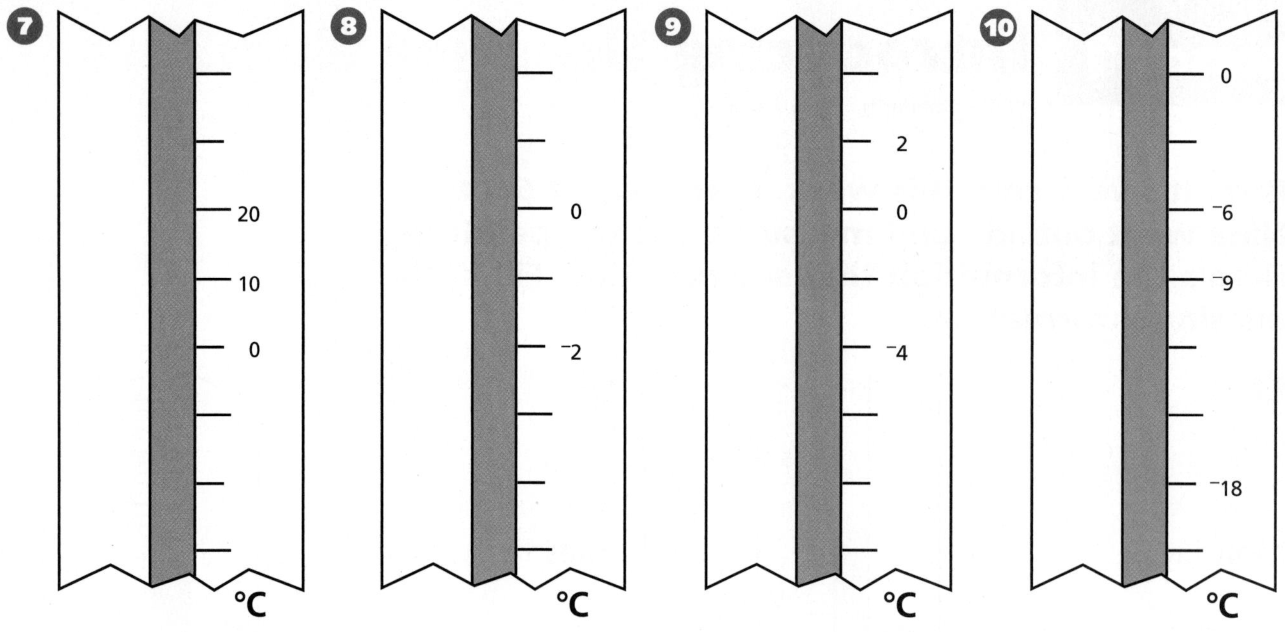

11 The lowest temperature this March was 5° Celsius.

In June, the lowest temperature was 13°C warmer than in March.

In January, the lowest temperature was 30°C colder than in June.

What was the lowest temperature in January? ___________

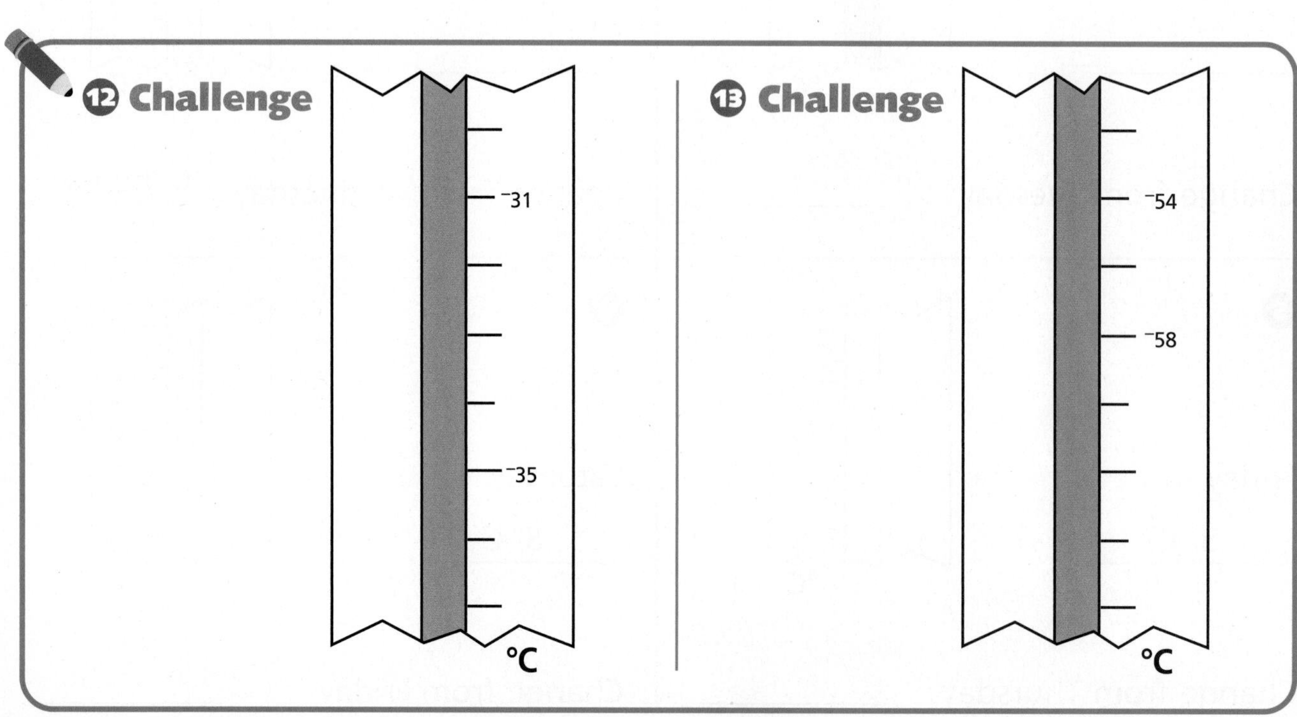

Chapter 12
Lesson 2

Name ______________________ Date ____________

Negative Numbers on the Number Line

NCTM Standards 1, 4, 6, 7, 8, 9, 10

Fill in the missing numbers on each number line.

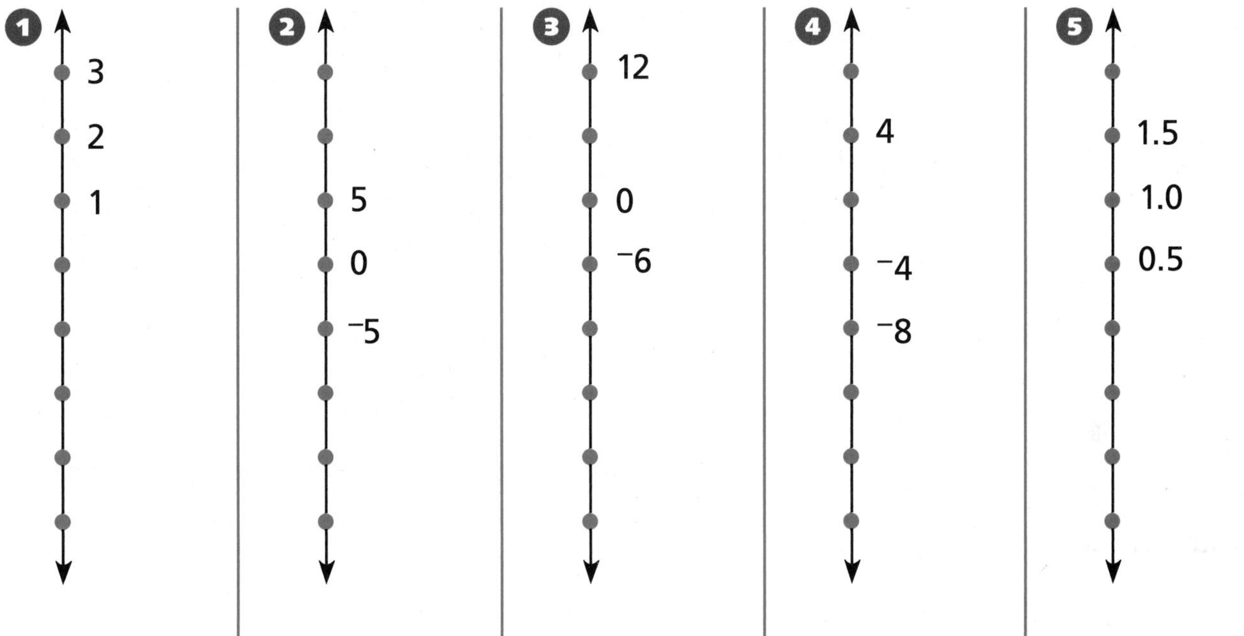

6

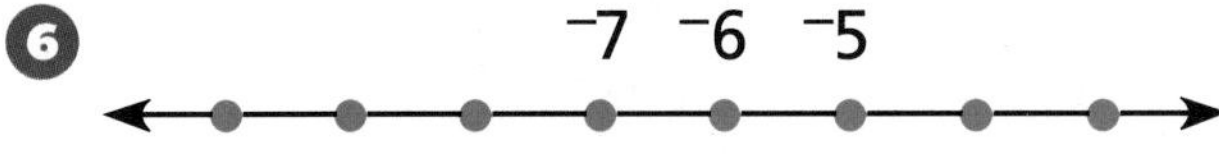

7

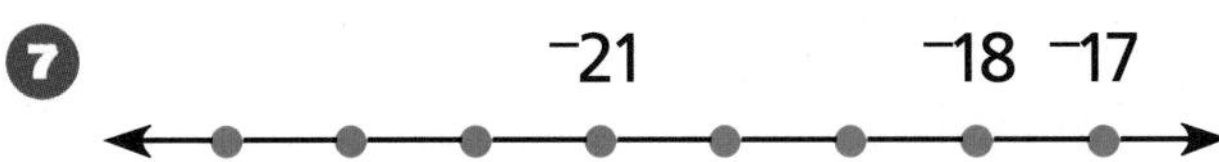

8 −3.3 −3.0

9 −24 −18 −6 −3

10 −34 −32

−12 −11 −10 −9 −8 −7 −6 −5 −4 −3 −2 −1 0 1 2 3 4 5 6 7 8 9 10 11 12 13

Use this number line to help answer the questions.

11 Start at 2. Jump backward 4 spaces.

Where are you? ___________

12 Start at −7. Jump forward 3 spaces.

Where are you? ___________

13 Start at −5. Jump forward 6 spaces.

Where are you? ___________

14 Start at 4. Jump backward 4 spaces. Then jump backward 3 spaces.

Where are you? ___________

15 Start at −11. Jump forward 5 spaces. Then jump forward 1 space.

Where are you? ___________

16 Start at −4. Jump forward 2 spaces. Then jump forward 3 spaces. Then jump backward 4 spaces.

Where are you? ___________

17 Yesterday's highest temperature was 10° Celsius. Today's high temperature was 15° colder than yesterday's. The forecast says tomorrow's high will be 3° warmer than today's.

What is the predicted high temperature for tomorrow? ___________

18 **Challenge**

Start at $2\frac{1}{2}$. Jump forward 3 spaces. Then jump backward 10 spaces.

Where are you? ___________

19 **Challenge**

Start at 1. Jump forward 1 half space. Then jump backward 4 half spaces.

Where are you? ___________

Chapter 12
Lesson 3

Name ______________________ Date ____________

Navigating on a Coordinate Grid

NCTM Standards 1, 4, 6, 7, 8, 9, 10

Aaron's house is in the center of the map. The lines on the map are the streets in his neighborhood.

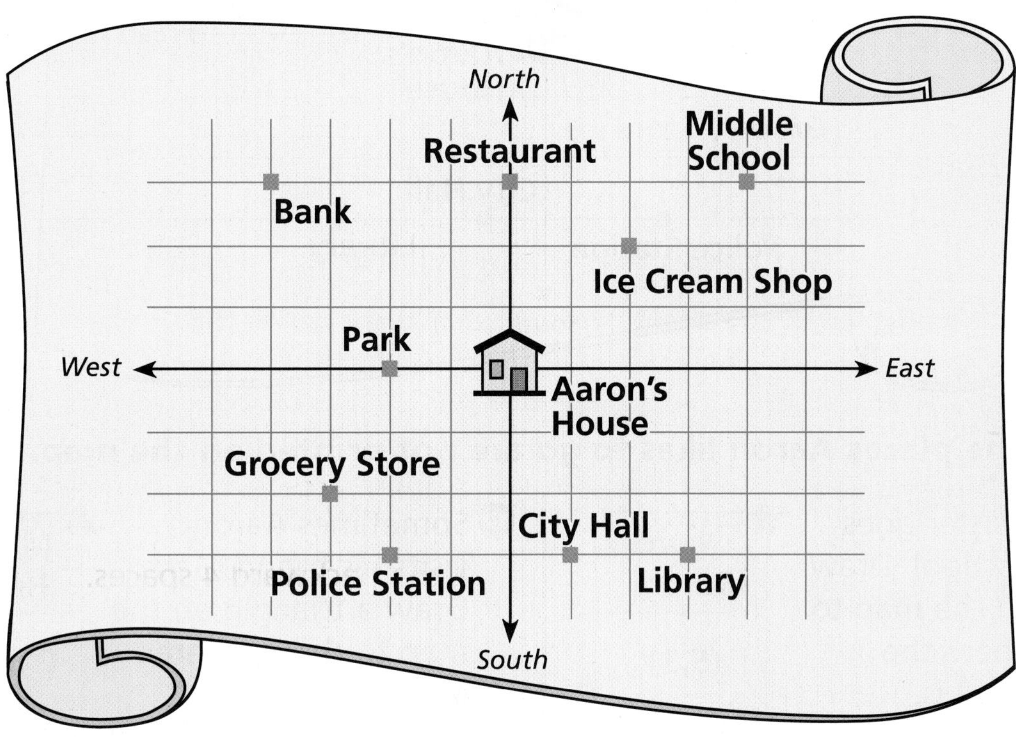

Aaron is new in town. He started making some cards to remind him how to get to different places from his house. Because the streets in town form a grid, he recorded each building the way mathematicians would. Complete each card.

1 School	2 Library	3 Bank	4 Grocery Store	5 Home
(4,3)	(3,⁻3)	(___,___)	(⁻3,⁻2)	(0,___)

6 Ice Cream shop	7 Park	8 Restaurant	9 ________	10 Police Station
(___,___)	(___,0)	(___,___)	(1,⁻3)	(___,___)

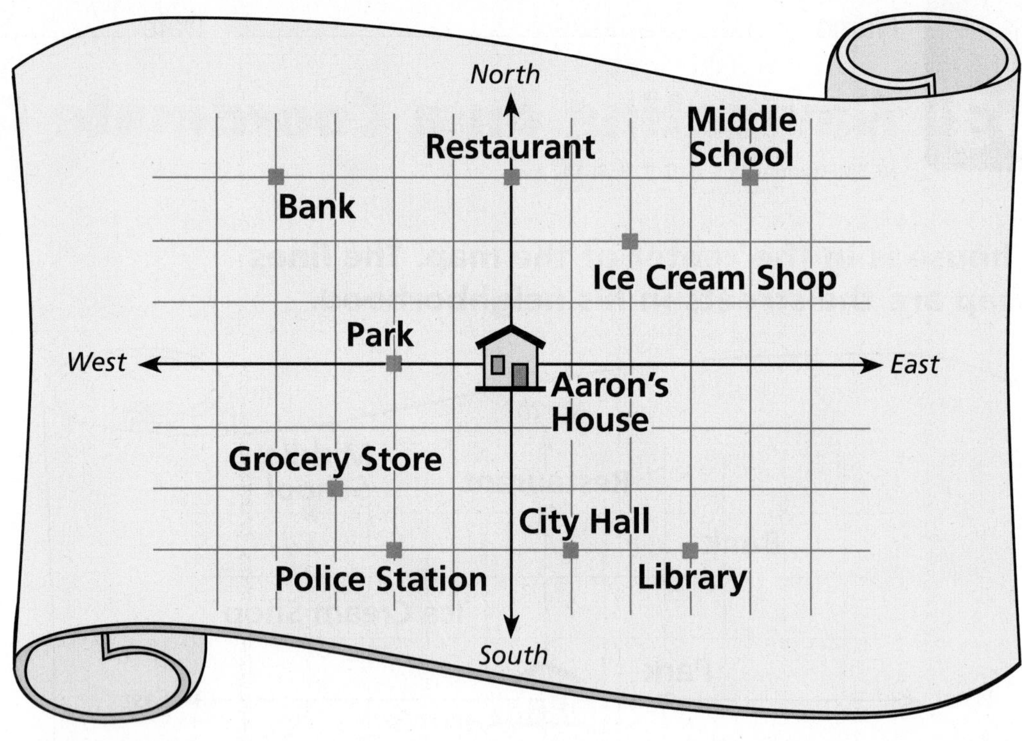

Some of the places Aaron likes to go are not printed on the map.

11 Aaron's sister goes to high school. Draw a star on the map to show where the high school is.

High School
(5,3)

12 Sometimes Aaron visits his friend Mark. Draw a triangle on the map to show where Mark's house is.

Mark's House
($^-5$,$^-3$)

In these questions, "How far" always means "How many blocks, walking along the streets."

13 How many blocks is the middle school from the restaurant? ______

14 How many blocks is Aaron's home from the park? ______

15 How far is City Hall from the library? ______

16 How far is the police station from City Hall? ______

17 How far is Mark's house from the library? ______

18 How far is the police station from the park? ______

19 How far is the bank from the middle school? ______

20 **Challenge** How many blocks is the shortest route from the high school to Mark's house? ______

Name ______________________ Date ____________

Chapter 12
Lesson 4

Points and Lines on a Grid

NCTM Standards 1, 4, 6, 7, 8, 9, 10

Follow the directions below.

1. Mark A at ($^-4$,3).

   Mark B at (3,3).

   Mark C at ($^-4$,$^-2$).

   Draw $\overline{AB}$.

   Draw $\overline{BC}$.

   Draw $\overline{AC}$.

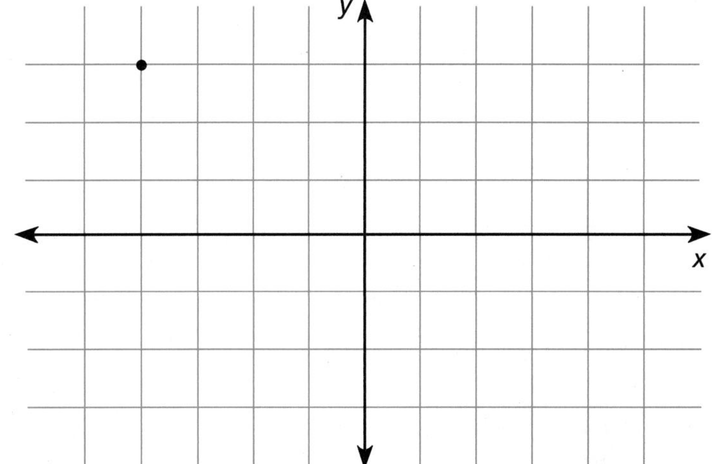

   What figure did you draw? ______________________

---

2. Mark D at (3,$^-2$).

   Mark E at (3,2).

   Mark F at ($^-3$,2).

   Mark G at ($^-3$,$^-2$).

   Draw $\overline{DE}$.

   Draw $\overline{EF}$.

   Draw $\overline{FG}$.

   Draw $\overline{GD}$.

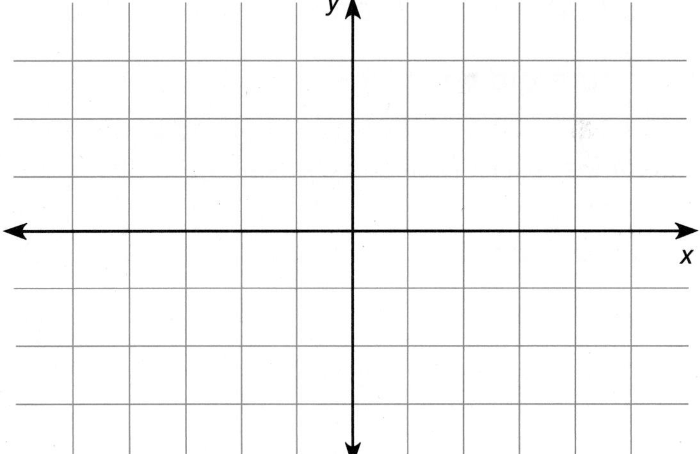

   What figure did you draw? ______________________

   What is its perimeter? ______________________

   What is its area? ______________________

3 Mark H at $(^-3,1)$.

Mark I at $(^-1,^-3)$.

Mark J at $(3,^-1)$.

Mark K at $(1,3)$.

Draw $\overline{HI}$. Draw $\overline{JK}$.

Draw $\overline{IJ}$. Draw $\overline{HK}$.

What figure did you draw?

____

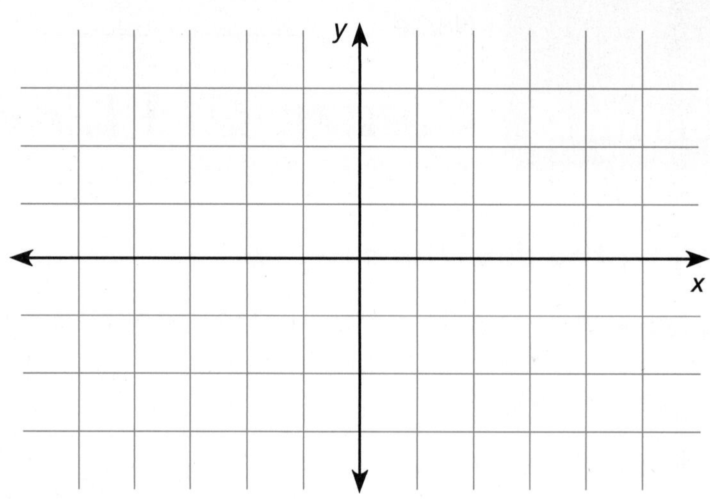

4 Mark L at $(^-3,1)$.

Mark M at $(^-1,3)$.

Mark N at $(3,3)$.

Mark O at $(3,^-1)$.

Mark P at $(^-1,^-1)$.

Draw $\overline{LM}$, $\overline{MO}$, $\overline{ON}$, $\overline{NP}$, and $\overline{PL}$.

What figure did you draw?

____

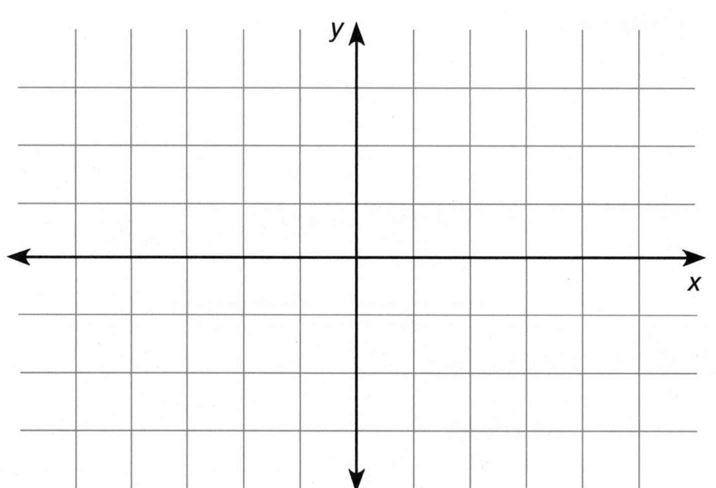

5 Challenge

Mark Q at $(^-2,3)$. Mark U at $(^-3,0)$.

Mark R at $(2,3)$. Mark V at $(0,^-1)$.

Mark S at $(0,2)$. Mark W at $(3,0)$.

Mark T at $(^-4,1)$. Mark X at $(4,1)$.

Draw $\overline{TU}$, $\overline{VW}$, $\overline{WX}$, and $\overline{VU}$.

What did you draw?

____

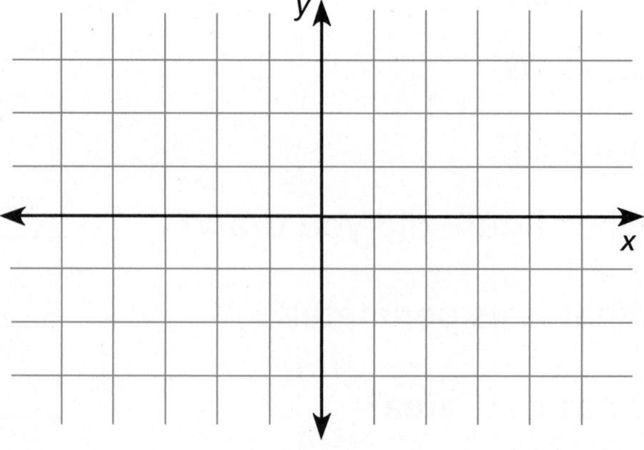

Chapter 12

Lesson 5

Name ______________________________ Date ______________

Drawing Figures on a Coordinate Grid

NCTM Standards 1, 4, 6, 7, 8, 9, 10

Write the directions for drawing each of the pictures below. Tell which points to mark and which connecting line segments to draw.

1

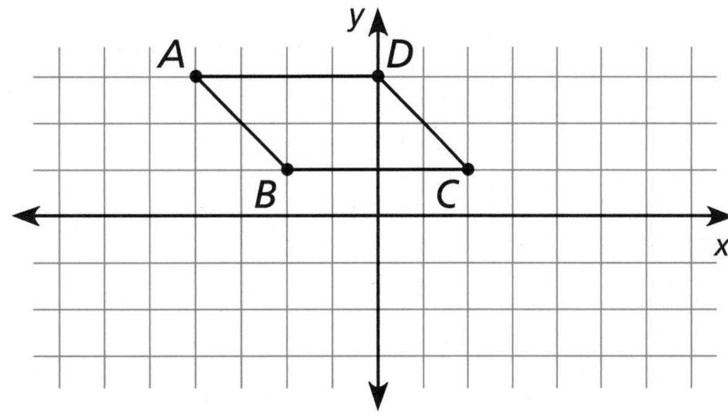

Mark *A* at (___,___). Mark *B* at (___,___).

____

____

2

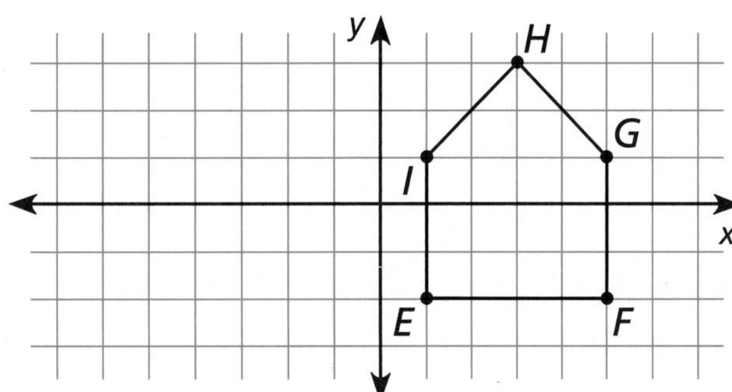

____

____

____

3 Challenge Draw a star like this one ☆ on the grid. Write directions describing how to draw it.

____

____

____

____

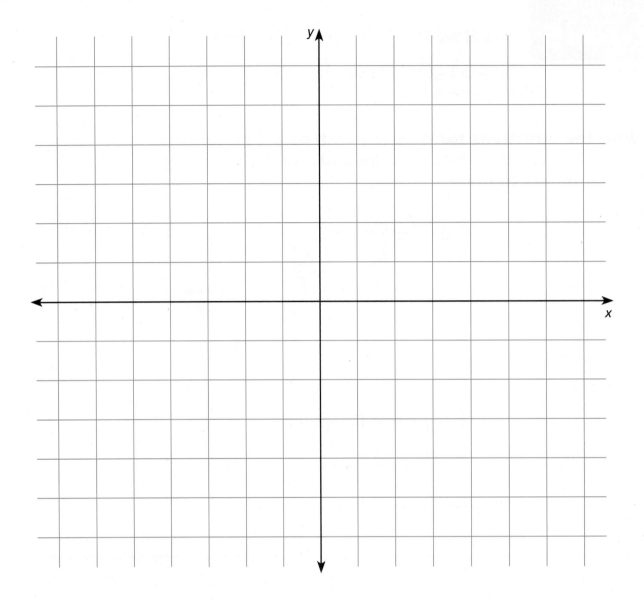

Name ______________________ Date ____________

Chapter 12
Lesson 6

Moving Figures on a Coordinate Grid

NCTM Standards 1, 2, 3, 6, 7, 8, 9, 10

1 Complete the table and draw and label figures H, I, and J.

A	H	I	J
(x,y)	$(x + 5,y)$	$(x,y - 5)$	$(x - 4,y + 4)$
(6,6)	(11,6)		
(6,9)			(2,13)
(8,6)		(8,1)	

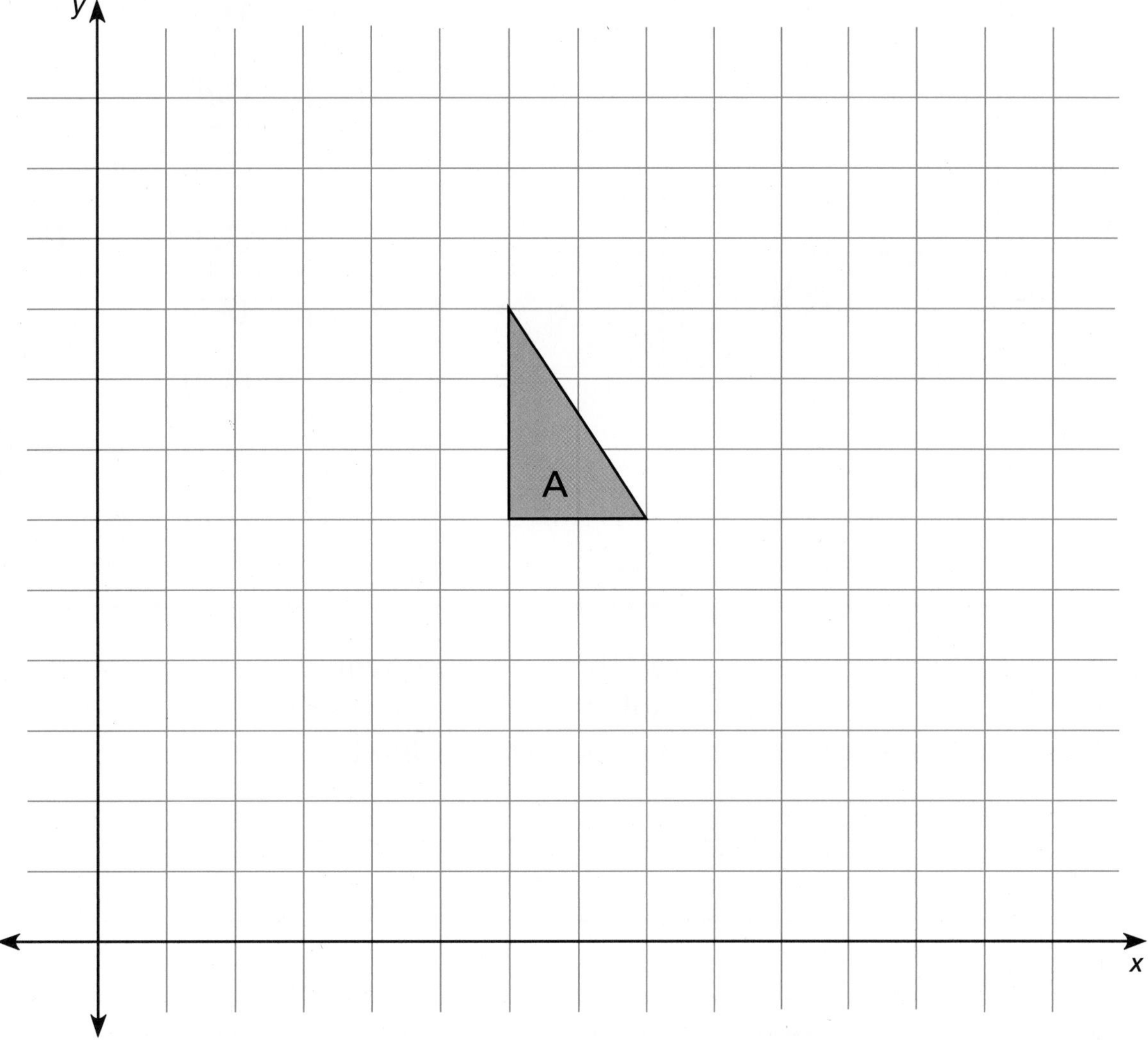

2 Slide this figure 4 spaces to the right.

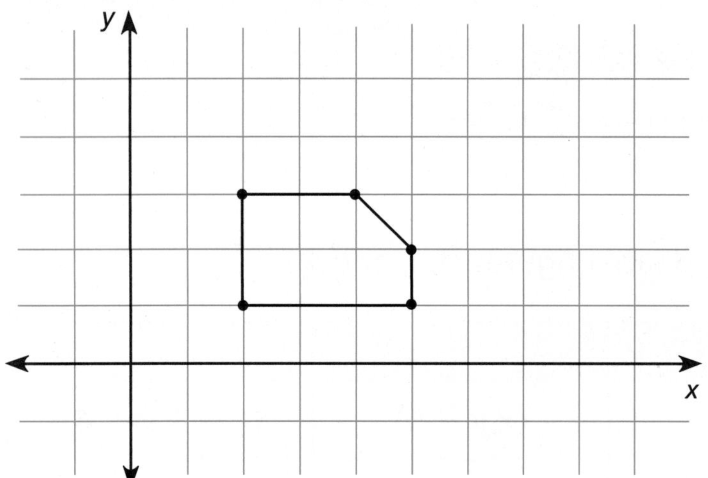

Original Points	New Points

3 Follow the rule to fill in the pairs of coordinates in the table. Then place and connect the new points to make a new version of the figure.

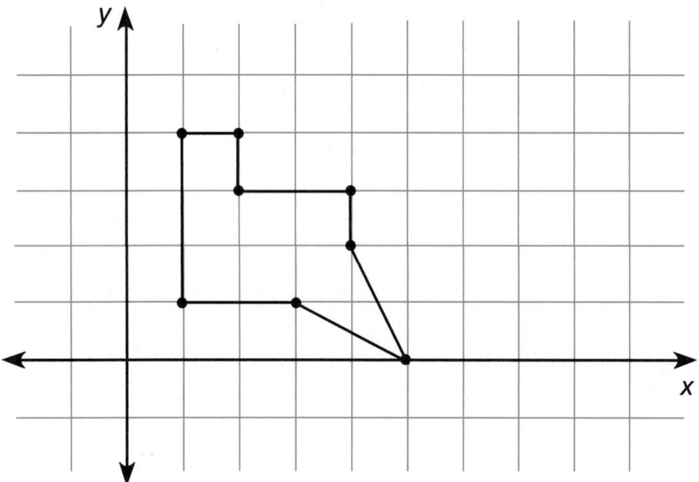

Original Points	New Points
(*x*,*y*)	**(10 − *x*,*y*)**
(1,1)	**(9,1)**
(1,4)	
(2,4)	
(2,3)	**(8,3)**
(3,1)	
(4,3)	
(4,2)	**(6,2)**
(5,0)	

How did the figure move?

____

4 **Challenge** Describe how you think a figure would move if, for each point, you subtracted 3 from the first coordinate and added 2 to the second coordinate.

____

____

____

Chapter 12
Lesson 7

Name ______________________ Date ______________

Number Sentences and Straight Lines

NCTM Standards 1, 2, 3, 6, 7, 8, 9, 10

1 Graph the line whose points all fit the sentence $y = x - 3$.

Fill in and use the table to help you find some points on the line.

(*x*,*y*)
(6,3)
(0,____)
(____,0)
(5,____)
(____,4)
(⁻3,____)
(____,⁻1)
(____,⁻5)

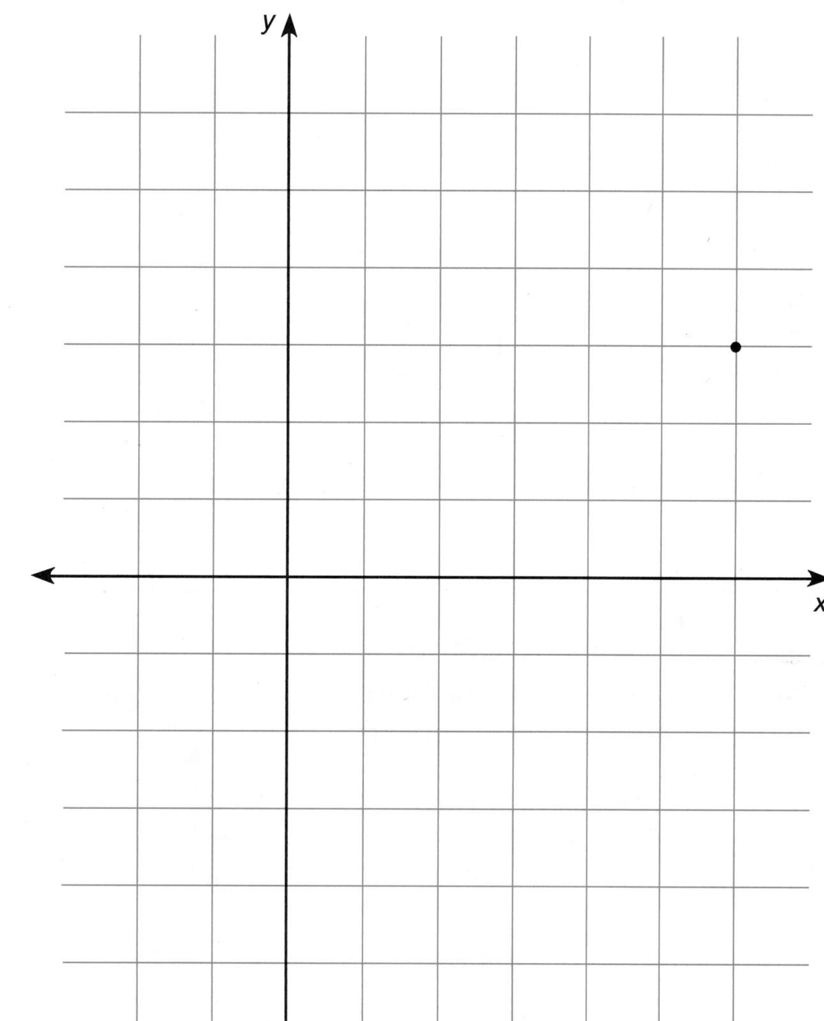

2 Mark the points and draw the line connecting them. Then, fill in the line table and write a number sentence to describe the rule.

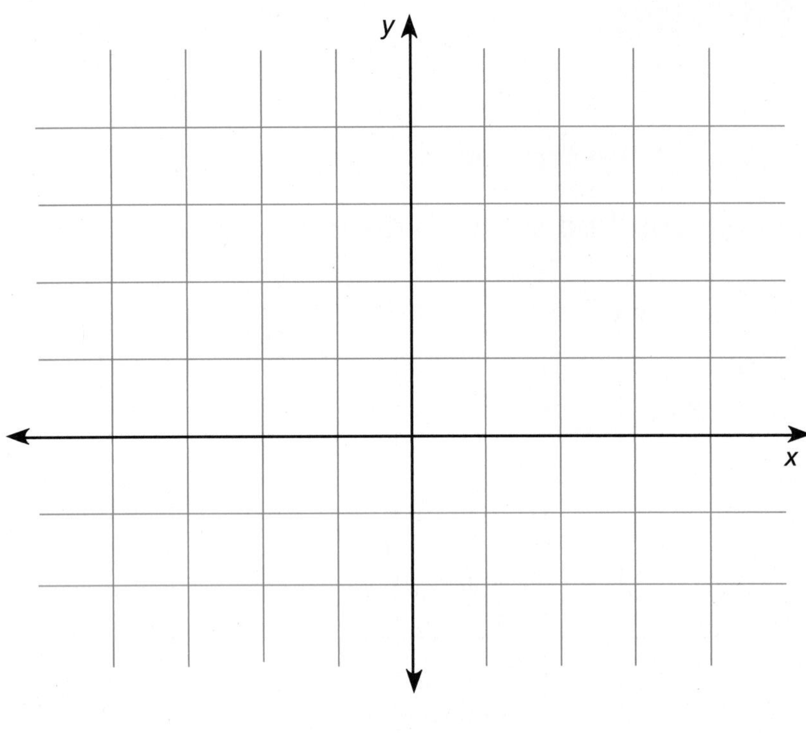

(x,y)
(1,3)
(0,2)
(____,0)
($^-$4,____)
(3,____)
(____,4)
(____,1)
($^-$5,____)

$y =$ _______

3 Challenge Sometimes the Generous Bakery delivers more cookies than a customer orders.

The clerks use this graph to tell how many cookies to send to a customer.

Suenita ordered 8 cookies.

How many cookies did the bakery send her? _______

When will you get more cookies than you order?

____

____

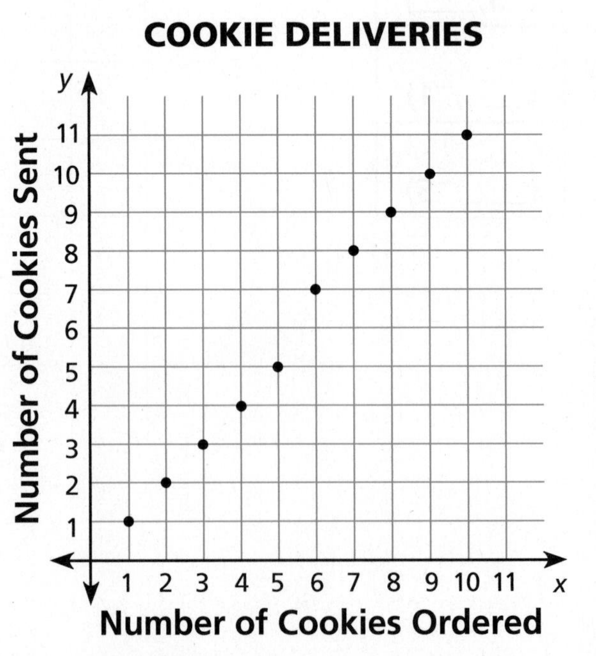

Chapter 12
Lesson 8

Name ______________________ Date ____________

Problem Solving Strategy

Draw a Picture

NCTM Standards 1, 2, 6, 7, 8, 9, 10

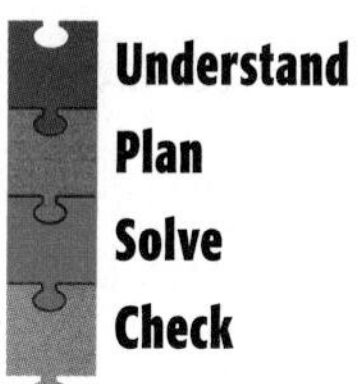

1. Jessica looked at the thermometer every three hours and recorded how the temperature changed. At 6:00 A.M., the temperature was $^-10$°C. At 9:00 A.M., it was 9° warmer. At noon, it was 3° warmer than at 9:00. At 3:00 P.M., it was 5° colder than at noon. At 6:00 P.M., it was 8° colder than at 3:00.

   What was the temperature at 6:00 P.M.? ____________

---

2. Ian and Jenwa played a card game in which you score points for combinations of cards and lose points for cards left in your hand. They played 6 rounds. Here is their score sheet:

	Ian	Jenwa
Round 1	6	$^-4$
Round 2	$^-7$	6
Round 3	5	$^-3$
Round 4	$^-4$	$^-5$
Round 5	$^-6$	9
Round 6	3	$^-5$

   What was Ian's final score? ____________

   What was Jenwa's final score? ____________

   Who had the higher final score? ____________

---

3. A snail fell down a hole and is crawling up to the surface. Every day the snail crawls up 3 feet, but every night it slides back down 2 feet. On Monday morning, the snail is 5 feet under ground.

   On what day will the snail get out of the hole? ____________

Problem Solving Test Prep

Choose the correct answer.

1. What will the temperature be if the temperature drops 9°C?

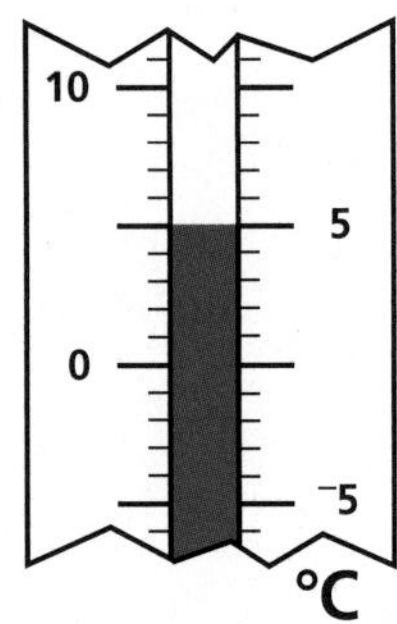

A. 5°C
B. 4°C
C. ⁻4°C
D. ⁻5°C

2. A rectangular prism is 8 cm long, 4 cm wide, and 2 cm high. What are the length, width, and height of a cube with the same volume?

A. 8 centimeters
B. 4 centimeters
C. 3 centimeters
D. 2 centimeters

3. Line segment $\overline{AB}$ is parallel to $\overline{CD}$. Which could be the coordinates of point D?

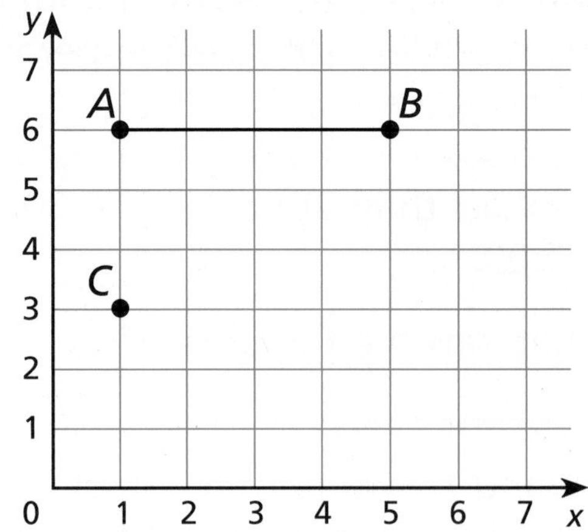

A. (5,6)
B. (1,6)
C. (6,1)
D. (5,3)

4. Which transformation is shown?

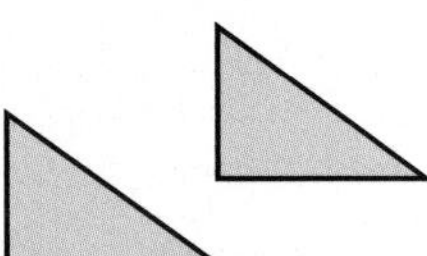

A. reflection
B. rotation
C. translation

D. translation and rotation

Show What You Know

Solve each problem. Explain your answer.

5. A game spinner has 6 equal sections labeled 1–6. Name an outcome that would give two players an equal a chance of winning. Explain.

____

____

____

6. A bar graph shows that the Tigers won 9 baseball games in April, 3 more than that in May, and 2 fewer in June than in April. How many games did the team win in the 3 months? Explain.

____

____

Name ______________________ Date ____________

Chapter 12 Review/Assessment

NCTM Standards 1, 2, 6, 7, 8, 9, 10

Every day at 6 A.M., Ming went outside and measured the temperature. Here's the information that she recorded. Fill in the missing information. Lesson 1

1. 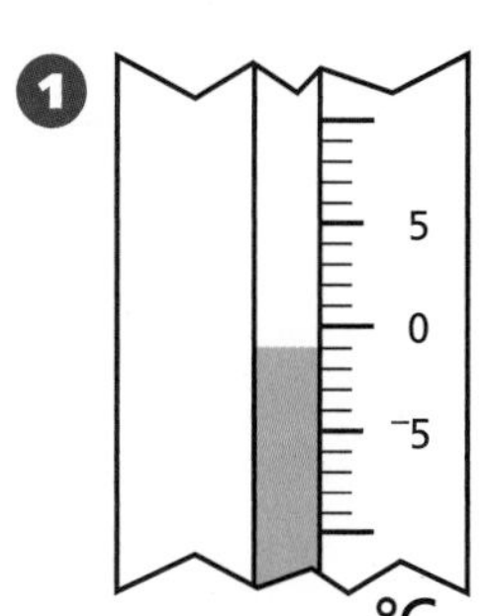

Monday

__________ °C

2. 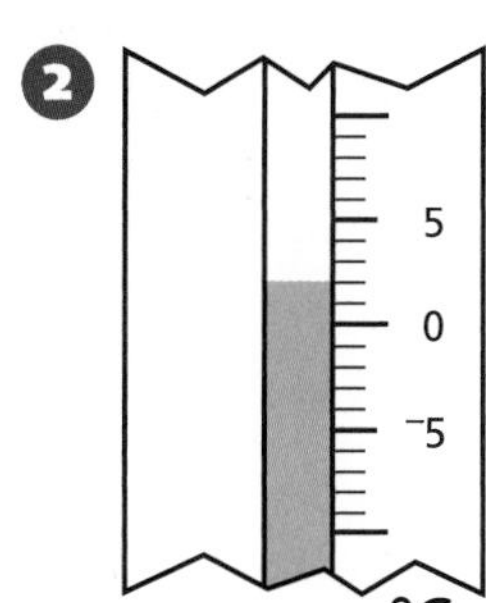

Tuesday

____

Change from Monday

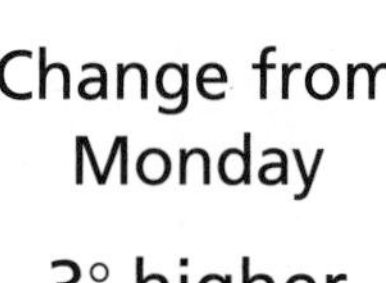

3° higher

3. 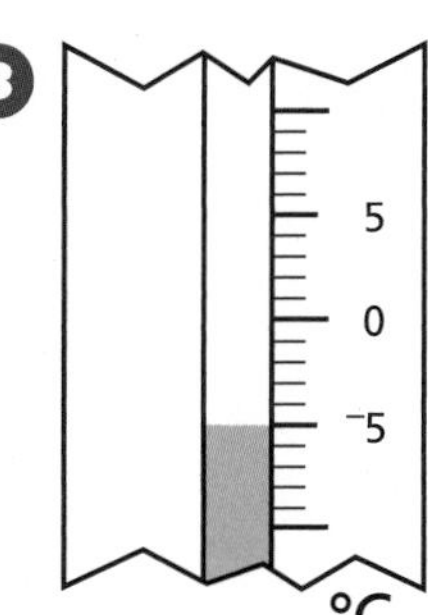

Wednesday

⁻5°C

Change from Tuesday

____

4. 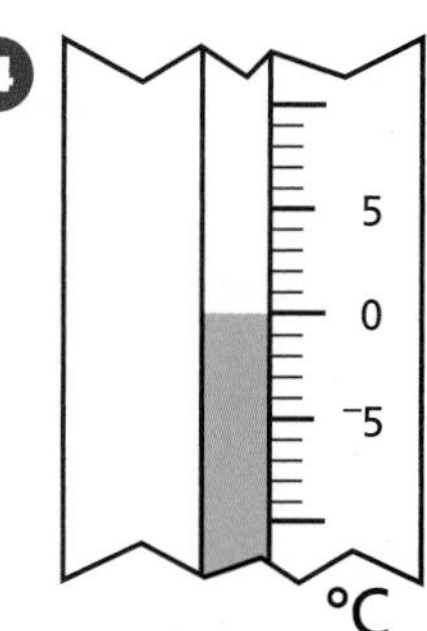

Thursday

____

Change from Wednesday

5° higher

Use this number line to help answer the questions below. Lesson 2

⁻12 ⁻11 ⁻10 ⁻9 ⁻8 ⁻7 ⁻6 ⁻5 ⁻4 ⁻3 ⁻2 ⁻1 0 1 2 3 4 5 6 7 8 9 10 11 12 13

5. Start at ⁻5. Jump backward 6 spaces. Then jump forward 3 spaces.

   Where are you? __________

6. Start at 10. Jump backward 8 spaces. Then jump backward 5 spaces.

   Where are you? __________

7. Start at 3. Jump forward 3 spaces. Then jump backward 7 spaces.

   Where are you? __________

8. Start at ⁻8. Jump forward 10 spaces. Then jump backward 6 spaces.

   Where are you? __________

9 Mark A at (0,2) Draw $\overline{AC}$ Lessons 3 and 4

10 Mark B at (2,0) Draw $\overline{AD}$

11 Mark C at (2,$^-$2) Draw $\overline{BD}$

12 Mark D at ($^-$2,$^-$2) Draw $\overline{CE}$

13 Mark E at ($^-$2,0) Draw $\overline{BE}$

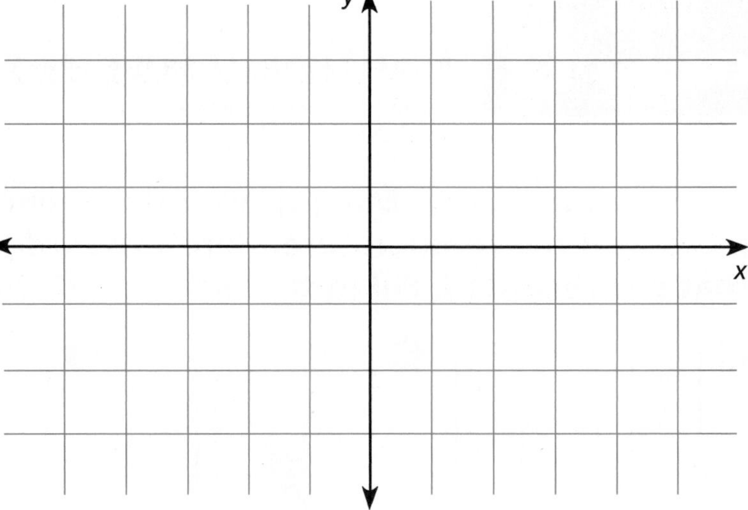

What figure did you draw?

____

14 Write the directions for drawing the figure below. Tell which point to mark and which connecting lines to draw. Lesson 5

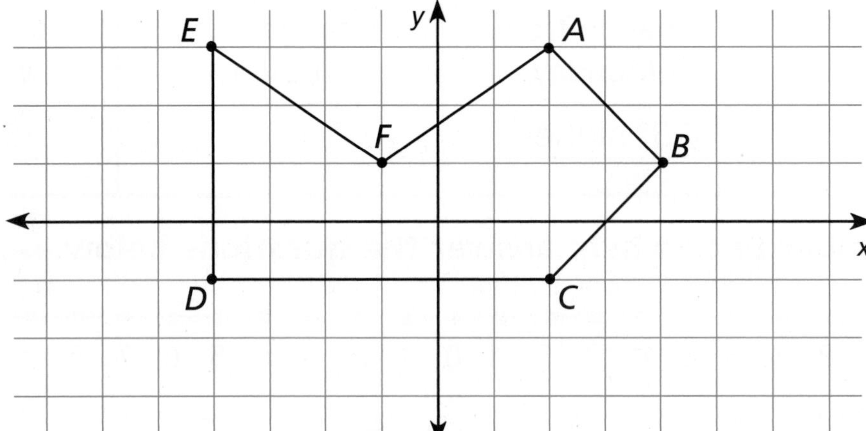

____

____

____

____

Chapter 13

Lesson 1

Name ______________________ Date ____________

Finding Missing Dimensions

NCTM Standards 1, 2, 4, 6, 7, 8, 9, 10

Find the missing length or width of the following rectangles.

1

☐ cm

6 cm

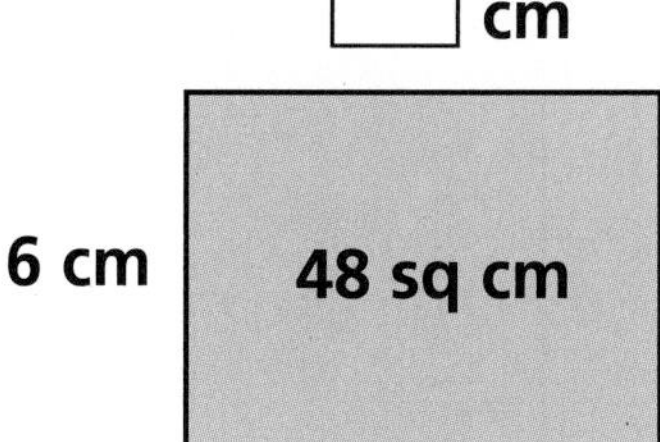

2

12 cm

☐ cm

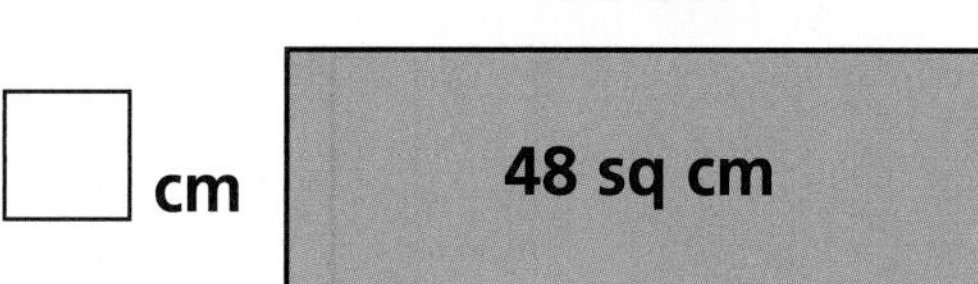

3

☐ cm

7 cm

35 sq cm

4

12 cm

☐ cm

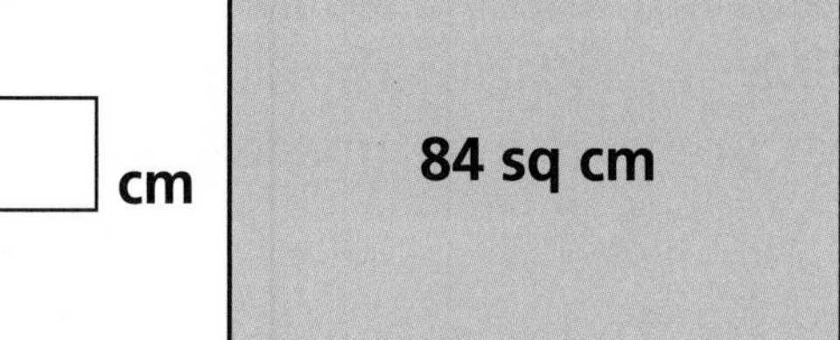

5

☐ cm

☐ cm

35 sq cm

84 sq cm

Total Area = ______ sq cm

6

☐ cm

☐ cm

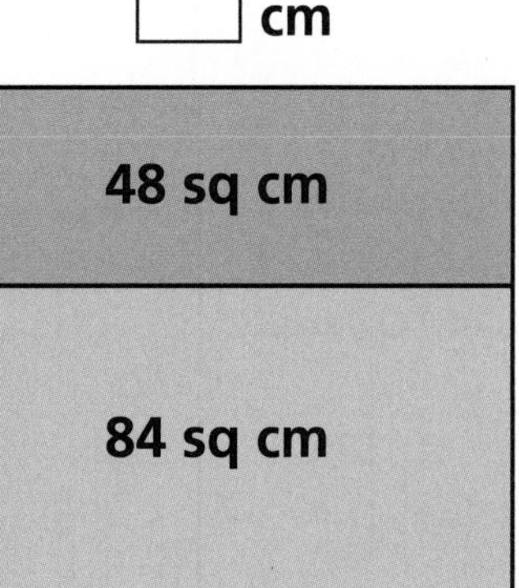

Total Area = ______ sq cm

Solve.

7 Antonio put all 216 of his songs on 18 CDs. When he was finished, he was surprised to notice that each CD had exactly the same number of songs. How many songs were on each CD? Show your work.

______ songs

8 There are 840 inches in the perimeter of Mr. Yang's classroom. How many feet are in the perimeter? Show your work.

______ feet

9

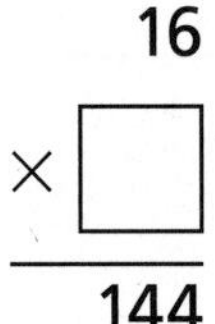

$$\begin{array}{r} 16 \\ \times \square \\ \hline 144 \end{array}$$

10

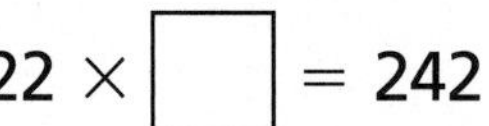

$22 \times \square = 242$

11 $\square \times 12 = 96$

12 **Challenge** Put one digit in each box to make a true sentence.

$\square\square \times \square\square = 2\square5$

Name ______________________ Date ____________

Chapter 13
Lesson 2

Finding Missing Factors

NCTM Standards 1, 2, 4, 6, 7, 8, 9, 10

Complete the multiplication puzzles.

Rule I: Only 0, 1, 2, 4, 8, or 16 can go in the **green** hexagons.
Rule II: The number in the **orange** hexagon must be the sum of the numbers in the **green** hexagons.

0	1	2	4	8	16

1

$4 \times 8 = \square$
$4 \times 1 = \square$
$4 \times 0 = \square$

$4 \times 9 = \square$

2

$7 \times 4 = \square$
$7 \times \square = \square$
$7 \times \square = \square$

$7 \times \square = 42$

3

$9 \times 4 = \square$
$9 \times \square = \square$
$9 \times \square = \square$

$9 \times 5 = \square$

4

$4 \times \square = \square$
$4 \times 2 = \square$
$4 \times \square = \square$

$4 \times 10 = \square$

5

$3 \times 2 = 6$
$3 \times \square = \square$
$3 \times \square = \square$

$3 \times 3 = 9$

6

$7 \times \square = \square$
$7 \times \square = \square$
$7 \times \square = \square$

$7 \times 7 = \square$

7

$3 \times \square = \square$
$3 \times \square = \square$
$3 \times \square = \square$
$3 \times \square = \square$

$3 \times 12 = \square$

8

$5 \times \square = \square$
$5 \times \square = \square$
$5 \times \square = \square$
$5 \times \square = \square$

$5 \times \square = 55$

9

$6 \times \square = \square$
$6 \times \square = \square$
$6 \times \square = \square$
$6 \times \square = \square$

$6 \times \square = 42$

Again, use 0, 1, 2, 4, 8, or 16 to build the missing factor in the orange hexagon.

0	1	2	4	8	16

10

□ × ⬡ = □

□ × ⬡ = □

□ × ⬡ = □

6 × ⬡ = 54

11

8 × ⬡ = □

□ × ⬡ = □

□ × ⬡ = □

8 × ⬡ = 56

12

□ × ⬡ = □

□ × ⬡ = □

□ × ⬡ = □

3 × ⬡ = 18

13

4 × ⬡ = 32

14

5 × ⬡ = 35

15

3 × ⬡ = 42

16 Challenge Lu is doing work on her house. She's tearing down the wall that separates the kitchen from the dining room. The width of each room is 12 feet. The new room will be a long rectangular space. The old kitchen floor had an area of 144 square feet, and the old dining room floor had an area of 120 square feet. What is the length of the new joined room?

12 ft	144 sq ft kitchen	120 sq ft dining room

_____ ft   _____ ft   _____ feet

Name ______________________ Date ____________

Chapter 13
Lesson 3

Finding Missing Factors More Efficiently

NCTM Standards 1, 2, 6, 7, 8, 9, 10

Rule I: Use only numbers from the **green** block to fill in the **green** hexagons.
Rule II: Try to use the largest number possible at each step.
Rule III: Use a zero for any green hexagon that you do not need.

0	1	2	3	6	9	18

1 starting number: **45**

9 × ⟨3⟩ = ☐

What's left? ☐

9 × ⟨ ⟩ = ☐

What's left? ☐

9 × ⟨ ⟩ = ☐

What's left? ☐

9 × ⟨5⟩ = **45**

2 starting number: **42**

7 × ⟨6⟩ = ☐

What's left? ☐

7 × ⟨0⟩ = ☐

What's left? ☐

7 × ⟨ ⟩ = ☐

What's left? ☐

7 × ⟨ ⟩ = **42**

3 starting number: **96**

8 × ⟨ ⟩ = ☐

What's left? ☐

8 × ⟨ ⟩ = ☐

What's left? ☐

8 × ⟨ ⟩ = ☐

What's left? ☐

8 × ⟨ ⟩ = **96**

4 starting number: **75**

5 × ⟨ ⟩ = ☐

What's left? ☐

5 × ⟨ ⟩ = ☐

What's left? ☐

5 × ⟨ ⟩ = ☐

What's left? ☐

5 × ⟨ ⟩ = **75**

5 starting number: **104**

8 × ⟨ ⟩ = ☐

What's left? ☐

8 × ⟨ ⟩ = ☐

What's left? ☐

8 × ⟨ ⟩ = ☐

What's left? ☐

8 × ⟨ ⟩ = **104**

6 starting number: **98**

7 × ⟨ ⟩ = ☐

What's left? ☐

7 × ⟨ ⟩ = ☐

What's left? ☐

7 × ⟨ ⟩ = ☐

What's left? ☐

7 × ⟨ ⟩ = **98**

Again, use 0, 1, 2, 3, 6, 9, or 18 to build the missing factor in the orange hexagon.

0	1	2	3	6	9	18

7 starting number: **32**

$2 \times \bigcirc = \mathbf{32}$

8 starting number: **51**

$3 \times \bigcirc = \mathbf{51}$

9 starting number: **275**

$25 \times \bigcirc = \mathbf{275}$

10

$15 \times \bigcirc = \mathbf{195}$

11

$4 \times \bigcirc = \mathbf{132}$

12

$9 \times \bigcirc = \mathbf{225}$

13 **Challenge** Soo Jin wants to give 12 stickers to each of her 8 friends. She has 71 stickers. How many more stickers does Soo Jin need? Show your work.

_____ stickers

Chapter 13
Lesson 4

Name ______________________ Date ____________

Estimating Missing Factors and Quotients

NCTM Standards 1, 2, 6, 7, 8, 9, 10

Complete the puzzles. Begin by rewriting each division sentence as a multiplication sentence.

Rule I: Use only numbers from the **green** block to fill in the **green** boxes.
Rule II: Try to use the largest number possible at each step.
Rule III: Use a zero for any **green** box that you do not need.

0	1	2	3	4	5	6	7	8	9
0	10	20	30	40	50	60	70	80	90

Hint: Fill in the **green** boxes before the **blue** boxes.

1 $136 \div 8 = \square$

$8 \times \square = 136$

$8 \times 10 = 80$

What's left? 56

$8 \times \square = \square$

What's left? $\square$

$8 \times \square = \square$

What's left? $\square$

2 $712 \div 8 = \square$

$\square \times \square = \square$

$8 \times \square = \square$

$\square$

$8 \times \square = \square$

$\square$

$8 \times \square = \square$

$\square$

3 $216 \div 9 = \square$

$\square \times \square = \square$

$9 \times \square = \square$

$\square$

$9 \times \square = \square$

$\square$

$9 \times \square = \square$

$\square$

Use numbers, words, or pictures to solve these problems.

4. Tim and four of his friends found 185 nickels! They shared the coins so that each ended up with the same number of nickels. How many nickels does each have? Write a number sentence to explain your answer.

_______ nickels

5. The police department spent $357 to buy seven identical winter coats for their officers. How much did each coat cost? Write a number sentence to explain your answer.

$_______

6. **Challenge** State Elementary School is having a field day. All 283 students were put onto six different teams as evenly as possible. Did all the teams have the same number of students? Explain your answer.

____

____

____

____

Name ______________________ Date __________

Chapter 13
Lesson 5

Dividing Using Multiplication Puzzles

NCTM Standards 1, 2, 6, 7, 8, 9, 10

Complete the puzzles. Rewrite each division sentence as a multiplication sentence. Choose numbers for the green boxes from this list:
0, 1, 2, 3, 4, 5, 6, 7, 8, 9, 10, 20, 30, 40, 50, 60, 70, 80, 90

1

☐
30
$7\overline{)238}$

7 × 30 = 210
28
7 × ☐ = ☐
☐
238 ÷ 7 = ☐

2

☐
☐
$9\overline{)432}$

9 × ☐ = ☐
☐
9 × ☐ = ☐
☐
432 ÷ 9 = ☐

3

☐
☐
$8\overline{)536}$

8 × ☐ = ☐
☐
8 × ☐ = ☐
☐
536 ÷ 8 = ☐

4

☐
☐
$6\overline{)582}$

6 × ☐ = ☐
☐
6 × ☐ = ☐
☐
582 ÷ 6 = ☐

5

☐
☐
$4\overline{)312}$

4 × ☐ = ☐
☐
4 × ☐ = ☐
☐
312 ÷ 4 = ☐

6

☐
☐
$9\overline{)153}$

9 × ☐ = ☐
☐
9 × ☐ = ☐
☐
153 ÷ 9 = ☐

Complete the puzzles. Rewrite each division sentence as a multiplication sentence. Choose numbers for the green boxes from this list: 0, 1, 2, 3, 4, 5, 6, 7, 8, 9, 10, 20, 30, 40, 50, 60, 70, 80, 90

7

3) 291

3 × ☐ = ☐

3 × ☐ = ☐

291 ÷ 3 = ☐

8

8) 272

8 × ☐ = ☐

8 × ☐ = ☐

272 ÷ 8 = ☐

9

5) 245

5 × ☐ = ☐

5 × ☐ = ☐

245 ÷ 5 = ☐

10 Challenge Write a word problem to match 138 ÷ 6 and then solve it.

Name ______________________ Date ____________

Chapter 13

Lesson 6

Completing Division Sentences

NCTM Standards 1, 2, 6, 7, 8, 9, 10

Complete the puzzles.

Rule I: Use only numbers from the **green** block to fill in the **green** boxes.
Rule II: Try to use the largest number possible at each step.
Rule III: Use a zero for any **green** box that you do not need.

0	1	2	3	4	5	6	7	8	9
0	10	20	30	40	50	60	70	80	90
0	100	200	300	400	500	600	700	800	900

1.

☐
☐
☐
5) 545
☐
What's left? ☐
☐
What's left? ☐
☐
What's left? 0

545 ÷ 5 = ☐

2.

☐
☐
☐
3) 396
☐
☐
☐
☐
☐
0

396 ÷ 3 = ☐

3.

☐
☐
☐
6) 558
☐
☐
☐
☐
☐
0

558 ÷ 6 = ☐

Divide.

4

$15\overline{)225}$

$225 \div 15 =$ ☐

5

$5\overline{)1{,}380}$

$1{,}380 \div 5 =$ ☐

6

$6\overline{)3{,}126}$

$3{,}126 \div 6 =$ ☐

7 Mr. Green has had 300 students over the course of his teaching career. One-fourth of his students have been 6 years old, one-third have been 7, and the rest have been 8. How many students of each age has Mr. Green taught?

_____ 6-year-olds

_____ 7-year-olds

_____ 8-year-olds

8 **Challenge** Write a division problem that has an answer between 111 and 222. Explain the solution.

____

____

____

Name ______________________ Date ______________

Chapter 13

Lesson 7

Problem Solving Strategy

Working Backward

NCTM Standards 1, 2, 4, 6, 7, 8, 9, 10

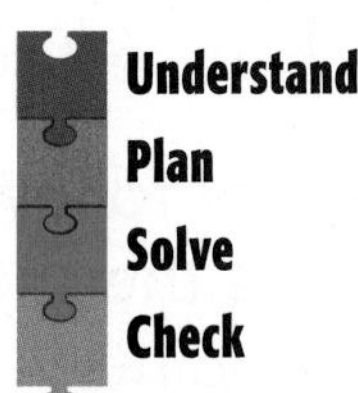

1. Charles measured his rectangular playground and found the area to be 432 square feet. He recorded the length as 24 feet but forgot to record the width. What was the width? Show your work.

______ feet

2. Mr. Tran made a list of some items he sells in his store. He has 10 umbrellas, 8 beach balls, 13 shovels, and 13 sunglasses. There are beach towels stacked equally on two shelves. Mr. Tran determined there are 76 items. How many towels are on each shelf?

3. There are 192 people at a dinner party. An equal number of people are sitting at each of 12 tables. Fifty-seven people ordered steak and 63 people ordered salmon. The same number of people at each table ordered chicken. How many chicken dinners should be served at each table? Explain.

Problem Solving Test Prep

Choose the correct answer.

1 By following the grid lines, what is the shortest distance between points *A* and *B*?

A (1,5) and *B* (4,3)

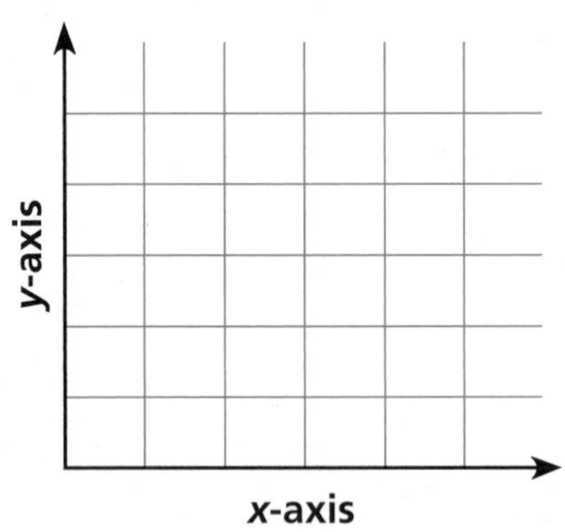

A. 3 units **C.** 5 units

B. 4 units **D.** 6 units

2 Jerome wants to change 42 inches to feet. Which number sentence should he use?

A. 42×12 **C.** 42×3

B. $42 \div 12$ **D.** $42 \div 3$

3 You toss a number cube labeled 1 to 6. What is the probability that you will toss a 5?

A. $\frac{1}{5}$ **C.** $\frac{1}{6}$

B. $\frac{5}{5}$ **D.** $\frac{5}{6}$

4 Ms. Carpenter drives 19 miles from home to work. How far does she drive each day going to work and then returning home?

A. 21 miles **C.** 38 miles

B. 28 miles **D.** 39 miles

Show What You Know

Solve each problem. Explain your answer.

5 Jean Marie planted 9 rows of tomatoes and 9 rows of beans. Each row has the same number of plants. In all, there are 396 plants. How many plants are in each row? Explain.

____

____

6 Pablo is walking on a rectangular path. He walks 35 feet, turns right, and walks some more. He turns right and walks another 35 feet. He turns right and walks back to where he began. In all, he walks 100 feet. What is the area of the rectangle? Explain.

____

____

Chapter 13

Name ______________________ Date ____________

Review/Assessment

NCTM Standards 1, 2, 6, 7, 8, 9, 10

Complete the multiplication and division sentences. Lessons 2 and 3

1

5 × ⬡ = 135

5 × ⬡20 = ☐

What's left? ☐

5 × ⬡ = ☐

What's left?  0

5 × ⬡ = 0

What's left? 0

2

7 × ⬡ = 861

7 × ⬡ = ☐

What's left? ☐

7 × ⬡ = ☐

What's left? ☐

7 × ⬡ = 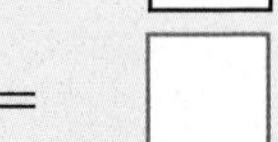

What's left? 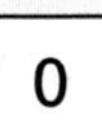 0

3

324 ÷ 9 = ☐

9 × ☐ = 324

9 × ☐ = ☐

9 × ☐ = ☐

9 × ☐ = ☐

4

427 ÷ 7 = ☐

☐ × ☐ = 427

☐ × ☐ = ☐

☐ × ☐ = ☐

☐ × ☐ = ☐

Circle the best estimate for each problem. Lesson 4

5 $32 \times ? = 2656$

800 80

1,200 60

6 $1{,}200 \div 48 = ?$

400 30

24 6

Complete the division problems. Lessons 5 and 6

7

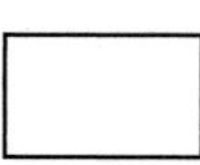

5) 805

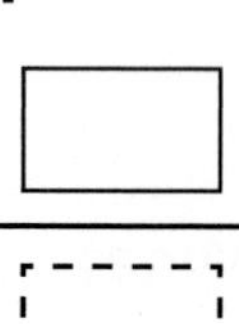

0

8

5) 290

9 Mikaela worked at the school carnival. She sold a school hat for \$10 and some T-shirts for \$13 each. She collected \$101. How many T-shirts did she sell? Show your work. Lesson 7

Name ______________________ Date ____________

Chapter 14
Lesson 1

Number Puzzles

NCTM Standards 1, 2, 6, 7, 8, 9, 10

1 Complete the chart.

	Think of a whole number between 0 and 10.	Multiply by 9.	Add the digits in your product.
A			
B			
C			
D			
E			
F			
G			
H			
I			

2 What do you notice?

____

____

3 Can you think of any numbers that don't follow this pattern?

____

____

____

____

As you complete this puzzle, look for patterns. The number in each blue box is the difference between the numbers in the green boxes above it. The number in each black box is the difference between the numbers in the blue boxes above it.

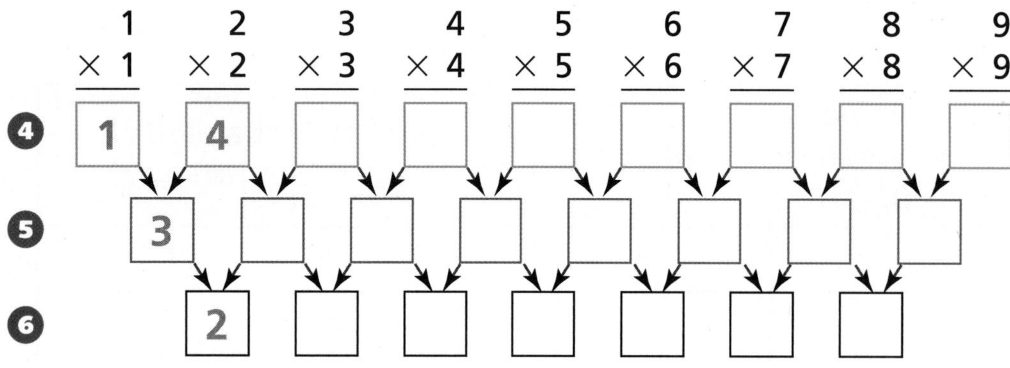

7 Describe the pattern in row 4.

____

____

8 Describe the pattern in row 5.

____

____

9 **Challenge** Two fourth-grade classes have the same number of students. Each student in these classes made a card for his or her first-grade buddy. One of the teachers also made a card. In the end, there were 49 cards. How many students are in each of the fourth-grade classes? Explain your answer. _____ students

____

____

____

Chapter 14
Lesson 2

Name ______________________ Date ____________

Introducing Variables

NCTM Standards 1, 2, 6, 7, 8, 9, 10

Fill in the missing numbers.

1

		A	B	C	D	E
Think of a number. Put that many counters in the bag.	bag	4	11			
Add 6. You now have the bag and 6 extra counters.	bag and 6 counters	10		21		
Double it. You now have two bags and 12 extra counters. How many counters all together?	2 bags and 12 counters	20			46	12

2

		F	G	H	I	J
Think of a number.	bag		4			
Double it.	2 bags			0		
Add 6.	2 bags and 6 counters					
Divide by 2. How many counters do you have all together?	bag and 3 counters	15			20	4

3

		K	L	M	N	O
Think of a number.	bag	7				
Add 7.	bag and 7 counters					
Add the number you thought of first.	2 bags and 7 counters					
Subtract 5. How many do you have all together?	2 bags and 2 counters		22	52	2	4

4. Choose steps to put in your puzzle. Then complete the puzzle.

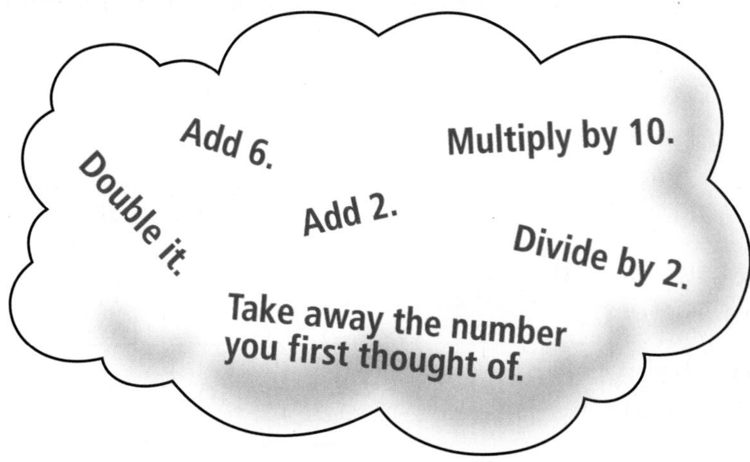

Add 6.
Multiply by 10.
Double it.
Add 2.
Divide by 2.
Take away the number you first thought of.

Think of a number.	6	20		12	

5. **Challenge** Fill in steps that give the correct final number from the given starting number.

Think of a number.	1	15	7	91	
	16	30	22	106	39

Chapter 14
Lesson 3

Name ______________________ Date ____________

Introducing a Shorthand Notation

NCTM Standards 1, 2, 6, 7, 8, 9, 10

Complete the puzzles.

1

Words	Pictures	A	B	C	D	E
Think of a number.	🝆	7				
Multiply it by 10.	10 🝆		10			
Add 130.	10 🝆 + 130			160		
Divide by 5.	2 🝆 + 26				50	
Divide by 2.	🝆 + 13					35
Subtract the number you thought of first.						

2

Words	Pictures	Shorthand	F	G	H
Think of a number.	🝆	x	3	5	
Add 47.	🝆 + 47	$x + 47$	50		
Double it.	2 🝆 + 94	$2x + 94$			
Subtract 75.	2 🝆 + 19	$2x + 19$			
Subtract the number you thought of first.	🝆 + 19	$x + 19$			
Subtract 18.	🝆 + 1	$x + 1$			54
Subtract the number you thought of first.					

3

Pictures	Shorthand	I	J
[bag]	x	8	
[bag] ••••	$x + 4$		
[bag][bag] ::::			
[bag][bag] :::			10
[bag][bag][bag] :::			
[bag] :			
:			

4

Pictures	Shorthand	K	L
[bag]		19	
[bag] + 50			
2 [bag] + 100			
2 [bag] + 148			
[bag] + 74			154
74			

5 Challenge Describe each step in the puzzle with words.

Words	Shorthand
Think of a number.	x
	$2x$
	$2x + 5$
	$4x + 10$

Chapter 14

Lesson 4 Using Shorthand Notation to Complete Number Puzzles

NCTM Standards 1, 2, 6, 7, 8, 9, 10

Name ____________________ Date __________

Find the missing numbers in these puzzles.

1

		A	B
Think of a number.	[bag]		0
	[bag][bag]··	52	2

2

		C	D
Think of a number.	[bag]		6
	2[bag] + 26	40	

3

		E	F
Think of a number.	x		
	$3x + 6$	18	33

4

		G	H
Think of a number.	x		
	$4x + 7$	11	35

5

If x is:	then $30x + 75$ is:
10	375
20	
25	
35	

6

If:	then x is:
$2x + 10 = 50$	20
$x + 17 = 92$	
$10 + 13x = 23$	
$8x - 2 = 22$	

7 Choose the correct answer.

Johanna has 6 boxes of erasers and 3 loose erasers. She counted all of her erasers and found she had exactly enough to give 1 eraser to each of the 81 fourth graders in her school. Which equation can be used to figure out the number of erasers in a box?

A. $81 \div 3 = 6x$

B. $81 \times 3 = 6x$

C. $6x + 3 = 81$

D. $3x + 6 = 81$

8. Use the clues in the table to find the missing parts of the puzzle. You do not need to fill in the **Words** column.

Words	Shorthand	A	B	C	D	E
Think of a number.	x		0			
		12	0	30		75
	$3x + 6$	18	6	36		
			6	26	16	56
Divide by 2						
Subtract the number you thought of first.	3					

9. Describe how you found the shorthand notation for the second row of the above puzzle.

10. **Challenge** Rosie brought 2 boxes of tissues and 1 pocket pack of tissues for her class to use. There are 12 tissues in the pocket pack. Rosie announced that she had brought 212 tissues. Which of the following describe this situation?

A. $212 - 2x = 200$

B. $2x + 12 = 212$

C. $x + 212 = 412$

D. $2x - 12 = 212$

Chapter 14

Lesson 5

Name ______________________ Date ____________

Using Square Numbers to Remember Other Multiplication Facts

NCTM Standards 1, 2, 6, 7, 8, 9, 10

Complete the diagrams and number sentences.

1

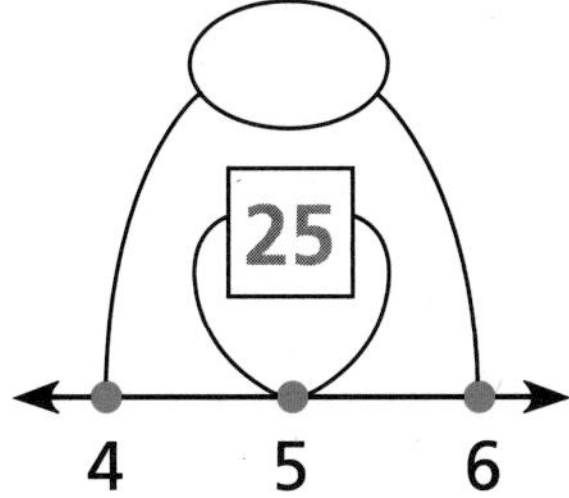

5 × 5 = ☐

4 × 6 = ◯

2

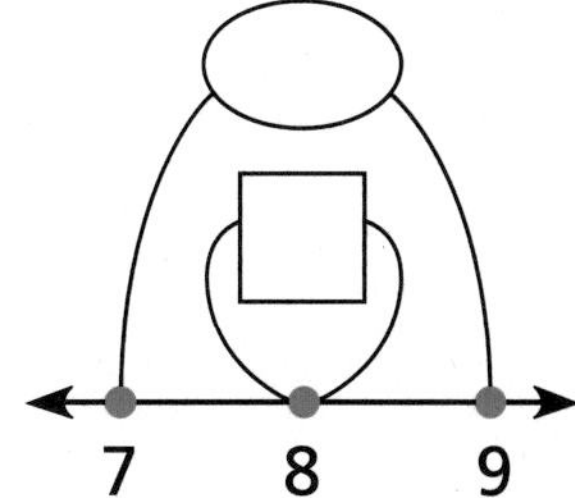

8 × 8 = ☐

7 × 9 = ◯

3

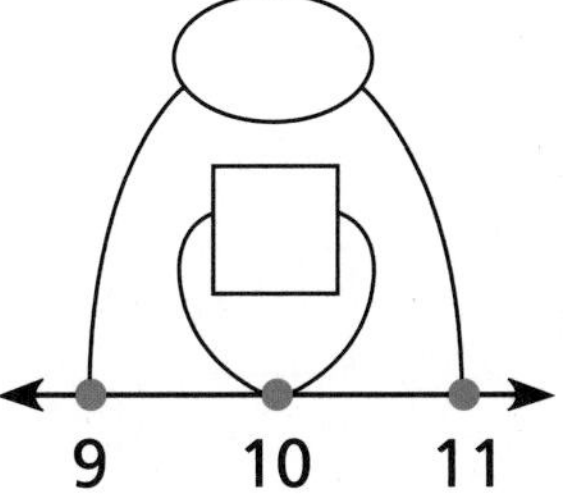

10 × 10 = ☐

9 × 11 = ◯

4

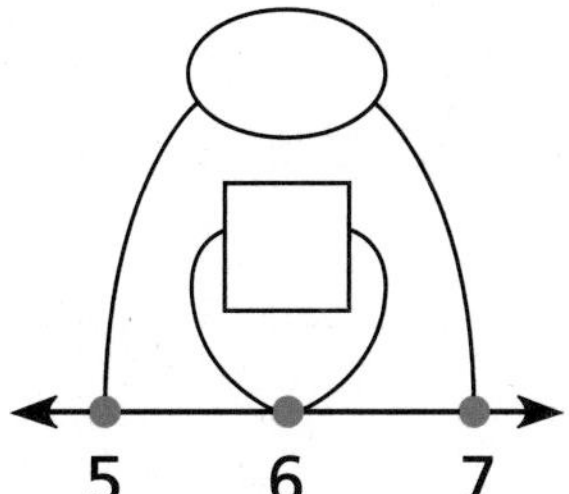

6 × 6 = ☐

5 × 7 = ◯

5

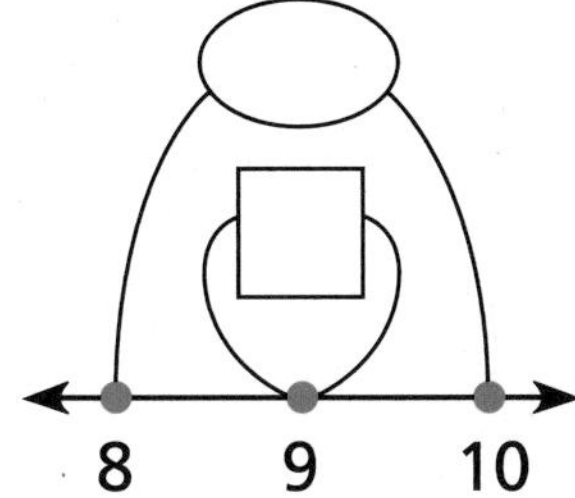

9 × 9 = ☐

◯ × ◯ = ◯

6

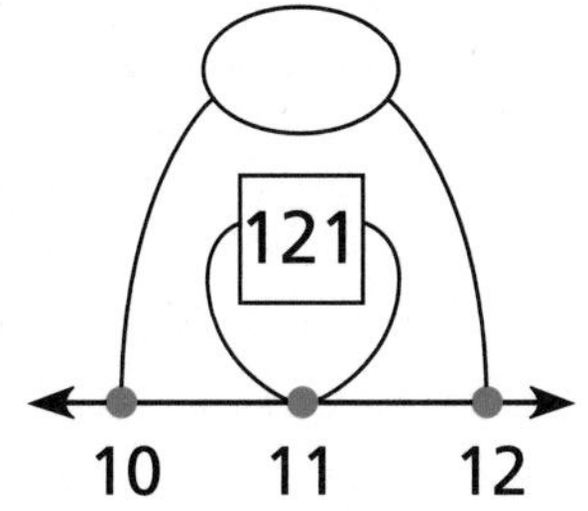

☐ × ☐ = ☐

10 × 12 = ◯

Complete the related number sentences.

7

$12 \times 12 = \square$

$11 \times 13 = \bigcirc$

8

$20 \times 20 = \square$

$19 \times 21 = \bigcirc$

9

$15 \times 15 = \square$

$\bigcirc \times \bigcirc = 224$

10

$25 \times 25 = 625$

$24 \times 26 = \bigcirc$

11

$\square \times \square = 324$

$17 \times 19 = \bigcirc$

12

$\square \times \square = \square$

$\bigcirc \times \bigcirc = 899$

13 **Challenge** Write two examples that show that:

$$A \times A - 1 = (A + 1) \times (A - 1)$$

____

____

Chapter 14

Lesson 6

Name ____________________ Date ____________

Generalizing a Multiplication Pattern

NCTM Standards 1, 2, 6, 7, 8, 9, 10

1 Complete the chart.

Try some examples of your own.

Words	Shorthand	Ben	Al	Mary	Jane	A	B	C
Think of a number.	n	3	5	11	4			
Multiply your number by itself.	$n \bullet n$	9						
Subtract 1 from the product.	$(n \bullet n) - 1$	8						
Add 1 to the number you thought of.	$n + 1$	4						
Subtract 1 from the number you thought of.	$n - 1$	2						
Multiply your results together.	$(n + 1) \bullet (n - 1)$	8						

2 Draw a picture to show that $(5 \bullet 5) - 1 = (5 + 1) \bullet (5 - 1)$.

Use square numbers to help you find the products below.

3. $31 \cdot 29 =$ ☐

   Hint: What's $30 \cdot 30$?

4. $51 \cdot 49 =$ ☐

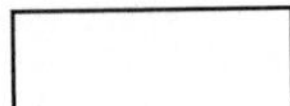

5. $13 \cdot 11 =$ ☐

6. $101 \cdot 99 =$ ☐

7. $41 \cdot 39 =$ ☐

8. $71 \cdot 69 =$ ☐

Use nearby products to find square numbers.

9. $(31 \cdot 31) - 1 =$ ☐

   Hint: What's $30 \cdot 32$?

10. $(51 \cdot 51) - 1 =$ ☐

11. $(41 \cdot 41) - 1 =$ ☐

12. $(101 \cdot 101) - 1 =$ ☐

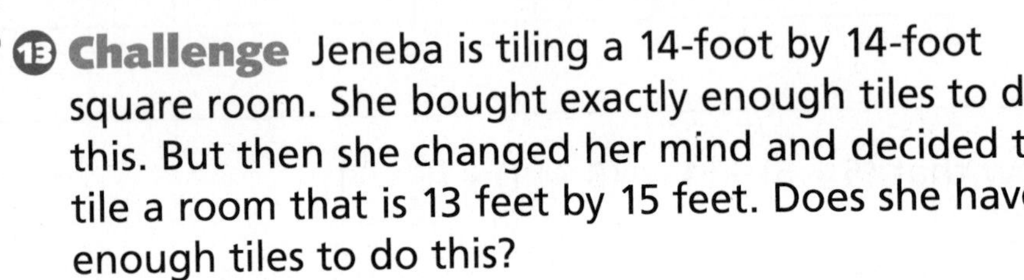

13. **Challenge** Jeneba is tiling a 14-foot by 14-foot square room. She bought exactly enough tiles to do this. But then she changed her mind and decided to tile a room that is 13 feet by 15 feet. Does she have enough tiles to do this?

Draw a picture and write a number sentence to explain how you found the answer.

Chapter 14
Lesson 7

Name ______________________ Date ____________

Problem Solving Strategy
Work Backward

NCTM Standards 1, 2, 6, 7, 8, 9, 10

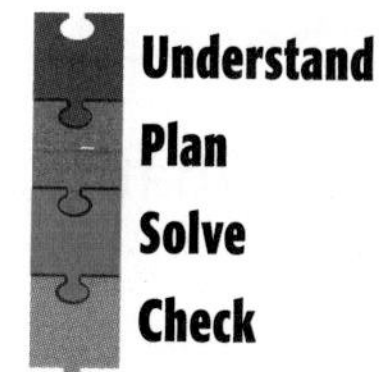

1 On Monday, Lorenzo bought x marbles. On Tuesday, he bought the same number he bought on Monday. On Wednesday, he gave 3 marbles to his brother. On Thursday, he bought 5 more marbles, giving him a total of 14 marbles. The equation $2x - 3 + 5 = 14$ represents the number of marbles Lorenzo had on Thursday.

Fill in the table to find how many marbles Lorenzo bought on Monday.

	Shorthand	Number of Marbles
Monday	x	
Tuesday	$2x$	
Wednesday	$2x - 3$	
Thursday	$2x - 3 + 5$	14

Lorenzo bought _____ marbles on Monday.

---

2 Jean ended up with 8 when she completed this number puzzle. What number was Jean thinking of? Fill in the table to find out.

Think of a number.	
Double it.	
Add 2.	
Divide by 2.	
Subtract 1.	8

Problem Solving Test Prep

Choose the correct answer.

1. What is the area of the figure?

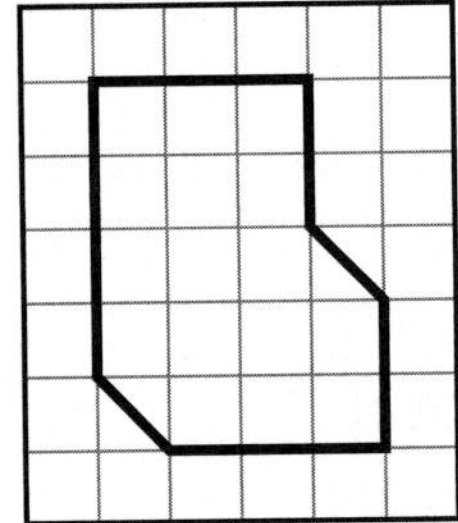

A. $16\frac{1}{2}$ square units
B. 17 square units
C. $17\frac{1}{2}$ square units
D. 18 square units

2. Which expression has the same product as 80×427?

A. 800×42
B. 400×827
C. 80×42.7
D. $8 \times 4{,}270$

3. Which fraction should go in the box on the number line?

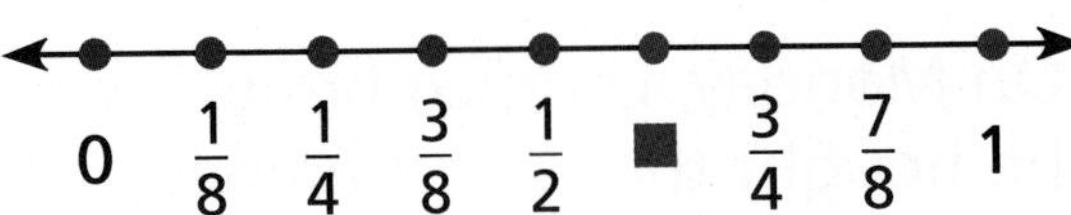

A. $\frac{2}{3}$
B. $\frac{5}{6}$
C. $\frac{5}{8}$
D. $\frac{6}{8}$

4. Athena has two $\frac{1}{2}$-gallon containers and one 1-quart container of orange juice. How many 1-cup servings can she make in all?

A. 5
B. 10
C. 20
D. 24

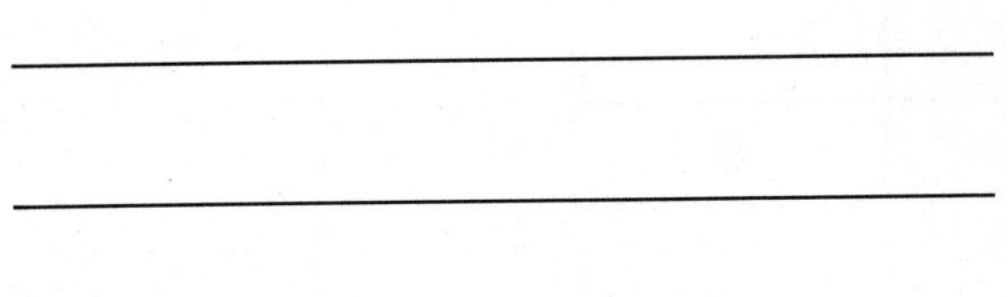

Show What You Know

Solve each problem. Explain your answer.

5. Carmen has $1.43 when she gets home from school. She paid $0.35 each way on the city bus, bought lunch for $1.45, and had a snack for $0.79. How much money did she leave home with?

____

____

____

6. Curtis cut his birthday cake into equal pieces. Six pieces were eaten at the party, and half of the leftover pieces were eaten the next day. The last 3 pieces were eaten two days later. Into how many slices was the cake cut?

____

____

____

Name ____________________ Date ____________

Chapter 14 Review/Assessment

NCTM Standards 1, 2, 6, 7, 8, 9, 10

1 Complete the puzzle. Lessons 1, 2, 3, and 4

Words	Pictures	Shorthand	A	B	C	D
Think of a number.		x	5			
Multiply by 2.						
Multiply by 2 again.		$4x$			24	
Add 6.						
Subtract the number you thought of first.						33
Divide by 3.		$x + 2$				
Add 8.				20		
Subtract the number you thought of first.						

2 What was each person's original number? Lessons 1, 2, and 7

Words		Jason	Sami	Joel	Rachel
Think of a number.					
		12	24	30	38

3 Computer Mart sold 147 printers for $147 each.
Printers Plus sold 146 printers for $148 each.
Which store made the most money in printer sales?
Explain how you know. Lesson 5

____

____

____

Complete the diagrams and number sentences. Lesson 5

4

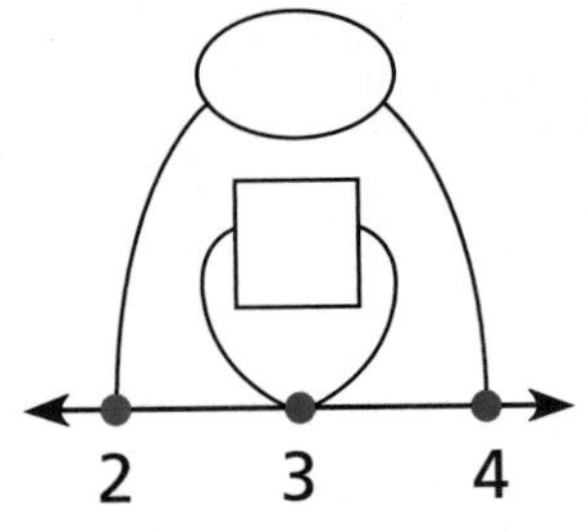

3 × 3 = ☐

2 × 4 = ◯

5 9 × 9 = ☐

8 × 10 = ◯

6 ☐ × ☐ = 2,401

48 × 50 = ◯

7 Draw a picture to show that
$(4 \bullet 4) - 1 = (4 + 1) \bullet (4 - 1)$ Lesson 6

8 Finish this puzzle so that no matter what number someone chooses, the final number will always be 2. Lessons 4 and 7

Think of a number.	x			
Double it.	$2x$			
Add 20.	$2x + 20$			
Subtract the number you thought of first.	$x + 20$			
		2	2	2

Chapter 15
Lesson 1

Name ______________________ Date ______________

Estimation Strategies

NCTM Standards 1, 6, 7, 8, 9, 10

Use estimation to help you answer these questions.

1. 116 − 58

   A. 93 **C.** 38

   B. 58 **D.** 104

2. 179 + 85

   A. 354 **C.** 304

   B. 204 **D.** 264

3. 23 × 5

   A. 108 **C.** 95

   B. 115 **D.** 150

4. 656 ÷ 8

   A. 91 **C.** 82

   B. 9 **D.** 50

5. 83 × 19

   A. 1,063 **C.** 1,477

   B. 1,277 **D.** 1,577

6. 908 + 86

   A. 1,194 **C.** 1,054

   B. 994 **D.** 1,624

7. How many people can sit in a concert hall if there are 57 rows with 79 seats in each row?

   A. 4,003 **C.** 3,003

   B. 4,503 **D.** 3,503

8. How many buses are needed to transport 4,224 people if each bus can hold 66 people

   A. 81 **C.** 64

   B. 54 **D.** 51

Refer to the inventory list to answer the following questions.

6 boxes of shorts	12 boxes of shirts
18 boxes of laces	24 boxes of balls
7 boxes of sweatshirts	16 pairs of socks
124 pairs of pants	19 umbrellas

9 If there are 22 shirts per box, how many shirts does the store have?

A. 200　　C. 324
B. 204　　D. 264

10 When Jack unpacked the boxes of balls, he had 168 cans of 3 balls. How many cans of balls are in a box?

A. 15　　C. 25
B. 7　　D. 21

11 There are 4 shelves for pants. How many pairs of pants should go on each shelf?

A. 31　　C. 51
B. 25　　D. 111

12 Jack unpacked the boxes of shorts and put them on 4 shelves. He put 48 shorts on each shelf. How many shorts are in each box?

A. 26　　C. 32
B. 52　　D. 42

13 **Challenge** If half a box of sweatshirts has 34 sweatshirts, how many sweatshirts does the store have?

A. 426　　C. 476
B. 238　　D. 526

14 **Challenge** If 210 is a third of the store's laces, how many laces are in each box?

A. 6　　C. 70
B. 630　　D. 35

Chapter 15
Lesson 2

Name ______________________ Date ____________

Estimating and Checking Length and Perimeter

NCTM Standards 1, 3, 4, 6, 7, 8, 9, 10

Estimate the perimeter and area of the following figures. Use the fact that the area of an orange tile is 1 square centimeter.

1. 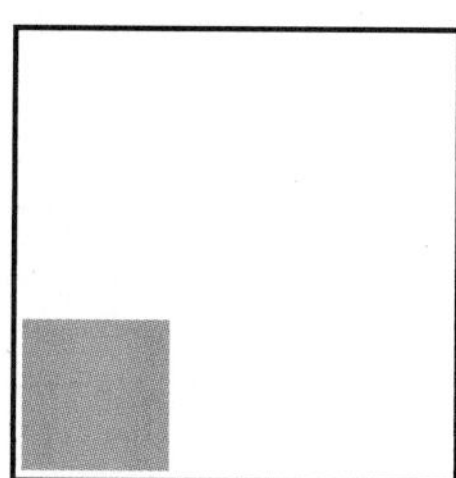

The perimeter is about ________ cm.

The area is about ________ sq cm.

2. 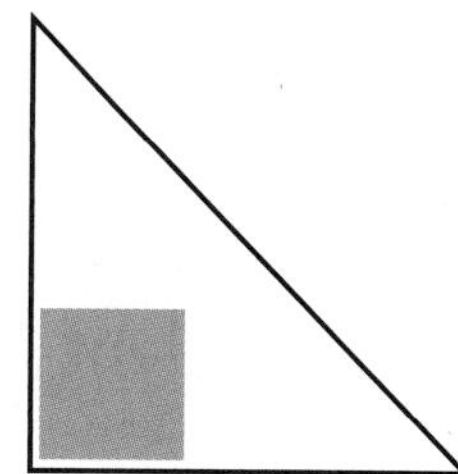

The perimeter is about ________ cm.

The area is about ________ sq cm.

3. 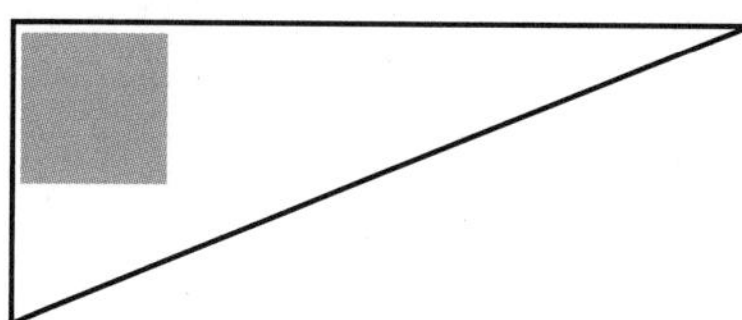

The perimeter is about ________ cm.

The area is about ________ sq cm.

4.  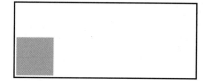

The perimeter is about ________ cm.

The area is about ________ sq cm.

Say whether the given measures are likely or unlikely.

5.  height = 6 meters

likely or **unlikely**

6. 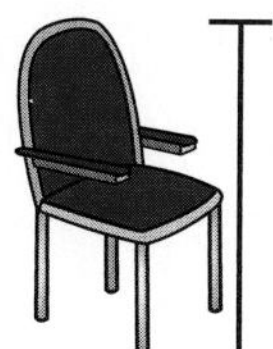 height = 80 cm

likely or **unlikely**

7.  area = 2 square meters

likely or **unlikely**

8.  area of a book's cover = 8 sq cm

likely or **unlikely**

Use the picture to answer the questions.

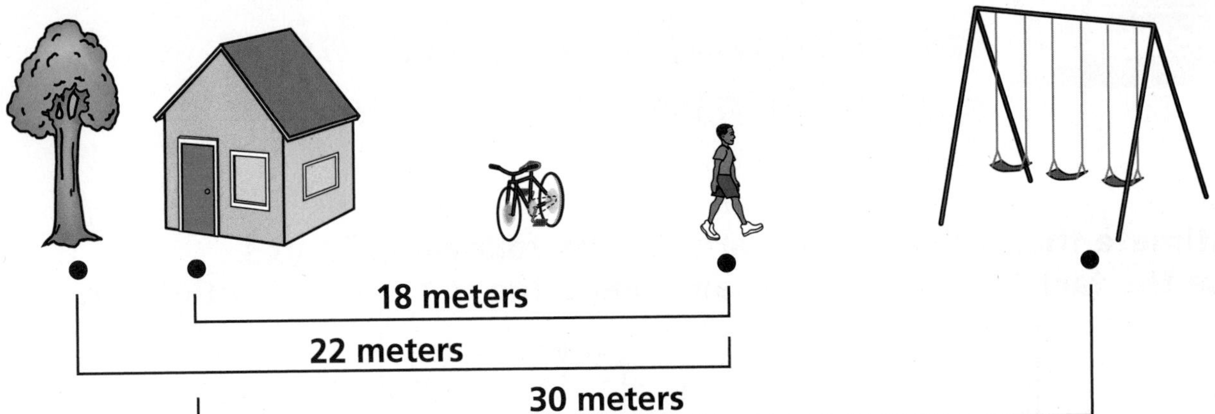

9. How far is the student from the swingset? _______ meters

10. How far is the tree from the house? _______ meters

11. How far is the tree from the swingset? _______ meters

12. What can you say about the bicycle's location?

____

____

____

____

13. **Challenge** Charlotte used her hand to estimate the perimeter of a drawing. She knows her hand is about 5 cm wide. If she found the perimeter to be 38 hand widths, what is her estimate of the perimeter, in centimeters and meters?

5 cm

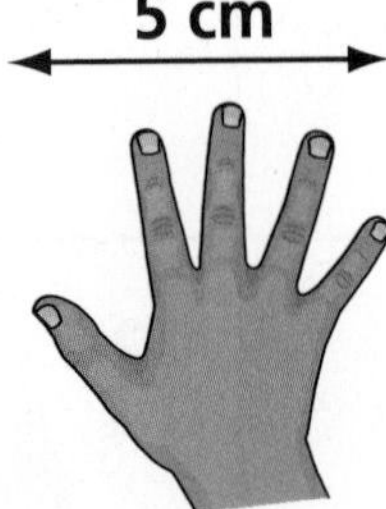

_______ centimeters _______ meters

Name ______________________ Date ____________

Chapter 15
Lesson 3

Designing a School

NCTM Standards 1, 3, 4, 6, 7, 8, 9, 10

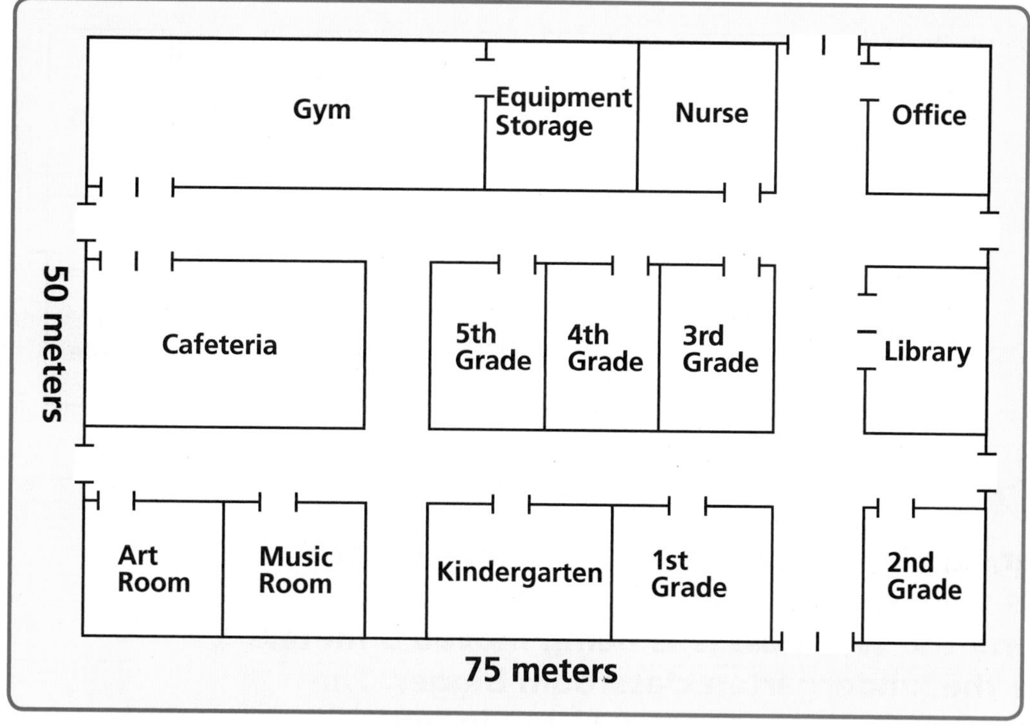

Use this school's floor plan to answer the questions below.

1. Which room has the largest area? ____________

2. Which grade's classroom has the smallest area? ____________

3. One wall in the office is 15 meters long and another is 10 meters long. Including the door, what is the office's perimeter? ______ meters

4. One wall of the cafeteria is 20 meters long and another is 15 meters long. What is the area of the cafeteria's floor? ______ sq m

5. The back wall of the 3rd, 4th, and 5th grade classrooms is actually one long 35-meter wall. The side walls are each 15 meters long. Approximate the area of the 5th grade classroom's floor. about ______ sq m

6. Approximate the perimeter of the 4th grade classroom. about ______ meters

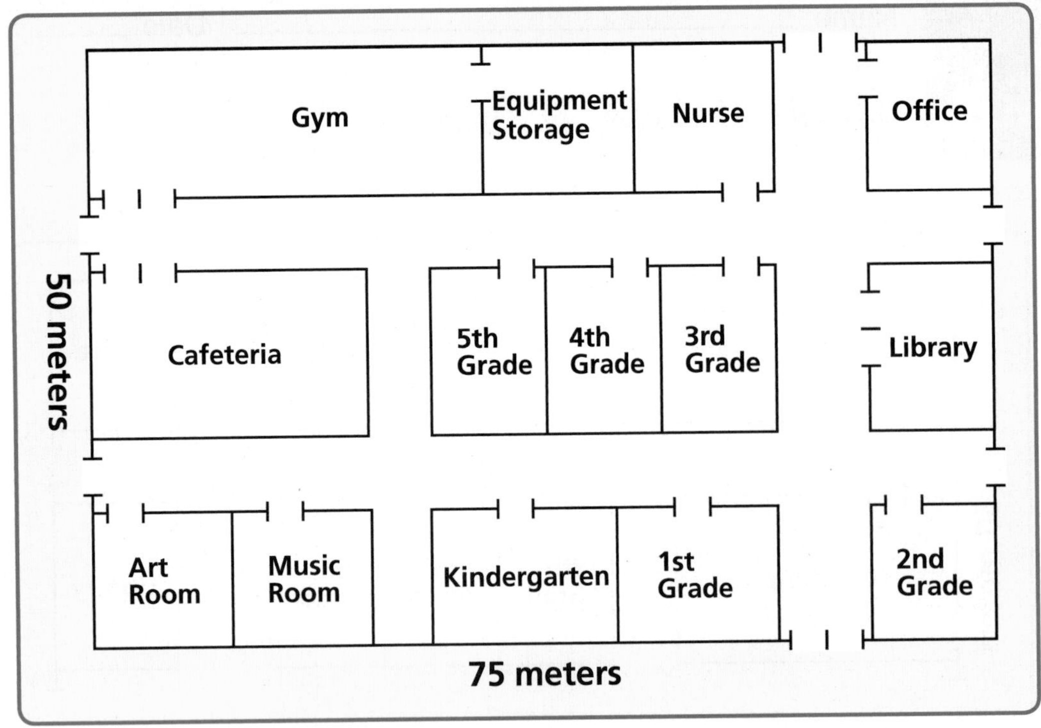

This year, the kindergarten class has many more students than the 1st grade class, so the wall separating the two classes is being moved 5 meters to make the kindergarten classroom bigger. The classrooms were the same size to begin with.

7. If the old perimeter of the kindergarten classroom was 55 meters, what is the new perimeter? _______ meters

8. What is the new perimeter of the first grade class room? _______ meters

9. The long wall in the kindergarten classroom is now 22.5 meters in length. What is the new area of the floor of the kindergarten classroom? _______ sq m

10. What is the new area of the floor of the first grade classroom? _______ sq m

11. **Challenge** Estimate the total perimeter of all the hallways. _______ meters

12. **Challenge** Estimate the total area of the floor space of all the hallways. _______ sq m

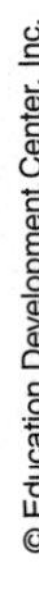

Name ______________________ Date ____________

Chapter 15

Lesson 4

Estimating and Checking Capacity

NCTM Standards 1, 4, 6, 7, 8, 9, 10

How can you use these containers to measure the amounts given in Problems 1–2?

a 3-liter jug

an 8-liter bucket

a 330-milliliter can

a $1\frac{1}{2}$-liter bottle

1. $7\frac{1}{2}$ liters

____

____

____

2. 1 liter

____

____

____

How can you use these containers to measure the amounts given in Problems 3–4?

a 1-gallon container

a 12-ounce can ($1\frac{1}{2}$ cups)

a quart container

3. $1\frac{1}{2}$ quarts

____

____

____

4. 4 ounces ($\frac{1}{2}$ cup)

____

____

____

Say whether the estimated capacity of each object is reasonable. If it is not, give a reasonable estimate.

The bucket's capacity is about 5 gallons.

Is this a reasonable estimate?

yes **no**

If not, what's a reasonable estimate?

about ______ gallons

6

The tub's capacity is about 5 liters.

Is this a reasonable estimate?

yes **no**

If not, what's a reasonable estimate?

about ______ liters

The glass's capacity is about 20 ounces.

Is this a reasonable estimate?

yes **no**

If not, what's a reasonable estimate?

about ______ ounces

8

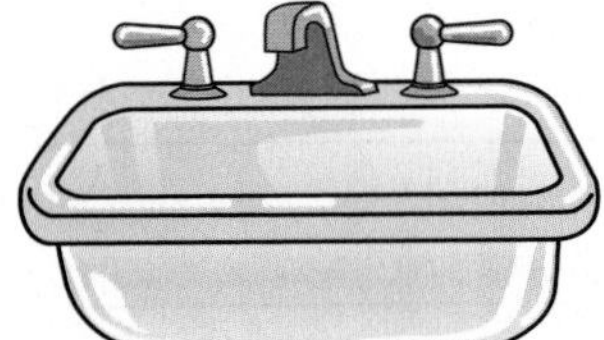

The sink's capacity is about $1\frac{1}{2}$ quarts.

Is this a reasonable estimate?

yes **no**

If not, what's a reasonable estimate?

about ______ quarts

9 Challenge Give an example of a container with a capacity of about 1 pint.

____

____

Chapter 15
Lesson 5

Name ____________________ Date ____________

Comparing Units of Capacity

NCTM Standards 1, 4, 6, 7, 8, 9, 10

Use estimation to help you compare these capacities. Use <, >, or =.

1 18×16 gallons ◯ 19×16 gallons	2 67×8 cups ◯ 66×4 pints
3 74×19 liters ◯ 74×19 quarts	4 83×4 quarts ◯ 87×1 gallon
5 38×27 pints ◯ 38×14 quarts	6 22×82 cups ◯ 21×22 quarts

Answer the questions.

7 The soccer coach brought 2 gallons of water to the game and the assistant coach brought 1 gallon of fruit juice. The drinks were shared equally among the 24 kids on the team. How many cups could each player have?

____

8 Before driving 456 miles to grandpa's house, Jen's mom filled the car with gas. The car holds 18 gallons of gas. If the car uses 10 gallons to go 240 miles, will Jen's mom need to fill the car with gas again during the drive? If so, how much more gas will she need? If not, how much will they have left in the tank?

____

____

____

Compare. Use <, >, or =.

9 $\frac{1}{2}$ gallon ◯ 2 pints	10 1.1 gallon ◯ 4 quarts
11 4.5 quarts ◯ $\frac{3}{4}$ gallon	12 $\frac{10}{10}$ pints ◯ 10 cups
13 $\frac{7}{8}$ gallon ◯ 10 cups	14 3 liters ◯ 2 quarts
15 5 cups ◯ $2\frac{1}{2}$ pints	16 4 pints ◯ $3\frac{1}{2}$ liters
17 1.7 liters ◯ 5.07 cups	18 $\frac{3}{4}$ cup ◯ $\frac{3}{4}$ pint
19 7.5 cups ◯ $\frac{6}{12}$ gallon	20 987.5 ml ◯ $\frac{1}{2}$ gallon
21 $\frac{5}{6}$ quart ◯ 0.5 liter	22 24 cups ◯ 1.5 gallons

23 **Challenge** Fill in the blanks to make the statements true.

67 × _______ cups = 8 quarts × 67

2.5 pints × 17 = _______ cups × 17

$\frac{1}{2}$ gallon + 2 cups = _______ pints + 1 cup

$\frac{9}{10}$ pint > _______ cups

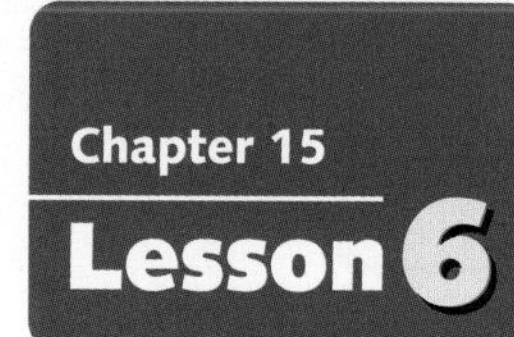

Name ______________________ Date ______________

Estimating and Checking Weight

NCTM Standards 1, 4, 6, 7, 8, 9, 10

Answer the questions.

1. An elevator can hold 2,000 kilograms. An average adult weighs 64 kilograms. About how many people can go on an elevator at once?

about _____ people

2. The Ramon family is moving to another country. They will ship all of their belongings on a boat. The cargo space they are renting can hold 1,000 kilograms. They have 4 beds that each weigh 50 kilograms, 4 sofas that each weigh 55 kg, 4 dressers that each weigh 60 kg, and a table and chairs that weigh 112 kg. About how much more weight can they ship?

about _____ kg

3. The second floor of a factory stores boxes that weigh about 15 kg each. The floor can hold 4,590 kg. About how many boxes can be stored on the second floor?

about _____ boxes

How can these weights be used to measure the following weights on a balance scale?

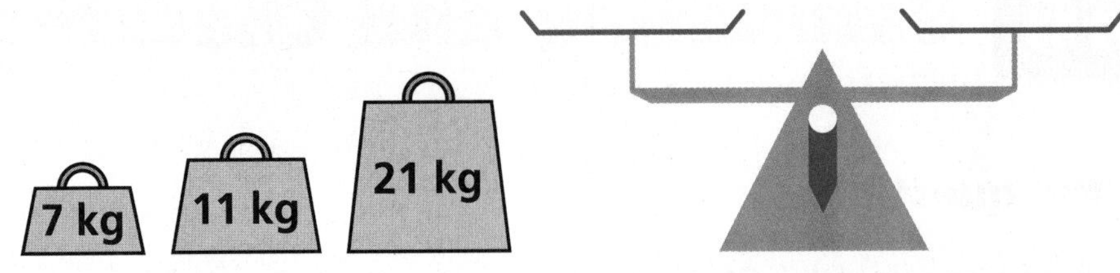

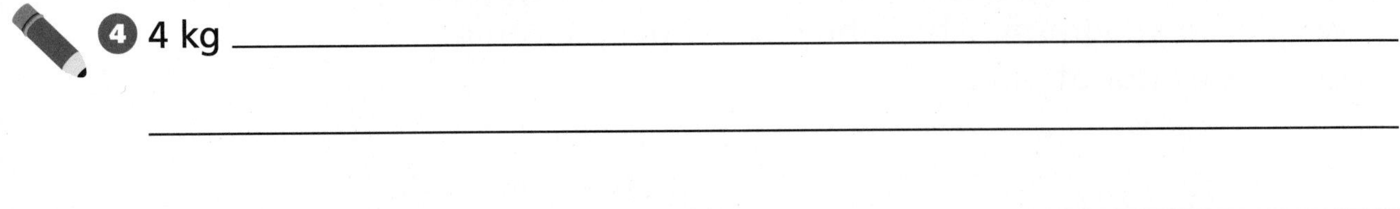

4 4 kg ______

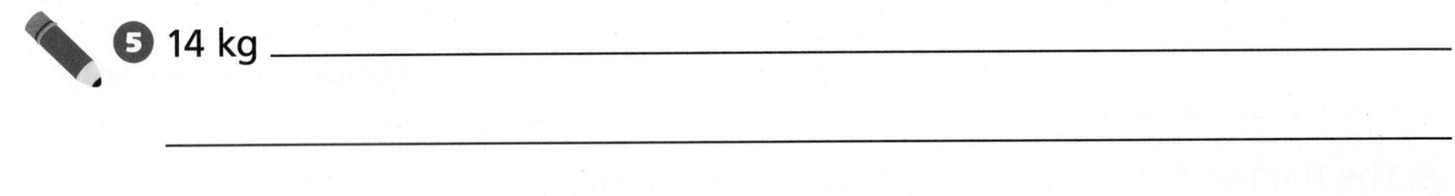

5 14 kg ______

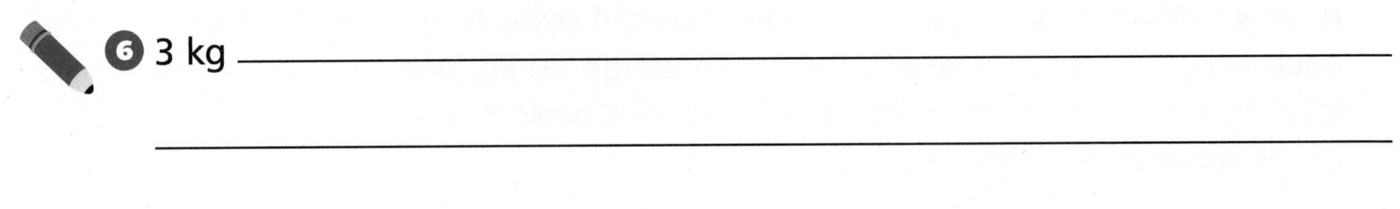

6 3 kg ______

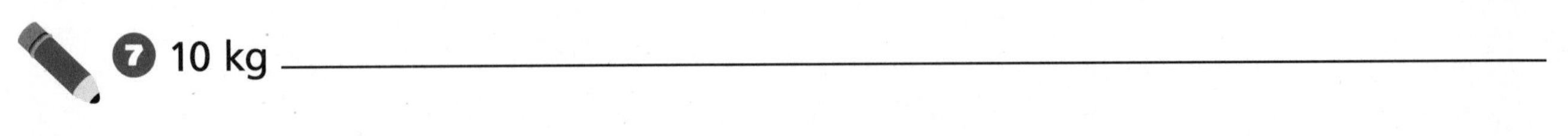

7 10 kg ______

8 **Challenge** Are there any other weights that can be measured with just a balance scale and a 7 kg, an 11 kg, and a 21 kg weight?

Chapter 15

Lesson 7

Name ______________________ Date ______________

Comparing Units of Weight

NCTM Standards 1, 4, 6, 7, 8, 9, 10

Choose the closest weight.

1. A box weighs 3 pounds.

   A. 3 kg **C.** 6 kg

   B. 30 kg **D.** 1 kg

2. A bicycle weighs 5 kilograms.

   A. 5 lbs **C.** 10 lbs

   B. 50 lbs **D.** 2 lbs

3. A plate weighs 8 ounces.

   A. 8 kg **C.** 1 lb

   B. 8 g **D.** 250 g

4. A notebook weighs 15 grams.

   A. 15 oz **C.** 1 lb

   B. $\frac{1}{10}$ lb **D.** 0.5 kg

5. A mug weighs 350 grams.

   A. 0.35 kg **C.** 35 kg

   B. 3.5 kg **D.** 350 oz

6. A wood table weighs 20 kilograms.

   A. 2,000 g **C.** 200,000 g

   B. 20,000 g **D.** 200 g

7. A cell phone weighs 0.25 pounds.

   A. 4 oz **C.** 12 oz

   B. 8 oz **D.** 16 oz

8. A book weighs 1 kilogram.

   A. 100 g **C.** 2 lbs

   B. 1,000 oz **D.** 0.5 lbs

9 Put these weights in order from lightest to heaviest.

1 kg	1 ton	2 kg	2 g	2 oz	3 lbs	2 lbs

____, ____, ____, ____, ____, ____, ____

Answer the questions.

10 What are two ways of comparing weights of objects?

11 Can 1 gallon of oil be heavier than 1 gallon of water? Why or why not?

12 **Challenge** Do you think that 1 kilogram of feathers can fit into a 1 gallon jug? Why or why not?

Name ______________________ Date ____________

Chapter 15

Lesson 8

Using Equations to Estimate

NCTM Standards 1, 2, 4, 6, 7, 8, 9, 10

Using shorthand notation, write an equation to describe each picture.

= 1 kg = 1 lb

1 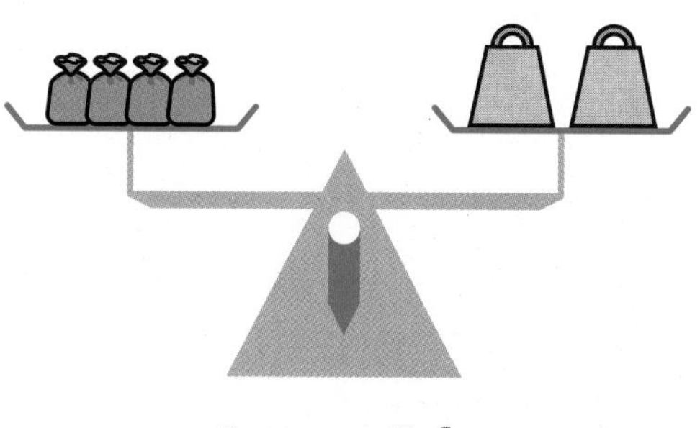

4x = 2 kg

2 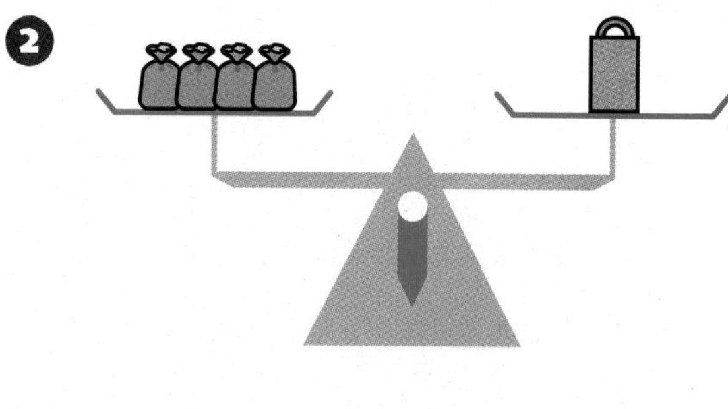

_____ = _____

3 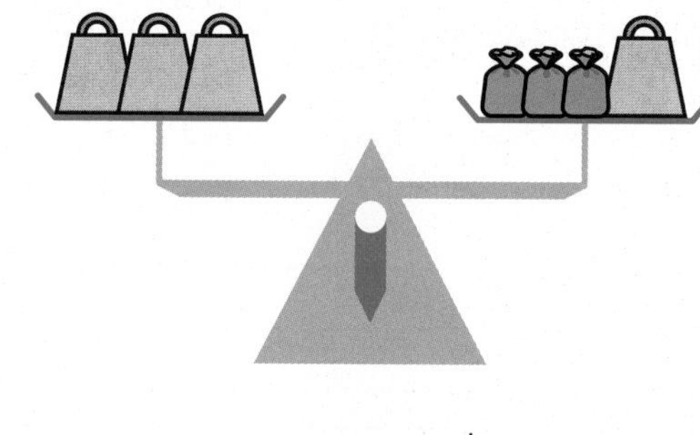

_____ = _____ + _____

4 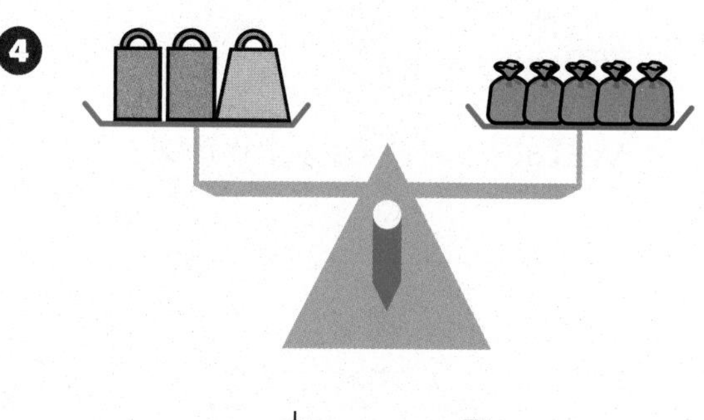

_____ + _____ = _____

Draw a picture to match the equation.

5 $5x = 3$ lb

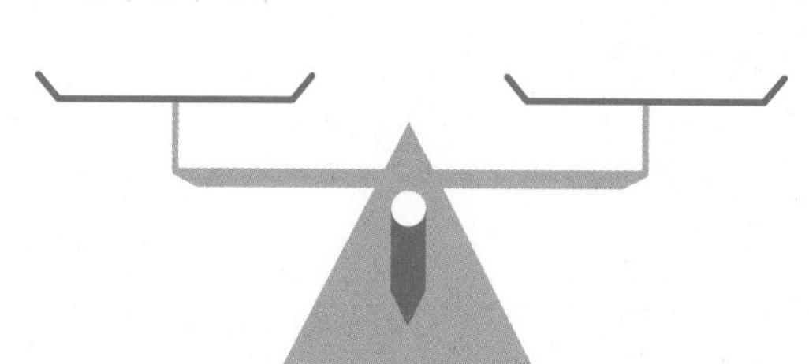

6 $2x + 1$ lb $= 5$ kg

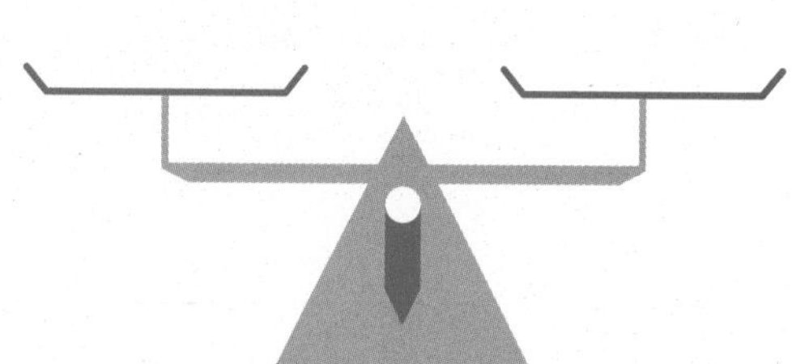

Complete the number sentences.

7. ________ g = 1 kg

8. ________ oz = 1 lb

9. ________ oz = 5 lb

10. ________ g = $\frac{1}{2}$ kg

What is *x*?

11. $x + 750$ g = 1 kg

x = ________

12. 1 lb − x = 12 oz

x = ________

13. 3 kg = x + 2,000 g

x = ________

14. 3 oz + x = 2 lb

x = ________

15. **Challenge** 9 bags weigh 5 kg, and 13 boxes weigh 6 kg. Which is heavier, a bag or a box? Explain your answer.

____

____

____

Chapter 15
Lesson 9

Name ______________________ Date ____________

Problem Solving Strategy

Act It Out

NCTM Standards 1, 2, 4, 6, 7, 8, 9, 10

Understand
Plan
Solve
Check

1. Xavier has several 3¢ stamps and 7¢ stamps in his desk drawer. He has weighed several letters and knows what postage each one needs. Can he use only the stamps he already has and put the exact postage on each letter?

A

27¢

B

11¢

C
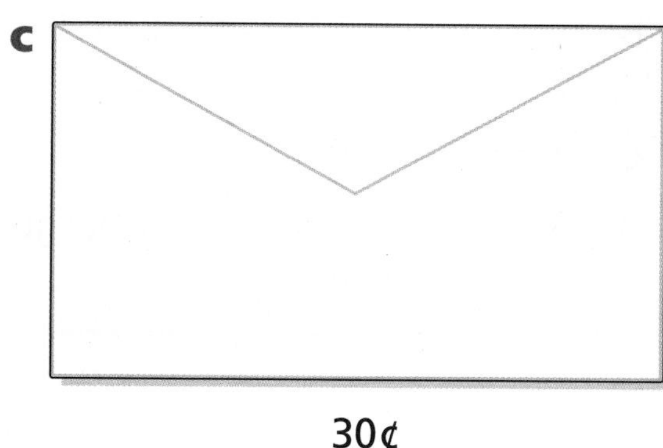

30¢

D

37¢

---

2. Sally is taller than Jake and Laura. Miguel is taller than Jake but shorter than Laura. Selby is shorter than Jake. Robert is taller than Sally. Put these six students in order from shortest to tallest.

______, ______, ______, ______, ______, ______

Problem Solving Test Prep

Choose the correct answer.

1. The value of 18×18 is 324.

   Which expression has a product that is the same as $(324 - 1)$?

   A. 17×19 **C.** 18×19

   B. 17×18 **D.** 16×20

2. Which CANNOT be the value for the variable *n*?

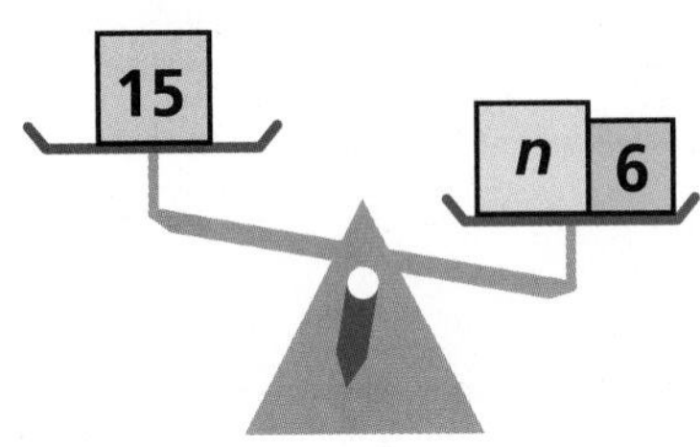

   A. 9

   B. 10

   C. 15

   D. 21

3. Choose the best estimate.

   $9\overline{)741}$

   A. 60 **C.** 80

   B. 70 **D.** 90

4. Which statement is NOT true of the reflection of the triangle over the line?

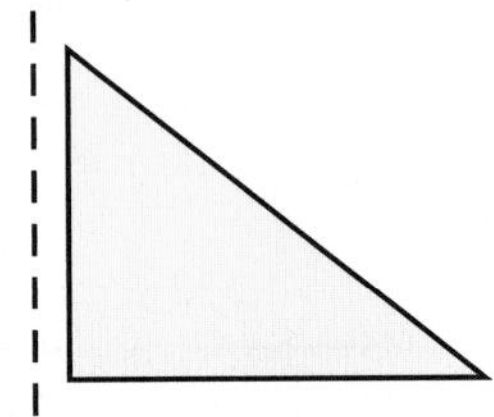

   A. It is congruent to the original.

   B. It faces the opposite direction of the original.

   C. It is a right triangle.

   D. It is the same shape but larger than the original.

Show What You Know

Solve each problem. Explain your answer.

5. Evan has several 3-pound and 5-pound weights. Can he use a balance scale to show all whole-number weights between 15 and 20 pounds? Explain.

   ___

   ___

   ___

   ___

6. Corey has 20 small cubes. What is the least number of additional cubes he needs to build a larger cube that uses all the small cubes? Explain.

   ___

   ___

   ___

Chapter 15

Name ________________________ Date ____________

Review/Assessment

NCTM Standards 1, 2, 4, 6, 7, 8, 9, 10

Use estimation to find the answer. Lesson 1

1. 267 + 843

A. 1,010
B. 1,210
C. 1,110
D. 1,020

2. 911 − 365

A. 696
B. 546
C. 646
D. 596

3. 37 × 22

A. 814
B. 614
C. 1,014
D. 684

4. 324 ÷ 9

A. 51
B. 25
C. 45
D. 36

5. The orange square is 1 sq cm. Lesson 2

Perimeter:

A. 14 cm
B. 25 cm
C. 26 cm
D. 50 cm

6. The orange square is 1 sq cm. Lesson 2

Area:

A. 24 sq cm
B. 18 sq cm
C. 12 sq cm
D. 6 sq cm

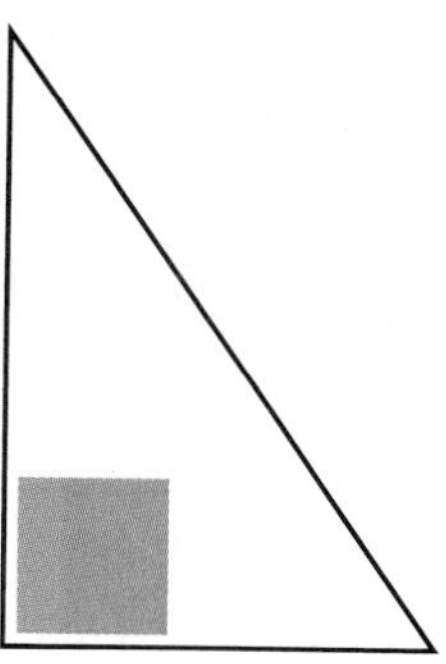

7. **Capacity:** Lesson 4

A. 1 gallon
B. 8 ounces
C. 3 quarts
D. 1 liter

8. **Weight:** Lesson 6

A. 0.25 tons
B. 15 kilograms
C. 8 pounds
D. 2 grams

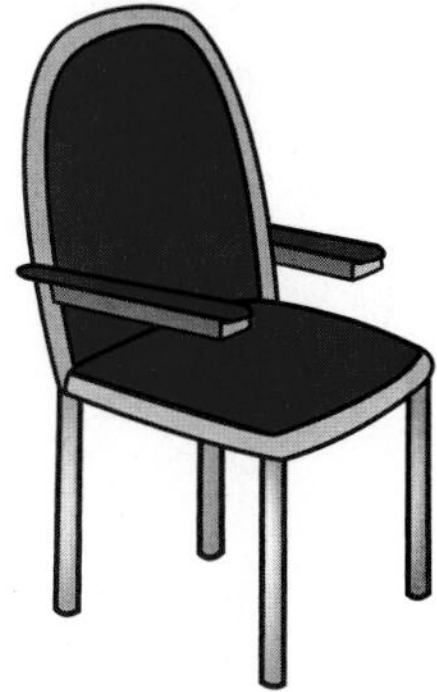

Compare. Use >, <, or =. Hint: Use estimation. Lessons 5 and 7

9 28 gallons × 9 ◯ 28 cups × 16	10 54 cups × 27 ◯ 27 pints × 54
11 33 quarts × 42 ◯ 66 pints × 33	12 81 cups × 17 ◯ 22 quarts × 18
13 55 × 12 liters ◯ 55 × 12 quarts	14 19 liters × 52 ◯ 18 × 52 quarts
15 24 kg × 31 ◯ 93 × 24 lbs	16 47 lbs × 21 ◯ 25 kg × 21

17 **How can you use 8-inch pencils to estimate the perimeter of a classroom window? What might be a reasonable estimate of the perimeter in feet?** Lessons 3 and 9

____

____

____

____

____

= 1 kg = 1 lb

Lesson 8

18

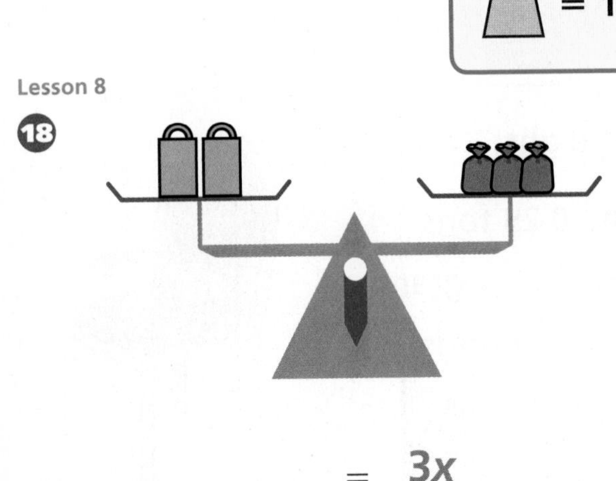

_____ = 3x

19

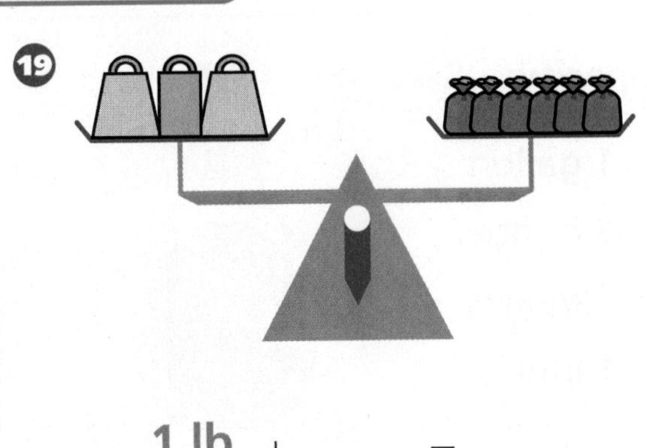

1 lb + _____ = _____